Boundaryless Hospital

Horst Albach • Heribert Meffert •
Andreas Pinkwart • Ralf Reichwald •
Wilfried von Eiff
Editors

Boundaryless Hospital

Rethink and Redefine Health Care Management

Springer

Editors
Horst Albach
Center for Advanced Studies in Management
HHL Leipzig Graduate School of Management
Leipzig, Germany

Heribert Meffert
Center for Advanced Studies in Management
HHL Leipzig Graduate School of Management
Leipzig, Germany

Andreas Pinkwart
Center for Advanced Studies in Management
HHL Leipzig Graduate School of Management
Leipzig, Germany

Ralf Reichwald
Center for Advanced Studies in Management
HHL Leipzig Graduate School of Management
Leipzig, Germany

Wilfried von Eiff
Center for Health Care Management and Regulation
HHL Leipzig Graduate School of Management
Leipzig, Germany

ISBN 978-3-662-49010-5 ISBN 978-3-662-49012-9 (eBook)
DOI 10.1007/978-3-662-49012-9

Library of Congress Control Number: 2016930828

Springer Heidelberg New York Dordrecht London

Printed on acid-free paper

Springer-Verlag GmbH Berlin Heidelberg is part of Springer Science+Business Media (www.springer.com)

Preface

The title of this book is taken from an article which was published in the Australian and New Zealand Journal of Medicine in 1994. The authors J. Braithwaite, R. Vining, and L. Lazarus applied a vision of the organization that Jack Welch, former CEO of General Electric (GE), had developed to make his company successful: *boundarylessness*. In the 1990 Annual Report of GE, Welch projected, "Our dream for the 1990s is a boundaryless company, a company where we knock down the walls that separate us from each other on the inside and from our key constituencies on the outside."

For Jack Welch, boundarylessness was the way to increase productivity. In his CEO letter to GE's shareholders, he wrote one year later, "1991 did, however, once again remind us how absolutely critical productivity growth is in the brutally Darwinian global market places in which virtually all of our businesses compete. [. . .] But to increase productivity, you first have to clear away all the impediments that keep you from its achievement—primarily the management layers, functional boundaries and all the other trappings of bureaucracy."

Welch stressed boundarylessness as an instrument for productivity growth through cost-cutting, which is important in order to survive in highly competitive markets. The hospital is not primarily considered an organization which provides services on competitive markets. Though, the hospital of today, which is a fact, also faces tough cost pressures. However, the goal of hospital management is higher efficiency of health care and good effectiveness. It is the key to achieving the target triangle (quality, access, and affordability) of health care based on a sustainable reimbursement system. The objective of hospital managers is to ensure the provision of high-quality care and healing environment services despite increasing financial constraints.

With the book in hand, the Center for Advanced Studies in Management (CASiM), the interdisciplinary research center of HHL Leipzig Graduate School of Management, aims at addressing this challenge. This requires more than planning and control of a firm. It goes beyond accounting and digitalization. The patient is more than a mere customer. Efficiency management in a hospital is based on both a profound understanding of medicine and nursing on the side of the manager and a deep understanding of business economics and health services on the side of the medical scientist. And for both sides as well as for the regulator, a deeper understanding of the impact of the regulatory framework on the outcome of the health care system is indispensable. The former traditional boundaries between health professionals, administrators, and nursing staff have to be removed to enable new effective forms of cooperation. The successful hospital of the twenty-first century is a *boundaryless hospital*.

And above all, managing the hospital requires a deeper and holistic understanding of the patient. To achieve this, on the one hand, the experience of the medical and nursing staff should be taken into consideration and recommendations should be monetarized against the background that a significant proportion of the healing success is actually psychology, and on the other hand, the new field of so-called *personalized medicine* should be further developed. Personalized medicine is a vision for health care. There may be similar concepts in other fields, particularly in marketing consumer products, where business economists talk about "markets of one" or "lot size one," but in medicine the concept is different. Our author Manfred Dietel defines personalized medicine as "the intention to diagnose and treat patients more precisely adapted to their individual needs." This new development has its background in modern tendencies: globalization with boundaryless markets, digitalization with boundaryless IT tools, demographic aging, and increasing risk.

All health care systems try to cope with the rising expenditures of health care, but the systems differ from country to country. Insurance—public or private—is one way to finance the costs of health care. Insurances may cover all expenses or they may require the sick persons to pay their health expenditures themselves. Regardless of the particular health care system, Jan P. Beckmann provides in his introductory contribution a philosophical underpinning for our approach to reach more efficiency and better outcomes with new economic instruments.

Boundarylessness in our understanding does not mean that there are no rules. On the contrary: The boundaryless hospital has to work on the basis of codes of conduct and contracts with regard to both internal and external relations. From Hirschhorn and Gilmore, we already know about the importance of internal "boundaries of the boundaryless company," as they called it in the Harvard Business Review in 1992. They argued that the players in a boundaryless company "must figure out what kind of roles they need to play and what kind of relationships they need to maintain in order to use those differences effectively in productive work."

Regarding the external boundaries, Alvin Roth, a 2012 Laureate of the Nobel Memorial Prize in Economic Sciences, gives a striking example of the positive impact of market design on the supply of donor kidneys. In his 2015 book on matchmaking and market design, his explanation of the entire process of establishing a kidney transplant network impressively shows the potential of synergies which can be exploited if the formidable obstacles caused by different logics on different sides can successfully be overcome: "Garet's frustrations led him in late 2007 to form an exchange network he called the National Kidney Registry. It [. . .] aims to facilitate potentially quite long non-simultaneous chains by recruiting hospitals and non-directed donors. If a hospital sends a non-directed donor, the NKR promises to end one of its chains at that hospital. That ensures that the hospital doesn't "lose" a transplant by sharing its donor: Keep in mind that hospitals earn revenue on their transplants; they're commercial enterprises as well as caregivers."

Cooperation and Big Data are the key words for the new developments in health care. They are the topics of this book. Cooperation in our understanding of a boundaryless hospital does not only refer to scientists from various disciplines and practitioners from different medical branches working together but also to the overall management of the value chain in the health care process and a new form of relationship between the doctor and the patient. As an example, Florian Kron and his coauthors present a new form of organization which provides the medical services cancer patients need—the Comprehensive Cancer Center (CCC): "The CCCs are the forefront to fight cancer. From an organizational perspective these large centers are highly complex. They cannot operate as standalone organizations but rely on cooperation in a network of hospitals and office-based physicians." Big Data means huge databanks with information about individual patients with individual diseases and individual methods for treating those diseases. But it is more than "number crunching" and repository management: Big Data solutions generate decision-relevant information. They aim at improving diagnosis and accelerating start of therapy to increase therapeutic effectiveness and patient outcome.

The papers in this book address international and interdisciplinary aspects. After introductory contributions in Part I, Parts II and III seize the previously identified opportunities across countries and disciplines and analyze whether the new concept is suitable to meet future challenges better. They elaborate and comment on the health care systems of Finland, Germany, Malta, the Netherlands, Portugal, and Switzerland. They deal with different diseases such as cancer, heart diseases, epilepsy, and inflammatory bowel disease, and with chronic care. The new developments also lead to new professions. Maarten Janssen and his coauthors draw attention to the "physician assistant" (PA) in the Netherlands. "Increasing experience, developed routines, specialization and trust among the medical and nursing staff enables PAs to gradually expand their occupational place, highlighting the fluidity of its boundaries." In the final Part IV, the boundaryless hospital is particularly reflected from the patient's perspective. Among other topics, the authors discuss the relevance and importance of patient involvement and its innovative potential for further development of health care.

Each book publication is the result of a considerable collective effort, and the completion of an edited volume always requires additional coordination. We would like to use this opportunity to thank all contributors collectively for their important efforts in realizing this project.

Some contributors we would like to praise individually. Specifically, we thank all authors for their highly stimulating papers and all reviewers for their critical and constructive feedback.

This book project also benefited greatly from fruitful discussions with the members of the board of CASiM. We would like to acknowledge their important support. Special thanks go to Prof. Dr. Thomas Gehrig (University of Vienna,

Austria) and Prof. Dr. Peter Letmathe (RWTH Aachen University, Germany), who also acted as reviewers in the double peer review process.

We would particularly like to thank our partners Siemens AG, B. Braun Melsungen AG, and McKinsey & Company, Inc. Without their expertise and financial support the publication would not have been possible in its current form.

Furthermore, we would like to thank Dr. Martina Bihn, Editorial Director at Springer, for her professional guidance and the constructive discussions throughout the publication process.

Last but not least, we owe special thanks to Daniela Neumann and Dr. Lukasz Swiatczak from the Executive Office of CASiM who managed this book project. They successfully coordinated all activities of the authors, reviewers, and editors and provided continuous editorial support.

We hope this publication will not only provide interesting reading but will also encourage further discussions and academic research on the boundaryless hospital and other innovative approaches to coping with the challenges and opportunities of health care in the twenty-first century.

We welcome your feedback via casim@hhl.de.

Leipzig, Germany
September 2015

Horst Albach
Heribert Meffert
Andreas Pinkwart
Ralf Reichwald
Wilfried von Eiff

Contents

Part I

Challenges and Opportunities of Health Care Management in the Twenty-First Century

Network Management: Strategic Option for the Boundaryless Hospital

Wilfried von Eiff

Abstract

Due to the phenomenon of the aging society, the number of patients suffering from multi-morbidity and/or chronic diseases has rapidly increased. Simultaneously, the cost-intensive progress in medical technologies leading to more precise diagnostic and innovative surgical interventions, enables treating patients with complex illnesses, as well as elderly people, more effectively.

Bearing this development in mind, it is fair to comment that patient-centered, successful medical services based on sustainable financial sources have to be organized in cross-sectoral medical networks consisting of primary care physicians, specialized clinics and rehabilitation facilities. The concept of the *boundaryless hospital*, in combination with the *value chain approach*, provides the theoretical basis for an effective and efficient network design. In this article, the nature, aims and impacts of network management in medicine are described. Furthermore, the traps and pitfalls of insufficient and inefficient network structures are discussed, and different types of network configurations, as well as limiting factors of network design are reflected. In addition, selected network concepts like the portal clinic approach, cross-sectoral contracting, managed care opportunities and emergency network designs are depicted.

Keywords

Medical networks • Network management • Strategy • Value chain • Cooperation • Integrated care • Network design

W. von Eiff (✉)
Center for Health Care Management and Regulation, HHL Leipzig Graduate School of Management, Jahnallee 59, 04109 Leipzig, Germany
e-mail: wilfried.von.eiff@hhl.de

H. Albach et al. (eds.), *Boundaryless Hospital*, DOI 10.1007/978-3-662-49012-9_1

1 Initial Situation

The highly developed health care systems of the Western countries will generally face similar challenges over the next 5–10 years:

- The phenomenon of the aging society causes a rising number of multi-morbid patients, and age-related diseases will increase.
- In addition, the number of chronic diseases will rise, especially those related to an unhealthy lifestyle (work stress, poor nutrition, lack of activity).
- Medical-technological progress enables more precise diagnoses and innovative intervention techniques, which also makes it possible to treat aged people more effectively.
- It is evident that there is a growing mentality of entitlement among patients regarding the diagnostic and treatment potential of modern medicine.

On the one hand, these trends will undoubtedly contribute to a rising demand for qualified health services. But on the other hand, strict financial limitations narrow the policy option for health care provision. Moreover, ethical questions arise and dominate the discussion surrounding the ethics and fairness of health services distribution and the limits that medical interventions have to respect: "Should we administer any medical service to patients that we basically can?", "Do the economic factors override the medical aspects?" and "Is rationing an appropriate approach for balancing an excess demand for health services and the limitations of financial resources?" These questions will have a central impact on the design of medical service structures in the future. In other words, the increasing demand for state-of-the-art medical services, performed in a healing environment, has to be achieved with limited budgets.

Against this background, it is necessary for a viable structuring of the health care system in future, to find medical supply forms that:

- conform to patients' expectations,
- ensure the fair distribution of effective evidence-based medicine to the community and
- integrate innovative treatment into the health care system in a way that ensures clear benefits and financial viability.

These organizational forms of provision, which focus on therapeutic effectiveness and efficient use of resources, require the goal-driven cooperation of different medical specialists.

Therefore, the economic component, as a design parameter for medical service structures, plays a more and more important role. This is confirmed by the efforts the German government, as well as of the statutory health insurance companies, which invest to steer the quality and service transparency of the hospital in terms of a pay-for-performance system. In connection with a so-called "purchasing system" of the insurance companies and the scrapping of the obligation to contract with hospitals holding a public supply mandate, it would be possible for the payers to take out individual quality-related (and possibly cost-related) contracts with the hospitals.

As a consequence, the successful organization and management of a hospital requires:

- a patient-centered medical service portfolio, which is strictly oriented to the needs of the health care market,
- offering selected, highly specialized and innovative medical services ("light-house" performance), as well as state-of-the-art care provision for the basic medical needs of the population in a limited catchment area,
- strict orientation of the design of internal processes to patient needs,
- goal-driven and economic cooperation with highly qualified external partners who are capable of contributing to the successful treatment of patients suffering from complex diseases,
- a holistic approach to the diagnosis and treatment of patients along the care continuum and
- ensuring complementary treatments for multi-morbid patients.

In this scenario of supply structure and contract options, it is essential for the hospitals to develop service structures in which qualified medicine is performed at financially sustainable levels. Experiences from the turnaround in the automotive industry in the 1980/1990s show that efficient structures can neither be professionally nor cost-effectively produced on an individual basis, but are characterized by network-oriented cooperation along the value chain. A comparable development can be found in the health economy, characterized by three design elements, which change the strategic role of the hospital and which enable new organization and steering forms for the medical supply of a country. These are the *boundaryless hospital*, the value chain as a factor combination and the network as an expression of decentrally allocated medical expertise.

2 The Boundaryless Hospital and the Value Chain in Health Care

The *boundaryless hospital* is patient-oriented, provides a safe environment, the medical knowledge is state-of-the-art and limited resources are used in a goal-oriented (effective) manner and without waste (efficient). Furthermore, the boundaryless hospital overcomes typical negative characteristics of hospitals: multi-bed rooms, lack of privacy and lack of self-control. Therefore, the boundaryless hospital approach incorporates the mission of transforming a typical health care setting into a healing environment that improves patient outcomes and employee motivation through the creative use of evidence-based design (von Eiff 2007).

Internal boundaries, caused by a silo mentality between professions and departments, with the consequence of poor communication and process efficiency, are teared down by interdisciplinary delegation, center organization and an incentive system that connects both ethical and economic decision criteria.

To realize *external integration* approaches like telemedicine, cluster strategy, portal clinics, networks for infection prevention, emergency supply and managed care concepts are used. The basis for a structured implementation of these concepts is the value chain approach.

The medical value chain approach refers to the sequence of supply stages for the complete treatment of a disease (e.g. cardiovascular diseases; diabetes) with regard to the individual and personal situation of the patient. The medical value chain is defined independently of institutions.

The hospital value chain (Porter and Teisberg 2006) includes all internal and external resources and institutions which are necessary to treat a disease comprehensively. This value chain approach focuses on the division of labor between medical service providers and aims at the appropriate design of outsourcing, cooperation and networks as supply forms (Fig. 1).

Infrastructure	Competence Centers, Community Health Centers, Telemedicine, Portal Clinics, Innovative Technology, Healing Environment							
Knowledge Management	Surgery Techniques, Innovative Medical Products, Prozess Optimization/Organisation, Good Medical Practice, Guidelines, Patient Datenbase, Bio Database							
Information Management	Quality Reports, Critical Incident Reporting, Patient Information, Enlightenment and Education, Patient Compliance Programs							
Measuring and Documentation	Resulty Quality, Process Quality, Patient Record Management							
Access Management	Incentive Systems, Setting Approach, Screening Program, Disease Management, Case Management, Hospitalist, Homecare Management							
Phases of value added	**Lifestyle Prevention**	**Monitoring Prevention**	**Central Emergency Department**	**Diagnosis**	**Therapeutic Intervention**	**Recovery Rehabilitation**	**Health Care Support**	**Nursing Home Management**
Tasks	• Health supporting lifestyle and environment • Impact of risk factors • Family anamnesis	• Screening • Targeted prevention programs • Risk factors • Genetic pre-disposition • Causes of death	• Triage and qualified initial treatment • Patient control • Bed occupancy management • MRSA-Screening • SOP - Manchester - Wells - Hamm • Discharge functional diagnostic, ICU, wards	• Admission diagnosis • Anamnesis • Tests • Functional diagnois • Specialis consultation • Treatment plan	• Procedures • Medication • Discharge diagnosis • Rehabilitation plan • Treatment plan	• Early rehabilitation • Therapy adjustment • Rehabilitation • Follow-up plan	• Monitoring and influence of patient's condition • Influencing patienten compliance • Monitoring of changes in lifestyle	
Benefits	Delay • Entry into the system • Severity level	Risk detection and preventive therapy	Clinical and economic control of patients	Precision, liformation value	Clinical effective/ Outcome-oriented	Recovery social/occupational mobility	Support and control	High quality of life in old age

Value Chain
Advantage
Patient's Benefit
Outcome
Medical Result
Process Costs

Fig. 1 The health care value chain

3 Networks in Medicine and the Health Business: Rational Network Design

Networks in medicine constitute a specific organizational type for providing a population or group of patients with health care services. The added value of networks, in comparison to individual (centralized) forms of supply organization results from the following medical and economic aspects:

- Networks are virtual knowledge centers. They mobilize and distribute expert knowledge and make it broadly available.
- Networks create near-to-patient services by dividing up specialized tasks and continuous medical care duties in a capability- and demand-oriented manner.
- Networks enable resource sharing and ensure secure investments and utilization efficiency.

The benefit of networking between medical service providers in the health care system is not only motivated by a desire to improve quality or to optimize resources, but is also fostered considerably by the German legislator. Social Security Code regulations §§ 39, 112, 140 a-f and 301 SGB V (Sozialgesetzbuch V 2015) indicate that a medically efficient and cost-effective cooperation along the value chain (in the sense of the patient care process from initial treatment until the completion of follow-up treatment) is supported by networks.

The aim of networks is to

- increase patient/customer satisfaction (Nagyrapolt 2008);
- improve patient's well-being (patient outcome);
- decrease costs per case;
- optimize the patient's pathway through the entire health care system in a case-oriented manner, meaning shortening the process and simultaneously performing it at lower cost;
- increase the quality of medical and social care of patients (and relatives) by mobilizing the best medical know-how, as well as nursing and physiotherapeutic capabilities;
- improve image so as to develop a brand status.

Given these aspects, a network can be seen as a target-oriented organized form of cooperation with the aim of meeting the requirements of the health care market in a customized, medically sound and cheaper manner (Fottler and Malvey 1995).

Networks serve to

- close identified supply gaps in a customer-oriented manner. The underlying reason is that the expert knowledge which is available in one's own organization is normally not sufficient to fully meet the market requirements (case requirements) or to set a new standard in the market.

- decrease the costs of preparation and distribution of a product/service, so that, e.g. one's own cost structure is disburdened by cooperating with the cost leader, or so that a higher medical supply level can be achieved by cooperating with the quality leader.
- open up new fields of business (added-business variant), which is not possible for a single hospital, because of a lack of market access or because the necessary expertise is not (yet) available to the required extent.
- mobilize know-how that is not available in one's own hospital or which has not yet been established for economic reasons (insufficient utilization of highly specialized and expensive capacities).

Furthermore, networks in health care, with their holistic patient-care approach, are the basis for a regional supply concept. However, they also serve the purpose of improving the quality of medical service processes and of simultaneously containing costs. Such organizational linkages affect medical processes (e.g. disease management programs) and complement supply processes (e.g. supply of medical products, radiology services or catering services).

For a hospital network, connections are possible or useful in three phases:

- Connections to general practitioners, e.g. by joint investments in high-tech medical devices with the aim that the general practitioner preferably refers patients to the partner hospital.
- Connections to support service processes in the hospital; this can affect para-medical professions (physiotherapist, speech therapist, etc.) as well as secondary service providers (radiology) and tertiary service providers (logistics).
- Connections to follow-up institutions, to generate a consistent treatment of patients on the basis of standardized coordinated therapy and rehabilitation approaches (aim: consistent quality assurance on the basis of proven guidelines and evidence-based medicine).

However, these networks can only work effectively, if

- the organizational structures and service processes of the network partners are coordinated according to the value chain approach (principle of corresponding organizations);
- common interests are present or can be achieved;
- the service provision, reimbursement and cost structures are transparent according to an open-book mentality;
- the partners act in the spirit of agreement in exceptional situations;
- a commonly accepted incentive system, which automatically reaches a uniform level of care provision of the partners and which has a process-coordinating effect, is the basis for cooperation.

Depending on aims, intentions, organizational and market-oriented frameworks, networks can be designed differently (Epstein and Harris 1995). These design alternatives are developed according to the following criteria:

- object/area of agreement (definable business field, definable operative task or the entire company, or a complex strategic task);
- temporary or unlimited agreement;
- core business-orientation or concerning the tertiary area;
- retaining or giving up legal or economic autonomy;
- level of organizational integration of the reporting system, level of decentralization, nature of incentive system, number of decision-making levels, influences on decisions, etc.

4 Restrictions of an Effective Network Design

There are four main obstacles in health economic practice which impede the development of effective network structures:

- Silo mentality within departments and between professions, including the associated inadequate communication. This refers especially to the demarcation of tasks, competencies and responsibilities between nurses and physicians, as well as the delegation of doctor's services to nurses.
- Incentive systems which favor hospital boundaries. This affects, e.g. economically motivated goals, which induce leading physicians to treat patients themselves, instead of referring them to qualified specialists.
- Sectoral financial budgets impede payment to qualified outpatient services performed by hospitals in the case of particularly serious diseases.
- Cross-sectoral contracts intended to secure the medical supplies are carried out by different institutions with their own objectives. In consequence, hospital planning and that of medical practices (general practitioners) are not coordinated; inpatient and outpatient sectors are not interlinked.

5 Types of Networks and Their Purposes

Oriented around the characteristics of a *boundaryless hospital*, networks are characterized by:

- their unique form of cooperation,
- the use of special technology,
- concentration on selected treatment process,
- the integration of both similar and different actors,
- strategic intent.

Intramural networks are formed within a hospital with the aim of meeting the special requirements of different patient types/diseases which do not occur regularly. Such a function is fulfilled by, e.g. rapid response teams which consist of different professions from different departments (trauma surgery, anesthesia, emergency medicine) in order to treat patients with life-threatening conditions, as well as uncertain diagnoses. The cross-departmental and interdisciplinary organization of internal innovation networks, with the aim of developing more effective and efficient diagnosis methods and therapy approaches (translational medicine), as well as the establishment of tumor conferences, are typical examples of intramural network structures.

Horizontal networks integrate medical service providers from the same supply sector (same stage in the value-added process), e.g. with the aim of designing the medical service portfolio according to market requirements and economically, so as to meet quality requirements or to share expensive resources. The mutual allocation of patients on the basis of a specialization strategy is also typical of horizontal cooperation. A significant motivation includes the mobilization of horizontal synergy effects like:

- Cost reduction through merging organizational units, whose services are needed in two or more hospitals, but can be performed regardless of location (laboratory, pharmacy, reprocessing of medical products, kitchen, laundry);
- achievement of procurement advantages through bundling of demand;
- coordination of medical service structures to avoid duplicated provision of resources (e.g. devices for radiology: MRI, PET/CT) or to fulfil minimum quantities for particular interventions (e.g. merging two orthopedic departments to reach the minimum quantity of 50 hip replacements, according to the expert associations and payers' requirements).

Vertical networks pursue service integration along the value chain. Typical network aims include market development by binding the referral physicians, e.g. by follow-up cooperation, consistent treatment of complex diseases (diabetes, multiple sclerosis, oncological entities) on the basis of organized patient pathways, as well as guidelines and a cross-sectoral approach of standardized treatment cases with an elective character (e.g. integrated process for total hip replacement patients). Vertical networks also arise through forward integration, for instance, if a hospital with a large orthopedic department (more than 1000 hip treatments per year) takes over an orthopedic rehabilitation clinic, or through backward integration, e.g. if a portal clinic (referral clinic) or a community health center is taken over.

The forward integration creates markets for the takeover target (the hospital secures the utilization of the target's rehabilitation clinic), the backward integration aims to secure referral markets for the hospital.

Lateral networks consist of actors from different supply sectors, those with different responsibilities (e.g. financing medical services) and actors from the medical industry. This network type includes managed care networks and legal constructs which connect the financing function (insurance companies) with the service provider function (hospital). Also, exclusive supplier partnerships in the procurement area of a hospital (single sourcing), as well as public-private-partnership projects are included in this type of networks.

Hybrid networks are a special kind of lateral networks. They are present if an integration of several lateral partners takes place: For example, an industrial (non-hospital) company takes over a hospital chain, which exclusively uses the products of this particular company (intention: securing markets and innovations). Simultaneously, there are exclusive supplier partnerships with a low number of technology suppliers, which at the same time assume operator responsibility (risk sharing). Additionally, a cross-sectoral, regionally concentrated (cluster) medical service portfolio guarantees a consistent treatment of patients or particular diseases (on the role of the industry in medical networks see Burns and Danzon 2002).

6 Factors Constraining Network Design

Limiting factors determine the supply character of networks, they constrain the organization options and define the success factors for operating the network.

The most important limiting factors are:

- The *time*, available between the triggering event (e.g. an acute life-threatening disease) and the therapeutic countermeasure (e.g. lysis to treat a stroke);
- *resources*, which are normally short term and/or expensive like expert knowledge for second opinions, special technology (PET-CT), etc.;
- *room* in terms of the size of the catchment area;
- *population density* (occupational intensity);
- *population structure* (age distribution, as well as prevalence and incidence of diseases);
- *complexity* of a disease or of a treatment case or treatment form (chronic diseases, oncological entities, orphan diseases, refractory wounds);
- *costs* and cost-containment potential;
- *efficiency and earnings potential*;
- *quality* and quality improvement potential;
- *service-supply level* of the population in a region.

7 Forms of Organization

7.1 King-Pin and Resident Principle

The *King-Pin Principle* of network design is used if a leading hospital provides combined conventional and special services for the other network partners (hospitals, general practitioners, rehabilitation clinics).

These services may entail expensive technical resources (e.g. cardiological interventional diagnostics and therapy), which are provided by the leading hospital and from case to case for the network partners. Knowledge services (second opinion) or diagnostic services (teleradiology) are also possible.

The leading hospital (king) is a service provider and investments by the leading hospital are co-financed by the net partners (pins).

The *Resident Principle* goes beyond the King-Pin Principle insofar as it has its own residents, in other words specialists, on-site in the pin hospital, organizationally integrated, who have access to the resources of the king hospital at any time. The Resident-Principle is often used to build up decentralized know-how in the pin hospitals or these positions are parts of a job rotation system for personnel development.

Both principles are, e.g. used in medical technical service centers. Any expensive test equipment and calibration stations are provided centrally. The repair sets can be found on-site. Resident technicians look after the medical devices on-site in heart surgery operation rooms, ICUs, diagnostic functional areas, with the aim of ensuring a high level of availability of the devices.

7.2 C + C Model

The C + C-Model (cooperation and coordination model) represents a designing principle for oncological networks that differentiates between coordinating and cooperating hospitals or general practitioners. To differentiate the tasks between cooperating and coordinating network partners, the C + C Model uses three criteria:

- the range of experts, which refers to the number of participating service providers of different complimentary specialist disciplines,
- the depth of specialization (with regard to oncological entities) and
- the separation of specialized tasks, which are performed in the acute inpatient area (e.g. tumor surgery, proton therapy, radiation therapy) and routine tasks which are performed close to the patient and due to guidelines in the outpatient sector (e.g. chemotherapy).

8 Selected Examples of Network Cooperation

8.1 The Portal Clinic as an Element of a Referral Physicians Network

Portal clinics (Münch and Scheytt 2014) are of particular importance for providing a comprehensive supply of medical services (also for highly specialized ones): Such clinics are highly qualified primary/secondary institutions for health services, which provide precise diagnoses in order to decide whether or not a patient needs a specialized treatment. They are associated with specialized clinics (e.g. pulmonary/thorax surgery; neurology; etc.), qualified service providers (e.g. radiology centers) and maximum providers by a telemedical IT infrastructure. Patient records are documented and distributed electronically. This enables fast and precise diagnoses, second opinion consultations via conference calls and targeted acute care (Fig. 2). Portal clinics are also of particular importance in emergency care. They give first aid in trauma networks with telemedical connections to maximum care providers.

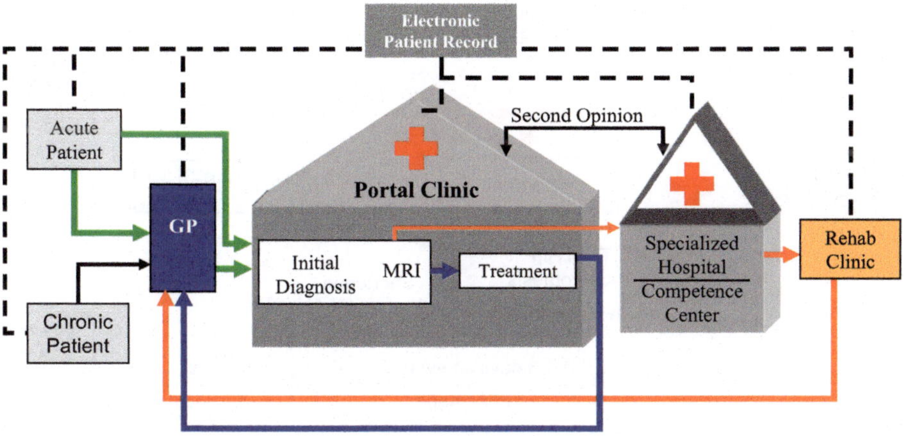

Fig. 2 The portal clinic is a decentralized hospital for basic medical supply and has the function of a gatekeeper

8.2 Integrated Cross-Sectoral Supply Models as a Strategic Option

Cross-sectoral supply models (Preusker 2015) reflect a strategy of bundling the entire medical service portfolio, which is necessary to treat a disease cross-sectorally and comprehensively, subject to uniform control at a single site or in a single region. These are diseases which on the one hand have an elective character and for which the treatment process can easily be standardized (e.g. total endoprosthesis). On the other hand, these medical provision concepts enable new forms of care for treating multi-morbid patients or those with complexity levels which require intensive medical care in the acute and rehabilitation sector (e.g. stroke treatment, cardio-surgical patients, transplantations).

8.2.1 Contracts of Integrated Care

Primary care by family practitioners or specialist physicians, diagnosis and treatment in acute care, rehabilitation and outpatient follow-up are cross-sectorally integrated and allocated to a central case management, which leads to shortened stays in the system, with a simultaneous decrease in treatment costs.

Such care is the basic idea behind integrated care contracts (Fig. 3). Diagnosis, therapy and rehabilitation are integrated and achieved without unnecessary waiting times. Follow-up home services enable an earlier discharge.

8.2.2 The Integrated Care Net: Supply with Managed Care Character

The integrated supply net connects medical service providers of different specializations with the aim of treating diseases without high complexity levels, so as to provide appropriate care and treatment at comparably low cost.

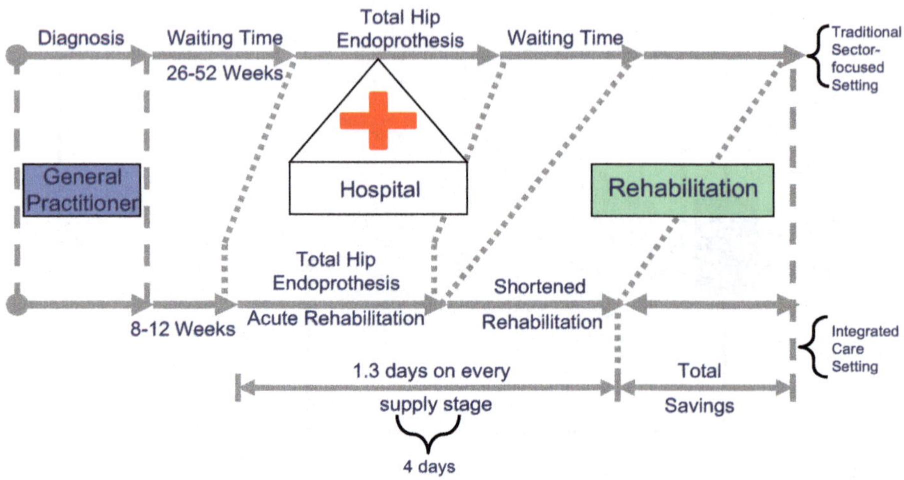

Fig. 3 Integrated care provision process flow using the example of hip endoprosthesis

On the one hand such network structures connect medical service providers at different supply stages (family practitioner, hospital, rehabilitation clinic, nursing home, etc.). On the other hand the medical service portfolio of such networks is the basis for insurance services, which can be obtained at particularly favorable conditions (Herzlinger 1997). Accordingly, the insurance service can be offered together with the medical service from a single source (in a single-contract package = managed care principle). Telemedical services are increasingly integrated into such managed care concepts (Kaufmann 2014) (Fig. 4).

8.3 Networks in Emergency Care

Emergency care is more efficient and effective when there is a smooth and quick link between the medical sectors (outpatient first aid, treatment in the ambulance, complementary inpatient treatment, acute rehabilitation and outpatient emergency follow-up). This can be demonstrated by the example of stroke treatment.

Annually, 250,000 people in Germany are affected by a first or repeated stroke event. 20–30 % of the patients die within the first 4 weeks. In 2013, 18,883 people died because of a stroke (women: 12,078; men: 6805; Statistisches Bundesamt 2014) and it is the second leading cause of death in the world (Müller 2013). The number of patients suffering from this acute disease is increasing, because of the aging society. Strokes occur especially at an advanced age. Men are aged 70 on average when suffering from the first stroke and women about 75. The World Health Organization (WHO) labels strokes as the “upcoming epidemic of the twenty-first century”.

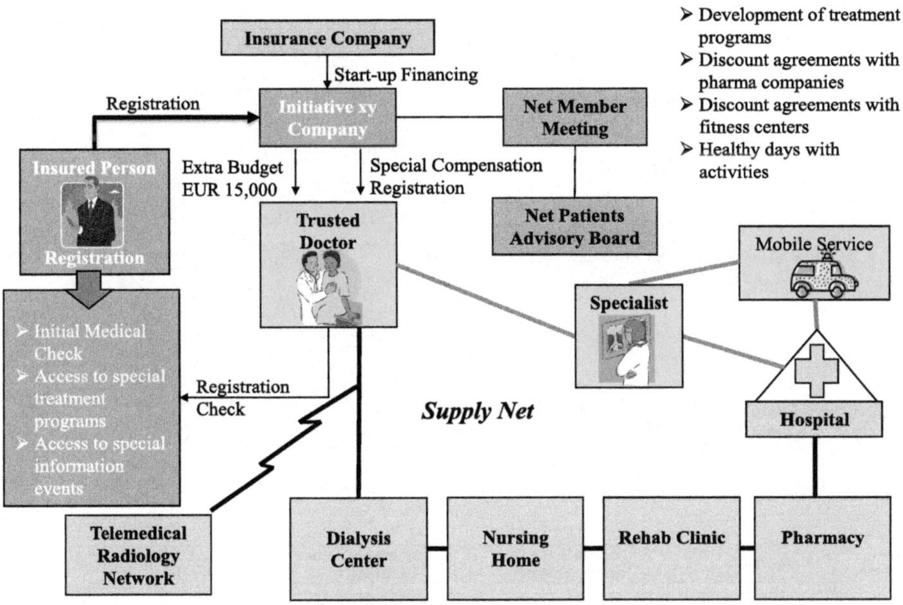

Fig. 4 Medical supply networks with a managed care character

In the case of a stroke, rapid emergency care is needed. Two rules reveal complementary and economic effects:

- *Time is brain*: The faster the stroke is treated, the larger the range of effective diagnostic and treatment options and the more positive the prediction regarding a return to a normal and largely self-determined life. One third of the patients remain permanently in need of care, which could partly be avoided by more rapid specialist care.
- *Time is money*: Rapid treatment enabled by integrated diagnostic and treatment approaches decreases individual treatment costs.

It is important that the key actors in the stroke value-added process match and perform their medical services promptly according to the guidelines (Figs. 5 and 6).

To do so, it is necessary to:

- train the rescue teams (emergency doctors, ambulance staff), to recognize stroke symptoms fast and clearly,
- concentrate the transport route on a hospital with stroke competencies,
- obtain the initial diagnosis in hospital (by CT/perfusions-CT/MRI) immediately after admission,
- have the therapeutic team (neurology, stroke nurse, physiotherapist, speech therapist) immediately available and
- ensure the immediate start of rehabilitation (no more than 6 h after the stroke event).

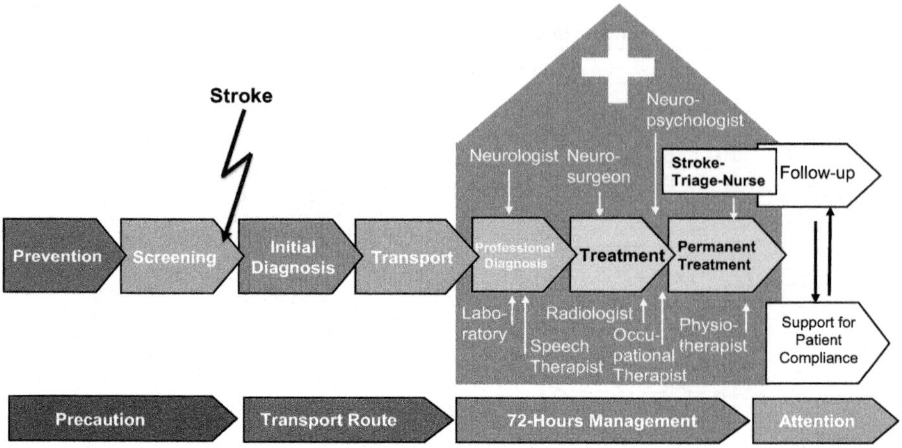

Fig. 5 Treatment according to the stroke management process

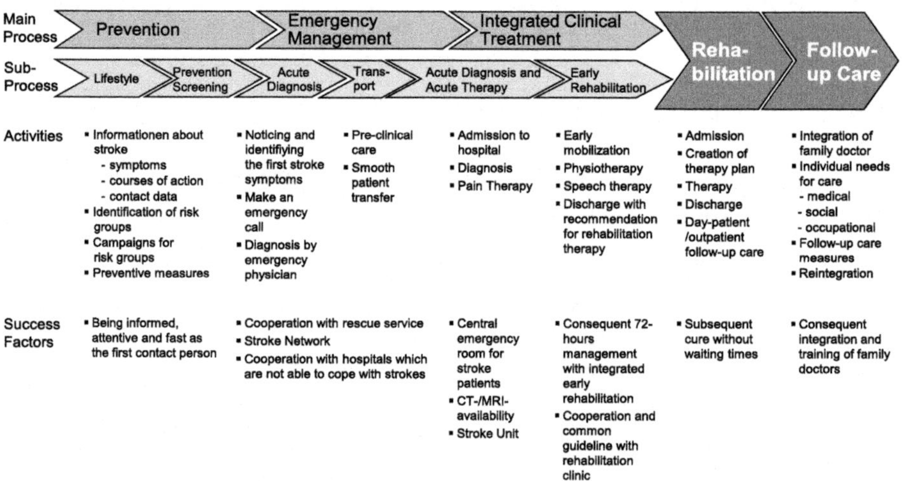

Fig. 6 Stroke management before and after admission to a hospital

8.4 Medical Clusters

Clusters (Porter 2008; von Eiff 2012) are regional (local) concentrated aggregations of medical service providers at different vertical stages in the value chain (Preusker 2015). They enable economies of scale by centralizing tertiary services (catering, cleaning, laundry, procurement, logistics, administration), through economies of scope by means of special offers (care concepts, assisted living, dementia care, Parkinson's disease care) an by economies of management (negotiations with payers from a single source for integrated services along the entire value chain) (Fig. 7).

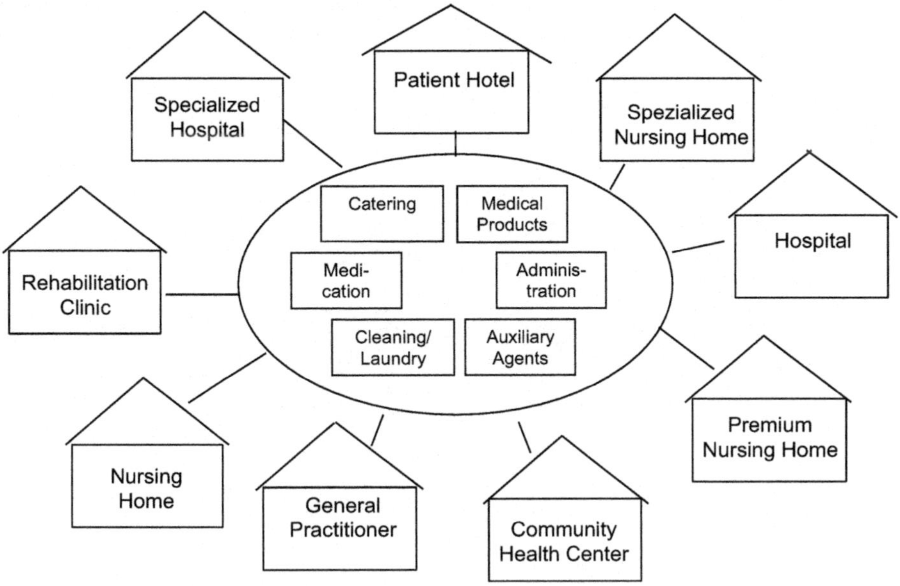

Fig. 7 Clusters facilitate economies of scale through regional centralization of tertiary services and economies of scope by additional social services (based on von Eiff 2013)

8.5 The Campus Concept

A campus is a local concentrated association of complementary medical service providers, with the aim of ensuring complete and comprehensive care for complex diseases (e.g. orphan diseases, cancer, cardiovascular diseases) (Fig. 8).

The campus concept facilitates interdisciplinary medicine, which is designed to provide complementary service structures for patients with complex diseases, multi-morbidity and special treatment requirements. The campus concept enables specialization and complementary differentiation of a medical service portfolio in acute care, as well as in elective care, with the aim of providing complete and full treatment (life cycle of care). The campus medical treatment approach is oriented towards the causal connections of diseases: 35 % of all heart attack patients are simultaneously diabetics and 20 % of all cardiovascular patients suffer from strokes. Diabetics are affected more than average by vascular complaints (diabetic foot; vascular stenosis). The campus concept brings together cardiology, cardiothoracic surgery, vascular surgery, diabetology, rheumatology and neurology. At the same time, the campus concept is cross-sector oriented: Outpatient services are offered, as well as acute care, rehabilitation and nursing services. Finally, the campus is a location for interdisciplinary medical research.

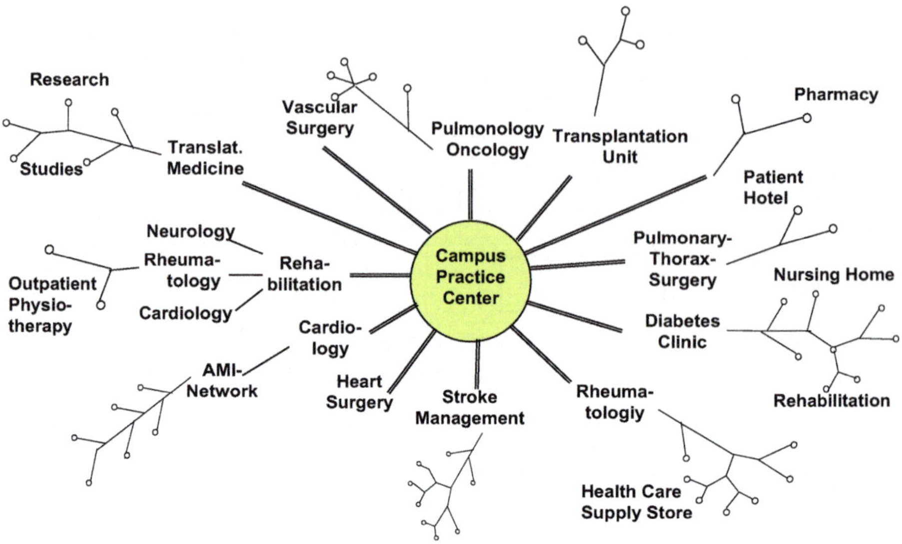

Fig. 8 The campus practice center

9 Conclusion

Networks in medicine are a powerful form of organization for meeting the challenges of the aging society, medical and technological progress, as well as the increasing number of more both medically and behaviorally demanding patients. Networks are the *organization of choice*, if complex illnesses are to be treated effectively. Rapid reaction to emergency situations is required and the competitive position of a hospital should generally be improved. Networks for the treatment of complex illnesses, such as in oncology, combine special services offered by maximum provider institutions (e.g. teaching hospitals) with routine services (e.g. transarterial chemoembolization) given at decentralized primary care physicians' offices. Within this type of network, distributed knowledge is the basis of design.

The critical success factor for designing an emergency network is time. In order to ensure that patients with life-threatening conditions get to the right hospital fast enough, the rescue chain has to orchestrate pre-clinical and acute care activities.

Furthermore, networks can be built and steered by *financial incentives*. Such *managed care networks* give patients the choice between different insurance options in combination with the option to request treatment only by selected physicians under contract with a health maintenance organization.

Networks contribute toward enhancing medical quality for the broader population and specific patient groups and toward simultaneously containing costs in the health system. In networks, duplicated diagnostic work can be avoided and purchasing advantages mobilized by bundling the demand for medical products. However, networks may also suffer from limiting factors of design such as aspects related to resources, catchment area, illness complexity and age structure of the population. The efficiency and effectiveness of networks depend on the level of commitment of the network and on the nature of partner behavior. It is a fact that low-commitment networks tend to foster "maverick behavior".

References

Burns LR, Danzon PM (2002) Pharmaceutical manufacturers. In: Burns LR, Wharton School Colleagues (eds) The health care value chain. Producers, purchasers and providers. Wiley, San Francisco, pp 219–249

Epstein JD, Harris SF (1995) Legal structure of health care delivery system. In: Wolper LF (ed) Health care administration. Principles, practices, structure and delivery, 2nd edn. Johns & Bartlett Learning, Gaithersburg, pp 589–599

Fottler MD, Malvey D (1995) Multiprovider systems. In: Wolper LF (ed) Health care administration. Principles, practices, structure and delivery, 2nd edn. Johns & Bartlett Learning, Gaithersburg, pp 489–515

Herzlinger R (1997) Market driven health care. Who wins, who loses in the transplantation of America's largest service industry. Perseus Books, New York

Kaufmann S (2014) Herausforderungen des Versorgungsmanagements aus Sicht einer Schweizer Gesundheitskasse. In: Fink U, Kücking M, Walzik E, Zerth J (eds) Solidarität und Effizienz im Gesundheitswesen. Ein Suchprozess. medhochzwei Verlag, Heidelberg, pp 261–268

Müller T (2013) Jeder Zehnte stirbt an Schlaganfall. In: ÄrzteZeitung online, 29.10.2013. http://www.aerztezeitung.de/medizin/krankheiten/herzkreislauf/schlaganfall/article/848989/welt-schlaganfall-tag-jeder-zehnte-stirbt-schlaganfall.html. Accessed 17 Sept 2015

Münch E, Scheytt S (2014) Netzwerkmedizin. Ein unternehmerisches Konzept für die altersdominierte Gesundheitsversorgung. Springer Gabler, Wiesbaden

Nagyrapolt ASG (2008) Value adding service delivery strategies. In: Ginter PM, Swayne LE, Duncan WJ (eds) Strategic management of health care organizations, 6th edn. Wiley, Chichester, pp 293–333

Porter ME (2008) On competition. Harvard Review Press, Boston, 2nd revised edition

Porter ME, Teisberg EO (2006) Redefining health care. Creating value-based competition on results. Harvard Business School Press, Boston

Preusker U (2015) Das deutsche Gesundheitssystem verstehen. Strukturen und Funktionen im Wandel. 2. Auflage. medhochzwei Verlag, Heidelberg

Sozialgesetzbuch V (2015) Sozialgesetzbuch (SGB) Fünftes Buch (V). http://www.gesetze-im-internet.de/bundesrecht/sgb_5/gesamt.pdf. Accessed 17 Sept 2015

Statistisches Bundesamt (2014) Gesundheit. Todesursachen in Deutschland 2013. https://www.destatis.de/DE/Publikationen/Thematisch/Gesundheit/Todesursachen/Todesursachen2120400-137004.pdf?__blob=publicationFile. Accessed 17 Sept 2015

von Eiff MC (2007) The healing environment. Eur Hosp 16(5):46

von Eiff W (2012) Wettbewerbsstrategie. Bedeutung des Porter-Ansatzes für Kliniken. Health Care Manag 3(5):14–17

von Eiff CA (2013) Mergers & Acquisitions auf dem deutschen Gesundheitsmarkt. Eine wirtschaftliche und rechtliche Betrachtung von M&A + Transaktionen im Krankenhaussektor. medhochzwei Verlag, Heidelberg, p 38

Wilfried von Eiff is Professor of Health Care Management at HHL Leipzig Graduate School of Management and is the Director of the Center for Hospital Management, a research institute linked to the University of Münster, Germany. Both institutions are well-known for international and national research, consulting and government advisory activities in the fields of cost–benefit analysis of medical technology and clinical procedures, strategic management and mergers and acquisitions in the health care sector, business ethics in medicine, risk management and health service research. Prof. von Eiff is a founding member of the initiative 'Best Practice Management in Healthcare and Hospital Management', which is part of the European Hospital Management Association (EHMA). He is member of various boards of directors in health care and industry. Before, he was Director and Member of the Board of the University Clinic of Giessen, Germany, and also Managing Director of an international automotive company overseeing the fields of organization, process, logistics and IT management. He holds a doctoral degree from the Faculty of Business Administration, University of Tübingen, Germany, as well as a doctoral degree from the Faculty of Medicine, University of Giessen.

Cancer Care: New Value Chains Challenge German Hospital Structures—A Comprehensive Cancer Center Perspective

Florian Kron, Andreas Bernschein, Anna Kostenko, Jürgen Wolf, Michael Hallek, and Jan-Peter Glossmann

Abstract

The medical and economic impact of cancer is a major challenge for hospitals in every country. Comprehensive cancer centers (CCC) are at the forefront to fight cancer. From an organizational perspective these large centers are highly complex. They combine patient-oriented cancer care with basic, translational and population-based cancer research. These centers cannot operate as stand-alone organizations but rely on cooperation in a network of hospitals and office-based physicians. The medical progress in recent years—which is often referred to as *personalized* or *precision* medicine—comes with hope for patients but also with diagnostic, organizational and financial challenges. Especially clinical trials are time-consuming and costly but indispensable being the backbone of treatment progress. A growing economic pressure results from a policy of increased competition on the one hand and a strict separation of ambulatory and inpatient care on the other hand. In this article we discuss the challenges and opportunities from the perspective of the Center for Integrated Oncology (CIO) Köln Bonn which is one of the largest CCCs in Germany. The political, scientific and economic challenges and opportunities are described as well as possible solutions including practical experience.

Keywords

Comprehensive cancer center • CCC • Cancer genomics • Sectorization • Economic challenges • Networks of cancer care • Germany • Oncology

F. Kron • A. Bernschein • A. Kostenko • J. Wolf, M.D. • M. Hallek • J.-P. Glossmann, M.D., M.P.H. (✉)
First Department of Internal Medicine, Cologne University Hospital, Kerpener Straße 62, 50937 Cologne, Germany

Center for Integrated Oncology Köln Bonn, CIO Köln Bonn, Cologne University Hospital, 50924 Cologne, Germany
e-mail: jan-peter.glossmann@uk-koeln.de

H. Albach et al. (eds.), *Boundaryless Hospital*, DOI 10.1007/978-3-662-49012-9_2

1 Introduction: Challenges and Opportunities

In the near future more people in Germany will die of cancer than of cardiovascular disease. Parts of Europe are already reaching a 'tipping point' where cardiovascular disease is no longer the leading cause of death (Nichols et al. 2014). There are new and promising developments of diagnostics and treatment leading to personalized cancer medicine. The prerequisites for good cancer care are complex and they especially challenge large comprehensive cancer centers (CCC). In the following we describe current medical and political developments as well as economic challenges from the perspective of the Center for Integrated Oncology (CIO) Köln Bonn.

1.1 Barriers in the German Health Care System

With the new millennium the Advisory Council for the Concerted Action in Health Care in Germany published the report Appropriateness and Efficiency and identified the overuse, underuse and misuse of diagnostics and treatment in the German health care system (Schwartz et al. 2000). Various deficits especially apply to cancer care. Most importantly there still is the strict separation of the ambulatory and inpatient care. This fragmentation of the in- and outpatient sector, sometimes referred to as sectorization, results in a lack of coordination in patient care and contributes to overuse (e.g. unnecessary referrals and repetition of diagnostic tests) and underuse (e.g. exclusion from medical services). The consequences are loss of information, inconsistent documentation, suboptimal therapies, avoidable harm and last but not least psychological stress for the patient. Recent health care reforms over the last decade have also tried to solve these structural problems although the main focus has been on cost containment. The relevant changes regarding the sectorization will be discussed in Sect. 1.3.

1.2 Cancer Genomics Changes Medical Practice

Cancer is a medical field on the verge of a paradigm shift towards personalized medicine and customization of health care (Goldstein et al. 2012). These changes also have an impact on how hospitals and office-based oncologists cooperate. Especially targeted therapies are currently revolutionizing cancer treatment. These drugs interfere with specific molecules involved in cancer cell growth and survival. Traditional chemotherapy drugs, by contrast, act against all actively dividing cells (National Cancer Institute 2015). The targeted therapy approach is based on the molecular understanding of the cancerous cell. Because cancer progression is facilitated by activation of oncogenes (tumor promoting proteins) and inactivation of tumor suppressors, the tumor can be eradicated by reversing these alterations. The key technology needed to identify the genetic alterations is DNA sequencing and genotyping. This technology is costly and currently

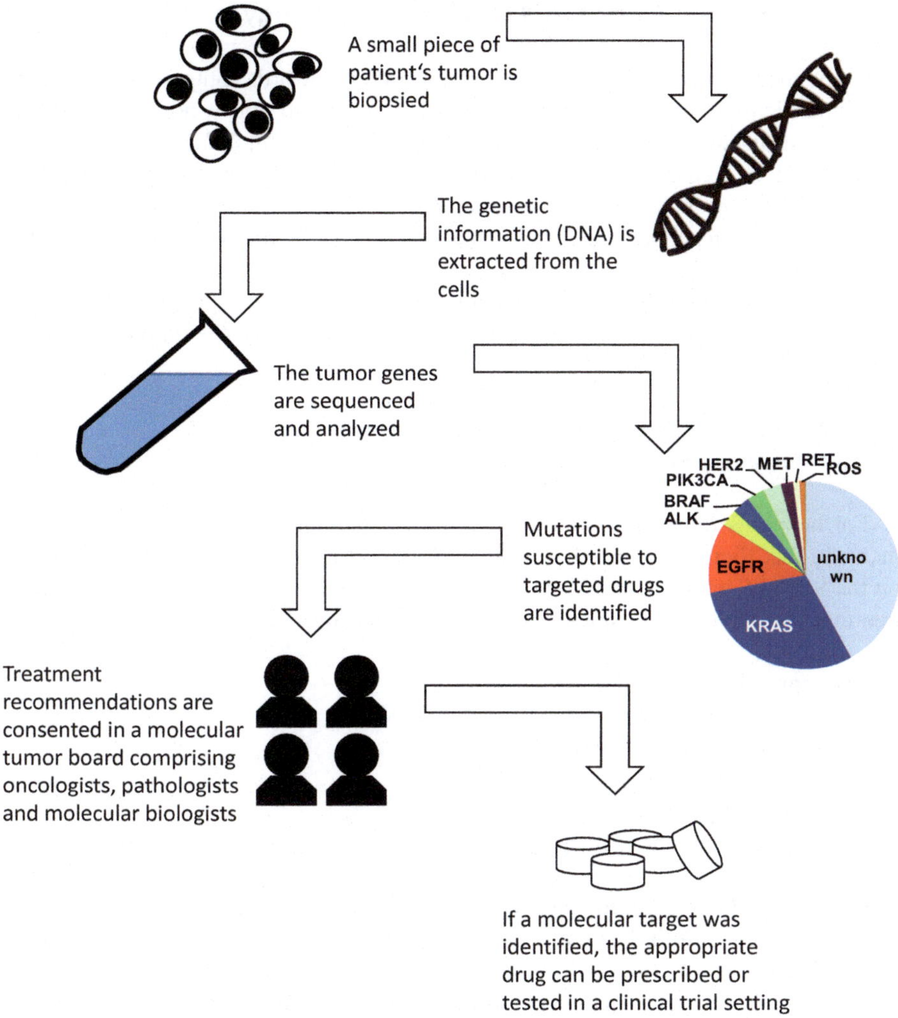

Fig. 1 Basic steps from biopsy to targeted therapy

improving at a fast pace. For example, at the CIO Köln Bonn the methods and machinery have been updated almost on a yearly basis between 2012 and 2015. The more advanced the technique, the less tumor material is needed for an increasing number of genetic alterations to be identified. Furthermore, expert knowledge of molecular biologists, pathologists and oncologists is required to interpret the vast data and to conclude treatment options for the patients. Fortunately, the patient does not have to travel to the next CCC to get the results since only a sample consisting of a few cells is needed (Fig. 1).

1.3 Economic Trends in Ambulatory Oncology

The advances in oncology reinforce the trend towards outpatient treatment ('ambulantization'). Less side effects and a patient-friendly administration of drugs (oral instead of intravenous application) are two major factors contributing to this trend. In recent years the German health policy sought to adapt to the medical trends and to overcome the strict separation of ambulatory and inpatient care (Jahn et al. 2012). In this context the question arises how economic issues can follow the medical progress.

The outpatient reimbursement system in Germany is heterogeneous. Numerous reforms over the last years led to a growing diversification of the outpatient sector. Basically there are two separate systems:

(a) the outpatient system for office based physicians and
(b) the outpatient system in hospitals.

For hospitals there is no consistent form of reimbursement of outpatient treatment. In fact there are more than a dozen different reimbursement systems. Based on the Social Security Code V (SGB V) and also in the context of research-related treatment at university hospitals the major options are (Lüngen 2007):

- Appropriations, § 95 SGB V
- Disease management program, § 137 SGB V
- Integrated care, § 140 SGB V
- University outpatient system, § 117 SGB V
- Outpatient surgery in hospital, § 115 SGB V
- Outpatient treatment in hospital, § 116 SGB V

Especially this fractured legal framework makes it difficult to overview and control different reimbursement systems in the outpatient hospital sector (Lüngen and Rath 2010).

Since a few years the economic impact of the outpatient units in hospitals has continuously been increasing. The following figure of § 116b registrations and related health fund costs illustrates the development. From 2007 to 2011 there was a steep increase in registrations and costs in this specific ambulatory reimbursement system (Fig. 2).

With two major health care reforms in 2007 and 2012 ("Gesetzliche Krankenversicherung Wettbewerbsstärkungsgesetz GKV-WSG' and "Versorgungsstrukturgesetz GKV-VStG") the options of outpatient reimbursement in hospitals were extended. One of the main goals was to improve intersectoral cooperation between the traditional outpatient sector and the hospital. The § 116b SGB V comprises the diagnostics and treatment of complex diseases including cancer and also requires special qualifications of personnel, interdisciplinarity and special medical equipment.

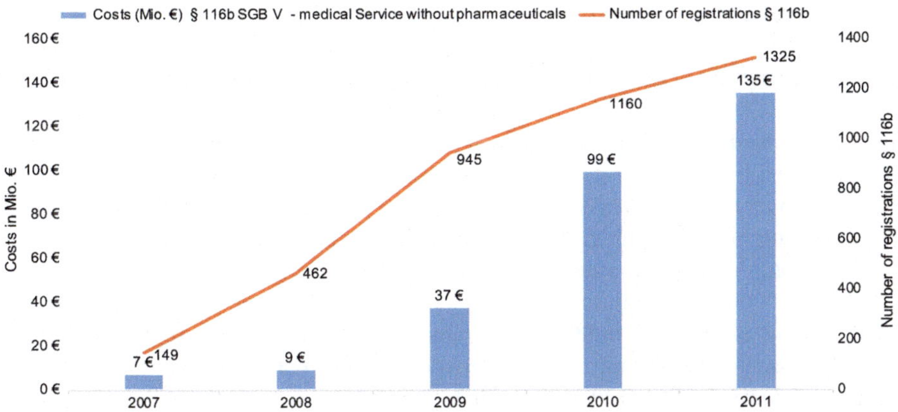

Fig. 2 Development of ambulatory care in hospitals § 116b SGB V (based on Schmedders 2012)

Inclusion criteria for § 116b are:

- diseases with severe course of disease
- rare (orphan) diseases with a small number of cases and
- diseases which require highly specialized diagnostic and therapeutic measures.

The participation in the reimbursement according to § 116b depends on many preconditions which have to be fulfilled by the health care providers. The directive of the Federal Joint Committee contains specific requirements for the process and structural quality e.g. requirements concerning organization, documentation, minimum quantities of cases, quality assurance and collaboration with office-based physicians. One of the biggest future challenges will be to fulfill personnel requirements such as providing a leading team, a core team and a supporting team from the two different sectors (Jahn et al. 2012). There has been a slow development of the § 116b SGB V: The requirements of the first oncological disease—gastrointestinal tumors—were defined as late as 2014.

Outpatient units in university hospitals are essential for medical research, teaching and the training of the students and young doctors. Based on § 117 SGB V university hospitals are allowed to do clinical research in an outpatient setting (Wissenschaftsrat 2010). In practice, these units are fully integrated in the whole ambulatory and teaching process at universities. Therefore, these outpatient departments are also involved in patient treatment beyond clinical research. A study on outpatient units at university hospitals from 2003 revealed that these units also play an important role in the regular outpatient care (Lauterbach et al. 2012). A lump sum is reimbursed and there is no cost-based re-financing (Lüngen 2007). In 2010, the German Council of Science and Humanities recommended to reform the standard fee system to a more differentiated and performance-based remuneration (Wissenschaftsrat 2010).

2 Potential Solutions

2.1 Cross-Sectional Organization Design in Oncology

Traditional hospital structures follow a functional organization approach and are characterized by departments in which each unit follows a profession (see Fig. 3). This top-down hierarchy classification requires a high degree of standardization and formalization but the complexity in dynamic health care markets limits this type of organization. As a development from the function-orientation the divisional form includes the concept of clinical governance that tries to integrate quality improvement, patient-orientation and financial transparency. Highly specialized and autonomous departments generate an isolated perspective that emphasizes the lack of interdisciplinarity. To avoid the conflict of integration and specialization cross-sectional structures can be implemented. Especially in cancer treatment the combination of divisional and matrix modules allows an integrative cancer center structure that is essential for multidisciplinary treatment (Lauterbach et al. 2010).

In Germany, several types of cancer centers have been established at federal level by the Federal Government (National Cancer Plan 2012), the German Cancer Aid (Deutsche Krebshilfe, DKH) and the German Cancer Society (Deutsche Krebsgesellschaft, DKG). These centers are typically located at hospitals—in this setting many specialized medical and supportive departments work together at central space. Three types of cancer centers can be distinguished: *organ centers (C), oncology centers (CC) and comprehensive cancer centers (CCC)* (Fig. 4).

Organ centers are specialized in organ-related treatment of one cancer entity (e.g. intestinal cancer or lung cancer). Hospitals with three or more organ centers can consolidate those in an *oncology center*. These two types of cancer centers are evaluated and certified by the DKG by certain quality requirements (Krebsgesellschaft). Comprehensive cancer centers are located at university hospitals. In addition, they perform basic and *translational research* (Pfaff et al. 2011). A selected group of these academic centers are funded as *Oncology Centers of Excellence* by the DKH. As of spring 2015, there are 13 *Oncology Centers of Excellence* in Germany (Fig. 5).

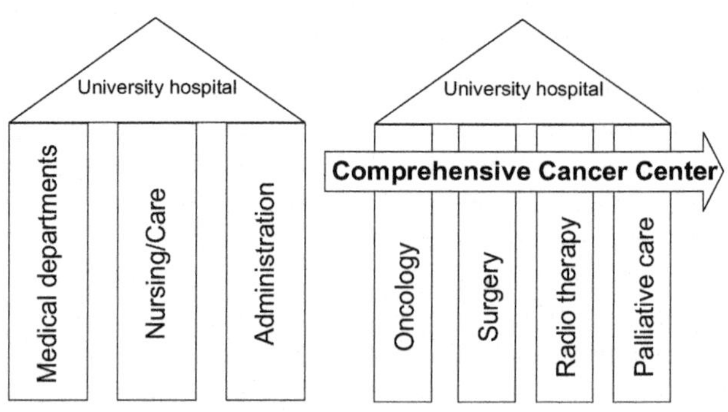

Fig. 3 Functional-orientation in hospitals and process-based cancer organization

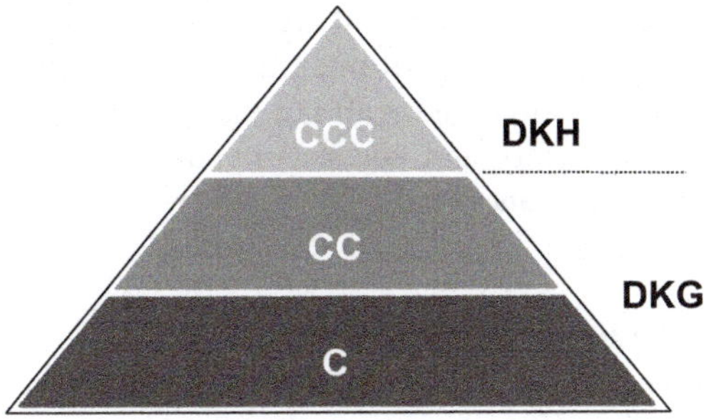

Fig. 4 Three stage model of oncology care in Germany

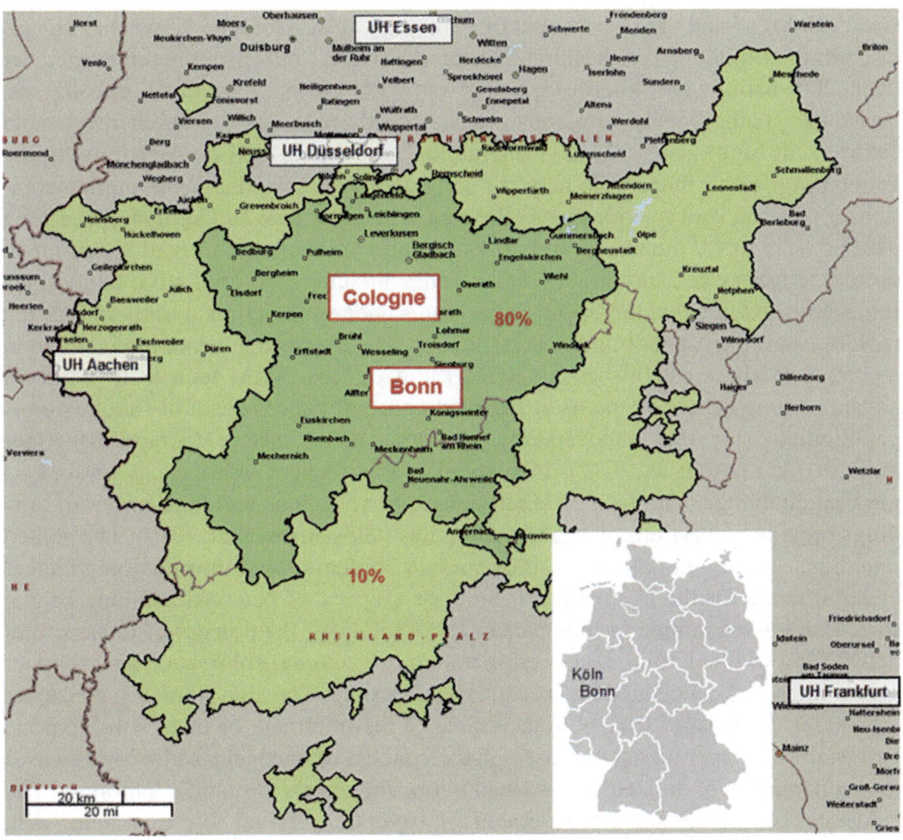

Fig. 5 Catchment area of the CIO Köln Bonn (own illustration, based on standard administrative data of the university hospitals Köln and Bonn)

The CIO Köln Bonn serves a catchment area of 4.5 million inhabitants, and it is one of the largest CCCs in Germany. It integrates the university hospitals in Köln and Bonn. All clinical units involved with the therapy and care of cancer patients work together to systematically and consistently improve all medical and allied health services provided for cancer patients.

2.2 The Future Lies in Networking

Within networks including office-based oncologists and regional hospitals patients can be treated close to their home. Molecular diagnostics should be limited to research-driven comprehensive cancer centers whereas patient treatment can be provided in local practices and hospitals. For example, the Network Genomic Medicine (NGM) Lung Cancer was founded in March 2010 by the Lung Cancer Group Cologne and the Department of Pathology at the Cologne University Hospital. Initially limited to North Rhine-Westphalia (NRW) but currently represented by over 200 nationwide interdisciplinary network partners (clinical oncologists, molecular pathologists, surgeons etc.), NGM provides comprehensive and centralized high-quality Next Generation Sequencing (NGS)-based multiplex genotyping for all inoperable lung cancer patients and stands for the implementation of personalized medicine into the routine cancer care in Germany. The lung panel covers DNA mutations and structural aberrations with a broad spectrum of proto-oncogenes and tumor suppressor genes including all predictive biomarkers for established targeted therapeutics, for drugs undergoing clinical trials and for the rapidly emerging cancer immunotherapeutics. The obtained information is stored in a central database established by NGM Lung Cancer. NGM focuses its work on advanced lung cancer as the most frequent cause of cancer death in Europe and is paradigmatic for the achievements of personalized cancer therapy (Buettner et al. 2013; Levy et al. 2012). In particular, lung cancer treatment is not only a medical challenge. The lack of curative treatment options and high prices of new drugs raise new questions on health economics (Glossmann et al. 2010). The gained mutational and immunologic profiles contain epidemiologic information which is of importance for the evaluation of the cost efficacy of personalized lung cancer care. Using the example of lung cancer as a prototype, the transfer of intersectoral networking to other solid cancer entities (e.g. melanoma, colorectal cancer, upper gastro-intestinal cancer and breast cancer) is possible. The algorithm of lung cancer biomarker diagnostics may be transferable to the treatment of other solid tumors. Personalized cancer therapy is based on the concept of oncogene addiction and uses the vulnerability of molecularly defined tumor subgroups to specific inhibitors. The evidence of significant improvement in overall survival by treatment with personalized medicine compared to standard chemotherapy in lung cancer patients who have previously been successfully genotyped (*EGFR*-mutant or *ALK*-rearranged) is given (A genomics-based classification of human lung tumors 2013). A broad implementation of personalized medicine in Germany has to accomplish comprehensive access of patients to molecular diagnostics and drugs,

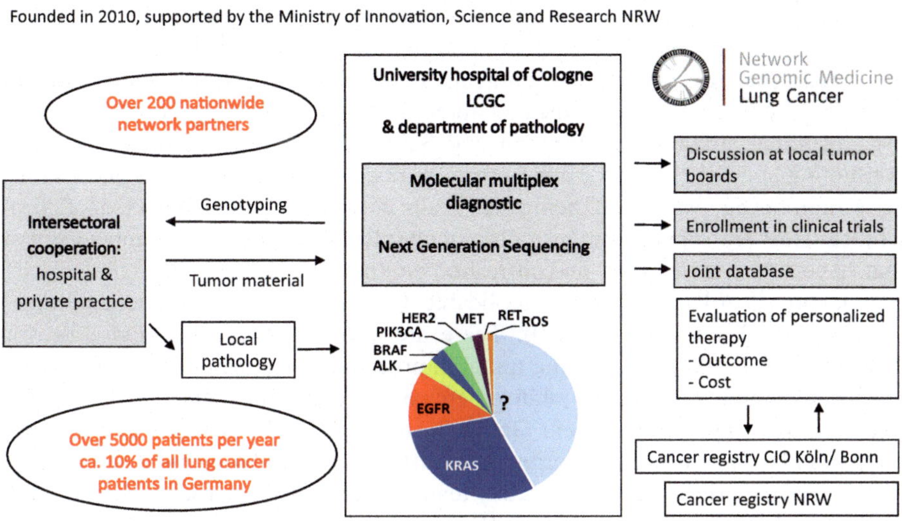

Fig. 6 Network Genomic Medicine

education of physicians and patients, evaluation of personalized treatment and cost-reimbursement strategies. The AOK Rheinland/Hamburg, one of the largest public health insurances in Germany, has contracted with NGM for full reimbursement of molecular multiplex testing and initiation of a joint evaluation program in April 2014. In 2015, further nationwide public and private health insurances followed this example and joined the integrated care contract. NGM reinforces networking by focusing on centralized molecular diagnostic of tumor material and by giving feedback to constituent partners to promote decentralized patient treatment and improve know-how transfer. The establishment of further regional diagnostic centers is planned to reinforce patients access to personalized treatment approaches that are already in clinical evaluation. Apart from the participation in clinical trials, the intersectoral networking enables data collection and evaluation and improves non-commercial research within new therapeutic areas e.g. off-label use. These data can be used by federal authorities as e.g. the Joint Federal Committee (G-BA), for decision making related to the approval of new drugs, approval enhancements etc. (Fig. 6).

2.3 Clinical Trial Management: The Backbone of Innovation

Conducting clinical trials is one of the main challenges for CCCs. Clinical trials are time-consuming and expensive, but in oncology with focus on the evidence-based medicine the process of conducting clinical research is indispensable being the backbone of treatment progress and bringing benefits to patients through research activity. In addition to evidence, in the long-term clinical research has a general impact on the conduct of care of those individuals who failed to join clinical trials. Thus, clinical trials enable treatment opportunities besides the standards, complement daily practice and improve clinical care (Selby 2011). High-quality clinical trials in oncology require dedicated interdisciplinary experts and well-defined organizational structures (Herrmann and Sehner 2011) Clinical trials are time-consuming and cost-intensive due to strict protocol-related regulations and continuous monitoring, with staff being the main cost factor (Emanuel et al. 2003). Clinical sites are supposed to establish standardized operating procedures (SOPs) that have to be maintained and refreshed continually, and provide regular staff training in accordance with the applicable law, all of which require additional resources (Fink and Wicke 2010). There are only a few official guidelines for cost calculation related to specific research procedures, e.g. assessment of adverse events. Common German reimbursement systems for inpatient and outpatient treatment (e.g. Diagnosis-related Group System, DRG) do not take into account the particular tasks of study coordinators, different hourly-based rates considering the level of experience of various study team members and high-level personnel or institutional overheads. Hence, trial-related staff costs, e.g. set-up cost, recruitment cost and study management effort beyond the patient treatment need to be calculated severally. Structural links and organizational interrelationships among participating departments, hospital administration, external study groups, authorities, clinical sponsors and clinical/ contract research organisations (CRO) etc. make the trial-related intra- and inter-institutional coordination and study management a big time-consuming and cost-intensive challenge. The CIO Köln Bonn comprises world leading study groups (e.g. German CLL Study Group, German Hodgkin Study Group and Lung Cancer Group Cologne) and several decentralized clinical trial units subordinated to various internal departments. Developing and maintaining an appropriately trained study team is essential to the success of the quality of clinical trials (Baer et al. 2011). Not only medical staff (physicians and study nurses) but also project/data managers, controllers and study coordinators are involved to conduct clinical trials, especially on purpose of investigator initiated trials (IIT). To improve transparency of the research site costs the Clinical Trials Center Cologne (CTCC) offers various services to decentralized clinical trial units (CTU) at the Cologne University Hospital. It has developed the STudy site bUDGEting Tool (STUDGET). The STUDGET fee schedule can be used for further budget and contract negotiation, the site personnel can expeditiously compare the proposed budget with the STUDGET fees. In addition, STUDGET can be used by investigators to calculate case payments including institutional overheads for participating sites during the planning of mono- or multicentre IITs (Arenz et al. 2014). Having a good handle of site costs is essential to foster a transparent relationship between CTU and trial sponsor. Both commercial and non-commercial sponsors prefer working with CTUs with a clear overview of their research site costs being able to conduct the budget negotiation in a professional and timely manner (Baer et al. 2010). Further challenges for investigators and interdisciplinary study team members result from an increasing complexity of regulations, the time and financial constraints and growing business aspects, e.g. the complexity of contracts and CRO pressures (English et al. 2010). Therefore, adequate reimbursement is essential to establish and to manage successful CTUs and study groups with broad opportunities and workforce excellence, which in turn affects data quality, patient outcome, the overall duration of trials and then again keeps the overall cost at a low level (Arenz et al. 2014).

2.4 Standardized Care and Interdisciplinarity

The kaizen quote by Taiichi Ohno[1] '*Without standards there can be no improvement.*' applies especially to cancer care. Doctors and nurses should have access to up-to-date standards to be able to treat patients with the best available care. Online standard operating procedures (SOPs) are therefore a key tool. These electronic documents are based on current national guidelines and are blended with center-specific information. The specific information includes detailed descriptions on the active clinical trials (e.g. of Cologne University Hospital) with in- and exclusion criteria, hints on when to involve early intervention palliative care depending on tumor entity and stage, an algorithm for psycho-oncological support and directions on when to present the patient at a tumor board. SOPs are written by interdisciplinary oncological project groups (IOP). The IOP coordinators are responsible for keeping the SOPs updated and in consensus with all the group members from various medical specialties. Comprehensive interdisciplinary cancer care embraces an individualized, face-to-face medicine as well as the best available treatment based on translational research and supplemented by supportive care.

The core structure is the interdisciplinary tumor ambulance. The key person is the patient navigator. These navigators are trusted persons for the patients and their families and they also organize all necessary steps of care including scheduling interdisciplinary consultation hours, initiating molecular diagnostics and contacting the study physicians for recruitment of patients into clinical trials. Furthermore, they arrange early palliative care consultations, psycho-oncological support and contact to self-help groups. Whenever avoidable, patients should not be sent from one specialist to the next but rather the specialist to the patient. The interdisciplinary tumor ambulance concentrates all these activities on one spot. For instance, in the ambulance, early phase clinical trial teams take care of patients participating in clinical trials. Also, the patient is not sent to the palliative care facilities but (members of) interprofessional early palliative care teams meet with the patient in the ambulance. These organizational structures are supported by services like patient pathways, interdisciplinary tumor boards and special consultation hours for first contact and second opinion for all cancer entities.

[1] The Japanese business man Taiichi Ohno is considered the father of the Toyota Production System, which became/the precursor of lean manufacturing in the United States.

3 Practical Experience

3.1 Comprehensive Cancer Centers as Hubs of Regional Care Networks

From an organizational perspective the structures in a CCC should all be in line with the purpose to provide the best available care for the cancer patient (Fig. 7). There are four modules to be managed: Medicine and Care, Education and Science, Hospital Management and CCC Organization.

These modules are embedded in a framework of quality standards and economic limits and influenced by defined processes and regulatory limits of in- and outpatient care (*sectorization*). Beyond these internal aspects, a CCC is part of a local health network.

In cancer networks regional cooperation with external health care providers is essential. These networks include office-based physicians as oncologists and pathologists, specialized hospitals and CCCs. Based on the three step model of oncology centers in Germany CCCs are university hospitals dedicated to do research on more effective approaches to prevention, diagnostics and treatment of cancer.

Within the network the CCCs function as hubs to bring innovation to the patients including molecular diagnostics, high-resolution functional molecular imaging and new drugs within clinical trials as well as new concepts of early integration of palliative care or integrating physical exercise during cancer treatment (Beckmann et al. 2007).

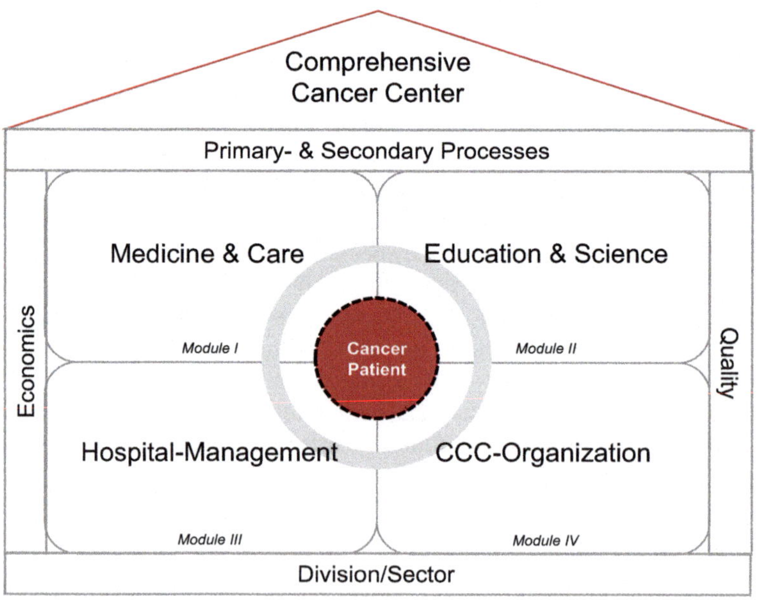

Fig. 7 Functionality of comprehensive cancer centers

3.2 Palliative Medicine and Psychosocial Care

Palliative medicine is mainly concerned with medical and nursing care of seriously ill and dying people and it aims to reduce suffering from a disease. For a long time, palliative medicine has been integrated only at a late stage of illness. Nevertheless, current evidence of clinical trials shows that an early involvement of palliative health care professionals significantly influences the course of disease. Effects are e.g. improvement of the patients' quality of life, prolonged survival or a reduction of number of hospital stays (Pott and Domagk 2013).

In the field of oncology a unique concept has emerged in recent years: From the time of diagnosis of incurable cancer the treating physicians involve the palliative care team to ensure a broad oncologic care. Based on the patients' symptoms and needs these teams develop an appropriate supportive treatment together with the patient. This approach of 'early palliative care' or 'early integration' is recommended e.g. by the American Society of Clinical Oncology (ASCO) (Gaertner et al. 2013). Figure 8 illustrates the intensity of palliative cancer care needed over the course of disease (Gaertner et al. 2011).

Palliative medicine has become tremendously important and, like psycho-oncology (see below), an integral part of the treatment and care of cancer patients [Arbeitsgemeinschaft der Wissenschaftlichen Medizinischen Fachgesellschaften e.V. (AWMF) 2014].

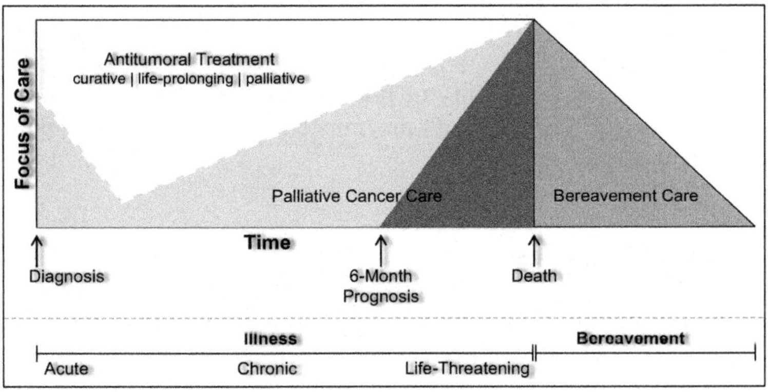

Fig. 8 ASCO approach of integration of specialized palliative care with permission

3.3 Psycho-Oncology

Psycho-oncology is a young discipline (Herschbach and Mandel 2011) which aims to implement scientifically approved psychosocial aspects into the treatment and care of patients (Holland et al. 2010). Psycho-oncology encompasses a wide range of tasks aimed at supporting cancer patients and their families in dealing with the disease and treatment effects, reduce mental stress and maintain a high level of independence and thus quality of life. It is essential to recognize a psychosocial burden at an early stage. The key element is the consequent use of diagnostic screening tools for psychological distress and psychosocial needs (e.g. the Hospital Anxiety and Depression Scale (HADS) (Herschbach and Weis 2010). Based on the screening result a demand-oriented care approach of psycho-oncological interventions can be offered at any time (psychosocial support in the diagnosis, treatment, rehabilitation, aftercare and palliative care) (Mehnert 2014). Today psycho-oncological care is part of oncological guidelines and a criterion for certification as a cancer center by DKG and DKH. In addition, its importance is reflected in the National Cancer Plan (Herschbach and Mandel 2011).

3.4 Oncological Training Therapy

Studies have shown a positive influence of sport therapeutic interventions on cancer (Schmitz et al. 2010). Numerous side effects, such as fatigue, nausea, vomiting, lymphedema, incontinence, atrophy etc. can be minimized by sports therapy. There is evidence that especially in breast cancer, prostate cancer and hematological diseases exercise programs can positively influence physical fitness, muscular strength, the psyche and the quality of life (Hayes et al. 2009). The oncological training therapy at the CIO Köln Bonn transfers recent scientific findings into practical sports therapy.

3.5 Cancer Registries

Cancer registries store information about all cancer patients. There are two different forms of cancer registries: population-based registries and clinical registries. The second form discerns state-related as well as institution-related cancer registries. The population-based registries only collect basic data such as name, date of birth, sex, address, tumor type and stage. This data is used primarily to gather information about the regional and national development of the cancer burden. These data sets are also collected by the country-related cancer registries. In addition, they record the diagnostic procedures as well as histological, molecular, treatment-related and follow-up data.

Typically, each federal state in Germany runs a population-based cancer registry and a state-based registry. They receive information of cancer cases from the whole state by physicians, medical practices and hospitals (here, the institution-related

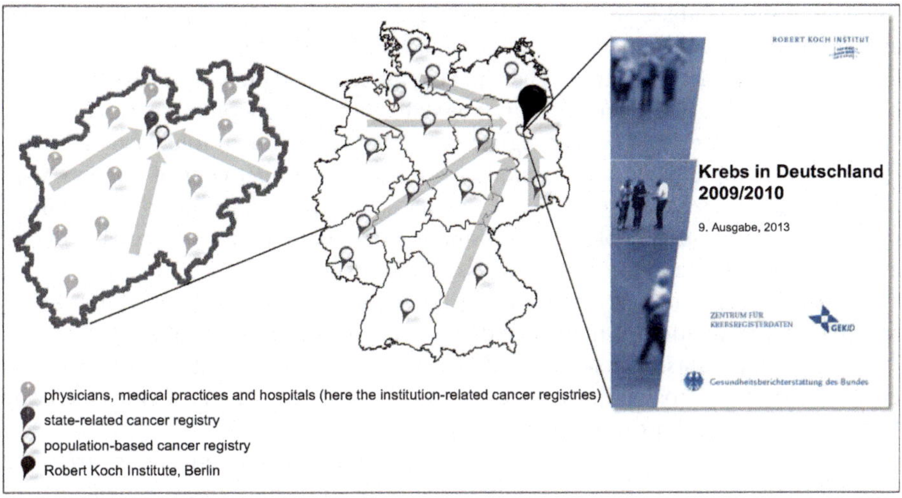

Fig. 9 Flow of registry data in Germany

cancer registries) (Robert Koch Institute). In most countries with cancer registries data is forwarded to a central country registry (in Germany the Center for Cancer Registry Data (ZfKD) at the Robert Koch Institute in Berlin. All the collected data enables public health professionals to better understand and address the cancer burden. Registry data is essential for programs which are focused on risk-related behaviors (e.g. tobacco use and exposure to the sun) or on environmental risk factors (e.g. radiation and chemical exposures). Such information is also essential for detecting when and where cancer screening efforts should be enhanced and for monitoring the treatment provided to cancer patients. In addition, solid registry data are crucial to a variety of research efforts, including those aimed at evaluating the effectiveness of cancer prevention, control or treatment programs. Figure 9 illustrates the flow of registry data in Germany.

In general, the quality of any registry database clearly depends on a careful process that defines any element of the database to be collected. In Germany, this task is assumed by the *Working Group of German Tumor Centers* (ADT) and the *Association of Population-based Cancer Registries in Germany* (GEKID) (Bundesministerium für Gesundheit 2012). These groups published a joint working paper that includes all items necessary (standard oncologic basic data set) (Bundesministerium für Gesundheit 2014). It is the theoretical background for any cancer documentation.

However, the quantity and the level of diversification of medical and biological information of patients with cancer has grown notably in the last years due to new diagnostic and treatment options. All these data sets are saved in many different and independent IT systems (e.g. clinical information system, pathology's or radiology's database). Only by merging the data sets of all patients it is possible to create a big database that can deliver the necessary output for sound scientific evaluation. Physicians, medical practices and hospitals deliver their single data to the mentioned cancer registries. The aim is to gather a complete summary of patient history, diagnosis, treatment and survival status for each oncologic patient.

The institution-related cancer registries are playing a crucial role. Usually, these registries are implemented at hospitals with a focus on treatment of patients with oncologic diseases. They collect on a smaller scale (in comparison to the country-related registries) any oncological information of usually their own patients in one database. In addition to the tasks discussed above, the captured data is utilized for e.g. certifications and—at institutions like comprehensive cancer centers—for research and evaluation of their own developments and patients' treatment.

Merging the datasets poses one of the major challenges in the process but is crucial. Only then cross-linking of data becomes possible which provides the basis for medical and health-economic research.

The progress and the expansion of the structures of all cancer registries are facilitated by national law. In Germany, several laws have been established in the last two decades on national and federal state level. The first task was to define the population-based data set. The latest laws aimed to foster the development of the clinical cancer registries. With the Cancer Detection and Register Law the cornerstone for the recording of clinical cancer information on the national level was laid (Bundesministerium für Gesundheit, 2013). Tumor documentation requires a lot of personnel resources which are currently not regularly financed. Nevertheless, a lot of institutions run their own institution-related cancer registries.

4 Summary and Outlook

Cancer care is complex and challenges a comprehensive cancer center in a number of ways. From an organizational perspective the structures need to be in line with the purpose to provide the best available care. These structures include standardized care and interdisciplinarity, clinical trials, DNA sequencing and genotyping capacities and clinical cancer registries. Furthermore, the center needs to actively participate in regional health care provider networks.

From a medical point of view there is a clear trend towards personalized medicine. Beyond new diagnostics and treatment there are additional patient needs that must be met including palliative and psycho-oncological support as well as physical exercise.

From a political and financial perspective there is sectorization and a trend towards ambulantization. Refunding for ambulatory care in hospitals remains complex and inadequate.

From our perspective, cancer patients will survive longer with a good quality of life thus leading to cancer as a chronic disease rather than a fast killer. The gain comes with a downside: the financial burden for society will also increase and needs to be faced.

References

A genomics-based classification of human lung tumors (2013) Sci Transl Med 5(209):209ra153. doi:10.1126/scitranslmed.3006802

Arbeitsgemeinschaft der Wissenschaftlichen Medizinischen Fachgesellschaften e.V. (AWMF) (2014) d. K. e. V. D. u. D. K. e. V. D. S3-Leitlinie, Palliativmedizin für Patienten mit einer nicht heilbaren Krebserkrankung. Retrieved 19 Dec 2014, from http://leitlinienprogramm-onkologie.de/uploads/tx_sbdownloader/1.Palliativmedizin_Langfas-sung_Konsultation.pdf

Arenz D, Hero B, Eichhorst BF, Langer M, Pester L, von Tresckow J, Vehreschild JJ, Vehreschild MJGT, Cornely OA (2014) Estimating site costs prior to conducting clinical trials. Clin Invest 4(3):227–234. doi:10.4155/cli.14.3

Baer AR, Hohneker JA, Stewart TL, Verschraegen CF (2010) Negotiating for success: navigating the contracting process for an exemplary research program. J Oncol Pract 6(2):107–110. doi:10.1200/jop.091082

Baer AR, Zon R, Devine S, Lyss AP (2011) The clinical research team. J Oncol Pract 7 (3):188–192. doi:10.1200/jop.2011.000276

Beckmann MW, Adler G, Albers P, Bruns J, Ehninger G, Hauschild A, Neuhaus P, Schmiegel W, Schmitz S, Schmoll H-J, Weller M, Wiegel T, Bamberg M (2007) Onkologie Dreistufenmodell optimiert Behandlung unter Kostendeckung Wie die künftigen Strukturen der onkologischen Versorgung in Deutschland aussehen sollten. Dtsch Arztebl International 104(44):3004

Buettner R, Wolf J, Thomas RK (2013) Lessons learned from lung cancer genomics: the emerging concept of individualized diagnostics and treatment. J Clin Oncol 31(15):1858–1865. doi:10.1200/jco.2012.45.9867

Bundesministerium für Gesundheit (2012). Retrieved 19 Dec 2014, from https://www.bundesgesundheitsministerium.de/fileadmin/dateien/Publikationen/Praevention/Broschueren/Broschuere_Nationaler_Krebsplan_-_Handlungsfelder__Ziele_und_Umsetzungsempfehlungen.pdf

Bundesministerium für Gesundheit (2013) Gesetz zur Weiterentwicklung der Krebsfrüherkennung und zur Qualitätssicherung durch klinische Krebsregister (Krebsfrüherkennungs- und -Registergesetz—KFRG). Retrieved 19 Dec 2014, from http://www.bgbl.de/xaver/bgbl/start.xav?startbk=Bundesanzeiger_BGBl&jumpTo=bgbl113s0617.pdf#__bgbl__%2F%2F*[%40attr_id%3D%27bgbl113s0617.pdf%27]__1437126274677

Bundesministerium für Gesundheit (2014) Bekanntmachung. Aktualisierter einheitlicher onkologischer Basisdatensatz der Arbeitsgemeinschaft Deutscher Tumorzentren e.V. (ADT) und der Gesellschaft der epidemiologischen Krebsregister in Deutschland e.V. (GEKID). Retrieved 17 Jul 2015, from http://www.tumorzentren.de/tl_files/dokumente/Module%20zum%20Basisdatensatz/Bundesanzeiger_BDS_28.04.14.pdf

Deutsche Krebsgesellschaft. Retrieved 19 Dec 2014, from http://www.krebsgesellschaft.de/deutsche-krebsgesellschaft/zertifizierung.html

Emanuel EJ, Schnipper LE, Kamin DY, Levinson J, Lichter AS (2003) The costs of conducting clinical research. J Clin Oncol 21(22):4145–4150. doi:10.1200/jco.2003.08.156

English RA, Lebovitz Y, Giffin RB (2010) Transforming clinical research in the United States: challenges and opportunities workshop summary. Institute of Medicine, Washington, DC

Fink T, Wicke D (2010) Klinische Studie—Herausforderung mit signifikanter Auswirkung. Biotechnologie 10'/11'Kapital, Markt, Wirtschaft. Retrieved 20 Feb 2015, from http://www.portusco.com/images/Klinische_Studie_mit_siknifikanter_Auswirkung.pdf

Gaertner J, Weingartner V, Wolf J, Voltz R (2013) Early palliative care for patients with advanced cancer: how to make it work? Curr Opin Oncol 25(4):342–352. doi:10.1097/CCO.0b013e3283622c5e

Gaertner J, Wolf J, Hallek M, Glossmann JP, Voltz R (2011) Standardizing integration of palliative care into comprehensive cancer therapy—a disease specific approach. Support Care Cancer 19(7):1037–1043. doi:10.1007/s00520-011-1131-y

Glossmann JP, Walshe R, Bernschein A, Wolf J (2010) Ökonomische Aspekte des Bronchialkarzinoms. Der Onkologe 16(10):1003–1008. doi:10.1007/s00761-010-1907-6
Goldstein I, Madar S, Rotter V (2012) Cancer research, a field on the verge of a paradigm shift? Trends Mol Med 18(6):299–303. doi:10.1016/j.molmed.2012.04.002
Hayes SC, Spence RR, Galvão DA, Newton RU (2009) Australian Association for Exercise and Sport Science position stand: optimising cancer outcomes through exercise. J Sci Med Sport 12 (4):428–434
Herrmann U, Sehner N (2011) Klinische Auftragsforschung—Ein Geschäftsfeld im Krankenhaus. DZFK 5(6):77–82
Herschbach P, Mandel T (2011) Psychoonkologische Versorgung im Nationalen Krebsplan. Der Onkologe 17(12):1107–1114
Herschbach P, Weis J (2010) Screeningverfahren in der Psychoonkologie. Testinstrumente zur Identifikation betreuungsbedürftiger Krebspatienten. Eine Empfehlung der PSO für die psychoonkologische Behandlungspraxis, 2nd edn. Retrieved 21 Dec 2014, from http://www.dapo-ev.de/fileadmin/templates/pdf/pso_broschuere2.pdf
Holland JC, Breitbart WS, Jacobsen PB, Lederbarg MS, Loscalzo MJ, MccorKle RS (2010) Psycho-oncology, 2nd edn. Oxford University Press, New York
Jahn R, Farrenkopf N, Wasem J, Walendzik A (2012) Neuordnung der ambulanten Onkologie: Gutachten im Auftrag des Berufsverbandes der niedergelassenen Hämatologen und Onkologen eV, der Deutschen Gesellschaft für Hämatologie und Onkologie eV und der Deutschen Krebsgesellschaft eV. Retrieved 15 Dec 2014, from https://www.wiwi.uni-due.de/fileadmin/fileupload/WIWI/pdf/IBES_Gutachten_Neuordnung_der_ambulanten_Onkologie-1_final_3_3.pdf
Lauterbach K, Lüngen M, Schrappe M (2010) Gesundheitsökonomie, management und evidence-based medicine, 3rd edn. Schattauer, Stuttgart
Lauterbach S, Potthoff S, Lüngen K, Klostermann G, Stock S, Müller B (2012) Bestandsaufnahme der Rolle von Ambulanzen der Hochschulkliniken in Forschung, Lehre und Versorgung an ausgewählten Standorten (Hochschulambulanzenstudie). Retrieved 15 Dec 2014, from http://www.gesundheitsforschung-bmbf.de/_media/Gutachten_Ambulanzen_26.pdf
Levy MA, Lovly CM, Pao W (2012) Translating genomic information into clinical medicine: lung cancer as a paradigm. Genome Res 22(11):2101–2108. doi:10.1101/gr.131128.111
Lüngen M (2007) Ambulante Behandlung im Krankenhaus Zugang, Finanzierung, Umsetzung Gesundheitsökonomie: Politik und Management. LIT, Berlin (Bd. 3)
Lüngen M, Rath T (2010) Ambulante Öffnung der Krankenhäuser—Welchen Anteil können Krankenhäuser in der onkologischen Versorgung abdecken? In: Klauber JG, Geraedts M, Friedrich J (eds) Krankenhaus-report 2010. Schattauer, Stuttgart
Mehnert A (2014) Psychoonkologie. Gynakologe 47(6):427–434. doi:10.1007/s00129-014-3388-y
National Cancer Institute (2015) Targeted cancer therapies. Retrieved 20 Feb 2015, from http://www.cancer.gov/cancertopics/factsheet/Therapy/targeted
Nationaler Krebsplan (2012) Handlungsfelder, Ziele und Umsetzungsempfehlungen. Retrieved 15 Dec 2014, from http://www.bmg.bund.de/fileadmin/dateien/Publikationen/Praevention/Broschueren/Broschuere_Nationaler_Krebsplan_-_Handlungsfelder__Ziele_und_Umsetzungsempfehlungen.pdf
Nichols M, Townsend N, Scarborough P, Rayner M (2014) Cardiovascular disease in Europe 2014: epidemiological update. Eur Heart J 35:2950–2959. doi:10.1093/eurheartj/ehu299
Pfaff H, Neugebauer E, Glaeske G, Schrappe M (2011) Lehrbuch Versorgungsforschung: Systematik—Methodik—Anwendung, vol 1, 1st edn. Schattauer, Stuttgart
Pott G, Domagk D (2013) Integrierte Palliativmedizin: Leidensminderung-Patientenverfügungen-Sterbebegleitung-intuitive Ethik. Schattauer, Stuttgart
Robert Koch Insitut. Zentrum für Krebsregisterdaten. Retrieved 21 Dec 2014, from http://www.rki.de/Krebs/DE/Content/ZfKD/Aktuelles/unterschiede_epi_klin_reg.html
Schmitz KH, Courneya KS, Matthews C, Demark-Wahnefried W, Galvao DA, Pinto BM, Irwin ML, Wolin KY, Segal RJ, Lucia A, Schneider CM, von Gruenigen VE, Schwartz AL, American College of Sports Medicine (2010) American College of Sports Medicine roundtable

on exercise guidelines for cancer survivors. Med Sci Sports Exerc 42(7):1409–1426. doi:10.1249/MSS.0b013e3181e0c112
Schmedders M (2012) Einfluss der ambulanten spezialfachärztlichen Versorgung auf die Gesundheitskosten. Retrieved 15 Dec 2014, from http://www.dgim.de:82/portals/pdf/korporative_MG/20121024_Schmedders_Herbstsymposium.pdf
Schwartz FW, Wille E, Fischer C, Kuhlmey A, Lauterbach K, Rosenbrock W, Scriba P (2000) Sachverständigenrat für die Konzertierte Aktion im Gesundheitswesen. Bedarfsgerechtigkeit und Wirtschaftlichkeit. Gutachten, 2001
Selby P (2011) The impact of the process of clinical research on health service outcomes. Ann Oncol 22(Suppl 7):vii2–vii4. doi:10.1093/annonc/mdr418
Wissenschaftsrat (2010) Empfehlungen zur Weiterentwicklung der ambulanten Universitätsmedizin in Deutschland. http://www.wissenschaftsrat.de/download/archiv/10052-10.pdf. Accessed 15 Dec 2014

Florian Kron gained his first practical experiences in health care management at the AMEOS Group based in Zurich in the department Mergers and Acquisitions. He obtained a diploma in health economics at the University of Cologne in 2012. At present he is the head of the economic division at the First Department of Internal Medicine at the University Hospital in Cologne. As member of the management team in the Center for Integrated Oncology (CIO) Köln Bonn he is focusing on economic issues in hematology and oncology. Florian Kron is writing his dissertation in economics of cancer treatment.

Andreas Bernschein has studied health economics at the University of Cologne with a focus on business policy, evidence-based medicine and health technology assessment. After graduating he has focused on health economic evaluation, business processes and quality management at the Center for Integrated Oncology (CIO) Köln Bonn. He is Head of the Clinical Cancer Registry and manages health economic issues. He is doing his doctorate on application of data of clinical cancer registries.

Anna Kostenko obtained a Diploma in Health Economics at the University of Cologne in 2012. Since April 2012 she is the Head Economist of the clinical trial unit at the First Department of Internal Medicine at the University Hospital Cologne and is focusing on financial aspects and personnel management in clinical trials (phase I–IV). In June 2014 she became scientific coordinator of the Network Genomic Medicine (NGM). She is currently writing her dissertation in the field of economics of clinical trials.

Jürgen Wolf is currently Medical Director of the Center for Integrated Oncology (CIO) at the University Hospital Cologne. He holds a professorship for Interdisciplinary Translational Oncology at the University of Cologne and is speaker of the CIO lung cancer program.

Prof. Wolf received his MD degree from the University of Freiburg. From 1986 to 1990 he spent his postdoctoral fellowship at the German Cancer Research Center Heidelberg in the tumor virology group of Prof. H. zur Hausen. In 1990 he started his clinical training in the Department of Internal Medicine, Cologne University Hospital. He is board-certified in internal medicine and haematology/medical oncology. From 1990 to 2003 he headed the Laboratory for Research on Hodgkin's Lymphoma in Cologne. From 2000 to 2004 he was co-chairman of the German Hodgkin's Lymphoma Study Group. Since 2004 he has been coordinating the establishment of the CIO at the Cologne University Hospital. In 2005 he initiated the lung cancer program at the CIO and founded the Lung Cancer Group Cologne (www.lungcancergroup.de) focusing on personalized early proof of concept trials. In 2010 he co-founded the Network Genomic Medicine (NGM) aiming at implementing lung cancer genotyping and allocation of patients to personalized treatment in routine clinical care (www.ngm.de).

Michael Hallek received his MD degree from the University of Munich, Germany, in 1985. He trained in pharmacology and internal medicine from 1985 to 1990 at the University and Technical University of Munich. From 1990 to 1992, he spent 2 years as a research associate at the Dana Farber Cancer Institute at Harvard Medical School, Boston, USA, before returning to the University of Munich, where he continued his training in internal medicine and in hematology and oncology. From 1994 to 2005, he was head of the Gene Therapy Program at the Gene Center of the University of Munich and at the National Centre for Research on Environment and Health (GSF), Munich. In 1994, he founded the German CLL Study Group and is its chairman until today. Since 2003, Dr. Hallek is Professor of Medicine, Director and Chair of the Department of Internal Medicine I at the University of Cologne. Since 2007, he is also the chairman of the Center for Integrated Oncology (CIO), the joint comprehensive cancer center of the Universities of Cologne and Bonn. Since 2011, he is a Member of the National Academy of Sciences (Leopoldina). He received numerous awards such as the Paul Martini Prize in 2012 and the Binet-Rai Medal in 2013.

Jan-Peter Glossmann was trained in medicine in Germany (Köln), Austria (Innsbruck) and Canada (Montreal). Additionally, he obtained a Master of Public Health in Boston at the Harvard School of Public Health with a focus on health care management followed by a fellowship in administrative management at Harvard Health Services. Back in Cologne he continued to focus on financial aspects and quality management in cancer care. He is a trained hematologist-oncologist and Chief Financial Officer of the Center for Integrated Oncology (CIO) Köln Bonn.

Health Care Under Market Conditions: An Ethical Analysis

Jan P. Beckmann

Abstract

Health care systems in many countries in the Western World face major challenges, esp. economic ones, due to both rising human life expectancy and to the enormous costs of technical innovations in medicine, e.g. in diagnostic imaging, in cell, tissue and organ transplantation, and possibly in near future of stem cell research. The central question raised by such developments is whether economic conditions are to be subordinated to the patient's needs or the patient's needs to economic conditions? The contribution of ethics consists in a critical examination of the justifiability of moral claims. This includes identifying normative preconditions and possible conflicts between norms. This must take place on both individual and collective levels of analysis. The following paper will thus fall into three parts:

1. an examination of the (collective) ethical foundation of providing sufficient resources for health care on the three levels involved:
   - the *macro* or resource-raising level,
   - the *meso* or resource-distributing level, and
   - the *micro* or resource-allocating level,
2. an analysis of the (individual) ethical basis of securing medical ethos under the condition of economic efficiency, and finally
3. an inquiry into the logic of the relation between prioritization and rationing from an ethical point of view.

J.P. Beckmann (✉)
Institute for Philosophy, FernUniversität in Hagen, Universitätsstr. 1/11, 58084 Hagen, Germany
e-mail: jan.beckmann@fernuni-hagen.de

H. Albach et al. (eds.), *Boundaryless Hospital*, DOI 10.1007/978-3-662-49012-9_3

The aim of the paper is not to argue for *acceptance* of the impact of economics on health care but to analyze ethical *acceptability* so as to refine the ability of both individuals and society to make informed ethical judgments.

Keywords
Diagnosis-related grouping • Macro or resource-raising level • Meso or resource-distributing level • Micro or resource-allocating level • Medical ethos • Norms of protecting human life • Respect for human life • Prioritization • Rationing • Norms of responsibility • Justice • Solidarity

1 Introduction

Intending the benefit of the patient and avoiding harm belong to the core of medical ethics; the challenge to this core presented by economic market conditions, however, is a fact. The central question that arises is whether economic conditions are to be subordinated to the patient's needs, or the patient's needs to economic conditions. Subordinating health to economic premises seems to lead to an unavoidable conflict with medical ethics (Beckmann 2011a).

1.1 Problems

The connection between the health care system and overall economic conditions is a natural one, a physician's help for a suffering patient being necessarily bound up with financial costs. Problems result with regard to the orientation of one side to the other, be it by subjecting the norm of saving human lives to economic restrictions, or by a physician's insufficient attention to financial limits. In both cases fundamental norms are at stake: The norms of respect for human life and of the duty of saving and protecting lives speak in favor of the priority of health care, whereas the norms of economic frugality and care in dealing with financial resources prioritize economy. In both cases values are involved, though they differ in kind: In health care, the foundation of all medical treatment rests upon fundamental human values: life, autonomy, and the individual's right to self-determination; in economy, it rests upon provision of the resources necessary to safeguard human lives. Raising the resources required for medical help represents the necessary *condition* of medical practice. Thus, what is needed is joint attention to the *value-relatedness* of economic action as well as to *value reflection* in medicine. Accordingly the problem in question is: *Can the medical ethos of helping and healing be preserved under the growing pressure of economic conditions, and if so, how?*

1.2 Background

The allocation of resources usually takes place under *limiting conditions*: Resources are neither economically nor logically unlimited. This, of course, as well holds true for the German health care system the cost of which has been rising drastically for years. Currently compulsory health insurance covers about 90 % of the German population, i.e. 70 million persons, but receives only 11 % of the gross domestic product (GDP) (Fleischhauer 2014; Deutscher Ethikrat 2011). As early as spring 2009, the then President of the Federal Medical Board (Bundesärztekammer) spoke in his opening speech at the 112th German Medical Assembly about "which therapies will be available for which patients in the near future and which may have eventually to be forgone" (Hoppe 2009). Ever since, the pressure to ration has been growing; an attempt is being made to reduce costs by improving efficiency reserves so as to make prioritization, not to speak of rationing, unnecessary (Schröder 2010). Yet, the potential for this does not suffice to counter-balance the rising costs. In spite of this, critical voices from the medical profession do not seem to be recognized (Zentrale Ethikkommission 2000, 2007).

The following five factors are mainly responsible for pushing up costs in today's health care:

1. constant progress in medical research and the enormous costs of new diagnostic and therapeutic means; e.g. in diagnostic imaging, in cell, tissue and organ transplantation, and possibly in the near future as a result of new therapies established on the basis of stem cell research;
2. costs resulting from insufficient innovation in the past, of over-therapy, and of the absence of institutional and structural co-operation;
3. changing understanding of health and disease, which calls for ever increasing resources;
4. rising life expectancy of men—the number of men and women who are over 90 years old has been rising from year to year;
5. last but not least the growing expectations and claims of patients, which push up financial engagements.

While each of these cost-raising factors leads to bottlenecks, it is obvious that all five together present an explosive mixture and, consequently, are straining health care already today. Politics has long since resorted to economic means for exerting pressure: *budgeting*, *diagnosis-related grouping (DRG)* and *rationing* form the well-known keywords of this development which renders undecided, whether this is *economy* in the sense of handling scarce resources rationally, or *economizing* in the sense of acting that is dominated first and foremost, if not completely by economic categories so as to increase shareholder value.

The keywords mentioned above apply especially to hospitals. It is foreseeable that as long as rising costs are not compensated by higher health insurance premiums or by public support, the medical profession is set under pressure. Is the hospital itself becoming a "sick house" (Deutscher Ethikrat 2014)? Without rationing, as authoritative voices from the medical profession, clinics and insurance entities tell, this development can no longer continue. What seems to be called for is a confluence of economic, social, legal, and last but not least ethical analyses (Hoffmann 2011; Busche 2011).

1.3 Contribution, Method, and Limits of Ethical Analysis

By its very method, ethics consists in a critical examination of the justifiability of moral claims. Ethical analysis is based on identifying normative preconditions of and possible conflicts between norms (Beckmann 2009). This identification has to take place on both individual and collective levels of analysis.

Now, economics seems at first sight to be concerned with *acting* and *facts*, while ethics is characterized by *analysis* and *reflection*. On closer inspection, however, it becomes obvious that both mean—each in its own way—acting as well as reflecting, and include both norms and facts: economics as sustained dealing with market options, ethics as reflective dealing with normative discourses regarding moral claims and argumentative analysis of conflicts between norms. Accordingly, the term 'ethics' denotes an *analytic* procedure not to be confused with the term ,morals' denoting the realm of *acting* under normative guidelines. Ethics, in a word, means critical reflection on moral claims.

With regard to the present topic the norms in question, on the side of society, are *responsibility* and *solidarity* in raising sufficient resources for the health sector and *justice* and *thriftiness* in allocating these resources; on the side of the physician there are the *patient's well-being* and the *avoidance of harm*; and on the side of the individual there is *self-determination* based on the principle of *autonomy*. The common aim is to secure compatibility between medical duties and economic limits. It is, however, not the aim of the following analysis to argue for *acceptance* of the impact of economics on health care, but rather to analyze the question of its ethical *acceptability*, so as to refine the ability of both individuals and society to make informed ethical judgments.

The following paper will thus fall into three parts:

1. an examination of the (collective) ethical foundation of providing sufficient resources for medical help on the three levels involved:
   - the *macro* or resource-raising level,
   - the *meso* or resource-distributing level, and
   - the *micro* or resource-allocating level,
2. an examination of the (individual) ethical basis of securing medical ethos under the condition of economic efficiency, and finally
3. an inquiry into the logic of the relation between prioritization and rationing from an ethical point of view.

2 An Examination of the (Collective) Ethical Foundation of Providing Sufficient Resources for Health Care on the Three Levels Entailed

Any medical action regarding an individual patient is necessarily connected with the allocation of financial resources that then are naturally no longer available for another patient. Now, it is obviously unthinkable to play-off one patient's need for medical help against another's, as doing so would violate both the norms of justice and non-discrimination and the medical ethos of helping every person in need of help. Equally obvious, however, is that one may not require physicians to draw on financial resources for one patient at the expense of helping another one: to do so would violate the societal *responsibility* for the benefit of everybody as well as of the social-ethical norm of *solidarity*. Thus, firstly an examination of the ethics of raising the necessary resources is called for.

Decisions regarding the *raising* of financial resources take place on the *macro* level, i.e. that of politics; decisions regarding the *distribution* of resources take place on the *meso* level, i.e. that of the clinic; and decisions regarding the *allocation* of resources take place on the *micro* level, i.e. that of the individual physician. Accordingly, not only do the decision makers differ from level to level, but also the addressees: Those on the macro level are completely unknown, and even those on the meso level (i.e. members of a group of patients) remain anonymous; the individual patient appears only on the micro level as the addressee of an allocation decision. These differences make it necessary to distinguish between a collective and an individual level of analysis.

2.1 The Macro or Resource-Raising Level

There are two questions to be answered regarding the macro level: first whether modern society acknowledges itself as such to be *responsible* for the costs of treating sick fellow human beings, and second whether in raising resources society adheres to the principle of solidarity.

2.1.1 Responsibility

'Responsibility' presents—logically speaking—a manifold predicate: Somebody or some institution is responsible *over against* somebody or to an institution *for* somebody *with regard to* something. The 'over against' refers to accountability, the 'for' to a duty, and the 'with regard to' to the reason for the responsibility. Thus, the individual has duties over against himself[1] and his social environment; at the same time he ought to give evidence regarding his actions, including the utilization of resources, as long as he can anticipate and influence them. Society on the other

[1] To facilitate reading, only the masculine form is used in this paper, designating always both sexes.

hand is responsible for securing the cost of life conditions in such a way that no individual member goes bankrupt because of the medical costs caused by his illness; at the same time the individual is responsible *over against* society or the group of insured, respectively, for making his own contribution to safeguard or maintain his health. In this respect, the norm of responsibility is closely connected with the norm of solidarity.

2.1.2 Solidarity

Solidarity (from the Latin 'solidus' = 'sound', 'firm') means the willingness to exert oneself for a fellow human being who is about to lose the solid ground under his feet—owing perhaps to the loss of his job or to age and/or illness (Beckmann 2011b). Solidarity therefore presupposes an awareness of being a part of a larger whole. As distinct from responsibility in which one 'stands', solidarity has to be 'declared'. The decision of the will stands in this case under the anthropological condition that man is essentially determined by his relation to his fellow human beings, as he is existentially a *social* being. Thus, to free oneself deliberately from solidarity would strictly speaking mean to try to put into question one's own status as part of a whole. By contrast, one shows solidarity with the other and his needs and concerns qua member of a *community* (Kerber 1999). This explicitly includes the acceptance of disadvantages: To exercise solidarity does not only mean to help the weaker and in doing so put their benefit into the foreground, but at the same time to accept that such help for fellow human beings in need of medical help may lead to restrictions on one's own benefit.

As regards the health care system this means not only that the healthy have to exercise solidarity with the sick, and the better-off with the less-well-off, but that they have to do so *at the price of a possible disadvantage to themselves.* For instance, the fact that in Germany, the self-employed are exempt from the compulsory health insurance is in line neither with the norm of solidarity nor with the economic principle of contributing according to one's own financial resources. Something similar can be said of the private health insurance in Germany: The principle of risk may be important in determining premiums, but to disregard the income of the privately insured is to fail to observe the norm of solidarity. The reason for this is that Germany's 'split' system for raising resources for health care is grounded upon completely different ethical norms: private health insurance upon the norm of *risk quantification*, compulsory health insurance upon the norm of *solidarity* (Sozialgesetzbuch 1976). The consequence is that roughly 10 % of the population, i.e. the privately insured, do not contribute a share to the financial risks of the roughly 90 % who are publicly insured (Marburger 2008). On the other hand, the privately insured have to pay for *each* family member and have to face rising insurance premiums, as they grow older. But even under the public insurance system solidarity is limited to the employee's income and does not depend upon his *taxable* income as a whole; and in addition to the maximum limit of currently EUR 4750 per month at present—both is not in line with the norm of solidarity according to which every person insured should contribute in a portion to his financial resources as a whole (Sozialgesetzbuch 2006).

The way out of this dilemma that politics seems to prefer is a (partial) shift from solidary to the private raising of resources for health care, which ethically means a shift from the norm of one-standing-with-the-other to the duty to help oneself. The presumptive consequence is a conflict with the ethical norm of *justice*, since not everybody with the same medical needs will get the same help, as this will partly depend upon one's private insurance premium.

2.2 The Meso or Resource-Distributing Level

On the meso level the collective ethical question is how a given clinic distributes resources to the various departments in accordance with the norm of justice.

Justice: In addition to the ethical norms of respect for the autonomy of the individual and his right to exercise this in form of self-determination and the patient's benefit, *justice* plays a role of rising prominence in medical ethics (Marckmann 2003). However, two kinds of justice should be distinguished from each other, 'commutative' and 'distributive' justice (Aristotle 1925). The idea of *commutative* justice is prominent among those who want the limited resources in medicine to be assigned according to the principle that "he who has paid a lot should receive a lot", while those who prefer *distributive* justice want the limited resources to be assigned according to the principle of "to equals equally, to un-equals unequally". Following the idea of distributive justice it would be absolutely unjust to treat people with one and the same medical need and, therefore, the same need for financial resources differently.

The concept of *commutative* justice is well suited for the utilization of resources with regard to the realm of well-being, while in the realm of securing existential needs the norm of distributive justice is relevant (Beckmann 2001). If one were to apply commutative justice in dealing with man's existential needs one would enter into conflict with the duty to protect human life, which may never be made dependent on financial resources. This protection can only be secured by *distributive* justice. In short: With regard to securing man's existential needs applying the norm of distributive justice has an egalitarian impact, while with regard to optimizing well-being has a non-egalitarian one. Normative background is the close connection between *distributive* justice and the norm of solidarity.

2.3 The Micro or Resource-Allocating Level

The two main questions on the micro or resource-allocating level are by which criteria are resources to be allocated to an individual patient, and who is responsible for the allocation decision.

In economic terms efficiency in allocation on the micro level stands under the maxim of *thriftiness*, according to which a maximum of efficiency ought to be achieved by a minimal use of resources. However, a physician's duty to help a patient independently of any financial value calculus may conflict with the requirements of economic efficiency. For in addition to his medical responsibility the physician has to assume responsibility for the financial implications and consequences of his actions, provided he is able to foresee them and to reconcile them with his ethos of helping and healing, and provided he can influence the extent of the use of resources.

However, the norm of responsibility—and this is usually overlooked—also applies to the patient, who is responsible for his own contribution to his recovery, i.e. to do everything that facilitates and accelerates it; at the same time the patient is also responsible to society or the solidarity community of the insured to restrict the use of resources necessary for his treatment to the minimum possible. For illness—considered medically as well as ethically—is a situation of need, not as such one of a right. There is no right to health, though there is a right to receive help if the former is at risk.

Owing to the German 'split' system for raising resources for health care there is no incentive in Germany for the patient to assume a share of economic responsibility for reducing costs entailed by his illness: 90 % of the population (i.e. those who are compulsorily insured) experience no incentive at all as they never see the physician's bill, which is settled directly by insurance. In consequence they can not realize that diseases entail costs and to what extent. Be that as it may, however, a physician has a duty to meet the *medical* needs of his patient, but also has to deny any claim exceeding these. Even the claims that the patient has on the community of the insured are only claims for the costs of safeguarding his health on the basis of a duty to keep the costs for it to the minimum necessary. Yet, realizing these normative requests may represent a potential to save costs in health care that has so far not been fully exploited.

2.4 Tensions on All Three Levels

As important as the distinction between the macro, the meso and the micro levels may be, i.e. between raising, allocating and distributing resources, the various tensions that may appear on each level seem unavoidable. Tensions on the macro level between economics and ethics arise between the efficiency of anonymous distribution on the one hand and the ethical duties of society on the other. Tensions on the meso level arise between large clinic departments with 'convenient' diagnosis-related groupings (DRGs) and smaller departments with 'less convenient' ones. On the micro level there are tensions between individual patient-related allocation and the general medical ethos of helping and of avoiding harm, both under the condition of economizing resources. The latter demands an (individual) ethical analysis and an inquiry into the conditions of the compatibility of physicians' duties and economic efficiency.

2.5 Social System or Market?

As mentioned above the present health care system in Germany neither quantitatively nor structurally fulfills the ethical norms of responsibility and solidarity. Unavoidable limitations in the allocation of resources on the meso level and especially on the macro level fall under the responsibility of politics and of society as a whole. From an ethical point of view however, one has to distinguish between a health care system qua social system and qua economic system, that is, between cost pressure resulting from the natural need to provide sufficient resources for medical action on the one hand and the pressure resulting from profit-oriented decisions for the sake of shareholder value on the other. The former is as natural as the latter is problematic:

- Natural: in so far as the German Code of Social Law V (Sozialgesetzbuch) expressly demands economic acting, too, though depending upon medical necessity. Any carelessness with financial resources would not only be economically inappropriate, but would also conflict ethically with the norm of justice that obliges both physicians and patients equally to do what is medically necessary as economical as possible. Infringements of this obligation violate the norm of justice, because the latter requires that resources provided by the solidarity community are not used beyond medical necessity.
- Problematic: because any economic restrictions on medical help for reasons of shareholder value stand in conflict with the norms of justice and solidarity. Profit turns health into merchandise; yet illness is neither merchandise nor is it a kind of 'mechanical defect' that may be 'repaired'. On the contrary, health and illness are *natural* aspects of human existence which on principle represents a value and does not have a price. To turn health into a merchandise that like any merchandise has a price, would anthropologically speaking be to turn man into a calculable economic phenomenon (Maio 2014).

2.6 On the Logic of the Difference Between Raising Resources and Profit

Medically necessary treatment inevitably involves financial resources. However, the need for the medically necessary resources and the aim to realize a profit by means of medical care differ categorically. The reason for this categorical difference lies in the different logic of the connection between economic resources and medically indicated treatment: While sufficient economic resources serve as *precondition* for medical treatment, striving for profit would be not the precondition, but the *function* of medical treatment. In a word, the principle underlying the connection between medical treatment and financial resources holds that "without resources medical treatment is impossible", while the principle underlying profit-orientation holds that "without medical treatment there is no profit". What in the first case is a precondition of medical treatment turns in the second into a function of medical treatment. Both manifest themselves in the process of rationing in medicine. As this mainly takes place on the individual level, a corresponding ethical analysis is called for.

3 An Analysis of the (Individual) Ethical Basis of Securing Medical Ethos Under the Condition of Economic Efficiency

According to the German Code of Social Law, a patient has a right to receive medical help within the limits of what is medically necessary, no matter what the costs are (German Code of Social Law 1988). But this legal requirement may be challenged by rationing such as budgeting or DRGs. If one understands 'rationing' as the deliberate and systematic withholding of medically indicated and effective therapies in order to save resources or because health insurance does not pay for them, it becomes immediately obvious that the normative problem is connected with the term "indicated". "Indication" means that a certain preventative, diagnostic or therapeutic action should be applied to the patient. If such an action is compulsory and urgent (serious illness, danger to life), one speaks of ,'absolute' or 'vital' indication; if the danger to the patient is limited or if there are equally effective means at hand, one speaks of 'relative' indication.

3.1 Protection of Life, the Patient's Benefit, and Respect for Autonomy-Based Self-Determination

It is obvious that rationing on the level of indications—at least if they are absolute or vital—would be in conflict with the fundamental ethical norm of the protection of life. For this reason the DRG model is based on a different ground, namely on the diagnosis, i.e. the classification of diseases (hence the term *diagnosis-related grouping*). Of prime importance in each singular case is the *main* diagnosis. Thus, it is no longer the individually different medical or nursing needs of an individual patient that are paid for by health insurance, but flat rate costs based on the main diagnosis. If the actual costs are below these rates, the clinic makes profit; if they are higher, the clinic has to absorb them. Even though it still is the *individual* patient who is being treated payment remains based upon *impersonal* diagnosis-related grouping. The consequence of this is that *medically* speaking the patient remains what he is: an unmistakably unique individual with his own medical needs, whereas *economically* speaking the patient is a 'case'. Logically as well as factually this means a transition from individuality to particularity: The patient is no longer seen in his uniqueness, but as 'part' of a certain group.

3.2 The Problems of DRGs

From an ethical point of view the problems of DRGs (Kettner and Koslowski 2011) are as follows:

1. That which is medically necessary for the patient—and patients exist in the form of individuality and unrepeatability *only*—is by its nature *not* abstract, external, particular and determinable a priori.
2. DRGs are by their very nature oriented not to the *result* of medical therapy, but a priori to a reductionist model, the so-called *main* diagnosis. From an economic point of view this is an invitation to skillful coding, which does not necessarily do justice to the medical needs of the individual patient. But by this means clinics make a profit, while less skillful coding leads to loss of profit.
3. The use of resources needed for the individual patient are determined *prospectively*. This may encourage, or even force, the clinic on one hand to limit the individually necessary therapy and on the other to apply something medically unnecessary for the patient. At the same time diagnostic and therapeutic needs of the patient that lie outside of the main diagnosis remain financially unremunerated.
4. If politics and society do not succeed in modifying the DRG model in the light of the medical duty to help the individual patient and to prevent harm, then the DRG concept may eventually lead to an erosion of the medical ethos or to a corruption of medical behavior as a result of economizing, as the patient will be considered a cost factor only.

Instead of adjusting the raising of resources adequately to the medical needs of the patient, the DRG concept in principle confronts the danger of adjusting the latter to the former by reducing the needs of the patient to the limited resources available. This outcome, however, conflicts with the central ethical norms of protection of life, medical help, and justice. Would prioritization help?

4 An Inquiry into the Logic of the Relation Between Prioritization and Rationing from an Ethical Point of View

'Prioritizing' in general means determining the priority of one thing over other things; with regard to medicine it means determining the priority of certain diagnoses and therapies over others (Zentrale Ethikkommission 2000, 2007). From an ethical point of view, prioritizing must precede rationing for the following reasons (Beckmann 2011a):

1. The *rule of non-discrimination*: Prioritizations must be valid on principle and without exception in order to be non-discriminatory. As a patient the individual may never unexpectedly be confronted with the withholding of medical help

because of cost-saving; rather he must know in advance thanks to prioritization that certain medical treatments are *generally* not covered by health insurance.
2. The *rule of fairness*: Prioritizations must be publicly accessible and transparent in order not to violate the ethical norms of solidarity and fairness (Rawls 1971) done by so-called silent rationing.
3. The *rule of facilitating provision*: The individual must be informed in good time about prioritizations, so that he can take action by changing his lifestyle, taking preventative measures, acquiring suitable insurance, etc. before becoming ill.

It follows from what has been said that from an ethical point of view prioritization must precede rationing, and not vice versa (Lohmann et al. 2010). And: If in medical treatment the absolutely necessary is distinguished from the advisable, and if both are distinguished from the useful, and if all of these are distinguished from the economically tenable, it becomes obvious that prioritization with the consequence of rationing is unjustifiable from an ethical point of view in the field of absolutely necessary treatment. This is so because of the norm of protection of life—taking the notion of the absolutely necessary to mean what will, if withheld, threaten human life or lead to serious lasting harm.

In the field of the medically advisable one may not, at least not without additional reasons, work with prioritizations insofar as the medically advisable is understood as that medical treatment which bears a sufficient chance of achieving a therapeutic result that is acknowledged to be important.

4.1 Levels and Addressees of Prioritizations

Prioritization may—ethically correctly used—never take place on the micro level, but only on the macro level. Prioritizing on the micro or meso levels would discriminate among individual patients or singular groups of patients which is incompatible with the norms of respect for the right of everyone to self-determination as well as for the protection of every life. The only level of prioritization which seems ethically justifiable is the macro level, as only this level is anonymous, universal, and transparent.

Furthermore the objects of prioritizations are goals of action, never medical indications or therapeutic processes or groups of patients. If one prioritized medical indications, one would run the risk of interfering with a physician's freedom of action; if one prioritized therapeutic processes, one would risk a conflict with the medical ethos of helping and never harming; if one prioritized certain groups of patients, one would risk discrimination. Correctly used, 'prioritizing' means putting goals of action into an order of priority or posteriority, respectively. Thus, the goal of acting to rescue and support human life is of a higher priority than the goal of acting to alleviate physical disturbances, and this again is of higher priority than the goal of acting to strengthen the human body's defences against diseases, and this again is of a higher priority than the goal of acting to enhance certain somatic or psychic human capacities. The highest goal of action is the norm of the protection of life; the lowest is the improvement of well-being. Between these the goals of action become more and more important upwards, and less and less important downwards, or in the terminology of prioritization, ascending they become ever more highly prioritized, and descending ever more highly 'posteriorized'.

The statement by the German Medical Assembly cited above rightly indicates that prioritizations may never be to the detriment of humanitarian empathy. "Humanity in the sense of § 70 Code of Social Law V is not posteriorizable" (Zentrale Ethikkommission 2000, 2007). This proposition has a logico-semantic as well an ethical background: 'Humanity' is a notion that neither logically nor semantically allows for increase or decrease: An action is either human or it is not; for there are no grades of intensity in between. Nor is the notion of humanity ethically variable, as it denotes that every human being ought to be treated humanely, i.e. according to his essential needs (Fuchs et al. 2009).

Here, a distinction between the absolute and the relative duty of a physician to be vigilant in the use of resources is at issue: *Absolute* is the duty to use financial resources thriftily in case of minor health problems and a high natural potential of self-healing; *relative* on the other hand is the duty to be vigilant in the use of resources in cases of life-threatening or otherwise severe diseases: As long as there is a chance of a positive result, no physician may be urged to withhold medical treatment for economic reasons. Here, a special danger of lists of priorities becomes obvious, i.e. of distinguishing only superficially among goals of treatment, while de facto distinguishing among patients or groups of patients (Schöne-Seifert et al. 2006; Schmitz-Luhn and Bohmeier 2013).

4.2 Is Compatibility of Medical Ethos and Economic Conditions Possible?

In order to avoid rationing in the fostering of human life which, as previously said, would inevitably lead to an unresolvable conflict with the fundamental norm of protecting life, society needs to raise sufficient resources on the macro level, according to the ethical norms of responsibility and solidarity. On the meso level, the ethical norm of justice requires an allocation of resources to the various medical departments that neither plays one department off against another nor posteriorizes groups of patients. And on the micro level the norms of the protection of life and avoiding harm and of the respect for the patient's autonomy-based right to self-determination may never become posteriorized for economic reasons.

As to the question of compatibility of medical ethos with market conditions it ought to be noted that saving financial resources and the medical ethos of help do not necessarily stand in each other's way. On the contrary, central economic norms like frugality, cost/benefit calculations and efficiency in the use of resources are compatible under certain conditions with the central ethical norms of justice, non-discrimination and responsibility. For a physician has a duty to do what is medically necessary; for everything below this threshold, however, he must adapt to economic conditions; otherwise he may face the problem that by failing to be vigilant over costs incurred for what is not medically necessary, he may endanger the financing of treatment of serious diseases in other patients. For the sake of *all* patients with severe diseases the medically necessary ought to be freed from economic constraints; by its very nature it cannot be subject to rationing. It is therefore imperative to organize the conditions of compatibility between medical duties and economic optimization in such a way that the higher the medical obligation, the lower the justifiability of economic influence—and vice versa.

5 Summary

1. With regard to the present structural change in Germany from a governmentally regulated to a free market health care system—in short, from a *social* system to a *market-driven* one—the position advocated here of a possible confluence of ethics and economics has an orientating function: The task is to uphold the norms of social justice, societal responsibility and solidarity so as to prevent them from becoming victims of economization, and yet to show that both can and must be co-ordinated with each other.
2. Co-ordinating justice and solidarity on the one hand and economic liberalization and individualization on the other is possible and promising, if the consensus persists that though the individual is responsible for his health to an appropriate degree, society has to take care that the individual is safeguarded from bankruptcy owing to the costs of medical treatment. Thus, reasonable economic risks and costs should be individualized, while unreasonable ones should be assumed by society.
3. From an ethical point of view, it seems hardly possible to counter the progressing danger of *economization* in medicine structurally on the micro level of physician and patient. Although both physician and patient bear responsibility for reducing the use of resources to the minimum necessary, the growing financial deficit in health care systems must be recognized and dealt with on the macro level.
4. Ethics does not aim at acceptance, but at an analysis of the *acceptability* of the influence of economics on medical treatment. The greatest obstacle to a rational and joint discussion of the topic "Medicine between Economy and Ethics" is the growing misunderstanding that health is to be considered as a ware and modern medicine is to be understood as a service undertaking, as if one could 'buy' and 'sell' health and as if the patient were a 'client' and the physician a 'purveyor'. The relation between economics and ethics (Albach 2005) may regarding medicine be characterized in a paraphrase of a famous dictum by Immanuel Kant: Economics without ethics would be blind, while business ethics without economics would be empty.

References

Albach H (2005) Betriebswirtschaftslehre und Unternehmensethik. In: Keutner T et al (eds) Wissen und Verantwortung, vol I. Alber, Freiburg, pp 249–267

Aristotle (1925) Nicomachean ethics (ed & tr. by Ross D, Oxford), Book V, Ch. 5, 1130b6–1132b20

Beckmann JP (2001) Gentests und Versicherungen. In: Sadowski D (ed) Entrepreneurial spirits (Festschrift Horst Albach). Gabler, Wiesbaden, pp 271–290

Beckmann JP (2009) Ethische Herausforderungen der modernen Medizin. Alber, Freiburg

Beckmann JP (2011a) Ökonomie und Ethik am Beispiel der Rationierungsdebatte im Gesundheitswesen. In: Busche H (ed) Philosophische Aspekte der Ökonomie. Königshausen und Neumann, Würzburg, pp 15–38

Beckmann JP (2011b) Über Solidarität und Individualismus. In: Busche H (ed) Solidarität. Ein Prinzip des Rechts und der Ethik. Königshausen und Neumann, Würzburg, pp 55–70

Busche H (ed) (2011) Philosophische Aspekte der Ökonomie. Königshausen und Neumann, Würzburg

Deutscher Ethikrat (2011) Nutzen und Kosten im Gesundheitswesen. Zur normativen Funktion ihrer Bewertung. http://www.ethikrat.org/dateien/pdf/stellungnahme-nutzen-und-kosten-im-gesundheitswesen.pdf. Accessed 3 Mar 2015

Deutscher Ethikrat (2014) Vom Krankenhaus zum kranken Haus? Klinikalltag zwischen ethischem Anspruch und Kostendruck. http://www.ethikrat.org/dateien/pdf/ht-22-10-2014-simultanmitschrift.pdf. Accessed 3 Mar 2015

Fleischhauer K (2014) Die Regulierung der medizinischen Versorgung in Deutschland. LIT, Berlin

Fuchs C et al (2009) Rationalisierung, Rationierung und Priorisierung—was ist gemeint? Deutsches Ärzteblatt 106(12):554–557

Hoffmann TS (2011) Wirtschaftsphilosophie. Matrix, Wiesbaden

Hoppe JD (2009) Verteilungsgerechtigkeit durch Priorisierung—Patientenwohl in Zeiten der Mangelverwaltung (Address). http://www.bundesaerztekammer.de/fileadmin/user_upload/downloads/112-DAET-Rede-Hoppe-1905092.pdf. Accessed 15 Mar 2015

Kerber W (1999) Solidaritätsprinzip. In: Ritter J et al (eds) Historisches Wörterbuch der Philosophie, vol 9. Schwabe, Basel, pp 1015–1017

Kettner M, Koslowski P (eds) (2011) Wirtschaftsethik in der Medizin. Wie viel Ökonomie ist gut für die Gesundheit? Fink, Paderborn, pp 67–153

Lohmann H et al (eds) (2010) Priorisierung statt Rationierung. Zukunftssicherung für das Gesundheitssystem. Economica, Heidelberg

Maio G (2014) Geschäftsmodell Gesundheit. Wie der Markt Gesundheit abschafft. Suhrkamp, Berlin, pp 25–41 and 91–105

Marburger H (2008) Die gesetzliche Krankenversicherung. Boorberg, Stuttgart

Marckmann G (2003) Verteilungsgerechtigkeit in der Gesundheitsversorgung. In: Düwell M, Steigleder K (eds) Bioethik. Eine Einführung. Suhrkamp, Frankfurt/aM, pp 333–343

Rawls J (1971) A theory of justice. Belknap Press of Harvard University Press, Cambridge

Schmitz-Luhn B, Bohmeier A (eds) (2013) Priorisierung in der Medizin. Springer, Berlin

Schöne-Seifert B, Buyx A, Ach JB (2006) Gerecht behandelt? Rationierung und Priorisierung im Gesundheitswesen. Mentis, Paderborn

Schröder KT (2010) Die Priorisierung von Gesundheitsleistungen widerspricht den Grundsätzen unseres Sozialstaates. In: Lohmann H et al (eds) Priorisierung statt Rationierung. Zukunftssicherung für das Gesundheitssystem. Economica, Heidelberg, pp 1–14

Sozialgesetzbuch (1976) Book I. Bund, Köln, § 1

Sozialgesetzbuch (2006) Book V. Deutscher Taschenbuch, München, § 6 Abs. 6

Zentrale Ethikkommission bei der Bundesärztekammer (2000) Prioritäten in der medizinischen Versorgung im System der Gesetzlichen Krankenversicherung (GKV). Deutsches Ärzteblatt 97(15):A1017–A1023

Zentrale Ethikkommission bei der Bundesärztekammer (2007) Priorisierung medizinischer Leistungen im System der Gesetzlichen Krankenversicherung (GKV). www.zentrale-ethikkommission.de/downloads/LangfassungPriorisierung.pdf. Accessed 15 Mar 2015

Jan P. Beckmann is Professor Emeritus of Philosophy at the Institute of Philosophy of FernUniversität in Hagen, Germany. In 1967 he was a Postdoctoral Research Fellow of the Max Kade Foundation, New York. 1968–1970 he served as Assistant Professor of Philosophy at Yale University, New Haven, Conn., USA. In 1979 he completed his habilitation in philosophy at Bonn University, Germany. He was member of the Selection Boards of the German Academic Exchange Service (Bonn 1970–1990) and the Studienstiftung des Deutschen Volkes (1971–2011). He also served for many years as Co-Director of the Institute of Science and Ethics and of the German Reference Centre for Ethics in the Life Sciences, both at Bonn University. In 2002 the German Federal Government made him a member of the Central Ethics Commission for Stem Cell Research (Berlin) of which he still is a member. He held guest professorships at the Universities of Oxford (1986), Bonn (1991, 1995) and Münster (1994). His fields of research include epistemology, ontology, ethics, esp. (bio-)medical ethics, and the history of ancient and medieval philosophy. He holds a Doctoral Degree in Philosophy from Bonn University and an Honorary Doctoral Degree from the Faculty of Medicine of the University of Duisburg-Essen, Germany.

Part II

Seizing the Opportunities Across Countries and Subdisciplines

Pathways Towards Health Care Systems with a Chronic-Care Focus: Beyond the Four Walls

Manuel García-Goñi, Peter McKiernan, and Francesco Paolucci

Abstract

Increasing health care expenditure is a matter of concern in many countries, particularly in relation to the underlying drivers of such escalation that include aging, medical innovation, and changes in the burden of disease, such as the growing prevalence of chronic diseases. Most health care systems in developed countries have been designed to *cure* acute episodes, rather than to *manage* chronic conditions, and therefore they are not suitably or efficiently organized to respond to the changing needs and preferences of users. Hospitals provide much of that health provision and they are in need of adapting to the needs of the population. New models of chronic care provision have been developed to respond to the changing burden of disease, taking into account the role of hospitals. Further, there is considerable practical experience in several different countries showing their advantages but also the difficulties associated with their implementation. In this paper, we focus on the international experiences in terms of policy changes and pilot studies focused on testing the feasibility of moving toward chronic care models. In particular, we discuss a framework that identifies

M. García-Goñi (✉)
Department of Applied Economics II, Universidad Complutense de Madrid, Campus de Somosaguas, 28223 Pozuelo de Alarcón, Madrid, Spain
e-mail: mggoni@ucm.es

P. McKiernan
Strathclyde Business School, University of Strathclyde, Glasgow, Scotland
e-mail: peter.mckiernan@strath.ac.uk

F. Paolucci
School of Management and Governance, Sir Walter School of Public Policy and International Affairs, Murdoch University, Perth, Australia

School of Economics and Management, University of Bologna, Bologna, Italy
e-mail: f.paolucci@murdoch.edu.au

H. Albach et al. (eds.), *Boundaryless Hospital*, DOI 10.1007/978-3-662-49012-9_4

and analyzes key prerequisites to achieving high performing chronic care-based health care systems and apply it to various countries and link this proposal with the concept of the *boundaryless hospital*.

Keywords
Chronic care • Integrated care • Health care policy • Health care strategy

1 Introduction

Health expenditures have increased in the last decades in most western economies with different types of health systems. The U.S. has the highest proportion of GDP devoted to health (about 17 % in 2012 from 12 % in 1990; OECD Health Data 2014). Its health system is mostly private, although the federal programs of Medicare and Medicaid are planned to cover most of people in need of health service provision. A lower proportion of GDP devoted to health is found in countries with social health insurance systems, e.g., The Netherlands. Their scheme is characterized by mandatory insurance with competition in the market of health care provision and with incentives for efficiency, although with some concern for risk selection—diminished through the use of risk-adjustment reimbursements of different kinds. The Netherlands has increased health expenditures from about 7.5 % of GDP in 1990 to 11.8 % in 2012 (see Fig. 1). Finally, countries such as the United Kingdom, Australia and Spain have a lower proportion of GDP devoted to health, i.e., 9–10 % in 2012 from 6 to 7 % in 1990. In those countries, health care provision is organized through a National Health System (NHS) that is mostly free at the point of use (with some variation across countries), although there is room for different levels of participation of private agents in the provision and funding of health services in different countries. For example, Australia has a higher

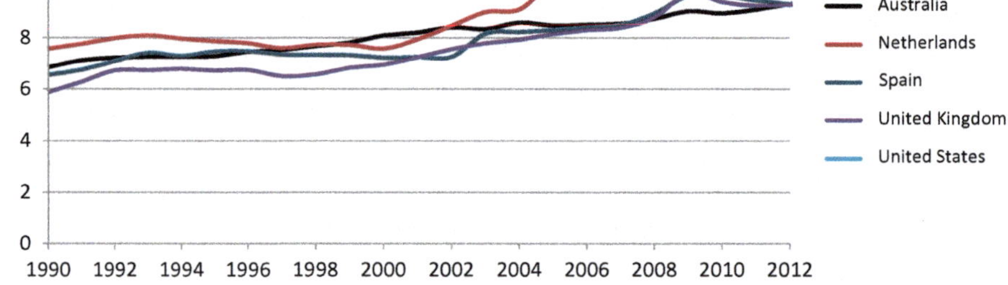

Fig. 1 Health expenditures as a percentage of GDP 1990–2012 (OECD Health Statistics 2014)

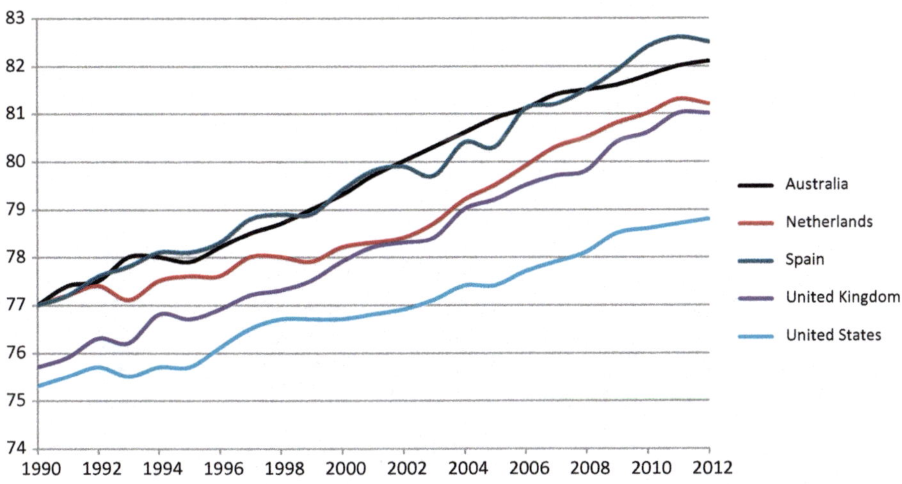

Fig. 2 Life expectancy in a selected group of developed countries. 1990–2012 (OECD Health Statistics 2014)

participation of private provision and funding while Spain has a regionalized version of an NHS (Ministry of Health, Social Services and Equality 2012).

No matter how each country's health system organizes provision and financing of health services, or the role of public sector, concern exists about the increasing relative weight of the health sector within the economy (Paolucci 2011). The health economics literature has pointed to health technology as the main determinant of this increase (Newhouse 1992; Barbash and Glied 2010), alongside the aging population (Paolucci et al. 2015). In this sample of countries (the U.S., The Netherlands, UK, Spain and Australia), life expectancy at birth has increased from 75–78 years in 1990 to about 79–82 years in 2012 (see Fig. 2). Together with the process of aging, the average type of patient has evolved and now, the burden of disease shows a greater prevalence of chronic conditions (Mathers and Loncar 2006; Samb et al. 2010) through an increase in the incidence of cancer (see Fig. 3).

The main goal of a health system is to deliver the necessary health services to the population with the highest quality of those services and through an efficient use and allocation of resources, including hospitals, primary care centers, and other health infrastructures. Because most international health systems were designed some decades ago, when health care was focused mostly on acute patients, they were designed to *cure* acute episodes rather than to *manage* chronic conditions. However, the care provision for chronic patients is different from the health provision for acute patients. Patients with acute conditions are in need of short-term treatments for a severe injury, an urgent medical condition, or some kind of health care in order to recover from a surgery. Differently, patients with chronic conditions suffer their illnesses for a long period of time and most likely they will not be cured. Once the condition appears, it usually affects the health status and worsens the quality of life of the patient.

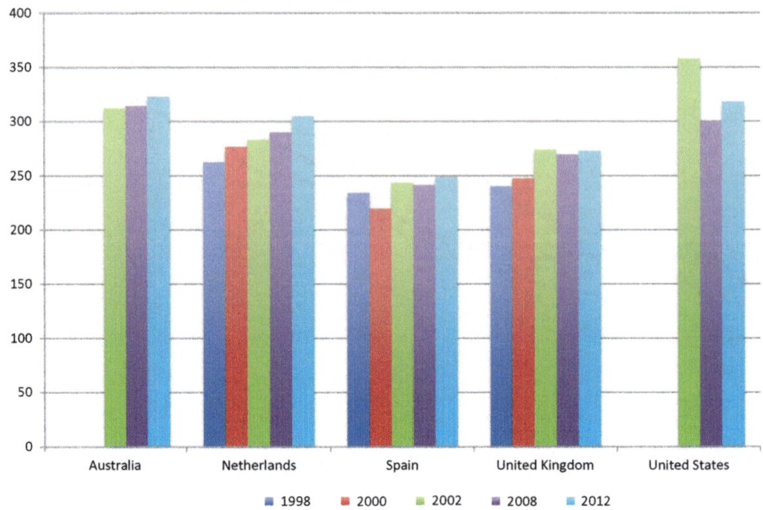

Fig. 3 Evolution of morbidity measured through incidence of cancer (malignant neoplasm) per 100,000 population (OECD Health Statistics 2014)

Nowadays, there is a common agreement about the challenge of adapting health systems to provide efficient care to chronic patients, for whom most health care expenditures are concentrated—for example, 78 % in the U.S. (Vogeli et al. 2007) or 7 % in Spain (Bengoa 2008). Furthermore, there is a growing proportion of patients living with more than one chronic condition (multi-morbidity) and the response to their needs has been recognized as one of the main challenges for health systems in the twenty-first century (Jadad et al. 2010). Orueta et al. (2014) find that within the entire population of the Basque Country, a region in Spain with more than two million inhabitants, about 24 % suffer from more than one chronic disease and concentrate 64 % of total health expenditures.

As an answer to this challenge, new models of chronic care provision have been developed, taking into account the role of hospitals. Considerable practical experience in different countries shows their advantages and the difficulties associated with their implementation. The two most important are the Chronic Care Model (CCM) (Wagner et al. 1996) and the Kaiser Permanente Pyramid Model (KPPM). The CCM was thought to improve quality of care, levels of satisfaction, and outcomes for chronic patients by looking at the adequate level of interactions between active and informed patients and prepared and proactive health personnel. The KPPM was designed to understand and identify different needs in different groups of patients by their risk levels according to complexity. Besides those models, Ham (2010) developed a framework identifying the ten key characteristics of a high-performing chronic care system. Most of the international experiences are related to the CCM or KPPM families of models and are focused on improving at least one of the key characteristics outlined by Ham's framework. In recent years, concern on the evolution of the role of hospitals has included a discussion of different innovative proposals, pointing to the concept of the *boundaryless* hospital. In this chapter we link both trends. The traditional fragmented type of care is characterized by a clear separation between different health providers. In contrast, a high-performing chronic care system needs to provide integrated care, including hospital, primary, ambulatory or specialist care, and whenever possible, social, community, or home care. Consequently, within this transition toward chronic care systems, the role of future hospitals needs to change and they should "pull down their walls" and intervene together with primary and community care.

The remainder of this paper is organized as follows: Sect. 2 describes how current health systems organize health care provision. Our main focus of attention is the role of hospitals, their activity and their size, and the concerns raised with the current trend in the burden of disease. Section 3 presents the main chronic care models and the framework provided by Ham. We show how those models improve not only the efficiency in the provision but also its quality within the pathway toward a high-performing chronic care system, and define, as one of their dimensions, the concept of the *boundaryless* hospital. Section 4 presents a summary of international experiences in dealing with the challenge of chronicity and the integration of health and social services. We organize our review of international experiences by health systems, attending to the different level of private sector provision and the consequences of their financial incentives. Here, we discuss the central role that hospitals might play in the future. Finally, Sect. 5 provides our conclusion.

2 Current Provision of Health Care in Hospitals

One of the first definitions of a hospital was provided by the World Health Organization (1957), which considered that a hospital was "an integral part of a social and medical organization, the function of which is to provide for the population complete health care, both curative and preventive, and whose outpatient services reach out to the family in its home environment; the hospital is also a center for the training of health workers and for bio-social research." Therefore, it is a health care institution that provides medical, diagnostic and specialized treatment to inpatients of different kinds with its health personnel (nurses, doctors, surgeons, etc.) and health technology equipment.

Nonetheless, the hospital has experienced a continuous increase in the types of activities and services during the last century (Lega and DePietro 2005) and that is a matter of concern because (a) it constitutes one of the main structures in the provision of health care and (b) it is one of the main determinants of their health expenditures. Here, we look at the current provision of health care in hospitals in the set of countries representing different health systems by looking at key indicators such as: their number of discharges, the number of beds and their average length of stay, with data obtained from the OECD Health Statistics (2014). At the same time, we evaluate whether that provision is evolving according to the burden of disease toward chronic conditions given the goal of efficient allocation of resources. It is important to note that health care provision and the mission of hospitals cannot be described with just one of those indicators. It is the analysis of all of them together that helps explain the functioning of hospitals and their role within the entire health system, taking into account the different participation between public and private sectors in the health care provision and funding under different systems, or their focus on the global aims of efficiency and equity.

2.1 Hospital Discharges and Size of Hospitals

Hospital discharges represent the formal release of a patient from a hospital after a procedure or course of treatment (OECD Health Statistics 2014). They occur when a patient leaves hospital after the termination of the treatment, when the patient leaves the hospital against medical advice, when transferred to another health care institution (but not when transferred to a different department within the same institution), or when the patient dies. Countries with different types of health systems present different trends in the number of discharges (Fig. 4). The Netherlands, with a social health insurance system, increased the number of hospital discharges by 24 % from 2000 to 2011. Australia, representing a National Health System but with high participation of private provision and funding in hospitals had a moderate increase of 5 % in hospital discharges from 2006 to 2011. However, Spain and the United Kingdom, both with National Health Systems and with a very important proportion of public provision and public participation of hospitals behaved differently in the same period. In Spain, the number of hospital

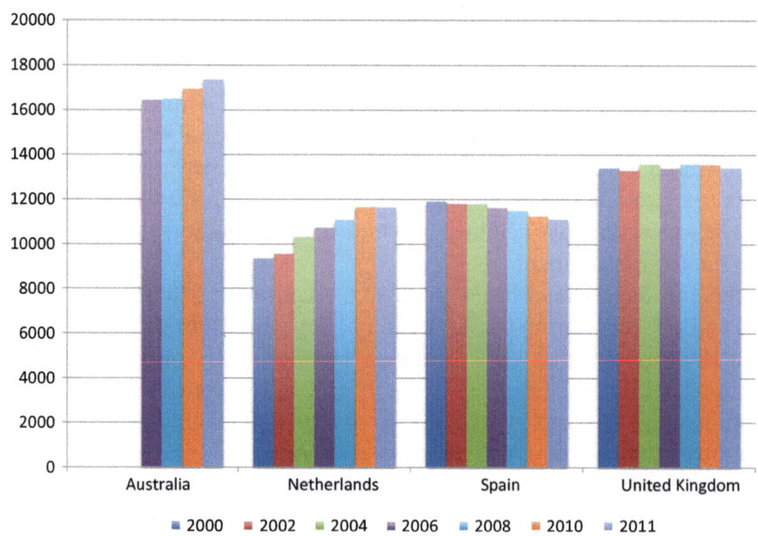

Fig. 4 Inpatient care discharges (all hospitals) per 100,000 population. 2000–2011 (OECD Health Statistics 2014)

discharges decreased by 7 % from 2000 to 2011 while in the United Kingdom, the number remained stable. Besides these trends, the levels are noteworthy. In Australia and the UK, the number of discharges is greater than in Spain or the Netherlands.

The evolution in the number of discharges is related to other indicators such as the size of the hospital given by its number of beds, or to the average length of stay that patients spend in the hospital. The evolution of number of beds is important because it provides information on how different health systems are modifying the capacity of hospitals. Recently, there has been a decrease in the number of acute beds in hospitals in countries with a National Health System: In Australia, the number of acute beds in hospitals per 100,000 individuals was of 3.6 in the year 2000 decreasing to 3.4 (about 6 %) in 2011. However, in countries with a greater participation of the public sector within an NHS, this trend has been more pronounced. Thus, in Spain in the same years, it decreased from 2.8 to 2.3 (about 17 %) and in the UK, it fell from 3.2 to 2.4 (about 25 %). The Netherlands, with a social health insurance system, again behaves differently and shows an increase in the number of acute beds in hospitals per 100,000 individuals from 3 in 2000 to 3.3 in 2011 (about 9.3 %).

2.2 Average Length of Stay

The average length of stay is another important dimension in evaluating the health provision performed in hospitals. Given that our challenge is to adapt to the burden of disease, we focus our attention on the difference between the length of stay of all inpatient stays in all hospitals, and the average length of stay of chronic patients. Figure 5a depicts the evolution of the length of stay for all inpatient stays and Fig. 5b the length of stay specific for cancer patients. In Australia, the length of stay for all inpatients decreased by 8 % from 2000 to 2011, while taking into account only cancer patients, the length of stays decreased by 9.2 % in the same period. The same decreasing trend occurs in the length of stay of other chronic conditions (22.7 % in endocrine, nutritional and metabolic diseases; 12.3 % in diseases of the circulatory system; 8.2 % in diseases of the respiratory system). Therefore, we can infer that a shorter inpatient stay in chronic patients explains the decrease in average length of stay for all inpatients. The United States exhibited a falling trend in the length of stay from 2000 to 2011. In the case of all inpatients stays, it decreased by 10.3 %, and for chronic patients the decrease was even smaller (3.5 % in cancer, 15.6 % in endocrine, nutritional and metabolic diseases, 2.1 % in diseases of the circulatory system).

The trend in the length of stay in the Netherlands, Spain and the UK is decreasing but is more pronounced than in the case of Australia or the U.S. Although data is incomplete, the trend in length of stays for all inpatient stays in the Netherlands decreased by 16.3 % from 2000 to 2006. For cancer patients it decreased by 32.7 % from 2000 to 2010; and for other chronic conditions, from 2000 to 2012, the decrease was also more pronounced (45.7 % in endocrine,

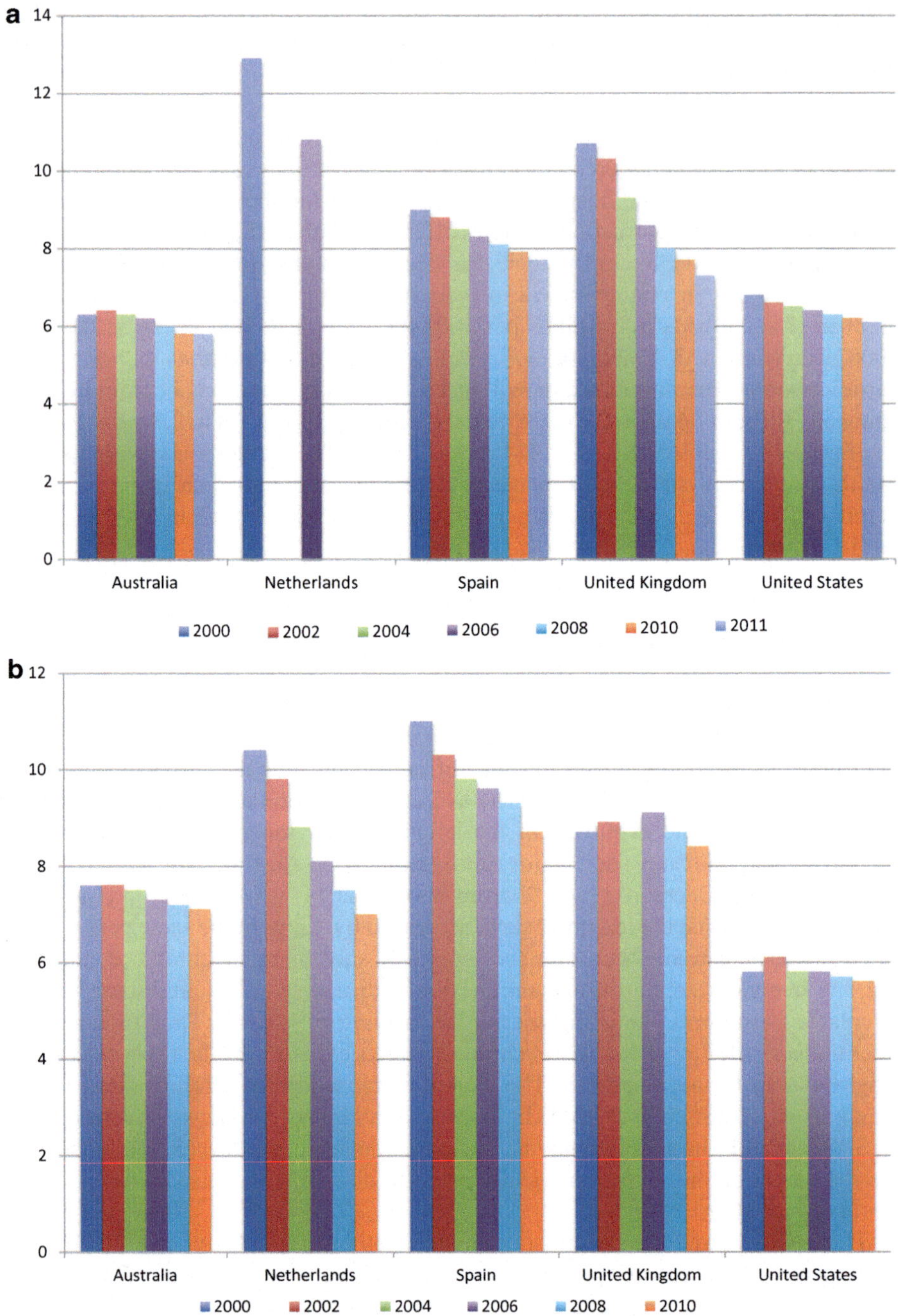

Fig. 5 (**a**) Evolution of the length of stay in days for all patients. 2000–2012 (OECD Health Statistics 2014). (**b**) Evolution of the length of stay in days for cancer patients. 2000–2012 (OECD Health Statistics 2014)

nutritional and metabolic diseases; 41.8 % in diseases of the circulatory system; 28.9 % in diseases of the respiratory system). In Spain, the decrease in the length of stay for all inpatient stays was of 15.6 % from 2000 to 2012, and as in the case of The Netherlands, it was more pronounced than in Australia for chronic patients (25.5 % in cancer; 37.9 % in endocrine, nutritional and metabolic diseases; 21.5 % in diseases of the circulatory system; 17.9 % in diseases of the respiratory system). With respect to the United Kingdom, the length of stay for all inpatients decreased by 32.8 % from 2000 to 2012 while for chronic patients, from 2000 to 2011 that decrease is more moderate (4.6 % in cancer; 21.8 % in endocrine, nutritional and metabolic diseases; 11.4 % in diseases of the circulatory system) showing a slightly increase of 4.2 % in the case of diseases of the respiratory system.

The decrease in the length of stay is significantly greater in the Netherlands, Spain and the UK relative to Australia or the U.S. and might be explained because Australia and the U.S. had the lowest average length of stay for all inpatients throughout the time period (6.3 and 5.8 in Australia; 6.8 and 6.1 in the U.S.; 10.7 and 7.3 in the UK; 9 and 7.7 in Spain in 2000 and 2011 respectively; and 12.9 in 2000 and 10.8 in 2006 in The Netherlands). Hence, it might be more difficult to accomplish further reductions.

It is worth noting that the U.S. has a private health system in which there is no equity in the access to health care and there are strong risk-selection incentives. At the same time, the Australian National Health System is characterized by a high proportion of private providers and funds. The Netherlands, with a social health insurance system with private provision, showed in year 2000 a length of stay for most conditions greater than other countries. Though, it has shown the greatest decrease in recent years it now presents a length of stay lower for most conditions than that of the UK or Spain. At the same time, The Netherlands and Australia (there is no data from the U.S.) show an increase in the number of hospital discharges while the UK maintains the same level and Spain has shown a slight decrease. Finally, it is in the UK and in Spain where the number of acute beds in hospitals per 100,000 individuals is lowest.

The fact that countries such as the UK and Spain have a lower proportion of acute beds, or a decreasing number of hospital discharges might be explained by the importance given to their primary and ambulatory care provision—one of the strengths of their systems. However, the Netherlands has decreased the average length of stay for chronic patients to levels lower than those of the UK or Spain, and is getting closer to the length of stay in the U.S. or Australia. Therefore, the current role of hospitals in the provision of health care depends on the health systems, as they present a different mix of utilization with respect to other health providers such as ambulatory, outpatient, home or social care. Those differences might be explained by financial incentives in the provision and the way in which health providers in general and hospitals, in particular, are reimbursed.

The role of hospitals in the provision of care is changing due to the need to adapt to the burden of disease and to provide efficient care to chronic patients. However, the numbers we have presented (with data until 2012) show that further reforms are needed. In the UK and Spain, the length of stay for chronic patients is still high and has decreased much less than in The Netherlands. At the same time, countries such as Australia, the Netherlands and the U.S. do not utilize as much primary care as the UK or Spain. Therefore, the efficient provision to chronic patients is not achieved and there remains a path to transit toward a better mix of utilization of hospitals and other health providers. Recommendations for following the right path can be found in different models and frameworks for chronic care provision.

3 Chronic Care Models and the Role of Hospitals

In spite of the increasing concern over chronic care and its associated concentration of health care expenditures, health planning and provision in most international health systems is still focused on the treatment and cure for acute patients instead of caring for chronic patients. Moreover, we have not observed dramatic changes in the way in which hospitals are utilized. As a consequence, there is an urgent challenge for international health systems to adapt and provide efficient care to chronic patients. The two most important models of chronic care provision developed for this goal are the CCM and the KPPM.

The CCM (Wagner et al. 1996) and the family of models that followed as the Expanded Chronic Care Model (Barr et al. 2003) provide a guide to improve quality of care, levels of satisfaction and outcomes. Their method is to look for adequate level of interactions between active and informed patients and prepared and proactive health personnel. The main model was thought to improve the quality of provision through interventions on four areas in the health system and clinical practice: self-management support, delivery system design, decision support and clinical information systems. The expanded version of the model added 'community' as another level of action, thus including population health promotion interventions as public health prevention and chronic disease management programs: "re-orienting health services involves encouraging those in the health care sector to move beyond the provision of clinical and curative services to an expanded mandate that supports individuals and communities in a more holistic way" (Barr et al. 2003). There is a clear link therefore in the CCM and the Expanded CCM between health systems and social and political and economic systems. Hence, under this model, the goal of the health care sector is to repair the health status of patients and to create the conditions for a healthier society advocating for the promotion of health in the environment.

The integration of health care, key in the CCM, provides a central role to the clinical practice at primary care. It differs from the traditional model of provision, which is characterized by the fragmentation of care with a clear separation between care provided to patients at hospitals and specialist care, and primary care. In the extended version, it includes the search for the optimal mix of interventions for chronic patients including treatment and preventive care. As a consequence, the CCM states intervention is required simultaneously across delivery system redesign, patient self-management support, decision support, clinical information systems, community linkages, and health system organization. Bengoa (2008) illustrates how within the transition toward a chronic care model, health interventions often work on the essential elements separately. Coleman et al. (2009) review and evaluate the different experiences of health interventions following the CCM and they find that even if the results are not definitive, there is a general improvement in the quality of care to chronic patients. Furthermore, following the evidence from observational studies, when those interventions are meant to change across different elements of the model simultaneously, the combined effect improves with respect to that of isolated interventions (Bodenheimer et al. 2002).

The KPPM was designed in the U.S. to understand and identify different needs in different groups of patients. In this set up, patients are considered as the first provider of health care through health promotion, prevention and self-management activities when they are healthy enough. This model looks for a greater importance of primary care together with the community interventions, modifying the role of hospitals and other health providers. The main idea is to classify individuals into risk levels according to their complexity. The model would add more formal health care provision the more complex the patient is, so that any unnecessary utilization of specialist care, hospital admissions, or any other formal health care provision are minimized (Garcia-Goñi et al. 2012). The basis of this model is to understand the concentration of health expenditures and health utilization by risk groups, and identify the most complex patients in order to provide the most efficient mix of health services for them. The KPPM allows for the use of predictive modeling to promote preventive interventions and hence, reducing health care utilization (Panattoni et al. 2011). In that way, risk stratification identifies patients at high risk or with expected high expenditures, being most of the patients with (many times several) chronic conditions. For those patients identified as high risk, the model provides intensive health care management.

The KPPM is based on the promotion of health care coordination toward functionally integrated health care teams, including doctors of primary and secondary care, nurses, pharmacists and other health personnel working with the same budget and within multi-specialty centers (Ham 2006). The aim is to empower patients so as to maximize self-care, self-management and choice, given the information available through their medical records. Different primary care trusts have applied the model, mostly in the UK and the U.S., and have found positive effects on the integration of services and reducing hospital admissions by providing for example, integrated primary care with the collaboration of general practitioners (GPs) and nurses (Ham 2006).

The pathways toward chronic care systems have been explored in the literature. Ham (2010) developed a framework identifying the ten key characteristics of a high-performing chronic care system, see the list below; being those supporting patients to self-manage their conditions, including the help by informal care-givers; adopting population-management approaches such as the stratification of people with long term conditions according to risk and the provision of commensurate support; integrating care to facilitate primary care access to specialist advice and support; and coordinating care effectively. Ham's framework provides a guideline to policy makers in which it specifies which are the strategies that would improve the quality of care for chronic patients. Although it does not address simultaneously important issues such as integration or coordination of care and reforms of funding systems (Campillo-Artero 2012), it provides a useful scenario to check what is needed under different health systems, taking into account not only the ten characteristics but also the environmental and cultural context.

Ten characteristics of a high-performing chronic care system (Ham 2010):

1. Ensuring universal coverage
2. Provision of care that is free at the point of use
3. Delivery system should focus on the prevention of ill health
4. Priority is given to patients to self-manage their conditions with support from care givers and families
5. Priority is given to primary health care
6. Population management is emphasized through the use of tools to stratify people with chronic diseases according to their risk and offering support commensurate with this risk
7. Care should be integrated to enable primary health care teams to access specialist advice and support when needed
8. The need to exploit the potential benefits of information technology in improving chronic care
9. Care is effectively coordinated
10. Link these nine characteristics into a coherent whole as part of a strategic approach to change

García-Goñi et al. (2012) applied Ham's model to Spain and analyzed how well those characteristics were present within the Spanish NHS. They found that most of the ten characteristics for a high-performing chronic care system were present, at least to some extent. However, some of them were still in the early stages of development or were being applied only in limited regions or clinical contexts. For instance, García-Goñi et al. (2012) found that there was a considerable margin for improvement in the coordination of care in primary care for patients with complex clinical and social needs.

Many of the international experiences in the search for efficiency in the provision to chronic patients follow variations of the two models for instance, in the UK (Ham 2010) or Canada (College of Family Physicians of Canada 2009; Vachon et al. 2013). Two common and central features of the KPPM and the CCM that are also present in the set of high-performing chronic care system characteristics exposed by Ham (2010) and enhanced by Busse et al. (2010), are the integration of care and the promotion of primary and ambulatory care in coordination with specialists. Those are highly dependent on the evolution in the role and the type of health services that are provided at hospitals and how they are related to other health providers. For example, both the CCM and the KPPM propose, in different ways, to decrease the inappropriate use of hospitals by increasing the utilization of ambulatory care, or nursing and residential care when appropriate. As a consequence, the integration of care should take into account health providers (hospital, primary or ambulatory care) and whenever possible, social care, home care and community care with multidisciplinary teams capable to deliver care to the most complex patients, who often suffer from several chronic conditions (multimorbidity patients). In other words, thanks to available technology and to risk stratification, the limits of hospitals are not visible any longer and integrated care from a multidisciplinary team could (and should) be provided in different places more efficiently instead of at the physical hospital. As Robertson et al. (2014) proposed, the evolution of hospital activities should involve specialists in "looking beyond the four walls of their hospital to work as part of a multidisciplinary team and develop services that address the needs of their local population at each stage of their journey from home to hospital", becoming as a consequence educators that advise and support other primary and community health workers to improve the diagnosis and treatment to patients at the community level.

In our understanding, this is what Braithwaite et al. (1994) were defining as the *boundaryless hospital*, consisting of "a core facility comprising only the most acute services, intensive care, operating theatres and an accident and emergency unit, with all other services and units linked by information technology to each other and to the core facility" (Braithwaite et al. 1995). Therefore, the concept of the *boundaryless hospital* is linked strongly to the process of integration of care recommended in the chronic care models (Fig. 6). This is in direct opposition to the fragmented-care approaches, with full separation of hospital care and ambulatory and primary care that is still present in most international health systems.

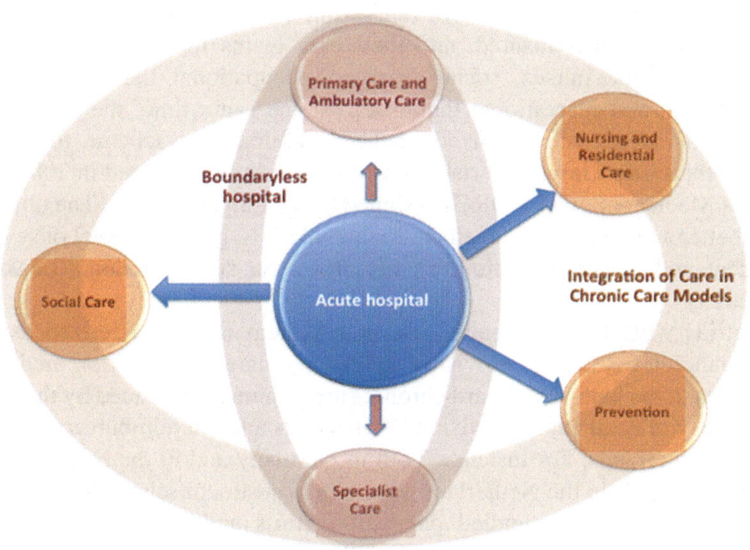

Fig. 6 Integration of care in the different Chronic Care Models and the boundaryless hospital concept

4 International Experiences with Chronic Care and the Evolution of Hospitals

The development of the CCM and the KPPM in the 1990s allows us to accumulate enough international experiences in the transition toward chronic care systems to infer some trends specific to different types of health systems. Here, we review some of those experiences ordered from higher to lower presence of private health care provision, paying attention to how much weight they place to financial incentives within the implementation of those strategies.

Both chronic care models were developed and first implemented in the U.S., within a private health system. The main evaluation for their health intervention programs is positive as shown in Coleman et al. (2009) or Panattoni et al. (2011) for the CCM or the KPPM, respectively, although results are inconclusive and there is still room for improvement. The basis of the implementation of the chronic care models in the U.S. is the full financial responsibility of the health care service provision by the provider, given the existing relationship between provider and insurer—even in the case of federal programs such as Medicare or Medicaid. As a consequence, the promotion of integrated care or the existence of multidisciplinary care teams is understood in the search for the efficient provision to the insured population. The Program of All-inclusive Care for the Elderly (PACE) (inserted in Medicare and Medicaid Programs), whose origin started back in the early 1970s in California (National PACE Association 2014), is an example of integrated care experience in the U.S. Its aim was to delay or avoid institutionalization of the elderly by providing appropriate daily health and social care (Calciori and Illinca 2011). Currently, it has expanded to 31 states. Providers have full financial risk and are responsible for the provision of delivering all the integrated health care and social services to their insured, and their care teams include physicians, nurse practitioners, clinic nurses, social workers, occupational therapists, dietitians, health workers and recreational therapists. At the same time, the importance of economic incentives is recognized in the reimbursement scheme for hospitals, estimated through an improved risk-adjustment formula, reformed in 2007 through the use of Medicare Severity DRGs assigned to each inpatient stay. The objective is to get a better adequate reimbursement for actual costs, given the level of severity of the patient and to avoid or diminish incentives for risk selection (Bienkowska-Gibbs 2013).

Countries with a social health insurance system are characterized as having public financing but private provision under a regulated competition model. Their experiences in the pathway toward chronic care systems are defined by the financial responsibility of health care provision by providers and the reimbursement scheme, e.g., The Netherlands. For instance, both in Germany and in the Netherlands, risk adjustment is used. In the Netherlands, the risk-adjustment scheme is more sophisticated, consisting of a bundled payment (Struijs and Baan 2011) to provide incentives for efficiency of care integration through finding a mix of health services, provided at a lower cost with the use of primary care and nurses and a lower utilization of specialists or hospital care. There has been an implementation of different disease management programs—diabetes, COPD or cardiovascular risk (De Bakker et al. 2012)—with coverage defined by the national disease-specific health care standards, but with prices negotiated individually between insurers and care groups to spur competition (Llano 2013). In addition, there has been a promotion of integrated care initiatives with the creation of multidisciplinary care groups in primary care that have obtained positive evaluations, but with inconclusive results (Kruis et al. 2014). In Germany, the implementation of integrated care programs such as the Gesundes Kinzigtal Integrated Care Initiative, including health care, social care, or preventive actions (Hildebrandt et al. 2010), and the evaluation of the different disease management and integrated care programs has been positive, although the health system is still fragmented (Schlette et al. 2009). Specifically with respect to the reimbursement scheme for hospitals, as in the U.S., The Netherlands reformed the formula in 2012, with the use of the diagnosed-based codes in order to adjust to actual hospital costs better and avoid duplication of treatments (Nucciarelli and Ivanovic 2013). The trend in those countries is to promote provider competition and to attract patients with improved quality of care and more holistic treatments and patient-centered strategies (Amelung et al. 2012; Nucciarelli and Ivanovic 2013). For hospitals, the bundled payment in The Netherlands might derive in the future merger of general hospitals, in which most of the reimbursement is obtained through increased volume of non-specialized activity with more small, specialized hospitals attracting specific patients.

There are multiple experiences of implementation of chronic care programs in countries with an NHS. Australia, characterized by a high presence of private provision and funding, launched the Practice Incentive Program (PIP) in 1998, with economic incentives to GPs focused on disease management activities for patients with diabetes or asthma (Commonwealth of Australia 2010). A second program (Chronic Disease Management program (CDM)—The Australian Institute for Primary Care (2008) followed in 2005 and focused on patients with chronic conditions and complex needs, and was comprised of a multidisciplinary team. Other programs in Australia, such as the GP Mental Health Care Program, in 2006, aimed to promote early intervention and prevention, as an integrated care strategy including GPs, psychiatrists, psychologists and other allied health professionals (The Australian Institute for Primary Care 2008). Evaluation of those programs is positive, but the health system seems to remain fragmented (Davies et al. 2009) and the concern about the future of the health system and its funding is shown in Paolucci and McRae (2012) and in The Productivity Commission (2011).

Other countries with an NHS place a lower weight on their chronic care interventions to financial incentives, without the full responsibility of providers. For example, in the UK, the Quality and Outcomes Framework, launched in 2004, consisted of disease management programs for specific patients and also included preventive actions. This program includes an annual reward as a financial incentive for GPs based on their results in clinical practice (Health and Social Care Information Centre 2014). The NHS and Social Care Model, launched in 2005, are focused on long-term care patients and integrate health care and social care provision. In Scotland, there is a further program for chronic patients that promotes the integration of primary care, social care, or local networks (National Health System 2003). The integration of health and social care and disease management programs for specific chronic patients are present in different programs implemented in Canada, including multidisciplinary teams (CHOICE Program in Alberta, launched in 1996; PRISMA Program in Quebec, launched in 1997; or the Mental Health Strategy). In Spain, a number of strategies have been implemented within different regional health services promoting the integration of health care providers for the entire population of an area, as the Bidasoa Integrated Health Organization or the Baix Empordà Integrated Health Service putting together primary care, specialist care, and hospital care. Other programs in Spain have focused on multi-morbidity patients, based on the creation of multidisciplinary teams with an increasing role given to nurses, and disease management programs for patients with specific conditions promoting educational and informational courses for patients encouraging their empowerment in prevention and lowering their need of health care utilization (Nuño-Solinís et al. 2012). Finally, with respect to the integration of health care and social care, the Spanish Parliament passed the Law of Dependence in 2006, enforced in 2007, that granted new rights to patients with long-term care needs as personal assistance (Guillén and Comas-Herrera 2012). However, at the moment, not all levels of need are funded and most beneficiaries receive allowances for the use of family informal care (Colombo et al. 2011). Further, in Italy, there are experiences of integrated care with multidisciplinary teams as the Patients Diagnostic Therapeutic Pathways Program, launched in 2007, or different disease management programs as the Rafaello, Abruzzo or Michelangelo programs for specific conditions. From the point of view of population-based integrated care of primary and specialist and hospital care, some examples of programs in Italy are the Expanded CCM in Tuscany, launched in 2008, and the Leonardo program, launched in 2007 in Puglia. Most of the programs implemented in the UK, Spain, Canada and Italy do not include financial incentives for health providers and the focus is placed more on their universality and equity in the access.

Hence, any modern evaluation of chronic care programs in countries with an NHS seems positive. The National Health System (2014) considered that there had been an improvement in the care to some chronic patients as cancer or cardiac, although still with variable quality. In Canada, Vedel et al. (2010) examine different programs on integrating hospital, nursing, home or social care and conclude that the health care system is becoming better integrated. García-Goñi et al. (2012) evaluate the current situation of the Spanish National Health System following Ham's framework and find that, even if the situation in terms of integration of care is improving, there is still room to improve. This is mainly because the health system is still quite fragmented and that fragmentation is even greater when considering the extant social system. The trends shown in the chronic care experiences in NHS countries show an increasing concern for the importance of prevention and public health programs and a better coordination between family doctors and hospitals, physical and mental health, or health and social care (National Health System 2014; Garcia-Goñi et al. 2012).

Some interesting proposals for the improvement of the integration of care from NHS countries are to allow the combination of multidisciplinary groups in what has been named in the UK "the Multispecialty Community Provider" (NHS 2014), to strengthen primary care with a better use of nurse practitioners, the information system, and collaboration between primary and secondary care (Vedel et al. 2010), or the introduction of a medical home as a patient-centered medical care setting (The College of Family Physicians of Canada 2009). With respect to the development of future hospitals, there are also some suggestions linked to the integration of care that point to the concept of the *boundaryless* hospital. For example, the Future Hospital Commission (2013), established in 2012 by the Royal College of Physicians, proposed that "care should come to patients and be coordinated around their medical and support needs." They propose to change the structure of the hospital and add three new components: the Medical Division (a multidisciplinary team to focus on complex patients with multi-morbidities), the Acute Care Hub (designed for patients with expected length of stay lower than 2 days, and others with intensive care needs), and the Clinical Coordination Center (coordinating the activities at the hospital site and by the Medical Division, including medical teams working into the community).

5 Conclusion

In the last decades, health care expenditure has increased and is expected to keep increasing in the future, given the cost of health technology, the process of aging in the population and the evolution in the burden of disease toward chronic conditions. There are three main types of health systems: private health systems, social health insurance systems, and national health systems. They differ in the way in which health financing, planning and provision are organized. However, the main goal for all of them is to deliver care to the population with the highest feasible quality through the efficient allocation of resources, including the utilization mix of hospitals, primary care centers, and other health infrastructures. As a consequence, international health systems should provide care to chronic patients efficiently. Conversely, as hospitals were designed to *cure* acute episodes rather than to *manage* chronic conditions, many are not suitably or efficiently organized to respond to the changing needs and preferences of users. This is what we find when we look at the evolution in the role of hospitals in countries with different health systems. The role of hospitals is in transition: countries with strong financial pressure for private providers present low or highly decreasing lengths of stay in their search for the efficient use of hospitals, including risk-adjustment strategies. If risk-selection incentives are solved, that is a good sign, as chronic care needs a lower rate of utilization of inpatient stays. At the same time, relative hospital discharges are increasing for countries with financial pressure, while remaining stable or decreasing in countries such as the UK or Spain, which have a lower proportion of acute beds. That might be explained by the greater importance placed upon primary and ambulatory care provision in countries without financial pressure in hospital provision. Also, this is a good sign of participation of other types of provision, less costly, than hospitals. Consequently, with or without financial pressure, the role of hospitals under different health systems does not seem to be efficient as far as the treatment of chronic patients is concerned.

New models of chronic care provision have been developed to respond to this challenge. The two most important ones are the CCM and the KPPM. In this paper, we briefly described their most important characteristics and also the framework provided by Ham (2010), identifying the ten key characteristics of a high-performing chronic care system. The most important feature that is common to the three of them is the *integration of care*: including hospital, primary, ambulatory or specialist care, and whenever possible, social, community, or home care. In order to do that, the creation of multidisciplinary teams is essential. Moreover, these must stretch beyond the four walls of the traditional hospital and act to re-define integrated health care. That integration of care is opposite to the traditional fragmented type of care, with clear separation between health providers, that is still present in most international health systems. In fact, the recommendation on the transition toward a chronic care system points to a radical change in the role that hospitals should perform. This defines the concept of the *boundaryless hospital*: Hospitals should pull down their walls and work in multidisciplinary teams addressing the real needs of their patients in terms of health care, but also providing education, advise and support to other primary and community health workers in order to improve the diagnosis and treatment at the community level.

Since the late 1990s, several countries have launched chronic care programs. The evaluation of them is generally positive, no matter what type of health system or what level of financial pressure in health providers. Increases in the quality of health care provision to chronic patients has followed. However, evaluations present inconclusive results in terms of the efficiency in the allocation of resources. They infer that there is still room for improvement in the integration of health care services. In countries with financial pressure, risk adjusted reimbursement schemes are focused on integrated care, so as to maximize incentives for efficiency in the mix of utilization of providers. This might result in mergers of general and specialized hospitals. In NHS countries, the discussion has focused on the re-structure of hospitals to provide efficient care through different multidisciplinary units to complex (multi-morbidity) patients, patients with acute health or intensive care needs, and a good coordination for care provided inside or outside the hospital walls. There is still a path to walk in the transition toward the creation of the *boundaryless hospital*.

Acknowledgement Manuel García-Goñi thanks the Ramon Areces Foundation for financial support under the research project "Envejecimiento y sistema sanitario y social. El gasto público y sus efectos en igualdad, dependencia y aseguramiento en España" [Ageing and the health and social systems. Public health expenditure and its effect in equity, dependency and insurance in Spain].

References

Amelung V, Hildebrandt H, Wolf S (2012) Integrated care in Germany—a stony but necessary road! Int J Integr Care 12(27)

Australian Institute for Primary Care (2008) System reform and development for chronic disease management. http://www.health.gov.au/internet/nhhrc/publishing.nsf/Content/038-aipclatrobe/$FILE/038%20Australian%20Institute%20for%20Primary%20Care,%20La%20Trobe%20University%20Attachment%20B.pdf. Accessed 29 Jul 2015

Barbash GI, Glied SA (2010) New technology and health care costs—the case of robot-assisted surgery. N Engl J Med 363(8):701–704

Barr VJ, Robinson S, Marin-Link B et al (2003) The expanded chronic care model: an integration of concepts and strategies from population health promotion and the chronic care model. Hosp Q 7(1):73–82

Bengoa R (2008) Curar y cuidar. In: Bengoa R, Nuño Solinís R (eds) Curar y cuidar. Innovación en la gestión de enfermedades crónicas: una guía práctica para avanzar. In the book series: Economía de la Salud y Gestión Sanitaria, by V. Ortún. Elsevier Masson, Barcelona (Chapter 2)

Bienkowska-Gibbs T (2013) Integrated care programmes in Canada. Eurohealth Inc Euro Obs 19 (2):13–14

Bodenheimer T, Wagner E, Grumbach K (2002) Improving primary care for patients with chronic illness. The chronic care model, Part 2. JAMA 288:1909–14

Braithwaite J, Vining R, Lazarus L (1994) The boundaryless hospital. Aust N Z J Med 24:565–571

Braithwaite J, Lazarus L, Vining R et al (1995) Hospitals: to the next millennium. Int J Health Plann Manag 10(2):87–98

Busse R, Blümel M, Scheller-Kreinsen D et al (2010) Tackling chronic disease in Europe: strategies, interventions and challenges. European Observatory For Health Systems And Policies, Observatory Study No. 20. ISBN: 978 92 890 4192 8, http://www.euro.who.int/en/health-topics/Life-stages/healthy-ageing/publications/2010/tackling-chronic-disease-in-europe-strategies,-interventions-and-challenges

Calciori S, Illinca S (2011) Organizing integrated care for frail elderly patients in Switzerland, Italy, United States and Canada. Chapter 12 in The Swiss Society of Administrative Sciences (SSAS) Yearbook 2011. Accessed 5 Dec 2014

Campillo-Artero C (2012) When health technologies do not reach their effectiveness potential: a health service research perspective. Health Policy 104:92

Coleman K, Austin BT, Brach C et al (2009) Evidence on the chronic care model in the new millennium. Health Aff 28:75–85

College of Family Physicians of Canada (2009) Patient-centered primary care in Canada: bring it on home. http://www.cfpc.ca/uploadedFiles/Resources/Resource_Items/Bring20it20on20Home20FINAL20ENGLISH.pdf. Accessed 3 Dec 2014

Colombo F, Llena-Nozal A, Mercier J, et al (2011) Help wanted? Providing and paying for long-term care, OECD Health Policy Studies, OECD Publishing. Available at: http://dx.doi.org/10.1787/9789264097759-en

Commonwealth of Australia (2010) Practice incentives program. Department of Health and Ageing Medicare Australia. The Auditor-General Audit Report No. 5 2010–11. Performance audit. http://anao.gov.au/~/media/Uploads/Documents/2010%2011_audit_report_no5.pdf. Accessed 30 Jul 2015

Davies GP, Perkins D, McDonald J et al (2009) Integrated primary health care in Australia. Int J Integr Care 9:e95

De Bakker DH, Struijs JN, Baan CA et al (2012) Early results from adoption of bundled payment for diabetes care in the Netherlands Show improvement in care coordination. Health Aff 31:426–33

Future Hospital Commission (2013) Future hospital: caring for medical patients. A report from the Future Hospital Commission to the Royal College of Physicians. Royal College of Physicians, London, p. xxiii

Garcia-Goñi M, Hernández-Quevedo C, Nuño-Solinís R et al (2012) Pathways towards chronic-care focused healthcare systems: evidence from Spain. Health Policy 108:236–245

Guillén M, Comas-Herrera A (2012) How much risk is mitigated by LTC protection schemes? A methodological note and a case study of the public system in Spain. Geneva Pap 37:712–724

Ham C (2006) Developing integrated care in the NHS: adapting lessons from Kaiser. Health Services Management Centre, University of Birmingham, Birmingham

Ham C (2010) The ten characteristics of the high-performing chronic care system. Health Econ Policy Law 5(Pt 1):71–90

Health and Social Care Information Centre (2014) Quality and outcomes framework. http://www.hscic.gov.uk/qof. Accessed 21 Dec 2014

OECD Health Statistics (2014) OECD, Paris. http://www.oecd.org/els/health-systems/health-data.htm. Accessed 22 Nov 2014

Hildebrandt H, Hermann C, Knittel R, Richter-Reichhelm M, Siegel A, Witzenrath W (2010) Gesundes Kinzigtal Integrated Care: improving population health by a shared health gain approach and a shared savings contract. Int J Integr Care 10:1–14

Jadad AR, Cabrera A, Martos F et al (2010) When people live with multiple chronic diseases: a collaborative approach to an emerging global challenge. Granada: Andalusian school of Public Health. http://www.opimec.org/equipos/when-people-live-with-multiple-chronic-diseases/. Accessed 3 Dec 2014

Kruis AL, Boland MR, Assendelft WJ et al (2014) Effectiveness of integrated disease management for primary care chronic obstructive pulmonary disease patients: results of cluster randomised trial. BMJ 349:g5392

Lega F, DePietro C (2005) Converging patterns in hospital organization: beyond the professional bureaucracy. Health Policy 74(3):261–81

Llano R (2013) Bundled payments for integrated care in the Netherlands. Eurohealth Inc Euro Obs 19(2):15–17

Mathers CD, Loncar D (2006) Projections of global mortality and burden of disease from 2002 to 2030. PLoS Med 3(11):e442

Ministry of Health, Social Services and Equality (2012) National health system of Spain, 2012. Ministry of Health, Social Services and Equality, Madrid. http://www.msps.es/en/organizacion/sns/libroSNS.htm. Accessed 4 Dec 2014

National Health System (2003) Partnership for care: Scotlands White Paper. http://www.scotland.gov.uk/Resource/Doc/47032/0013897.pdf. Accessed 26 Aug 2015

National Health System (2014) Five year forwards view. https://www.england.nhs.uk/wp-content/uploads/2014/10/5yfv-web.pdf. Accessed 29 Jul 2015

National PACE Association (2014) PACE and managed care: strategies for expanding PACE through new payer relationships. http://old.npaonline.org/website/download.asp?id=6406&title=PACE_and_Managed_Care_Strategies_November_2014.pdf. Accessed 14 Jul 2015

Newhouse JP (1992) Medicare care cost: how much welfare loss? J Econ Perspect 6(3):3–21

Nucciarelli A, Ivanovic A (2013) Hospitals in the reformed Dutch health care system: balacing products and services. Eurohealth 19(2):40–43

Nuño-Solinís R, Sauto R, Toro N (2012) Integrated care initiatives in the Spanish Health System/ Experiencias de integración asistencial en el Sistema Nacional de Salud de España: Abstracts from the Third Spanish Conference on Chronic Care, San Sebastián, 19–20 May 2011/ Resúmenes de Comunicaciones al III Congreso Nacional de Atención Sanitaria al Paciente Crónico, Donostia-San Sebastián, 19 y 20 de mayo del 2011. Int J Integr Care 12(Suppl 2):e35

Orueta JF, García-Álvarez A, García-Goñi M, Paolucci F, Nuño-Solinís R (2014) Prevalence and costs of multimorbidity by deprivation levels in the Basque country: a population based study using health administrative databases. PLoS One 9(2):e89787

Panattoni LE, Vaithianathan R, Ashton T, Lewis GH (2011) Predictive risk modelling in health: options for New Zealand and Australia. Aust Health Rev 35(1):45–51

Paolucci F (2011) Health care financing and insurance. Options for design. In: Frech HE, Zweifel P (eds) Developments in health economics and public policy, vol 10. Springer, Berlin

Paolucci F, McRae IS (2012) Healthcare delivery for our ageing population: what does Australia need to do? In: Pincus J, Hugo G (eds) A greater Australia: population, policies and governance. Committee for Economic Development of Australia (CEDA), Melbourne, pp 162–174. ISBN 085–8012790

Paolucci F, Sowa PM, García-Goñi M et al (2015) Mandatory aged care insurance: a case for Australia. Ageing Soc 35(2):231–245

Robertson R, Sonola L, Honeyman M, et al (2014). Specialists in out-of-hospital settings. Findings from six case studies. King's Fund report. October 2014. http://www.kingsfund.org.uk/publications/specialists-out-hospital-settings. Accessed 3 Dec 2014

Samb B, Desai N, Nishtar S et al (2010) Prevention and management of chronic disease: a litmus test for health-systems strengthening in low-income and middle-income countries. Lancet 376:1785–97

Schlette S, Lisac M, Blum K (2009) Integrated primary care in Germany: the road ahead. Int J Integr Care Apr–Jun; 9:e14

Struijs JN, Baan CA (2011) Integrating care through bundled payments—lessons from the Netherlands. NEJM 364:990–1

The Productivity Commission (2011) Caring for older Australians: report no. 53. Publisher, Canberra

Vachon B, Désorcy B, Camirand M et al (2013) Engaging primary care practitioners in quality improvement: making explicit the program theory of an interprofessional education intervention. BMC Health Serv Res 13:106

Vedel I, Monette M, Beland F et al (2010) Ten years of integrated care: backwards and forwards. The case of the province of Québec, Canada. Int J Integr Care 11:1–11

Vogeli C, Shields AE, Lee TA et al (2007) Multiple chronic conditions: prevalence, health consequences, and implications for quality, care management, and costs. J Gen Intern Med 22(Suppl 3):391–5

Wagner EH, Austin BT, Von Korff M (1996) Organizing care for patients with chronic illness. Milbank Q 74(4):511–544

World Health Organization (1957) Report of the Expert Committee on Organization of Medical Care. Techn Rep Ser 1957:122

Manuel García-Goñi is Associate Professor of Applied Economics at Universidad Complutense de Madrid. He acted as Visiting Scholar at Columbia University, Visiting Fellow at the Australian National University (Canberra, Australia) and Visiting Professor at Universidade Nova de Lisboa, Universitate de Vest din Timisoara, and Universidad Carlos III in Madrid. Professor García-Goñi obtained his Ph.D. in Economics and MA in Political Economy at Boston University with the field of specialization of health economics and industrial organization. Since 2004 he has been Academic Secretary and Director of the Spanish Encounter of the Drug Industry that takes place annually at Universidad Internacional Menéndez Pelayo in Santander, Spain. Manuel García-Goñi was also a guest lecturer of health economics at the University of Bologna, Erasmus University in Rotterdam, Management Center Innsbruck, and Hibernia College in Dublin. He has published in peer-reviewed economic journals as Health Economics, Health Policy, Research Policy, or European Journal of Health Economics among others, and was a member of the Boards of Directors of the Spanish Health Economics Association between 2006 and 2012, and Chair of the Scientific Committee for the Spanish Health Economics Conference in 2012.

Peter McKiernan is Professor of Management at the University of Strathclyde in Glasgow, Scotland. He has been Dean of the School of Management and Governance at Murdoch University in Perth. Previously he held the Chair of Management and was Head of the School of Management at the University of St Andrews. He has been President of both the British Academy of Management and the European Academy of Management and is a Fellow of both institutions. He was elected as the CEEMAN Institutional Champion in 2013 and is a Companion of the Association of Business Schools. His articles have been published in many international journals and his many books include the best seller *Sharpbenders*. His research has covered corporate turnarounds, SMEs, health care, scenario planning, productivity and innovation, business history and the business school sector. Peter McKiernan is the Director of the EFMD/EURAM Directors of Research Programme. With Peter Waring, he is currently setting up a new research center in Singapore—the Singapore Centre for Productivity, Innovation and Technology (SCRIPT).

Francesco Paolucci is Associate Professor of Health Policy and Economics at the School of Management and Governance and Head of the Health Policy Program in Sir Walter Murdoch School of Public Policy and International Affairs at Murdoch University in Perth, Australia and Associate Professor at the University of Bologna. Formerly Reader of Health Economics and Policy at the University of Northumbria in Newcastle, UK Associate Professor at the University of Western Australia in Perth and Fellow at the Australian National University in Canberra and researcher at the Erasmus Universiteit Rotterdam. Dr. Paolucci has also worked for government, non-government and private sector national and international organizations, and held visiting and adjunct appointments from the University of Oslo; Erasmus Universiteit Rotterdam; the Universitad Complutense de Madrid and the University of Newcastle, UK He has published and advised in the areas of health management, economics and policy focusing on health care systems governance and design, health care financing and insurance and decision-making and priority setting in various countries including Australia, Cambodia, Colombia, Italy, the Netherlands, Norway, Qatar, South Africa, Spain, The United Kingdom and the United States. He obtained a Ph.D. from Erasmus Universiteit Rotterdam in the Netherlands (2007) with a thesis subsequently published by Springer (2011) entitled "Healthcare Financing and Insurance: Options for Design".

The Importance of Time in Developing a Boundaryless Hospital: An Example from Northern Portugal

Luís Velez Lapão

Abstract

The role of time in developing a *Boundaryless Hospital* is explored, as time is a critical component in the dynamical evolution of a hospital's interaction with its neighborhood, especially when health systems are calling for more coordination. It is expected that the effective coordination of care would promote, with time, and by a step-by-step process, the removing of the boundaries that still exist in local health systems.

A Local Health Unit in Portugal, established in 1999, was revised using case study approach, combining both qualitative and quantitative data. Kingdon's "three-streams" theory was used to analyze the gaps between the intentions expressed by policy-makers and the reality of integration as perceived by performance results.

This Local Health Unit, within an organizational and legal framework aiming at optimizing services' response through an integrated management of various health care facilities, involved several governments and difficult conditions. However, it successfully is presenting today several *boundaryless hospital* characteristics—from full quality certification in 2012, to strengthened links with primary care to reduce hospital admissions and to an information system that was critical to support referral services and, further, in establishing new connections with patients and other local players. After 16 years of effort trying to build a more integrated organization, time was clearly a critical factor. Time enabled the establishment a culture of working together to solve problems, to learn and understand their different requirements. Time is necessary to nurture the "organizational thread" that bonds the different care levels. The challenge of

L.V. Lapão (✉)
Global Health and Tropical Medicine, WHO Collaborating Center for Health Workforce Policy and Planning, Instituto de Higiene e Medicina Tropical, Universidade Nova de Lisboa, Rua da Junqueira, 100, 1349-008 Lisbon, Portugal
e-mail: luis.lapao@ihmt.unl.pt

H. Albach et al. (eds.), *Boundaryless Hospital*, DOI 10.1007/978-3-662-49012-9_5

establishing a boundaryless hospital is multi-dimensional, but yields significant long-term benefits.

Keywords
Boundaryless hospital • Vertical integration • Implementation • Change management • Time • Portugal

1 Introduction

During a person's life there are many interactions with different care units of the health system, which leads to the importance of integration and care coordination. Recognizing the people's access to care patterns and understanding them is important, whether people receive the range of services suitable to their needs or whether the programs are well coordinated and integrated. Thus it is important to evaluate the adequacy of health services. Moreover, nowadays with the diversity of services available (no longer "the physician" but a "specialist integrated within a team of care professionals") the person can easily be lost in the system, and with it both quality and costs could be ruinous. Proper integration of care is, therefore, a necessity. This challenge has been addressed for many years, though with limited success so far (Starfield et al. 2005). It includes a better knowledge of each other's work in the system, where establishing a coherent system for referrals and improving the coordination among care units of different sorts would make care more efficient (Bodenheimer 2008). The perspective of a more "patient-oriented" care is only possible through a more coordinated care across settings and over time. Particularly for the increasing type of patients with long-term chronic and medically complex conditions, who may find it difficult to "survive" on a fragmented, and often anachronic, health care system, time seems to be an important factor.

The integrated management and the verticalization of health services is a complex issue, whose impact potential analysis has required to search for evidence to validate an implementation at large scale (Ramsay et al. 2009; Armitage et al. 2009; Suter et al. 2009). Clearly, the report of Pauly and Burns (2002) argues that vertical integration does not show significant economic improvements, with the exception of cases where the integration was built on a system based on precise clinical governance objectives and rules (Enthoven and Tollen 2005). Indeed, Ramsey et al. (2009) showed that there is evidence regarding the integration process, but less about the end results; there is also evidence of the critical role of information systems (IS), that enables the integration of capacity; of local partnerships and of adherence to guidelines. The impact on costs and cost-effectiveness seems to take more time and it is more difficult to predict. This is so because, in the short term, one should always consider the upfront investments required in an integration process (e.g. training, change management, information systems). However, there is evidence that health systems that adopted the focused "integrative" chronic care management model are predisposed to enable a significant reduction in costs, together with better outcomes (Singh and Ham 2005). Once again, the effect of a clear integration goal could be a determinant for its success.

The rationality brought about by an effective coordination of care would promote the system's transparency, which with time would encourage, step by step, the removing of the boundaries that still exist in most local health systems.

The challenge of establishing a more integrated and "boundaryless" hospital is multi-dimensional, but yields clear long-term benefits. For countries with national public health services, such as Portugal, the UK or northern European countries, it is even more functional, once there is an intrinsic potential for the integration of services.

The *boundaryless hospital* is fundamentally a governance architecture that promotes the ubiquiness of relations through the integration of the health care processes within the health units in a local network (Braithwaite et al. 1994). However, integration is in itself a complex process that involves creating and maintaining, over time, a common structure between independent partners (within the organizations), which aims at coordinating their interdependence and allowing for joint working under a shared strategic aim.

The concept of a boundaryless hospital should also be understood in the context of the new clinical management and primary care trends (Starfield 1998). Clinical management trends are showing that proper organization of services can both reduce the number of necessary beds and move beds into the home, based on the support of primary care services (McKee 2004). A well-organized primary care service could deal with the provision of patient needs and support the coordination of continuity of care.

As a matter of fact, two relatively recent health policy decisions made by the Portuguese Ministry of Health have opened the way to the *boundaryless hospital* approach:

(a) The development of the "Local Health Units" (ULS, integrating hospitals and health centers within the same organization), and
(b) The "Primary Health Care" (PHC) reform, initiated in 2007.

There is extended experience in Portugal for adopting the most relevant health care management trends (national planning, integration, care coordination, team work, commissioning, etc.), often following closely the developments in Britain's and the Northern European National health systems. Since there are significant differences in organizational and decision-making processes of clinicians and managers, the evidence-based practice needs to be properly "translated" for management rather than simply transferred (Walshe and Rundall 2001).

1.1 The Role of Time in Implementing and Developing a New Organization

The implementation of new organizations can take a long time (Weick and Quinn 1999; Lapão and Dussault 2012). Time is needed to study and design a new organization and train and prepare the professionals to the new way of working, as well as time required for adjustments, etc. However, these "times" are often not considered and even dangerously forgotten among the anxiety of policy-makers to promote fast change. Again, often this gap between the excitement of changing promotion and the reality of actual efforts leads to frustration, conflict and obstruction of the next attempts to implement change. It is recognized that change implies the close enrollment of professionals to both address process requirements and overcome professionals' barriers (Berg 2001; Weick 1995).

Perkins (2010) argues about the need to professionally manage change to control risks and deal with expectations by eliciting the professionals about all aspects of the process changing (Fig. 1). Figure 1 also shows that carefully managed change would start with lower, and more realistic, expectations while building on collaboration would probably reach faster and better results.

The literature in health services research also shows that there are several variables, including the governance model, leadership action and time required to implement, and learning and making a change happen (Ferlie and Shortell 2001; Grol and Grimshaw 2003).

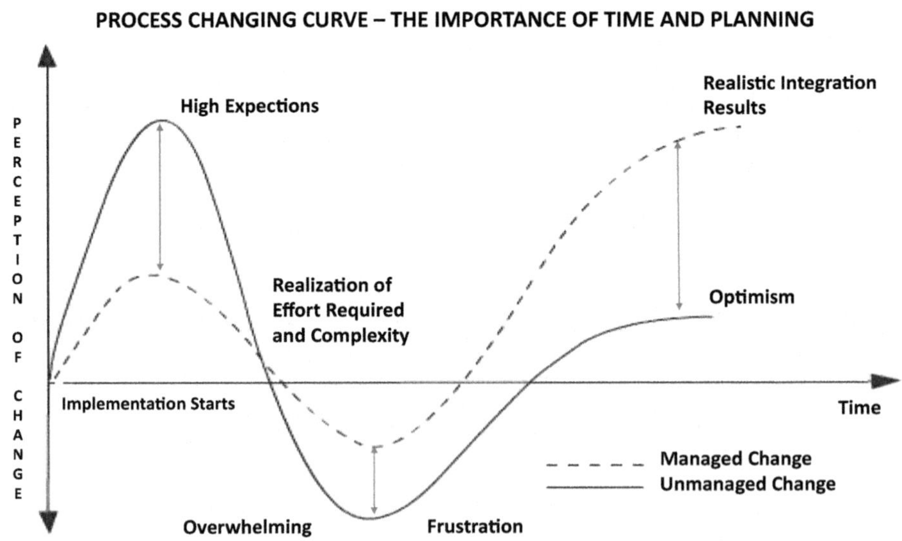

Fig. 1 The importance of managing change over time

1.2 The Definition of Local Health Units

A Local Health Unit (ULS) is a health care organizational and legal framework aimed at optimizing the response of services through an integrated management of various health care facilities within a region. Usually a ULS covers about 200,000–400,000 inhabitants, in urban or rural areas. The idea behind the concept of the ULS was to establish, through an integrated management and provision of all services framework, one way to improve the interconnection of the health centers with hospitals, and eventually with other entities—namely with continuum care units, through an extended process of vertical integration of these different levels of care.

The integration of health care services within the ULS was expected to have a prompt impact in reducing examination costs, including the internalization of services (since often, and for accessibility reasons, it was allowed to do the exams elsewhere in any private laboratories near the patient's home), thereby improving the utilization of the installed capacity.

The first time this model was put in place was with the creation of the Local Health Unit of Matosinhos (ULSM) in 1999, 16 years ago. This decision was made as the result of a study done by the National Institute of Public Administration. It took 8 years to create the second ULS in 2007: the Local Health Unit of North Alentejo (ULSNA), in a rural area. In the following year (2008) three new ULSs were established: the Local Health Unit of the Alto Minho (ULSAM), the Local Health Unit of Baixo Alentejo (ULSBA) and the Local Health Unit of Guarda (ULSG). In 2009, the Local Health Unit of Castelo Branco (ULSCB) was created and in 2011 the ULS Nordeste in Bragança district was created. The last case was the ULS of Litoral Alentejano in 2012 (Fig. 2).

The possibility of integrating services within a ULS is a direct and immediate result of the creation of a ULS, and represents a clear choice of health policy, which is expressed in paragraph 4 of Article 1 of Decree-Law No 127/2009 and states that the management should find a balance between the patient's "freedom of choice" (i.e. a patient perspective) and values of good governance (i.e., a business perspective). Naturally, this business perspective must be made compatible with other values such as quality and the professionals' satisfaction (Portugal 2009).

Hence, the regulator needs to control this balance with special care for such business procedures that are likely to harm users in putting into disregard the right to universal and timely access (delays, more costs, wasting time, etc.) of the users of the ULS It is also important to ensure that such health care service is provided by the best conditions of access and that it should not have a lower quality than those which prevailed before the creation of the ULS. This was to guarantee that one could expect an improvement from the new model of the ULS.

Although it was expected that vertical integration, through the ULS, would result in a better articulation between the different levels of health care and consequently provide greater benefits in accessing health care for users residing in the ULS's catchment area, it was necessary to control, in legal terms (the law on universal access), and in practical terms, whether there were any differences in procedures adopted within the ULS compared to other establishments of the NHS.

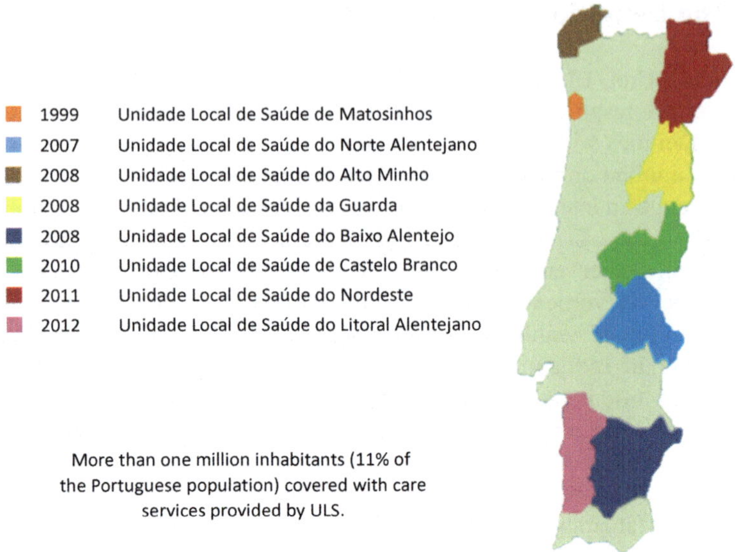

Fig. 2 Area covered by ULS boundaryless services in Portugal

There are now eight ULSs implemented in Portugal. The most remarkable one is located in the north of Portugal and it was created in 1999, i.e., with 15 years of continuous work on building a more integrated organization. This ULS encompasses the local district hospital and four health centers within the surrounding area, now integrated in a group of health centers—ACES (Lapão and Dussault 2012). The Decree-Law creating the ULS is very clear at proposing that "innovative ways of managing such means of flexible and appropriate management, such as the contracting activity based funding to pursue the establishment of incentives to health professionals and streamlining the hiring of means necessary for its operation."(1999b) The policy makers were quite aware of the need to address both change management and innovation to overcome the existing "integration" barriers, from different cultures on dealing with diseases, and from a more general perspective to a more specialized one. Weaknesses in clinical processes were hampering the possibility of a closer contact between care levels.

Theoretically, the aim of the "ULS model" was to integrate one or more hospitals, with a number of health centers based on geographic proximity, balancing of specialties and the existence of emergency medical service. The growing access to health care needs of the population, firstly calls for the reorganization of services, with increased levels of quality requirements, and for the integration of the management of existing resources within each geographical area (Bodenheimer 2008).

Therefore, a ULS aims at providing comprehensive health care to the population of its area, deploying services directly or indirectly through contractual arrangements (with other care units), as well as ensuring the public health activities and the necessary means to exercise the powers of the health authority in the geographical area covered. To deploy such integrated services one needs to correctly define, negotiate, plan and implement (and test) those services. These processes surely could take some time (Orlikowski 1996). Adding to this, the launching of the "Alert" information system to support referrals from the PHC enabled a faster way to manage and control the continuity of care. At the least, on a weekly basis, the referring coordinator of each hospital department accesses the referrals and guides them toward the right (by clinical governance means) physician of each department.

2 The ULS Matosinhos

In 1999, the creation of the ULS Matosinhos (ULSM) was an important step taken by the Ministry of Health to initiate a new approach toward the integration of health care levels. Many doubts and uncertainties were then discussed. Therefore, the ULSM's global performance proved to be of primary importance to analyze and validate the ULS model, in particular its intrinsic characteristics, which consisted of integrating the delivery of health care, and verifying that it was likely to have potential positive impacts on access for users residing in the ULS influence area. The comparison with the other users of the National Health Service (NHS) should be done to validate that the creation of the ULS has enhanced access to health care for the users covered.

The ULSM offers 24 health services, with an area of influence corresponding to an area of 62 km^2 and a population density of 2721.2 inhabitants per km^2. The number of Pedro Hispano Hospital doctors is 430 and 683 nurses. The ACES Matosinhos has 169 physicians and 138 nurses. The hospital has a ratio of doctors per 0.630 nurses while the ACES has a ratio of 1.225.

The ULSM is a public institution, fully integrated in the NHS, following an enterprise management model, with financial, administrative and patrimonial autonomy. The ULSM combines four main facilities: Pedro Hispano[1] Hospital, Pulmonology Diagnostic Center, the Convalescent Unit and ACES Matosinhos. ACES Matosinhos, that offers primary care services to the region, consists of four health centers (situated in four main locations):

1. *Leça da Palmeira*, which includes six health facility extensions in "Santa Cruz do Bispo", "Leça da Palmeira", "Lavra" and "Perafita", and the "Leça" and "Maresia" Family Health Units;
2. *Matosinhos*, which includes three health facility extensions of "Atlantida" and the Family Health Units of "Horizonte" and "Oceanos". Two other smaller units of Community Care in Matosinhos and Leça da Palmeira are also included.

[1] Pedro Hispano was a famous Portuguese physician from the XIII century who later became Pope John XXI.

Table 1 Health services at ULSM's health centers

Health care services	Treatments and other activities
Family and general medicine	– Child health (0–14 years) – Youth health (14–19 years) – Sexual and reproductive health (family planning)—women 15–49; maternal health – Seniors' health (>65 years) – Priority programs: diabetes mellitus; high blood pressure; cardiovascular risk; asthma; COPD; homecare; social service; clinical psychology; clinical nutrition; nursing consultation – SASU—Emergency basic unit; User's office – Consultations: stomatology; surgery; orthopedics; psychology; clinical hematology; endocrinology; physical medicine and rehabilitation; pediatrics; and tele-dermatology
Public health unit	Promoting programs and health education: School and oral health
Sharing health programs	PAII (Senior Integrated Support Plan) ADI (Integrated Homecare Support) CAJ (Youth Support Center)

3. *São Mamede de Infesta*, which includes two Family Health Units in "Infesta" and "Portas do Sol";
4. *Senhora da Hora*, which includes four health facility extensions of "Privada I", "Privada II" and "Privada III", and a Family Health Unit in "Lagoa". Three other health facilities are included, as providers associated with ACES Matosinhos the "Diagnostic Center Pulmonology", the SASU (emergency services) in Matosinhos and the Public Health Unit (USP).

The medical services offered by Hospital Pedro Hispano include the main specialties: anesthesiology, cardiology, general surgery, maxillofacial surgery, reconstructive plastic surgery, Dermato-venereology, infectious diseases, endocrinology and nutrition, gastroenterology, gynecology, clinical hematology, immuno-allergology, medical physical and rehabilitation, internal medicine, nephrology, neurosurgery, neurology, obstetrics, ophthalmology, orthopedics, otolaryngology, pediatrics, pulmonology and urology. These services cover ambulatory, inpatient and emergency routes.

The health centers, within ACES at ULSM, offer a set of medical treatments or activities described in Table 1.

3 Methods

A case study approach was used, collecting both qualitative and quantitative data allowing deeper analysis and understanding of the case (Yin 2001). It included interviews with selected managers and health care professionals combined with internal data and reports revision. A workshop was organized to validate the data.

Kingdon's (1995) theory was used to analyze political interventions. Kingdon's analysis could present gaps between the intentions expressed by policy-makers and the reality of integration as perceived by performance results. Kingdon's "three-streams" theory of policy development is useful to understand how an issue (e.g. integration mechanisms) reaches the policy agenda and eventually leads to an intervention. It can also be used to understand why a policy failed, or succeeded, to produce its expected results. The "problem stream", in which issues are recognized and brought to the public agenda, the "policy stream", in which alternative options are offered to policy makers, and the "political stream", in which political actors place an issue on their agenda, can be seen as a "set of processes" that can be reconstituted retrospectively to identify factors that influenced the conduct of the integration process.

4 Results: ULSM Integration and Openness Process

The care integration "problem stream" was recognized and brought to the public and to the political agenda. Several studies provided alternatives ("policy stream") and policy makers produced (from 1999 onward) a set of legislation and regulations ("political stream") that helped establish the "boundaryless" hospital concept.

The Local Health Unit of Matosinhos, EPE (ULSM) was established 16 years ago (in 1999) as the first formal integration of a hospital and a set of health centers aiming at optimizing the response of services through an integrated management board. EPE means that it follows a public enterprise-based management model. The Decree-Law 207/1999 of 9 of June, that created ULSM, highlighted the need to "undertake the reengineering of the health system organization, creating conditions for integration of care services, sharing problems that today confront each level of care alone, sharing responsibilities and resources" (Portugal 1999b). Thus, on the genesis of the ULS was the aim of creating a better connection between different levels: health centers, hospitals and other entities responsible for a regional or local health department.

It also refers to the adoption of "alternative management models", which represented a clear choice of policy-makers by introducing an innovative organizational model of care services from primary to secondary (hospital) health. The policy-makers "wanted to optimize the response of health services through an integrated management of the multiple health units of a region." Therefore, the creation of the ULS was also a choice of health policy for one specific format of integrated services; the local health system established by Decree-Law 156/99, of 10 May (Portugal 1999a).

Later another law, 27/2002—the new Legal Regime of Hospital Management (Portugal 2002a)—was approved, which enabled larger management flexibility for the ULS. This new scheme formalizes the scope of the integration of hospitals within the National Network of Health Care Delivery, covering all NHS establishments (open to all citizens), private institutions providing care to clients in the NHS and "pure" private establishments.

The "Legal Regime of Hospital Management" defined the possibility of the existence of four distinct types of public hospitals, according to the management model adopted:

1. *integrated hospitals* in the government sector (hereinafter SPA), as public institutions, with legal personality, administrative and financial autonomy, with or without patrimonial autonomy;
2. *hospitals-owned companies* (hereinafter EPE), as public institutions, with legal personality, administrative, financial and of a business nature;
3. *Hospitals limited company* (hereinafter SA), as limited companies wholly publicly owned; and,
4. *hospitals under public-private partnerships* (PPP) and private establishments, with or without profit, with which contracts are established for the provision of health care (they are not integrated in the NHS).

Under the "Public Administration Restructuring Program" (PRACE), a Resolution from the Council of Ministers 102/2005, it was decided there would be the "gradual extinction, by the end of 2006, of the health care sub-regions with the next redesign of regional health authorities and health centers functions, as well as the creation of local health units where conditions exist for the immediate integration of primary health care in hospital care" (Portugal 2005c). The creation of new Health Centers groups (ACES) completed the extinction of health care sub-regions, and allowed the management of health centers, as ACES, within a ULS [Art. 41 of Decree-Law 28/2008, which created ACES (Portugal 2008)]. This last point represents an advance in the direction of the "boundaryless" concept.

The creation of the ULSM represented an innovative organizational model of care services from primary and differentiated (hospital) health. The ULSM specificity was mainly the fact that a single body, the Board of Directors (which includes managers from the hospital and from ACES/primary-care), was provided the responsibility to define and implement an integration strategy, opening the many barriers among the different health facilities. Most of these barriers are cultural and organizational rather than legal.

The management rules kept changing through time. Only after 3 years of its establishment, the ULSM was transformed [by the Decree-Law 283/2002, (Portugal 2002b)] into a limited company owned exclusively by public funds, later through Decree-Law 93/2005 (Portugal 2005a). This law transformed 31 hospitals into EPE, also comprised the ULSM, which recuperated the nature of the EPE. The final organization and functioning rules of the ULSM were obtained with the "legal statutes, legal regime and governing rules" [Decree Law 233/2005 (Portugal 2005b)] together with its Rules of Procedure (the ULSM Rules of 26/08/2009, ULSM 2014).

Actually, the "Article 1" of ULSM Rules states that the ULSM "[...] is integrated into the National Health Service and aims to provide health care and may, incidentally, explore the services [...] to its object or which may facilitate or encourage their achievement as well as participate in joint stock companies whose capital is majority owned by ULSM and which have as their object the provision of health care, as well as other forms of association" (ULSM 2014). This set of "Rules" also included the ULSM "vision", consisting of "[...] simplified and facilitated accessibility, fairness guaranteed and committed effective integration, productivity and efficiency in resource utilization and decreased health needs" (ULSM 2014). Furthermore it defines its "mission" to "[...] satisfy all the health needs of the population, assuming the integration of different levels, from education for health and self-care, to long and palliative care and referral to other levels of the hospital network" (ULSM 2014). The network includes health centers, Pedro Hispano Hospital and the network of continuing care. Incidentally, the social intervention available to health partnerships, including new information technologies, provides hospital care to the population of Maia, and, as a second reference, to the hospital of Póvoa do Varzim-Vila do Conde.

The ULSM assignments were clearly defined (ULSM Regulation of 26/08/2009):

- To provide primary and continuing health care to all inhabitants of Matosinhos municipality;
- To provide differentiated health care to residents in the area of influence of ULSM;
- Ensure the public health activities and skills required to carry out the health authority in the Matosinhos municipality;
- Participate in the training process of pre- and post-graduated professionals.

The ULSM set of rules also defines the following units of care "[(A) Health Centers Group of Matosinhos—ACES; (B) Pedro Hispano Hospital—HPH; (C) Convalescence Unit] which should articulate [...] in order to provide health care focused on the specific needs of patients by promoting the integration and continuity of care" (ULSM 2014).

Within primary care services, Regulation ULSM of 26/08/2009 provides that health centers should develop specific activities of personalized care directed to the individual and to the family, users enrolled, and community health to residents "[...] and under care of the Pedro Hispano Hospital perform duties in the areas of providing differentiated supportive care, pre- and post-graduate training and research", and "the provision of specialized care takes place under outpatient or inpatient" (ULSM 2014).

Finally, regarding long-term care, it should be provided by the Department of Continuing Care, which includes a "Discharge management team", a "Unit of Palliative Care" and a "Unit of Convalescence".

Analyzing all these changes, one can realize that it took approximately 10 years to reach the ultimate version of the ULS integration management model. The regulator authority played an important role in this process. The reality is that the cycle of policy-making takes time to understand the health system dynamics while responding to changes in health care demand.

The regulator authority was very meticulous; its methodology for access evaluation took into account the analysis of a set of balanced indicators like "closeness", "capacity" and "temporal" analysis. The "proximity" indicator used is the number of services supplied by the ULS per square kilometer of geographical coverage. In fact, the larger the number of providers (i.e., the number of health facilities) per square kilometer, the higher the "proximity" indicator value (i.e. the ratio health care provider per user).

Considering the case of the ULSM, although having a relatively low number of providers, its smaller and concentrated surface (urban municipality), resulted in a high index of proximity. The ULSAM presents a relatively low level of "closeness", which is justified by the reduced number of providers. To evaluate the "scale capacity" two other indicators were constructed (ULSM 2014):

(a) the ratio between the number of doctors and the population density (capacity I); and,
(b) the ratio between the number of physicians and the population over 65 years of age (Max II).

The combination of these indicators assess to what extent the structure of a ULS addresses the need of users residing in the region, hence reflecting the responsiveness of the integrated ULS's care services.

The ULSM presents a low rate of capacity because, although showing a high number of doctors, it has too high a population density. Regarding the Max II index, the ULSM displays the best indicator in Portugal, as it has the largest number of doctors (599) combined with a low number (compared to other ULSs) of populations over 65 years.

It appears, therefore, that in relation to the ratios measuring the spatial dimensions, the reality among the ULSs is very heterogeneous. The ULSM globally, presents the best indicators of proximity and capacity (due to the high Max II index).

These high rates, in proximity and capacity, correspond to a meaningful assistive movement in the ULSM (Table 2).

4.1 ULSM Main Health Outcomes Since 1999

- Life expectancy in the ULSM is slightly lower than the Northern Region (RN) and Portugal as a whole (78.5 years). The birth rate, although it has been declining, is superior to the RN. The infant mortality rate reduced significantly, especially from 2003 onward.
- Within the mortality rate stand out the deaths from malignant tumors and infectious diseases, negatively compared with RN, especially in the age group of 25–44 years;
- The standardized mortality rate (by age) decreased between 2001 and 2005. Yet, the ULSM has values that rate well above the RN and Portugal for infectious and

Table 2 Assistive movement (number of patients) between September 2013 and 2014 (ULSM 2014)

Services		2013	2014
Outpatient consultations	First	52,134	56,118
	Next	126,147	137,846
Surgery	Ambulatory	4737 (58 %)[a]	5342 (62 %)[a]
	Conventional	3688	3601
	Emergency	1280	1357
Emergency	General	55,172	58,353
	Obstetrics	5973	6180
Inpatient	Clinical	7991	8193
	Programed surgery	3075	3014
	Emergency surgery	1503	1577
Average duration	Days	6.94	6.98
Day-hospital sessions		7461	8491

[a]Ratio of ambulatory surgery vs. programed surgery

parasitic diseases and malignant tumors. In these groups, deaths from AIDS and malignant tumor of the trachea, bronchus and lung stand out. This is mainly due to the fact that the region was an important industrial center;

- In 2013, ULSM causes for hospital admission (with higher values than RN and Portugal) were the infectious diseases, malignant and benign tumors, endocrine diseases, nutritional and metabolic, and musculoskeletal diseases. The high number of hospitalizations for pregnancy, childbirth and postpartum also stand out due to its population's lower age average. In a standardized hospitalization rate, the specific causes of hospitalization are essentially malignant tumors, ischemic heart disease and COPD;
- The ULSM presents values of incidence (new cases) of AIDS and tuberculosis well above the RN and Portugal, despite the sharp decline verified over the past years;
- Since March 2013, the patients who have earlier discharge are followed at home in an endeavor to push the hospital services closer to the patient. The Continuous Care nursing teams from ACES are supporting the patients with greater dependence.

4.2 Local Health Plan Development

ULSM has taken almost 12 years to define its "Local Health Plan" (LHP). An LHP is an important management tool for diagnosis of the health care status of the population to date, identifying the main health needs of the population, making a prognostic assessment of population's health situation, setting health goals and making recommendations for intervention, not only on health services, but also including other local stakeholders. It also enables the open planning exercise to include other relevant local players into a more integrated approach, to cut costs while improving the access of the population to a more coordinated care, and avoiding as much as possible the need of patients to move around. This was then an innovative process coordinated by the Public Health Unit and promoted by the Northern Health Authority with contributions of local health observatories. Together these institutions collected data and provided health information, analyzed and prognostically assessed problems and health needs of the population. The IS play a vital role in the future LHP monitoring and evaluation process.

Once more, time is a critical factor. The process of building an LHP is a continuous and dynamic process that does not finish with the preparation of the respective written reports. It is essential not to forget its instrumental utility, reinforced in the current context of economic crisis. The heads of institutions must create the necessary conditions (both internal and external) that allow the strengthening of the weakest aspects of each LHP. Moreover, regarding LHP implementation, the various functional units of the ULSM or their local partners (both inside and outside the health sector) must be coordinated in order to effectively improve the health status of the population.

4.3 Quality Policy Strategy

The ULSM, almost since its foundation, has defined a strategy focused on quality improvement. Assuming quality, based on the satisfaction of both their users and professionals, as a fundamental value it was critical to assure the development of a practice-based culture. In 2007, the ULSM defined a quality certification as a medium term objective. In 2012, 5 years later, the ULSM received ISO 9001: 2008 certification (International Standard Organization), becoming the first ULS with this distinction, as the result of its quality and continuous improvement policies. The ULSM board acknowledges that this is a continuous improvement process, however the results are already reflected in such different aspects as the monitoring of waiting times for consultations, surgery and care in the emergency room, ensuring that they are met, the safety of users, and the humanization of care.

The certification project of ULSM was also recently honored with a “Hospital of the Future” award, highlighting the work of the institution, its course and its organizational culture within the NHS.

4.4 Reduction in Hospital Admissions Sensitive to Primary Care

One of the areas that has been addressed by the ULSM is “hospital admissions” for ambulatory care sensitive conditions (Cardoso et al. 2014). Ambulatory care sensitive conditions (ACSCs) are those conditions for which hospital admission could be prevented by good access and interventions at the ambulatory and primary health care levels. Between 2008 and 2012, hospitalizations for causes sensitive to ambulatory care in ULSMs accounted for 2.6 % of total admissions, with an attributable cost of about EUR 4.6 M (ULSM 2014). The numbers of admissions for ACSCs, as well as their associated costs, have declined over that period. The three main causes of ACSCs' hospitalization, in the period between 2008 and 2012, were: heart failure (with 28.8 % of ACSCs' admissions), COPD (25.9 %) and epilepsy (16 %). These were also the ones with higher costs. The ULSM is adopting measures to reduce preventable hospitalizations and its economic impact.

4.5 Integration Between Primary and Secondary Care

The predominant forms of communication found in ACES also vary between individuals: while the informal written communication (e.g., email, chat), communication via intranet and oral communication (e.g., telephone) are the most used by all; the formal written communication (e.g., letter, legal documents) is widely used by the health facilities coordinators (but not by the Executive Director and the President of the Clinical Council, who prefer the telephone). The one-to-one, in person, oral communication is the less used by all (Lapão 2014).

An important feature found in the case of the ULSM, concerning communication, is the existence of an internal communication system, which connects all professionals (from primary care to hospital). By simply entering, and registering, in the personal computer, personnel are automatically connected to the system. It works similar to a chat system. According to the interviewed, this solves several issues very quickly (e.g., between secretariats; to clarify clinical questions with colleagues during primary care consultations) and it enables communication with colleagues without interruption. This system started working in 2009.

This is very interesting not only as interconnection tools and facilitating communication between the ACES and the hospital, but also from the point of view of the very activity of individuals who, as we have understood from the workshop, mentioned a constant interruption of the activities by telephone calls, by drop-by and internal requests.

All the professionals (physicians, nurses and managers) covered in the interviews felt that the ULSM allows an "almost perfect link" between levels of care due to communication tools such as instant messaging and the "internal telephone system", which links the ACESs' professionals with on-call specialists in the hospital. It was reported there was an increased sharing of information (e.g., patients' records, exams, X-rays) among all professionals through the information system. However, several years were required for the system to be optimized.

According to the hospital medical director, through this referral system, the general practitioners (GP) can get in touch directly with the medical specialist and immediately, if necessary, refer the patient to emergency care. There is one medical specialist available per medical specialty. This allows greater personalization of care and an economy of resources that otherwise would be spent on secondary care to situations that could possibly be answered at the primary care level. Moreover, as noted by one participant at the workshop, "the better the communication between specialties and GPs, the better the referral to specialists."

Despite these advanced infrastructures, communications and collaboration between the ACES and hospital, services are still regarded as only "reasonable" by several managers. It is perhaps for this reason that many participants considered that patients' referral to secondary care has only slightly improved in recent years. Another participant (a GP) pointed out that "medical specialists should also contact us to improve the discharge effectiveness."

The communication with continuous care, and referral processes with secondary care and long-term care are aspects considered as good or excellent by most participants. Two of the participants consider that communication and collaboration between teams within the ACES was the main aspect that has greatly improved in recent years, predominantly due to the improvement in the ACES management (i.e. reform).

However, even this small and specific process took some years to develop. As to the relationship between primary and secondary care, specifically in referencing there is a consensus that significant collaborative efforts have existed between the ACES and hospital services' directions to improve the referral process of patients.

Information systems (IS) seem to be, in this context, of utmost importance, especially in planning for contract awarding, monitoring indicators, organization of care, etc. Overall, these IS are mostly considered by participants as "good", with the exception of two that are "reasonable", and RNCCI (linking health services to continuous care) considered by a respondent as "bad". The information management in the ULSM improved remarkably over the last 15 years. The closure of the old District Hospital Matosinhos and the starting the new Pedro Hispano Hospital brought a new dynamic in the information available to professionals (Canastra and Ferreira 2014).

5 Discussion: The Importance of Time in the Evolution of ULSM

The ULSM presents several boundaryless hospital characteristics built during the last 16 years, since 1999, as a combination of policy-making, management and clinical governance activities following the "three-stream" cycle:

- ULSM's health units forms a relatively flexible health network (communication, referrals, training, etc.) connecting the hospital, the health centers, public health, palliative care, home care, patient associations. etc.;
- The ULSM is seriously addressing services quality improvement, through both the promotion of clinical protocol design and implementation, and the ISO 9001 certification (issued in December 2012).
- There is a strong focus on IS: There were clear efforts for combining a set of integrated (and others not-yet integrated) IS, like the ULSM single patient record, an imaging system, a hospital care referral system (Alert), etc (Kuhn et al. 2007).

- Telemedicine service is broadly used in several departments; for instance, in dermatology, only a small fraction of users who need specialized monitoring are referred to the hospital with most patients being monitored remotely.
- In 2011, the ULSM joined the "Integrated Children Care" network in the north region of Portugal, connecting all health units providing pediatric services.
- A "Walking Clinic" (i.e. an additional level of GP as a first line in emergency care, at the hospital) was created to reduce waste and costs.
- The ULSM has become an important school for health professionals, from which a significant part will join other health units within the ULS, having a good knowledge of the ULS culture and procedures.

It is very clear now that the IS played an important role in most of these developments. However the IS still need to be further aligned with the organization's actual processes, to simplify the communication and the management.

After 16 years of continuous effort trying to build a "more and more" integrated ULSM organization, and comparing to other existent ULSs in the country, the most important observation is that "time" seems to be a critical factor.

Time enabled the establishment of a culture of working together to solve problems, to learn and understand their different requirements and availability, with the conquest of several benefits for the organization leveraging the Kingdon's windows of opportunity (Kingdon 1995). However, there are still many problems to solve, but there are valuable changes that motivate further efforts.

Another important factor is the new professionals who, when they start working at the ULSM, are being trained in a more open and boundaryless culture, creating the mechanisms to go further in connection with the other services.

Although boundaries between levels of care are still difficult to transpose in Portugal, the case of the ULSM shows that a focused effort during a significant time makes it easier to overcome the resistance of such barriers. Primary health care (PHC) played an important role in the integration of care, assuming functions of coordination and case management. The case manager is, wherever possible, the user himself, duly supported by PHC. The communication interfaces enables a greater coordination between clinical PHC and clinical departments of hospitals, as well as other organs of governance—term care and the social sector.

As far as "integration" is concerned, the PHC reform became part of the government's program in 2005 after various policy alternatives had been proposed in reports and studies, for example on the cost-effectiveness of PHC services, and after pilot experiments were conducted between 1996 and 2004 (Lapão and Dussault 2012). The ideas of integration and PHC reform had been discussed for more than 20 years, but it was only in 1999 (integration) and in 2005 (PHC reform) that it reached the political agenda, in both cases when a newly elected government took power.

The process of integration was not a simple one (as was presented in the results), but the focus on rural areas had limited the impact and the controversy. The main challengers of the ULSM model are primary care associations and syndicates who have seen the ULS as a mechanism of controlling the health centers by the hospital. The facts show that both sides are right: the integration has improved the referrals and reduced costs, but there are also cases of transfer of "primary care resources" to "hospital services", mostly regarding investment in diagnosis equipment. The decision, however, of creating a ULS in Matosinhos was done quite easily as a test-bed for future developments. In 2002, a study compared the ULSM with other hospital systems presenting no significant benefits to the ULS [INA, 2002, Integration of Hospitals in Portugal. Instituto Nacional de Administração, Oeiras (unpublished)]. Probably, because of this, only in 2007, a second ULS was established, when the same political party came to power.

In the case of primary care reform, the Minister of Health delegated the responsibility for implementation to a task force, turning a policy objective into a technical issue. What had thus far been a policy commitment of the whole government became the responsibility of a technical agency; the implementation became the "problem" of a multi-disciplinary task-force, combining all the important stakeholders in the process (Lapão and Dussault 2012).

In the PHC reform, each of the three streams followed its own logic and had its own driving forces. Some coordinators of the GP's association were prominent members of the socialist party elected in 2005 and they helped bring PHC reform on the policy agenda. A technical document prepared, 4 years before, by their association advocating for the reform, became basically the government plan for PHC services' organization and delivery. The combination of government and professional associations' support, created a "policy window" favorable to the launch of the reform. Such "*policy windows, the opportunities for action on given initiatives, present themselves and stay open for only short periods*" (Kingdon 1995), and this was the case in Portugal. The task force organized a broad and demanding capacity building program involving all the new primary care managers (Lapão and Dussault 2011).

The window was narrow because not all stakeholders were supportive: professional councils, faculties of medicine, associations of medical specialists did not oppose the reform, but their support was rather lukewarm because they had not been associated in its conception. The time needed to put in place the technical, regulatory and administrative structure to accompany the reform slowed the momentum of the reform. When all was ready, the financial crisis had reached Portugal and support weakened even more. In summary, a mix of internal and external factors changed the environment from favorable to less favorable in a matter of just 2 years. However, the reform was very important and well defended within the ULSM, and it enabled a higher balance between primary and secondary care.

This example of the ULSM shows the benefits of combining the science of implementation and of integration with actual changing processes, covering both sides of primary and secondary care. Once these two main levels are integrated, the other levels are easily brought into the system as complementary services that are required to fully serve the patients. Beyond doubt, the decentralization of primary care management opens a multitude of opportunities to involve other local partners, from municipalities to citizens associations and local media. And another chapter of the *boundaryless hospital* is opened.

6 Conclusion

Regarding the experiences that have been developed in Portugal and, specifically, the case of the ULS model, initially developed to better understand the potential for integration of services, the key issue is to create a sustainable local structure, as a "mesh" of resources that addresses the comprehensive needs of populations. The necessary structure to ensure integration and continuity of care does not necessarily have to result from the merger of institutions, but, instead, in the result of fine tuning of referral networks of organizational rules, accountability mechanisms and technical consulting. The role of information systems is absolutely critical to both support the communication and the referral services and to further establish new connections with patients and other local players, like municipalities, NGOs and private care organizations.

The number of links necessary to be established among all the stakeholders and partners is very large. This will create a "thread" by trimming all the links, founding the bases of a boundaryless hospital that reaches the population in many ways, fitting the specificity of health needs with the combination of services. The quest for reaching a full boundaryless organization will take some time. It is necessary that the "organizational thread" grows and matures to properly deal with the different care levels' requirements. One must have in mind that the case of the ULS took at least 16 years.

References

Armitage GD, Suter E, Oelke ND, Adair CE (2009) Health systems integration: state of the evidence. Int J Integr Care 9:17

Braithwaite J, Vining RF, Lazarus L (1994) The boundaryless hospital. Aust NZ J Med 24(5):565–571

Berg M (2001) Implementing information systems in health care organizations: myths and challenges. Int J Med Inform 64(2):143–156

Bodenheimer T (2008) Coordinating care—a perilous journey through the health care system. N Engl J Med 358(10):1064

Canastra MA, Ferreira MA (2014) Perspetiva histórica da informação na ULSM. ICHI—International Congress on Health Information. ULS Matosinhos 39

Cardoso S, Lima G and Santos S (2014) Avoidable hospital admissions for ambulatory care sensitive conditions, ULS Matosinhos, 2008–2012

Enthoven AC, Tollen LA (2005) Competition in health care: it takes systems to pursue quality and efficiency. Health Aff 24(5):1383

Ferlie EB, Shortell SM (2001) Improving the quality of health care in the United Kingdom and the United States: a framework for change. Milbank Q 79(2):281–315

Grol R, Grimshaw J (2003) From best evidence to best practice: effective implementation of change in patients' care. Lancet 362(9391):1225–1230

Kingdon JW (1995) Agenda, alternatives, and public policies, 2nd edn. HarperCollins College, New York

Kuhn KA, Giuse D, Lapão L et al (2007) Expanding the scope of health information systems. Methods Inf Med 46(4):500–502

Lapão LV (Coordination) (2014) AVALACES: primary-care management models and integration with secondary-care. Project report. Instituto de Higiene e Medicina Tropical, Lisbon

Lapão LV, Dussault G (2011) PACES: a national leadership program in support of primary-care reform in Portugal. Leadersh Health Serv 24(4):295–307

Lapão LV, Dussault G (2012) From policy to reality: clinical managers' views of the organizational challenges of primary care reform in Portugal. Int J Health Plann Manage 27(4):295–307

McKee M (2004) Reducing hospital beds: what are the lessons to be learned? vol 6. WHO Regional Office for Europe, Copenhagen

Orlikowski WJ (1996) Improvising organizational transformation over time: a situated change perspective. Inf Sys Res 7(1):63–92

Pauly MV, Burns LR (2002) Integrated delivery networks: a detour on the road to integrated health care? Health Aff 21(4):128–143

Perkins J (2010) Digital school transformation. http://www.slideshare.net/joseph.perkins/digital-school-transformation-managing-change-with-effective-strategies. Accessed 20 Jul 2015

Portugal (1999a) Decree-Law 156/99. The definition of local health system. http://www.sindicatomedicosnorte.pt/portal/index.php/destaques/item/443-decreto-lei-156-99-de-10-de-maio. Accessed 20 Jul 2015

Portugal (1999b) Decree-Law 207/1999. The creation of the ULS Matosinhos. http://www.base-geral.com/pt/dr1/diploma-apresentar.asp?diploma=207___Decreto-Lei%5EDecreto-Lei&ano=1999. Accessed 20 Jul 2015

Portugal (2002a) Decree-Law 27/2002. The definition of the new legal regime of hospital management. http://www.acss.min-saude.pt/Portals/0/Circulares/Lei%2027%20-%2002.pdf. Accessed 20 Jul 2015

Portugal (2002b) Decree-Law 283/2002. The definition of limited company owned exclusively by public funds. http://dre.tretas.org/dre/158694/. Accessed 20 Jul 2015

Portugal (2005a) Decree-Law 93/2005. The actualization of the definition of limited company owned exclusively by public funds. http://www.sg.min-saude.pt/NR/rdonlyres/4D921E90-4382-4E9E-B682-3FE85F261D87/17862/36363637.pdf. Accessed 20 Jul 2015

Portugal (2005b) Decree-Law 233/2005. The definition of public enterprise entities. http://www.acss.min-saude.pt/Portals/0/DL%20n.°%20233.2005,%20de%2012-29%20(Consolidado).pdf. Accessed 20 Jul 2015

Portugal (2005c) Resolution from the Council of Ministers 102/2005. The creation of the "Public Administration Restructuring Program" (PRACE). http://www.dgaep.gov.pt/media/0701020000/Cap%C3%ADtulos%201%20a%204/cap1_3/cap%20I.pdf. Accessed 20 Jul 2015

Portugal (2008) Decree-Law 28/2008. The creation of new health centers groups (ACES). http://www.smzc.pt/attachments/132_DL_28_2008_ACES.pdf. Accessed 20 Jul 2015

Portugal (2009) Decree-Law No 127/2009. Definition of the National Health Regulatory Agency. http://www.sindicatomedicosnorte.pt/portal/index.php/legislacao/outra-legislacao/item/547-decreto-lei-n-127-2009-de-27-de-maio. Accessed 20 Jul 2015

Ramsay A, Fullop N, Edwards N (2009) The evidence base for vertical integration in health care. J Integr Care 17(2):3–12

Singh D, Ham C (2005) Transforming chronic care: evidence about improving care for people with long-term conditions. http://www.download.bham.ac.uk/hsmc/pdf/transforming_chronic_care.pdf. Accessed 20 Jul 2015

Starfield B (1998) Primary care: balancing health needs, services, and technology. Oxford University Press, Oxford

Starfield B, Shi L, Macinko J (2005) Contribution of primary care to health systems and health. Milbank Q 83(3):457–502

Suter E, Oelke ND, Adair CE et al (2009) Ten key principles for successful health systems integration. Healthc Q 13:16–23

ULSM (2014) Relatório de Actividade da Unidade Local de Saúde de Matosinhos ULSM, Matosinhos

Walshe K, Rundall TG (2001) Evidence-based management: from theory to practice in health care. Milbank Q 79(3):429–457

Weick KE (1995) Sensemaking in organizations. Sage, London

Weick KE, Quinn RE (1999) Organizational change and development. Annu Rev Psychol 50 (1):361–386

Yin RK (2001) Case studies—planning and methods, 2nd edn. Bookman, New York

Luís Velez Lapão is Professor of International Public Health and researcher at the Global Health and Tropical Medicine, Instituto de Higiene e Medicina Tropical, Universidade Nova de Lisboa. He is President of the NGO-AGO-Global Healthcare Cooperation and Development.

He holds a Ph.D. in Systems Engineering (health care management) from Technical University of Lisbon. He was Visiting Professor of Health Care Management at Karolinska Institutet, Solna, Sweden, in 2014 and at Dubai University in 2009. He was Visiting Professor of Medical Informatics Project Management at University of Porto (2007–2009). He is an active member of the World Health Organization Collaborating Center for Health Workforce Policy and Planning. He was Director of the PACES program (Ministry of Health of Portugal) responsible for training primary health care managers (2008–2010). He is auditor of the European Commission for the Health Care Information Systems since 2005.

His main areas of research are organizational development (leadership, organizational reengineering, management innovation, management of information systems and telemedicine (Telemedicine in Cape Verde, Angola and European Project Momentum).

Professor Lapao is Principal Investigator in four research projects: "HAITool" an EEA Grant to develop an Antibiotic Stewardship Information Systems; "OSYRISH-FCT" using an Information System to reduce health care-acquired infections (2013–2015); "ePharmacare-FCT" Collaborative information management in community pharmacies (2012–2014); and the AVALACES (INSA/Ministry of Health) to assess the Primary Health Care services management models. He is author and co-author of several papers and four books: Technology Commercialization (Kluwer 2002), Complexity and Reform of Public Administration (INA 2007), "Health Informatics—Best Practices and New Perspectives" (2007) and Handbook of Business Information Systems (World Publishing, 2010).

Networked Care: IT-Assisted Tools (Wearable Sensors) for Patients at Risk

Kurt J.G. Schmailzl and Hans H.Th. Sendler

Abstract

Networked care should be conceived as a paradigm shift in care. We shall discuss networked care with regard to feasibility (monitoring, transmitting, and interpreting of physiological data), user-network interfaces (patients, medical professionals), and perspectives (personalized risk management).

IT-assisted tools for patients should address the shortcomings of a health care system (due to its sectoral structure) and add something new to it (real-time physiological data, extension of care to preventive and rehabilitative measures, self-empowerment of the patient), which by and large is divided into delimited players.

IT-assisted tools for patients at risk are made up of digital companions, mainly external, some internal (implanted, such as pacemakers).

The objective is to build a mobile, virtual drop-in clinic (mobile health, mHealth) by

1. designing a health-care app to monitor patients at high risk,
2. monitoring with different kinds of wearable sensors and point-of-care blood tests,
3. developing the eHeart Center with telemedical services for data management and patient guidance.

K.J.G. Schmailzl (✉)
Ruppiner Kliniken, Fehrbelliner Strasse 38, 16816 Neuruppin, Germany
e-mail: kjg.schmailzl@ruppiner-kliniken.de; http://www.schmailzlonline.eu

H.H.Th. Sendler
Eusendor, Berlin, Germany
http://www.eusendor.com

H. Albach et al. (eds.), *Boundaryless Hospital*, DOI 10.1007/978-3-662-49012-9_6

We report about initial steps of networked care with the help of IT-assisted tools for cardiovascular patients at risk: as a new framework and a laboratory of care for similar regions.

Overall, the philosophy of a boundaryless hospital could lead to a patient-centered work-flow.

This work-flow can be organized by digital companions creating a sheltered way amidst individual health hazards and through the inevitable risks of life.

Keywords

Networked care • Paradigm shift in care • Personalized risk management • Preventive and rehabilitative measures • Self-empowerment • Mobile • Virtual drop-in clinic • mHealth • Wearable sensors • Point-of-care testing • eHeart Center • Patient-at-risk • Boundaryless hospital • Patient-centered workflow • Digital companions • POCT • Point-of-care testing • Implants • Implanted medical devices (like ICDs) with sensors on-board

Networked care can be considered as a trend in technology. More importantly, networked care should be recognized as a shift of borders in care. In fact, networked care implies a paradigm shift in care at all.

This said we shall not mistake ‘networked care’ as just exchanging data.

The exchange of data—i.e. transferring personal, medical data—in the smoothest way as fast and secure as possible, is required for but not equivalent to networked care.

The basics of modern electronic data traffic should long-since have been implemented into the system, at various levels. ‘Fighting’ for IT just for the purpose of *accelerating* processes of care, *interconnecting* institutions, *cross-linking* findings and experts, howsoever still necessary today, appears odd, given, say, the presence of social media or the elegance of our children’s cross-border gaming.

Claiming for uniform standards in eHealth, technically, legally, as well as cross-sectorial, just provides the preliminaries; indispensable, overdue but insufficient. To agree upon certain standards is, of course, on the agenda. It is the homework of all the stakeholders, the political ones, especially; bothersome, and running late as most homework. But linking hospital A to Dr. X does not upgrade care as far as it matters patients’ well-being or health and disease; it is only for the administration.

The paper in hand develops the increasing relevance role of IT-assisted tools for patients at risk.

‘Networked care’ is defined by the cross-linking of otherwise non-chained actions, players, institutions and levels of preserving health and confining ill health with all the help of today’s technically advanced networks.

Networked care is motivated, necessitated and driven by

- the increasing shortage of personal medical care offside the big cities, together with an increasing disparity of access to health,
- the unmediated discrepancy between the well-beloved family doctor and the amazing technical achievements of modern medicine, and, last not least,
- the imminent unpayability of the big pledges of social care, especially in the face of the brewing financial crisis.

We shall discuss networked care using the example of the *cardiovascular* patient at risk; particularly with regard to *feasibility* (monitoring, transmitting, and interpreting of physiological data), *user-network interfaces* (patients, medical professionals), and *perspectives* (personalized risk management, self-empowerment).

Beyond that, IT-assisted tools make up not only for the cardiovascular patient at risk but offer a *toolbox* and thus a *showcase for networked care in general*: equally suitable for the patient at *any* health hazard: the handicapped, the elderly, every patient suffering from a chronic disease, or even just the one living alone, wherever (in Brandenburg, the Mezzogiorno, the Midwest. . .).

1 Networked Care: The Cardiovascular Patient at Risk

1.1 Feasibility (Monitoring, Transmitting, and Interpreting Physiological Data)

Cardiovascular diseases account for EUR 196 billion (2009) of economic as well as human costs (around 40 % of all mortality) in the EU a year (European Heart Network and European Society of Cardiology 2012).

This burden will increase due to (1) an ageing population as well as (2) problems arising from a declining area-wide medical care in many European regions. This shows dramatically the need for concepts to sustainably reduce the expenditures, improve patients' outcome and ensure maximum care efficiency.

The cardiovascular patient *at risk* was described many times (World Heart Federation 2014) and was the subject of many eHealth studies (The George Institute for Global Health 2014; IN-TIME Study Group 2014). This is mainly due to the epidemiological impact of chronic cardiovascular diseases. The condition most often addressed in this context is heart failure. Heart failure is a chronic disease prone to acute ('acute-on-chronic') congestive episodes at shortening intervals. Monitoring heart failure most simply might be realized by monitoring bodyweight, on the assumption that deteriorating heart failure will soon appear as volume overload and thus weight gain. Instead of recording bodyweight traditionally—stepping on the scales every morning and writing down the weight—measured data are transferred immediately from scales digitally (Bluetooth) (Charité Universitätsmedizin Berlin 2014). In our view, this might be charming by it is technical elegance; however, there is no major added value.

This is supported by a study we conducted with 100 cardiovascular patients at risk who carry an implantable cardioverter defibrillator ICD (which records all arrhythmias). We handed out a diary to all and asked them to protocol their bodyweight and how they feel (on a simple ordinal scale: *excellent, good, middle, bad, terrible: will seek medical attendance soon)* each day carefully. To our surprise neither congestive heart failure did turn out as the most frequent reason for unplanned hospitalization, nor was it predicted more or less reliably by bodyweight. Hospitalization was instead triggered mainly by *arrhythmias* (e.g. tachycardic atrial fibrillation, shock delivery for fast ventricular tachycardia) and, to a lesser degree, therapy (drugs, implanted devices)-related *adverse effects*. This probably was due to the fact that after the implementation of new therapies in the late 1980s and 1990s, chronic heart failure changed its face. It appeared that chronic heart failure carries the risk of sudden death, but death in pulmonary edema has taken a back seat compared to death caused by arrhythmias.

We conclude that just digitizing things, we could get just as well analogically, does not upgrade care unequivocally.

The feasibility of networked care is dependent on the feasibility of monitoring and on monitoring the right things revealing what we are in fact trying to uncover.

We should know the indicators that signal when to adapt therapy.

Concerning the cardiovascular patient at risk this could be

1. the pump function (ejection fraction, usually determined by imaging techniques) of the heart,
2. the frequency and severity of episodes of ischemia and
3. arrhythmias,
4. pulmonary congestion, and
5. the technical integrity of implants (like artificial valves, ICDs or assist devices).

Some data are available today, but some are not yet at hand. What is needed seems to be research and development on biological signals *which make the difference*, or: What do we want to know basically?

If we knew these signals, they should be recorded as minimally invasive as possible, simply because the less invasive they turn out to be, the less complications we shall anticipate, and the higher the acceptance by the patient.

Transmitting biological signals is possible in many ways. The transmission is less a question of technical feasibility but of standards and data security. Standards mainly make up perspectives of usability and profit expectations. Data security, as E. Snowden unveiled, is a highly debatable issue; the more so, as information about the vulnerability of people is in the limelight.

Interpreting physiological data faces two problems: We surely need algorithms beyond clinical medicine to guide therapy *by biological signals*, and we need automated algorithms simply for the mere amount of data coming in continuously. Analyzing 3-lead-ECGs over periods of 3 (easily comprising 1 GB), 7 or 30 days would be extremely time demanding to browse through manually even just for some questionable episodes. Evaluating ischemic burden over and above arrhythmias could easily evoke an information overload. Thus, new kind of—to the greatest possible extent—automated analysis software seems mandatory. For very critical final judgement and action-guiding results, however, automated analysis is still going to be combined with human expertise.

Because there already is data analysis with algorithms, in the near future we shall not need the many people in the cardiovascular business dealing just with setting up and interpreting medical technology. In the medical 'internet of things' companies will create platforms (Rifkin 2014). Once running, they will be operated by algorithms, artificial intelligence at the end, and will be managed by some supervising cardiologists.

1.2 User-Network Interfaces (Patients, Medical Professionals)

Data streams can be directed to medical professionals as well as to the patients themselves.

The data transfer to the medical professional follows the traditional route. Today, a written medical report is sent by mail or e-mail. Networked care requires the language and its ways of transfer digitized. Data streams are sent into 'my' *cloud*. And this cloud is open for additional information like text or voice input, point-of-care (POC) diagnostics (done autonomously by the patient) and more.

Furthermore, as the network comprises ever continuing information about the delicate state of health of a very special person, either ill, or still healthy, or healthy again, for quantitative and qualitative reasons there is an apparent need for *processing and editing the data*: might it be a web portal dedicated to all medical professionals who are concerned with this particular patient operated by an eHealth Center, or a simple to handle and easy to understand app that is communicating with the patient via his end device, smartphone, TV, or any other.

Before data streams reach the final user, they pass an *interface*. There, signals will be processed, physiological data interpreted, and information matched. At the end, medically meaningful data will be presented.

In the simplest form, the physician will log in to a web portal to obtain information about a specific patient. This web portal can be run by a doctors' network, a professional association, a third-party company, a state-run organization, or a bigger regional supplier. It could be the job of the receptionist or ward secretary to retrieve the information from the web portal (licensed by contract) for just the particular patient sitting in the waiting room.

For the physician, the challenge remains to screen within seconds the information for the very valuable content that could guide actions. Presumably this too should trigger an amendment to traditional medical education: as it is neither self-evident nor included into common training to translate statistic tendencies into specific action. The interpretation of statistic tendencies is rather the job of epidemiologists, not of practitioners, whereas the practitioner's aim is to treat a person instead of covering an issue of relevance for the society as a whole. Concepts and instruments for a quite new component of our medical students' education are needed.

Just now we experience the brave new world of 'iHealth'. We monitor everything: our nutrition, fitness, sleep, and also vital signs such as respiratory rate, blood pressure, heart rate, and body temperature. Tracking ourselves in terms of health and disease, brought along with mobile health (mHealth) tools, meanwhile makes up a new responsibility. mHealth tools make data available to tune one's lifestyle, medication, and many other aspects based on longitudinal monitoring. *This addresses issues related to the self-management of health and diseases as well as to citizen engagement.*

2 Perspectives of Networked Care

2.1 Personalized Risk Management

To date, the management of the patient at risk is assigned to the primary care physician. He is the one who shall pilot the patient through the health care system. He is the first to meet particular problems and to forward the patient to respective consultants. For several epidemiologically relevant problems there are disease management programs agreed upon by the big health insurances presetting diagnostic and therapeutic measures. Progress and barrier at the same time, they mainly consist of *standards*. There are standards of diagnostic and therapeutic measures that should be observed. These standards change with the changing guidelines of the respective professional organization. The guidelines are built around clinical studies. True, a study has to define inclusion and exclusion criteria, and these criteria describe the 'ideal' patient for study purposes. In real life patients differ from study patients. Hence, albeit guidelines can set up standards and therefore avert that a particular patient misses those standards, they, at the same time, give individualized care a hard fight. The more so, if we look at preventive measures (the preventive use of statins may be a good idea for somebody, but not necessarily for everybody with high cholesterol).

Personalized risk management needs new tools and even newer insights.

New tools for patients should address the shortcomings of a given health care system, which by and large is divided between delimited players, and add something really new to it (real-time physiological data, extension of care to preventive and rehabilitative measures, self-empowerment).

IT-assisted tools for patients at risk should overcome the disembodiment of services and at the same time offer an added value.

We suggest designing these tools as *digital companions*, mainly 'external' (worn), and some 'internal' (implanted, such as pacemakers). These tools should be easy to use and barely perceptible. We favor the concept of *wearable sensors*, possibly connected to *implanted devices*.

Some of these digital companions are already at hand, ready for the market, but others are prototypes only, and others exist even only on a sketch block. We are equipped with mobile cardiac telemetry systems like Corventis NUVANT®, iRhythm ZIO® XT Patch, or AthenaDiaX ARES®. We could all be accompanied by wearable sensors for heart rate, rhythm, and ischemic burden, blood pressure, oxygen saturation, and much more, picking out the individually eligible match.

Compared to yesterday, value will be added not only by the diversity but by the constant update of the data pool. The view changes from examining a current state to understanding *trends*: Personalized risk management has to understand trends in health and disease of a given patient.

Furthermore, *digital companions* span a network from the particular patients (the only named constant in the equation of delivering health) in their everyday life to all the medical professionals around, each dedicated to the individual case.

This network—networked care—defines a crucial aspect of the 'boundaryless hospital'.

Personalized risk management can be looked upon both as *managing chronic diseases* like heart failure and/or as the *management of acute threats and emergencies* like an imminent heart attack.

If digital companions really work as a modern kind of guardian angels, without much doubt a question will pop up on the smartphone of a heart failure patient: 'How do you feel today? Did you take your daily pills?' *(establishing a dialog between man and machine)*, at the very same time while data about stroke volume and pump function are delivered into the cloud. If point-of-care diagnostics are implemented in the protective screen, our patient would be asked to get a single drop of blood and obtain BNP (point-of-care analysis of blood, e.g. immunological cardiovascular risk markers, electrolytes as well as metabolites).

Similarly, another patient with chest pain of acute onset will obtain troponin and myoglobin as markers for acute myocardial damage (while simultaneously sending his ECG together with a comment: '[Right now I am experiencing] chest pain'. Personalized risk management means: The first mentioned heart failure patient will get advice to consult his doctor soon, whereas in case of patient no. 2 supposedly an emergency ambulance will immediately be sent.

Possibilities and necessities exceed pure gimmicks and lifestyle tracking.

2.2 Self-Empowerment

Networked care is spelled not only in the language of expenditure, but can be rolled out in terms of disease prevention and thereby support the self-management of health. *The focus is to empower patients to monitor and manage their health/disease*: at home, underway, wherever. The monitoring can cover different aspects: (1) (interactive) health and life style Q&A's, (2) functional diagnostics, and (3) blood-based diagnostics. Based on these data, specific and patient-centered interpretations and recommendations are sent via the cloud to an eHealth Center. Thus, the management of health/disease without a next-door visit to the doctor's office but under supervision of medical staff is coming true: '*Medicine* comes to you by digital companions, but you go to your *doctor*.'

Saying that, the visit to the *doctor's* office will aim at physician-patient relations on a prevailing personal level, where empathy is wanted, but (more and more, and evermore crucial) *pure medical data* will be delivered from the patient to the eHealth Center (and from there to the caretaking doctor) with no need to leave home.

All too often we fail in disease prevention or management because, by way of example, our patient indeed may know (he reads it on every packet) that 'smoking kills', *but enlightenment and pure information fall short in changing behavior*.

A health app might work as a kind of bio-feedback, and (serious) gamification could support such advice (Kohl 2013a, b).

IT-assisted tools, applied in networked care, and extended from simple Q&A's ('How do you feel today?') to functional diagnostics (full disclosure ECG) and even blood diagnostics unlock the potential to enhance self-responsibility. Maybe, the old dilemma that knowledge does not simply translate into behavior hence will be alleviated. If we look at the hits and defeats of advertising psychology, we see that action-initiating messages function not simply because of the message itself, but and mainly due to *emotional carriers* which bring them to our perception. This holds true for these nerve-racking messages about health: Do not smoke! Avoid cholesterol, fat, and sugar! One of the very few successful campaigns about health in Germany was the one against AIDS. It worked with the help of sex and humor. Sex and humor operated as 'emotional carriers'. The intrinsic message—safer sex *is* smart—*surfs* on these carriers, en route circumventing defense mechanisms (against paternalism, cautioning, spoiling the party) and thereby effective.)

There is a dispute with regard to health education: Is it acceptable to utilize all the glitzy tricks of promo? In our view: Why certainly! As long as there is no lie.

Using the smooth, attractive force of an app, playfully put into effect, devoted to me personally and not least the awareness to be on the right track seems to be a very venial sin.

Self-empowerment of patients by 'wearables' (Fig. 1) is enabled within a personalized framework: The patient, in his everyday activities, wears an adhesive skin patch able to measure various physiological data. These data will be transmitted into a cloud. A regional eHealth Center will process the data technically and medically (analysis, reporting). If the patient uses a lab-on-chip-system (Nestler et al. 2010) (to do POC diagnostics, e.g. troponin, cholesterol etc.), also lab data will be transmitted and processed. All data, integrated in a patient file, could take two lines: back to the patient's smartphone (or the device of a person of trust, e.g. a family member), or to a medical call center which—if necessary—would contact the patient or his family doctor.

The medical professional will have the patient's data at hand, already well before the patient enters the practice, and the data will be by far more comprehensive as he is used to today.

Maybe more importantly, for the first time the patient gets easy-to-understand regular reports on the successful or poor efforts to stay healthy or to recover continuously.

There is simply no longer a traditional monopole by professionals on substantial patient-related health information.

With that said, it seems quite clear that we are talking about an eHealth system with a strong (mostly subliminal) educational component.

What has to be clarified is the—epidemiologically justified—medical content or: Which data, at the end of the day, will make the difference?

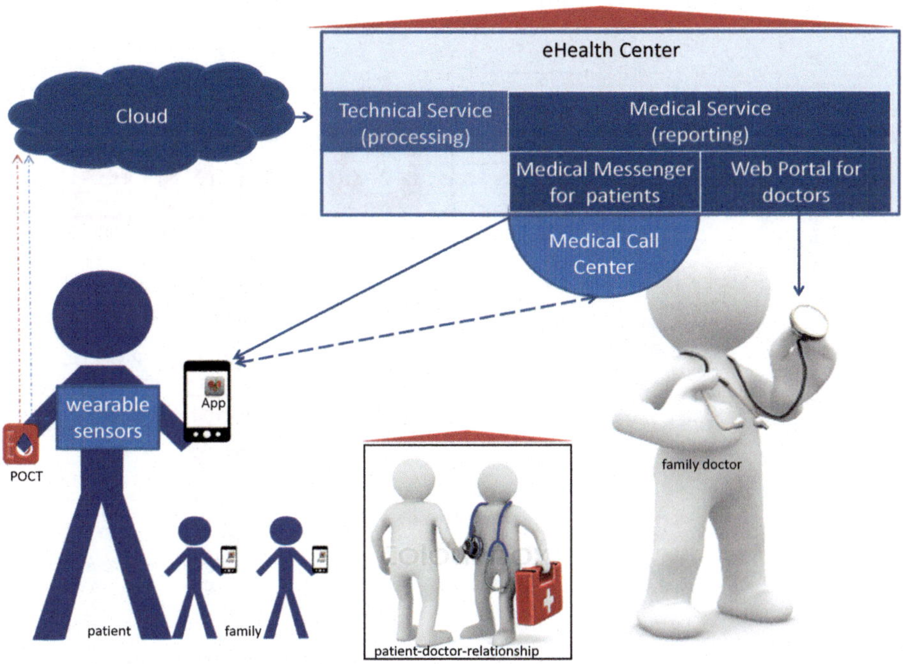

Fig. 1 *Self-empowerment* of patients by 'wearables' giving a personalized framework of every-day activities' health effects

3 Networked Care Adapted to Needs: Toolbox and Showcase

3.1 Toolbox

To translate networked care into different realities of care it is quite likely insufficient to just dispose new electronic gimmicks. iHealth—as marketed currently by Apple and others—has been a door opener. The addressee who goes through this door enters the land of countless medically interesting information: counting steps (accelerometer), gauging the intensity during workouts (heart rate sensor) to improve overall calorie tracking, 3D object recognition technology... The customer—in this regard our patient-at-risk—faces the difficulty to pick and combine the—for him personally—appropriate digital companions, to understand the personal impact of the information delivered for health and illness, and to draw the necessary action-guiding individual conclusions.

What we apparently need seems to be a new kind of medical infrastructure, partly real, partly virtual, to handle those new needs.

The toolbox, full of sensors and fascinating gimmicks, has to be integrated into a new conceptual framework of care (*boundaryless hospital*).

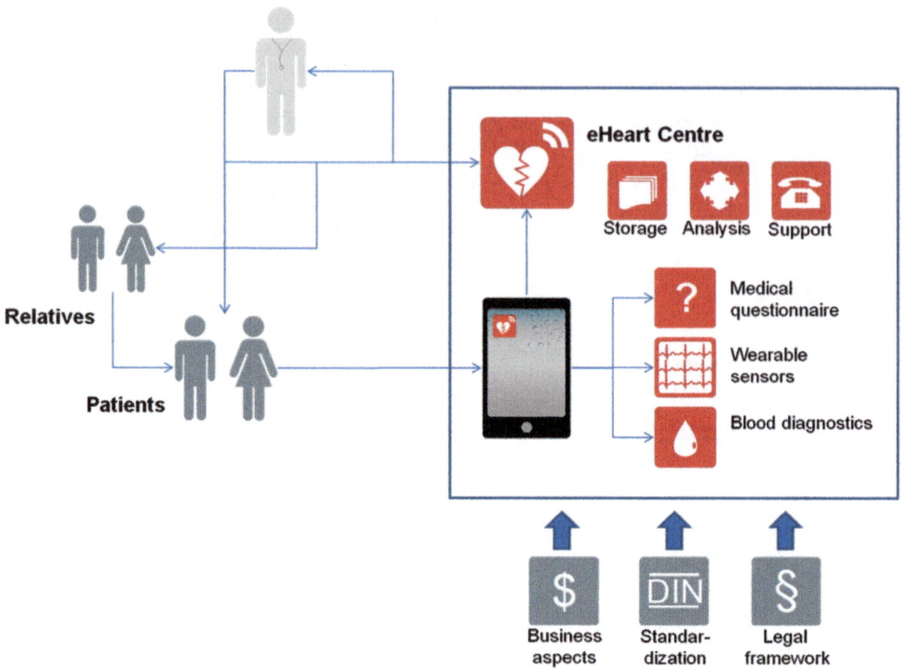

Fig. 2 mHealth system for cardiovascular patients at risk

If we talk about personalized networked care we are aware of data accessibility unknown before.

The proposed mHealth system for cardiovascular patients at risk (Fig. 2) is arranged around an eHealth Center (in this context called: eHeart Center). This eHeart Center has to deal with the storage, analysis of data, and the clients' support. The data from wearable sensors and POCT (blood diagnostics) could be broadened and complemented by medical questionnaires (angina, dyspnea, palpitations, quality of life. . .) sent to the particular app and, after being answered, resent again.

It is obvious, that those complex interactions will raise issues (business aspects, standardization, and legal framework) and prompt questions beyond technical aspects.

On these never running dry but more and more upswelling data a mobile (mHealth), virtual drop-in clinic is built. And it is built by

1. designing a health care app to *monitor* patients at high risk,
2. monitoring with different kinds of *sensors* and *point-of-care blood tests,*
3. developing the *eHealth Center* with telemedical services for data management and patient guidance.

Whereas the concept of combining sensors with an app is common and many different apps for 'lifestyle tracking' are available (Istepanian 2004), networked care to this effect provides a toolbox raising new answers to old questions:

- Addressing business aspects: evaluating health care cost benefits arising from the health app, elaborating a sustainable business and dissemination model for the health app system based on the evaluation of model regions, defining a sustainable telemedicine model by the integration of an eHealth Center guiding patients and physicians
- Addressing standardization: incorporating current standards and technical rules into the system as well as developing recommendations for new standards and technical rules which are currently missing
- Addressing the legal framework: elaborating a legal framework for patient data management in patient-physician communication as well as 'big-data analysis' with anonymized or pseudonymized data based on national and European law (from data management by health insurance companies to public health inquiries)

Parallel to these questions, the following technical functions will become development objectives (World Health Organization 2011):

- User-driven development of the app for intuitive use of the system
- Further development of easy-to-use wearable sensors for functional diagnostics such as ECG or blood pressure
- Further development of a system for point-of-care analysis of immunological cardiovascular risk markers, electrolytes as well as metabolites
- Establishment of an IT solution which collects data from wearable sensors, blood diagnostic and patient health questionnaires and transfers these into a cloud to be accessible to an eHealth Center

The data delivered into a cloud, analyzed, managed and shared out, in some cases will enable action-guiding conclusions, and hence suggestions could be provided. They could be passed to the physician in charge, and alternatively (or supplementary) they could be sent directly to the afflicted patient.

The patient himself is independent of the doctor's office while continuously being protected against his biggest individual health risks, might he be at home or underway. Thereby he is the *master of his data*, neither the medical professional nor the cost bearers. He decides with whom he wants to share his data.

These features *(informational self-determination)* justify the concept of networked care as patient-centered (in contrast to hospital- and professionals-centered care structures).

All data generated will be used in the first instance for individual health monitoring and treatment. The data will be managed within an eHealth Center. Its knowledge-based information system analyzes the data on a routine base. For that purpose, alerts and timers will be used to encourage patients to follow medical recommendations. These recommendations are individually addressed to the patient's needs.

A concept about data management and data security including a legal framework for patient data handling has to be elaborated.

Thus, it should be possible not only to guide patients, moreover, an outcome of public health will be generated subliminally. From that point of view it is possible to relate the *medical* impact of networked care to the impact concerning the whole society (cost-benefit).

The aim is a sustainable mHealth system which combines different information pathways: data generated by sensors unperceivable in daily life, Q&As from a dialog between a patient and his smartphone (automatic speech recognition), blood diagnostics requiring some kind of interaction between patient, point-of-care test cartridge and app (alluded via Bluetooth), et al. For each stakeholder (patients, family members, doctors as well as public health authorities), another messaging and *communication structure* will be used. Whereas patients will receive recommendations for a healthier life style or other factors, relatives of patients will be given information on how to support patients in their actions.

And the more diverse information pathways and communication structures turn out to be, the more data traffic has to be based and elaborated on state-of-the-art regulations and data security issues in order to ensure patients' privacy.

Partially, these developments are already reality if we look at commercially available, implanted devices like ICDs (Biotronik's Home Monitoring Service Center, Boston Scientific's Latitude NXT Patient Management System, or Medtronic's CareLink Remote Monitoring Network).[1] For instance, the Latitude NXT Patient Management System consists of a website (which provides quick access to important information such as device battery life, lead performance and patient arrhythmias), a weight scale and a blood pressure monitor providing in-home monitoring of weight and blood pressure, and the Latitude NXT Communicator that conducts scheduled interrogations. The Latitude NXT Mobile App allows clinicians easy access to see patient data from an iPhone. The read-only view allows clinicians to see alert information, review patient information, including events, leads, battery, leads and health measurements, review patient arrhythmia events since last reset, and generate reports to view, save, email, and print.

The scope of functional diagnostics invites barely limited technological innovations and fantasy. The characteristics and specific data cluster indicative of heart failure, obstructive airways disease, depressive syndrome, or complications during pregnancy (to mention just a few) provide the technological challenges.

Unfortunately, today not the disease provides a bunch of parameters, but conversely the parameters technically on hand provide the diseases being promoted in eHealth business (body weight: congestive heart failure).

---

[1] For more details visit www.biotronik.com, www.bostonscientific.com, and www.medtronicheart.com

The mHealth system currently being developed in Brandenburg, Germany (see Sect. 3.2), will address at first glance patients at risk of a serious adverse, cardiovascular event. This defined patient group is an exemplary patient group which is in special need for such a system.

This risk group is of uttermost relevance due to the high prevalence of cardiovascular diseases in the EU. In 2012, about 17.5 million people died from cardiovascular diseases worldwide (World Health Organization 2015). Estimations of prevalence show that in 2030 more than three quarter of all deaths will be ascribed to non-communicable diseases such as cardiovascular diseases (Fuster and Kelly 2010). Although the prevalence is high and the development of such a system will be beneficial, this is seen just as a first application of this mHealth model and should further be developed addressing different other kinds of health care burdens or in the world.

Definitely desirable measurements in cardiovascular medicine are ECG (rate, rhythm, and ischemic burden), blood pressure, ejection fraction, and oxygen saturation.

Supposed that sensors ideally should be unperceivable, in the long run devices which need bulky additional equipment such as scales or conventional blood pressure cuff and even Holter ECG presumably will be discarded.

Personal data has to be collected largely unperceived to become accepted. This even more applies to healthy people and preventive measures.

It is not until retrieving and rating the data, that a patient's intentness may be deserved. This is quite similar to the pedometer built into my sports shoe; nobody cares about metering, but everybody talks about the resulting statistics.

What's yet missing in most of today's professional systems (which are built for professionals) is: enabling the *patient* to access his own—edited and generally understandable—data.

'Patient-centered' systems on the market still are just toys. Transforming those life-style products into serious tools to monitor health and disease without losing its playful, motivating character remains a challenge (Cipresso et al. 2012).

Certainly this should be done without a wagering finger and long-winded chapters, perhaps just by something like a traffic light (do: green, think: yellow, don't do: red).

People at risk—with the help of digital companions—*shall be empowered to manage their health and disease self-reliantly and, if desired, in tight cooperation with the local health institutions as well.*

Accordingly, networked care personalized means: Based on imperceptibly recorded and continuously updated biological signals of a particular person medical information hits a new level. Data quantity turns into a new quality of the database (Van Doornik 2013). Evaluating software will undoubtedly provide conclusions of unprecedented predictive accuracy and pragmatic suggestions.

3.2 Showcase and Roadmap: Networked Care for Regional Development

In the federal state of Brandenburg in Germany, we develop *networked care* with the help of IT-assisted tools for cardiovascular patients at risk, and understand it as a contribution to regional development.

Until here, we have described the *idea* of networked care.

Currently, the following elements are already put into action:

- A wireless multi-sensor module combined with an adhesive skin patch for long-term registration, storage and transmission of physiological data (currently carried out: 3-lead ECG)
- An Android-based app and a local server
- An eHealth Center (under construction)
- A suitable platform for multiple point-of-care tests (relevant lab parameters are identified)

As this project may work *as a new framework and a laboratory of care*, we should like to delineate a *roadmap* to set up networked care with the help of IT-assisted tools for patients at risk (Fig. 3):

In our view, the very first building block is a sensor. The sensor should be at most practicable. In fact, it should be a platform/device able to measure multiple meaningful parameters to avoid countless accesses to the patient. The sensor could be wearable or implantable dependent on the chief aim and the expected benefit.

Next, it becomes important to define the target group. Layman or professional? Both? The answer triggers the needs of data processing (getting their impact across) and privacy.

Because of the many data accumulated, one of the key elements is data handling as defined by workflow. If processing, analyzing, interpreting, and drawing

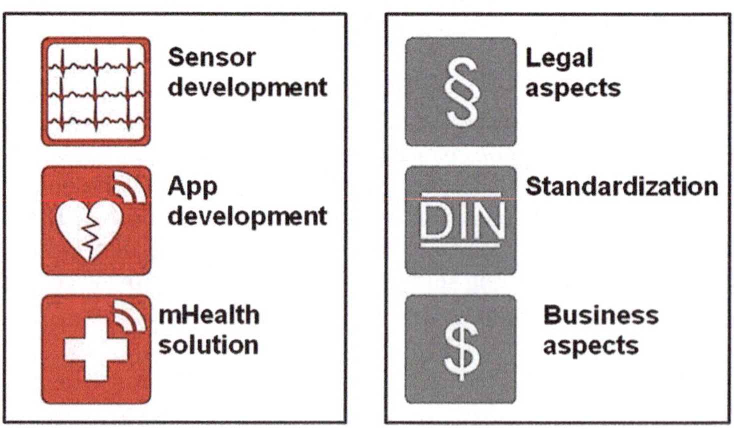

Fig. 3 Roadmap to set up networked care

consequences turns out to be too time-consuming, the project is doomed to failure. This concerns transmission time, computing time, and any manual operations. Possibly, new algorithms for evaluating big data have to be developed.

Not least: To fit networked care—understood this way—into the needs of a region the relevant regional players have to be involved because their commitment is vital to the success.

Significant regional players are

- local authorities (e.g. town council),
- the biggest health and care insurance providers in the particular region,
- GPs and physicians' networks,
- regional domain care companies.

This project *may* work *as* a new framework and a laboratory of care. This in particular holds true for deprived people and regions:

- people subjected to many and greater risks to health, and
- rural regions, facing the similar challenges of aging, evermore shutdown of country doctor's offices, rundown infrastructure and a continuing uneven access to adequate medical help.

In a nutshell, *the philosophy of a 'boundaryless hospital' leads away from a hospital-centered to a patient-centered workflow.*

This workflow will be organized by digital companions creating a sheltered way amidst individual health hazards and leading through the inevitable risks of life.

References

Charité Universitätsmedizin Berlin Study (2014) Telemedical Interventional Management in Heart Failure II (TIM-HF II). http://telemedizin.charite.de/en/research/fontane/telemedicial_interventional_management_in_heart_failure_tim_hf_ii/. Accessed 16 Nov 2014

Cipresso P, Serino S, Villani D, Repetto C, Selitti L, Albani G, Mauro A, Gaggioli A, Riva G (2012) Is your phone so smart to affect your states? An exploratory study based on psychophysiological measures. Neurocomputing 84:23–30. doi:10.1016/j.neucom.2011.12.027

European Heart Network and European Society of Cardiology (2012) European cardiovascular disease statistics. Sophia Antipolis, Brussels

Fuster V, Kelly BB (eds) (2010) Institute of Medicine (US) Committee on preventing the global epidemic of cardiovascular disease: meeting the challenges in developing countries, National Academy of Sciences

IN-TIME Study Group (2014) Implant-based multiparameter telemonitoring of patients with heart failure (IN-TIME): a randomised controlled trial. Lancet 384:583–90. doi:10.1016/S0140-6736(14)61176-4

Istepanian R (2004) Introduction to the special section on m-health: beyond seamless mobility and global wireless health-care connectivity. IEEE Trans Inf Technol Biomed 8(4):405–413

Kohl J (2013a) Interview with Anna Sort: gamification in health care Part 1. http://www.kohl.ca/2013/interview-with-anna-sort-nurse-teacher-consultant-and-gamer-part-1/. Accessed 16 Nov 2014

Kohl J (2013b) Interview with Anna Sort: gamification in health care Part 2. http://www.kohl.ca/2013/interview-with-anna-sort-gamification-in-health-care-part-2/. Accessed 16 Nov 2014

Nestler J, Morschhauser A, Otto T, Koger B, Brandenburg A, Wunderlich K, Ehrentreich-Foerster E, Bier FF, Gessner T (2010) Highly-integrated, low-cost in-vitro diagnostic platform for miniaturized assay development. http://www.rsc.org/binaries/loc/2010/pdfs/papers/418_1168.pdf. Accessed 16 Nov 2014

Rifkin J (2014) The zero marginal cost society: the internet of things, the collaborative commons, and the eclipse of capitalism. Palgrave Macmillan, Basingstoke

The George Institute for Global Health (2014) One for all: the Consumer Cardiovascular Disease (CVD) Risk Management eHealth Portal Development and Testing, Australia. http://www.georgeinstitute.org.au/projects/consumer-cardiovascular-disease-cvd-risk-management-ehealth-portal-development-and-testing. Accessed 16 Nov 2014

Van Doornik W (2013) Meaningful use of patient-generated data in EHRs. J AHIMA 84 (10):30–35

World Health Organization (2011) mHealth. New horizons for health through mobile technologies. http://www.who.int/goe/publications/goe_mhealth_web.pdf. Accessed 16 Nov 2014

World Health Organization (2015) Fact sheets: cardiovascular diseases (CVDs). http://www.who.int/mediacentre/factsheets/fs317/en/. Accessed 24 Aug 2015

World Heart Federation (2014) Cardiovascular disease risk factors. http://www.world-heart-federation.org/cardiovascular-health/cardiovascular-disease-risk-factors. Accessed 16 Nov 2014

Kurt J. G. Schmailzl is Head of the Department of Cardiovascular and Thoracic Diseases at Ruppiner Kliniken in Fontanestadt Neuruppin near Berlin. He served as founding dean of three universities and is now member of the faculty council of the newly founded MHB, Medizinische Hochschule Brandenburg, the first medical school in the federal state of Brandenburg, Germany.

Kurt J. G. Schmailzl studied physics, medicine, and social sciences. His professional career led him from Munich to Berlin and Hershey, PA, USA, focusing on artificial organs and cardiac imaging. He works on biosensors and eHealth concepts. Medicine, considered as delicate mission in a given social context, cannot be separated from political issues. Given that, Kurt J. G. Schmailzl develops health services research in the complementary framework of sociology, public health, international health management and life sciences.

He worked with Health ClusterNET, an NGO that advises the EU in health policy, and recently was involved in the restatement of the new 'masterplan' of the health region Berlin-Brandenburg.

Hans H. Th. Sendler After studies of law and economics and a doctorate on automation in social insurance he has for decades been holding roles encompassing different perspectives within the health and social systems in Germany: in the Medical Advisory Service of the German Association of Statuary Health Insurance Funds as well as in the Federal Association of Company Health Insurance Funds, in the Government of the German State of North Rhine-Westphalia and in the Federal Association of the German Pharmaceutical Industry. For many years he was member of the board of the German Association of Social Medicine and Prevention. Also by his literary work he interfered in made out necessities. He addressed required structural developments of the health and social systems by innovative projects—also with manifold European and international aspects. Now already for years he—with his concept agency EUSENDOR—contributes to coping strategies for the demographic change within the health and social systems, at the workplace and by volunteering. Together with Kurt J. G. Schmailzl he has developed the concept of Health and Social Contract Management.

Carving Out a Place for New Health Care Occupations: An Ethnographic Study into Job Crafting

Maarten Janssen, Iris Wallenburg, and Antoinette de Bont

Abstract

Over the past few years several new occupations have been introduced in health care next to those of vested professionals. In this chapter we analyze the introduction and development of the physician assistant (PA) as one of them. A PA is an allied professional or nurse who has obtained additional university training and who is allowed to work independently in health care practice, conducting certain medical procedures. The central question this chapter addresses is: '*How do new professionals craft their job by carving out a place in health care practice?*' To explore this topic we build on the theoretical notions of *place* (Creswell, Place: a short introduction. Blackwell, 2004) and *job crafting* (Wrzesniewski and Dutton, Acad Manag Rev 26(2):179–201, 2001). Data comes from two case studies; one in emergency care and one in neonatology. Through ethnographic research we analyze how new professionals continuously develop their job and how this changes their place in everyday health care practice. Our results show that increasing experience, developed routines, specialization and trust among the medical and nursing staff enables PAs to gradually expand their occupational place, highlighting the fluidity of its boundaries. PAs do not only create and *occupy* their place; they add specific meanings to it and in the process create both individually and collectively a new work identity for the PA as an occupation.

Keywords

Occupational development • Job crafting • Place • Health care • Ethnographic analysis • Physician assistant • Identity • The Netherlands

M. Janssen, MSc (✉) • I. Wallenburg, PhD • A. de Bont, PhD
Institute of Health Policy and Management, Erasmus University Rotterdam, Burgemeester Oudlaan 50, 3062 PA Rotterdam, The Netherlands
e-mail: m.janssen@bmg.eur.nl

H. Albach et al. (eds.), *Boundaryless Hospital*, DOI 10.1007/978-3-662-49012-9_7

1 Introduction

Occupational roles in health care are rapidly changing due to the introduction of new health care services, changes in health care education and demographic transitions. In recent years, several new professional occupations, such as the nurse practitioner and the physician assistant, have been introduced in the health care arena next to *vested* health care professions. New occupations continuously develop in practice and take over clinical tasks that used to be carried out by medical specialists such as conducting physical examinations and prescribing medication. These changes in workforce illustrate a trend described as the *replacement* of care from clear-cut and well-defined occupational groups (e.g. specialists, medical residents, nurses) to more situated professional roles and team-based work. To put it differently, boundaries between occupational groups seem to be fading, prompting new questions on task distribution, on responsibility and accountability of the delivery of care as well as on the relations between different health care professionals. Distributing tasks to new health care practitioners asks for new to-be-developed arrangements; legally, socially and in terms of skills and expertise (Oldenhof et al. 2015). In this chapter we aim to enhance the understanding of new occupational development by analyzing how a new health care occupation gets established. More precisely, we study the work that a new professional, in our study the physician assistant (PA), needs to conduct to obtain an own position in everyday health care practice. The PA has been introduced as a new occupation in countries such as the USA, the UK, the Czech Republic, Germany and the Netherlands.[1] PAs conduct a range of medical procedures that used to be preserved to medical specialists, e.g. the prescription of medication. We investigate how the PA has developed and gets integrated in the everyday practices of hospitals. We draw on ethnographic research in two case studies in the Netherlands to analyze how individual PAs act upon, give shape, add meaning, change and create their occupational role in daily practice.

For our analysis we introduce the notion of place (Gieryn 2000; Creswell 2004) as alternative to the often-used notion of *professional jurisdictions* that is key in traditional sociological and organizational literature on professional development (e.g. Abbott 1988; Currie et al. 2012). Literature on jurisdictions tends to emphasize how vested professionals protect existing boundaries and domains, and as such block developments that form a threat to their formal position and interests (Abbott 1988; Sanders and Harrison 2008; Suddaby and Viale 2011). Instead of going into these theoretical debates on professional jurisdictions, we argue that the allegedly clear legal boundaries and the defensive strategies and tactics of vested professionals do little justice to the exigencies of practice in which these and new

[1] In the UK, the term *physician assistant* was replaced by *physicians' associate*. Yet, the tasks and responsibilities of a Dutch PA are quite similar to that of the physician associate in the UK. A PA in the Netherlands does however bear more clinical responsibility and autonomy than a PA in Germany, which also illustrates the situated nature of the development of a new occupation (Wallenburg et al. 2014b).

occupations are produced, shaped and made meaningful (Barley and Kunda 2001). While the traditional literature on professions suggests there is almost no room for new professionals to develop and get embedded in an already institutionalized setting, practice shows ample examples of PAs who work in the core of care provision in hospital settings. Therefore, we describe the efforts of new professionals carving out their *place*—as an alternative conceptualization of a role, in an institutionalized health care setting with pre-existing identities and relations of, and between, vested professionals (Centellas et al. 2014). The need to *carve out* a place in interaction with others implies that such a place is not vacant and that new professionals, such as the PA in this study, cannot simply take possession of it. The central question our research addresses is: '*How do new professionals craft their job by carving out a place in health care practice?*'

In order to analyse *how* individual PAs do carve out an occupational place in practice we draw on job crafting theory. The notion of job crafting goes well with a practice-oriented research approach on place-making activities as it sheds a light on how such processes transform not only individual jobs, but also the place for new occupations in general. Hence, combing the notions of place and job crafting in this chapter enables us to take into account and render visible the dynamic processes of how new professionals actually create a role, conceptualized here as a place, through processes of job crafting.

This chapter is organized as follows. In the next section we develop our theoretical framework on the notions of place and job crafting. In Sect. 3, we describe the two case studies in more detail, as well as the research design and the methods used for data collection and analysis. The Results section describes job crafting practices of PAs and the consequences hereof for their place in hospital practice. In the fifth section we answer the main research question and show how this influences our conceptualization of professional boundaries in these processes. In the final section, the discussion, we reflect on our contribution to theories on place and job crafting and describe important implications for the concept of a *boundaryless hospital*.

2 Carving Out a Place Through Processes of Job Crafting

As already briefly touched upon in the introduction we build our theoretical framework upon the notions of *place* and *job crafting*. These concepts allow for a more dynamic analysis of how occupations are constantly constructed and shaped by and within the (inter)actions of individuals in health care practice.

2.1 On Carving Out a Place

Using the concept of place enables us to dynamically analyze how new professionals develop their occupational role which can also be conceived of as *a place*. This is more than an accumulation of separate tasks and responsibilities

(Strauss et al. 1985) as it also directly relates to meaning making and identity creation. Place has both a theoretical and empirical meaning. Here we will attend to the theoretical meaning as we will use the concept in a more heuristic and empirical manner. We chose to use the concept of *place* for our analysis of occupational development for new professionals especially for two reasons:

First, the notion of *place* offers a dynamic perspective on occupational development as it does not only reflect a location, physical context or passive environment for social processes, activities and experience (Andrews and Moon 2005). Places are not just *out there* to be discovered; they are actively produced through daily actions and the reiteration of mundane practices (Creswell 2004). Places thus need to be constructed and are shaped into being by people (Mesman 2009). This implies that places cannot simply be handed over or made available to others. In addition to being produced, places are in essence dynamic. Producing a place never stops as they are never completely finished or forever fixed (Barley and Kunda 2001). Moreover, places can be something very different for different actors as their boundaries are not always clear (Oldenhof et al. 2015). Assuming that places are constantly produced through the reiteration of seemingly mundane activities on a daily basis makes them *endlessly made* (Gieryn 2000) or *always becoming* (Creswell 2004). In this chapter we envision places as active doings in the development of occupations. Agentic individuals are able to create or carve out such places.

Second, we argue that using place better fits with the challenge new professionals face when they are introduced in health care practice. Although new professionals can often rely on an official legal framework that defines their rights and competences, they still have to develop their occupation that is *in place* at a specific department. Having a place in a team at a specific department is all about determining who and what belongs where and when, and what is considered deviant or *out of place* by all involved actors. People's perception of *being in place* emphasizes the importance of meaning rather than envisioning place solely as linguistic label or spatial metaphor (Creswell 2004; Ainsworth et al. 2009; Mesman 2009; Oldenhof et al. 2015). As people make places meaningful, they become the material for creating an identity. Individual actors are crucial in these processes of creating feelings of belonging. Bolstered by the accumulation of all that has happened to an individual, they make that places are endowed with meaning and value (Tuan 1977; Gieryn 2000).

In short, we argue here that places are accomplishments rather than givens. Carving them out takes effort. Places are social constructs or events rather than secure ontological things. They form the product of everyday practices with their unique gathering of things, actors, meaning and values (Creswell 2004) and we argue that individuals have the ability to carve out their place through job crafting processes (Wrzesniewski and Dutton 2001).

2.2 On Processes of Job Crafting

Job crafting theory focuses on the development of occupations by individual actors in day-to-day practice. Rather than defining a new occupation by functional definitions, job crafting highlights the crucial importance of the dynamics in which people work, with whom they work, what they actually do, and how they conceptualize their identities and the collectives they are part of, for acquiring an understanding of the development of new occupations (Barley and Kunda 2001). Job crafting theory thus enables us to dynamically study the processes of occupational development and their results in terms of occupational places in practice.

Literature on job crafting originates from critique of job design theory that has long been influential in debates on work within organizations. Job design studies analyze how individuals experience their jobs according to a list of motivating and stimulating job characteristics (Hackman and Lawler 1971; Hackman and Oldham 1976, 1980; Berg et al. 2010), and in doing so, it addresses mainly the structural characteristics of a job that can be enforced by managers (Miner 1987; Campion and McClelland 1993). This tends to deny that actual work relationships influence a certain job (Barley and Kunda 2001). In contrast to job design theory that would assume that new occupations are simply domesticated after their introduction, job crafting theory assumes that a new occupation emerges from a certain practice instead. Job crafting is a verb, suggesting a process in which individuals put effort in shaping, molding and redefining their own job. It argues that individuals proactively make physical and cognitive changes in the task or relational boundaries and characteristics of their own job[2] (Berg et al. 2010). Job crafting theory thus assumes that individuals are able to craft their job and its meaning at the level of the work floor. This turns a job not into a static entity but into something that is inherently changeable (Hughes 1971b). Analyzing new occupations from a job crafting perspective therefore does justice to the agency practitioners possess, and the creativity they exhibit, in shaping and reshaping their own work with its set of work activities and work identity (Wrzesniewski and Dutton 2001).

Literature on job crafting provides examples of *how* professionals conduct job crafting in practice, although it has no pre-established pathway (Blumer 1966; Wrzesniewski and Dutton 2001; Creswell 2004). *Tasks* and *interactions* are seen as the raw materials or building blocks that can be used to craft a job as individuals can change what they do (i.e. tasks) and with whom they do it (i.e. interactions) (Wrzesniewski and Dutton 2001; Berg et al. 2010). *Interactions* as building block become even more important as the provision of care is increasingly becoming a team effort. New forms of working may create or reduce dependencies and interactions between professionals so that *getting the work done* becomes more

[2] A job is by Ilgen and Hollenbeck (1992) defined as: "a set of task elements grouped together under one job-title and designed to be performed by a single individual" and described by Dubois and Singh (2009) as loosely coupled elements of education, training, skills, knowledge, experience, competences, tasks and responsibilities.

dependent on direct and indirect relations between professionals (Hughes 1971a; Strauss et al. 1985; Strauss 1993; Allen 1997).

Professionals can craft their jobs in three ways; by changing task, cognitive or relational boundaries within their work environment (Wrzesniewski and Dutton 2001). The first way describes how professionals make changes in the total set of tasks by setting or altering task boundaries, e.g. the number, type and scope of performed tasks (Barley and Kunda 2001). The second way describes how professionals cognitively change the interactions between different tasks, i.e. their perception of the entire set of task. Do they see their job as a sum of different tasks or as a whole with a slightly different meaning? Third and finally, professionals can craft their job by changing relational boundaries, i.e. the interactions with other professionals with whom they work (Wrzesniewski and Dutton 2001). With this way the frequency, content, quality and amount of interactions are altered (Barley and Kunda 2001). Taken together, these three ways of job crafting alter the design of the job and/or the environment in which the job is conducted (Barley and Kunda 2001).

The design and environment of a job are intrinsically connected with work identity as changes in the design and environment of a job may, in turn, change the meaning of the work and a person's *work identity*. The meaning of work reflects what people consider as the purpose of their work and what they perceive is achieved through it. An attempt to conceptualize the purpose of work differently is therefore considered to be a form of job crafting (Wrzesniewski and Dutton 2001). Related to this is the identity that people derive from their work, i.e. how professionals define themselves at work. In explaining what their work entails, people tend to refer to claims about who they are and why what they do matters (Ashforth and Mael 1989; Pratt et al. 2006). Individual professionals thus tend to strive to build an identity or self-view over time that they themselves, and even more importantly, others can also support, as an identity is built on feelings of both collegiality and autonomy (Clegg et al. 2011). Taken together, meaning and work identity turn job crafting into a set of meaningful actions to derive a new occupational identity from the work professionals conduct.

The importance of meaning and identity in processes of job crafting supports our approach of studying how individual professionals carve out a place in practice. Although individuals craft a job, they are not alone in their efforts as they are dependent on others within their organizational context. This interdependence of professional work has instigated increasing attention for collective forms of job crafting. For example, Leana et al. (2009) stress that processes of job crafting are extremely social and often consist of joined actions between professionals.[3] Job crafting can also be collectively performed by formal or informal groups of similar professionals (Leana et al. 2009). In addition to the work of individual agents,

[3] These interactions are visible in the building block of *relations* that individuals craft as the work itself is dependent on interactional alignments. In the respective actions of arrangements of people, this form of interaction is important (Blumer 1969).

employees together make "physical and cognitive changes in the task or relational boundaries of their work" (Wrzesniewski and Dutton 2001). So, although boundaries are often drawn around individuals, collectives of professionals may also find opportunities to alter, revise or craft jobs and as such carve out a place.

To summarize our theoretical arguments: We argue that individual PAs, as new professionals, are able to carve out a place for themselves and their occupation through processes of job crafting. In the following sections we analyze how PAs craft their job in practice by changing boundaries and by processes of meaning making. Yet we first turn to the methods section in which we also briefly provide background information on the PA as new occupation.

3 Research Design and Empirical Setting

3.1 Background

The PA has been introduced as a new occupation in Dutch health care in quite a rapid pace after their role was legalized by the revision of the Individual Health Care Professions Act in 2011 (Wallenburg et al. 2014a, b).[4] PAs work in the medical domain within a specific discipline (e.g. cardiology, internal medicine) and conduct a range of medical procedures that used to be preserved to medical specialists. Examples include endoscopies, injections, punctures and the prescription of certain medication. Individuals need to have a background and relevant work experience either as allied health care professional (e.g. as a physical therapist), or as nurse to enter the training to become a PA. They follow a 2-year training program on university level. These changes granted the PA the right to set diagnoses and carry out medical procedures that were previously reserved to medical specialists.

3.2 Case Studies

To empirically flesh out the development of the PA we build on two case studies that are part of a broader research project on new health care professionals in the Netherlands (2012–2015).[5] For this specific research we selected two case studies in hospital care in close consultation with the association of PAs: one in emergency care and one in neonatology (Table 1). Selection was based on the (perceived) successfulness of the introduction of the PA as we sought to gain insights into how

[4] In 2012 around 600 PAs were either trained as or were already working as a PA in health care practice in the Netherlands (personal communication, manager the Netherlands Association of Physician Assistants, Oct. 2014).

[5] In this broader research project on new professional roles *good examples* of task reallocation in the Netherlands were analyzed in nine different case studies. The research focused on the Physician Assistant and the Nurse Specialist as new occupations (Wallenburg et al. 2014b).

Table 1 Overview of the research settings of the two case studies

#	Case	Description
1	Neonatology	The neonatology department is an intensive care unit specialized in the care of newborns and preterm infants. Patients end up here because their lives are at serious risk due to different kind of complications linked to their delivery, congenital diseases, infections, or premature birth (after $\geq$24 weeks of pregnancy). Patients here are immunologically fragile and undergo many often complicated procedures in the course of their stay (Mesman 2009).
2	Emergency care	At the emergency ward, the main aim is to offer first aid, to stabilize patients that come in with specific symptoms that can come from an almost unlimited range of diseases and to transfer them to other departments where further treatment is provided when applicable (Ainsworth et al. 2009). Health care professionals from various medical disciplines work at the emergency ward (e.g. surgeons, cardiologists, internal medicine specialists), next to specialized practitioners (e.g. nurses specialized in emergency care, emergency physicians).

the role of PAs, and the places they carve out, develop in a health care setting. Although the care settings differ, they nonetheless show similarities: At both departments patient flows cannot be fully planned as the provided care is emergent. As a consequence, professionals cannot control the number of presentations which make the care and patients streams rather difficult to plan (Ainsworth et al. 2009). Yet the two case studies are unique and do provide a genuine opportunity to learn about crafting a new occupation in hospital settings.

In both the neonatology and the emergency care case study, the introduction of the PA started on an initiative of medical specialists and managers. In neonatology, the PA was introduced mainly to counteract the threats of a decreasing workforce capacity and to enhance the continuity of care. The emergency care department, in turn, faced the problem of rather inexperienced medical residents and increasing societal concerns about the quality of patient care (Gaakeer et al. 2013). Driven by political pressure to improve quality of emergency care, various hospitals introduced new professions such as the PA and the emergency physician to secure a higher level of specialized knowledge and skills.

3.3 Research Design and Data Collection

In order to gain insight into the dynamic processes of job crafting in practice, we conducted an ethnographic research in which we applied a combination of situated field techniques. Throughout our time in the field, we relied on observations, shadowing techniques and in-depth formal and informal interviews as data collection methods. This combination of research methods enabled us to analyze the current work of PAs, and to reflect upon the changes the PAs' job has undergone over the years. Respondents for both case studies were personally approached after close consultations with the participating institutions. Following the practice-oriented approach, and in order to remain open for the situated practices we studied, we did not select the respondents beforehand but decided upon the selection as the research evolved (e.g. Allen 2015).

We observed PAs during their daily activities and interviewed them about their work to analyze how they craft their job. At the neonatology department we observed and shadowed PAs for 15 days and/or nights during their work at the neonatal intensive care units (NICUs) (>120 h of observation).[6] PAs were shadowed while they provided and coordinated daily care to premature babies and their parents. We shadowed them while they were on call during night and weekend shifts, as they supervised nurses, during talks to parents and while they assisted medical specialists conducting certain clinical procedures. At the emergency ward we also observed and shadowed PAs during their day-to-day work (>60 h of observation).[7] Here, we observed how the PA treat patients with minor injuries, often picked up in and around the house, and major traumas caused by e.g. traffic accidents. In total, our empirical data comprise 180 h of observations and shadowing which were documented in elaborate transcripts.

In addition to the observations we conducted ten semi-structured 1-h interviews with key stakeholders such as managers, physicians, PAs and nurses. Interviews were both formal and informal. Formal interviews were semi-structured, leaving room to explore new relevant topics that were posted by the interviewees, shedding light on various aspects of job crafting such as motives, outcomes, challenges and successes. The interviews also offered the opportunity to reciprocally discuss initial findings with the interviewees. While interviews were useful to analyze views, meanings and related underlying developments, they are less useful for studying actual work practices (Schön 1983) as most work practices are so contextualized that people are seldom able to articulate "how they do what they do unless they are in the process of doing it" (Barley and Kunda 2001). Because of this we conducted numerous informal interviews during the times we shadowed the PAs in the course of their work. By means of this *real-time interviewing* on calm moments and in between activities, in which respondents were very willing to share ideas, we were able to collect in-depth insights into the job crafting practices of these new professionals.

Interviews were tape-recorded with permission of the interviewees and transcribed verbatim. During the observations, field notes were taken which were elaborated upon in detailed observation reports shortly after together with the informal interviews. Altogether this lead to thick descriptions (Geertz 1973) of everyday work practices of PAs.

---

[6] Observations and interviews were conducted by the first author between October 2013 and February 2014.

[7] Observations and interviews were conducted by research assistants under supervision of the authors between April and June 2014.

3.4 Data Analysis

We conducted a cross-case analysis, meaning that we did not aim to compare both case studies to reveal similarities and differences as such, but rather to come to an in-depth understanding of job crafting and place-making activities by continuously comparing both case studies (Sanders and Harrison 2008). Data generation and analysis proceeded concurrently after it started with a critical read of the transcripts to identify accounts on job crafting from the perspective of the PAs and with a focus on their interactions with other health care practitioners such as physicians, nurses and medical residents, and patients. We used the analysis method of abduction to identify themes and patterns (Lipscomb 2012). This implies that we coded our material inductively, yet constantly comparing codes with the concepts of job crafting and place. Further analysis consisted of a repeated process of interrogating the data with the use of theory. The abduction analysis approach (Tavory and Timmermans 2014) provided situational and theoretically-based generalizations of our findings. In the following Results section we provide the results of the analysis in a comprehensive manner and illustrate them by interview quotes and fragments from our field notes.

4 Results

PAs need to insert themselves into existing organizations and practices, carving out and creating a place next to other professionals such nurses, medical residents and medical specialists. In practice, PAs face all kinds of problems when they start working in a particular setting:

> When I'd just started I didn't receive a Christmas gift. The first month I didn't have a salary because nobody knew where I belonged. . .So I did not receive any salary, yet this has been solved now. . .[. . .]. . .Apparently this is very complicated. . .It's about all these details you run into (PA, neonatology department, 04-02-2014).

Although this interview fragment may describe a seemingly mundane issue, it shows that PAs are not fully incorporated in the organization the moment they take up their job. They still had to carve out their place. In this Results section we will analyze how the PAs managed to do so. We explain first how individual PAs craft their jobs by changing their set of tasks and their work relations after which we will go into how individuals craft their job by attaching meaning to it and by deriving an identity from it.

4.1 Crafting a Job Through Changing Tasks and Relations

At the neonatology department the PAs served at the wards, taking care of the premature infants under supervision of the neonatologists. PAs conducted tasks that were previously carried out by medical residents or interns, e.g. administrative work, making drip-lines, supervising MRIs and interpreting lab results. Although PAs received additional training and were legally allowed to perform these and other procedures, a precise set of their skills, competences and tasks was not given. In fact, PAs actively influenced their set of tasks, and how that changed over time:

> Gradually we were allowed to do things that are routine tasks for neonatologists. I mean making venous lines, administrating drugs through arteries, conducting ultrasounds of the brains and supervising transports. Those are examples of tasks that are certainly not delegated to medical residents, but that we are allowed to perform. So we developed from doing resident stuff to taking over tasks that formerly were reserved to the medical specialists (PA, neonatology department 28-01-2014).

4.1.1 Tasks

Following legal requirement, organizations must specify the tasks PAs are allowed to perform. We observed however, how these agreements changed over time, both formally and informally. The actual distribution of tasks and responsibilities gradually got shape. PAs needed time to gain experience in certain procedures in order to present themselves as intelligible, skilled and trustworthy practitioners. By gaining trust among the medical specialists, they were allowed to perform more complicated procedures, such as intubating newborns. Another important turnaround in the work of the PAs in neonatology was the shift to on-call work. At first, PAs only worked at day time. Yet, when PAs proved their skills, knowledge and trustworthiness they were also allowed to work in nightshifts:

> I really wanted to do nightshifts, because I mean...Being on call means you are challenged way more than at daytime. You have to make much more decisions on your own, and you learn a lot more and faster. During the day there's always someone around who gives you advice or suggestions about what to do. When you are here at night, you do not want to call a specialist for every trifle that comes up (PA, neonatology department 04-02-2014).

PAs considered the night shifts as a new phase and achievement in their professional development. It also meant a relief to the 24 h on-call duty of the neonatologists. Being able to work the nightshift, and doing so in a satisfying way, contributed to the PAs' position and status within the medical team.

Also in emergency care PAs gradually developed a more autonomous role in the course of time. Here, the work of PAs particularly focused on routine skills and tasks. PAs conduct physical examinations of self-referred patients (i.e. who visited the department on their own account) set diagnoses and take care of the minor traumas and relatively simple physical inconveniences. This means they mainly treat minor fractures, tendons, repositions and sutures. By deliberately focusing on what we may term *routine care*, they captured their own field of expertise. Within this field, PAs achieved a high level of independence and got recognized for it by the medical specialists:

> Partly because of their background as a nurse, PAs have more experience in dealing with things like sutures, tendons, and repositions. These tasks are really their thing. They perform those tasks often even better than we do (Emergency physician, emergency department, 14-05-2014).

PAs crafted their jobs in term of tasks and responsibilities by gaining competence in specific skills and procedures (the neonatology case), and by conducting specific sets of routine work (the emergency care case). This specific focus enabled them to change and develop their place in care provision at both departments. Other health care practitioners acted upon this. For instance, we observed how medical specialists consulted PAs in particular patient cases. This strengthened the PAs self-confidence, as they felt respected for the knowledge they possessed, and it contributed to their feeling of being "in place".

In addition to specialization, PAs crafted their jobs in terms of tasks in yet another way. Initially they worked in the clinic only, yet they gradually developed a role outside direct patient. They participated in several work groups and discussion forums on topics, varying from organization's policy on making drip lines, special nutrition, the use of needles, the development of new evacuation protocols and the expansion plans of the hospital. PAs contributed to these discussions from their own experience and perspective. PAs also started to take part in scientific research by co-authoring scientific publications and educating nurses and medical students on specific research and care related topics. This brief overview of non-care related tasks illustrates how the nature of PAs' tasks has shifted from care-oriented to more organization-oriented aspects of clinical work. Although opinions differed on these additional activities—some considered them a burden in time while others appreciated these additional responsibilities—PAs generally enjoyed them as they contributed to their feeling of belonging and doing meaningful work.

Notably, this *carving out* a place through specialization and expanding tasks exceeds the individual role. The PA who happened to be the first working at the neonatology department felt it to be her personal responsibility to make her work a success; not just for herself but also for the PA as an occupation in the hospital organization she was working:

> Yes, I mean that really felt as an enormous pressure. If I don't succeed in this than it [the function of the PA at this department] is over. That's why I worked so incredibly hard during my first year. I wanted to make sure that I wasn't the one who ruined the chances of the other PAs here. That was my biggest fear back then. I felt the pressure of the PAs that were not even here... (PA, neonatology department, 04-02-2014).

The PA in this extract explains how she felt that the work she does also influences the future position, role and work of other PAs. This indicates that carving out a place exceeds the individual. Crafting a job in term of tasks influences the place for PAs also in a more general sense as future PAs may profit, or suffer, from the work of the first PAs.

4.1.2 Relations

As outlined above, *carving out* a place does not happen automatically, or in a predictable and linear order. Just as the PAs had to insert themselves in the human resource system of the organization, as the example in the beginning of this section pointed out, they also had to give shape to their role within the clinical team. PAs had to develop a place within a team of vested occupational groups such as the medical specialists, nurses and medical residents. Hence, job crafting also entails the work that is needed to weave the PA in a (changing) professional context.

All PAs in our study had a nursing background and had worked as a nurse at the department prior to their PA training.[8] When qualified as a PA, they had to move out of the team of nurses and develop a new occupational identity. Although we expected this to cause some tension among the PAs and the nurses, the nurses mainly emphasized the benefits of working with a PA at the department. The fact that the nurses knew the PAs personally enabled them to have brief exchanges in case of minor questions or problems they faced in the course of their work. Nurses also appreciated the PAs because of their approachability. PAs, however, experienced more difficulties when they turned from a nursing role into a PA. Instead of being a colleague, they now had to accept a role as supervisor. This shift in hierarchical relations was not always visible in practice. We observed PAs doing nursing tasks when nurses had a busy shift. The inside knowledge of nursing work enabled the PAs to temporarily move into the nursing domain to *get the job done* at the ward (Allen 1997). Although PAs mainly worked in the medical domain, clear boundaries between them and the nurses did not seem to exist at these specific instances. However, at other times boundaries were made much more explicit. For example, a neonatology PA told a story about a conflict she had with a nurse who had accused her of not doing a certain procedure on a newborn patient. The PA had made clear to the nurse that the particular procedure was typically something nurses had to do, not a PA. This brief story reveals that also *not* doing something affects and defines the occupational role and position. In this case, it had made the PA realize that explicit boundaries between the nurses and the PAs are needed to establish an occupational place.

In addition to positioning themselves towards the nursing profession, PAs had to conduct work to position themselves in a medical team. Although PAs conduct medical work, they are seen as different. Medical specialists often referred to the differences in how they approach clinical problems compared to PAs:

> Let's assume there is a patient that has trouble breathing, what to do? In general, PAs learn a list of steps: first you increase breathing support, second you make an X-ray of the thorax, third you look for obstructions in the airway and if the problem is not solved by then, you call someone who knows what to do. . .Sometimes it's simply not enough to follow these steps, you need to have broader medical expertise to set the proper diagnosis (Neonatologist, neonatology department 27-02-2014).

The neonatologist quoted here points at the complexity and uncertainty that is sometimes inherent to clinical work. He doubts whether a PA is able to deal with the kind of clinical reasoning that goes beyond the medical textbook. The PAs in our

---

[8] This was also found in other research (Wallenburg et al. 2014b). This finding implies that PAs are not automatically introduced and embedded in health care practices. Work of individuals and trust between professionals is required for this to happen. It shows that it is important who the first new professionals at a specific department are and supports our argument about the need to carve out a place.

case studies acknowledged this as, according to them the most relevant question is how they can function with their *own* repertoire of knowledge and expertise. In emergency care, the distance between medical specialists and PAs was expanded through the introduction of the emergency physician, a new medical role in acute medicine. The emergency physicians, who were introduced to enhance quality and continuity of emergency medicine (Gaakeer et al. 2013; Schothorst et al. 2015), were positioned between the PAs and the medical specialists. We observed how the PAs and the emergency physicians functioned next to each other, an example:

> The results of a CT scan of a man with chest pain are available. It is still unclear what the man suffers from. The PA decides to ask the emergency physician for his view on this and explains that he performed all the regular examinations but that these show no deviations (Observation notes emergency department, 07-04-2014).

Emergency physician and PA closely worked together. We also observed how emergency physicians checked upon the PAs, supervising and controlling their work. The PAs, however, did not consider this hierarchy to be a problem as they pointed out that it also safeguarded their position as non-physicians; emergency patients are often vulnerable and clinically instable. Hence, practitioners constantly need to deal with situations in which there is high clinical uncertainty. Setting an initial diagnosis is of the utmost importance to determining what kind of care is needed, and hence puts a substantial responsibility on the shoulders of the PA. PAs argued that the emergency physicians added to their clinical knowledge and experience and, as such, secured the PAs' clinical role and responsibility. This interaction between the PAs and the emergency physician in emergency care illustrates that carving out a place is a highly interactive process and is about safeguarding a role just as much as it is about pursuing its expansion.

The interactions between PAs and medical specialists that we describe here raise questions about the boundaries of the place of the PAs. During our fieldwork, we observed that the boundaries between the work of the medical specialists and the PAs were often not that strict. It turned out to be not so easy to determine where these boundaries were precisely located, and also our respondents found it difficult to point them out to us. In the emergency care case, for example, we observed how emergency physicians allowed PAs to transfer patients to medical specialists sometimes when they were too busy to step in. A fragment from our observations at the neonatology department illustrates the duality of the professional and occupational boundaries, which seem not to be present at one point in time and rather strict at another:

> When asked after the boundaries between professionals, usually some general rules were formulated. At the neonatology department it was explained that it was a general rule that when an infant below 30 weeks of pregnancy was about to be born, a neonatologist had to be present to supervise childbirth. Yet, as one of the PA points out this was more a rule of thumb than strict regulation: "Sometimes we go alone, even below that threshold of 30 weeks. That is very much dependent on the situation at the department. Sometimes an extra pair of hands is needed and in the end it comes down to the question whether you are able to account for your actions. We always say if you are competent that you have the

> authority to do so, I believe that is even the way how the law is formulated. Where that ends? I don't know" (Observation notes neonatology department, 04-02-2014).

This fragment of our field notes shows that PAs provide care to the extent that they and other professionals feel they are competent, and that assessing this level of competence is rather context-specific. Individual practitioners must assess their own competences in judging whether they can or cannot perform a certain procedure or task. The examples above may suggest there are no clear decision criteria or rules. Yet at other times these rules appeared to be very strict and almost tangible. In emergency care, for example, we observed situations in which boundaries suddenly became very explicit:

> A patient at the emergency department is referred to the surgeon but a PA decides to take care of this patient right away without waiting for the permission of the surgeons. "I'll just check upon this patient and maybe I can put in a request for X-ray or run a blood test already. I know what to do and this saves time for the surgeons". After a while a trauma surgeon enters the room, looking highly agitated. He asks the patient to tell the story again as he does not fully trust upon the initial diagnosis set by the PA (Observation notes-, emergency department, 30-03-14).

What matters for the argument made here is, that the examples from both case studies show that boundaries between the work of medical specialists and the PAs do exist, yet they are not explicit all the time. Boundaries are situated and constructed in everyday practices. Moreover, they may differ between individual practitioners. For example, a neonatologist can be more willing to leave the care for a child to one PA and not to another. Boundaries may also shift over time as individual professionals develop themselves over time. As a consequence, PAs must continuously estimate what the boundaries of their acknowledged field of expertise are. The focus on the enactment of the boundaries and the uncertainty related to it, requires an embodied effort of PAs to continuously decide upon their room to act in order to avoid conflicts with medical specialists while also acting in the best interest of the patient. The fluidity of boundaries makes it also almost impossible to clearly define occupational boundaries in protocols. Instead, boundaries between professionals seem situational and constantly constructed and negotiated in daily practice (always becoming) by the individuals involved in a particular situations.

In this first part of the this section we have demonstrated how carving out a place involves job crafting in the sense that work activities and interactions are shaped, adapted and reshaped in the course of daily practice, and how in doing so, PAs relate themselves to other health care practitioners. After having discussed changes in the design of the job (tasks) and environment in which PA perform their job (relations), we now turn to the topics of meaning and identity which are also crucial to the understanding of how PAs carve out a place.

4.2 Crafting a Job Through Attaching Meaning and Deriving an Identity

Job crafting is also about giving meaning to the work that is conducted and deriving an identity from it (Berg et al. 2010). Individual professionals shape their identity by *coloring in* their work and relationships in a certain way, and as such construct meaning and professional identity claims.[9]

The way the PAs talked about their job shows that they frame the meaning of their work differently than when they worked as a nurse:

> Originally I'm a nurse and up to this moment I had to enroll in a new training or educational program every five years to keep updated and also motivated. But now, as a PA, I see everything changing in my day to day work. Partly because the care itself is changing. We now take care of babies born after only 24 weeks of pregnancy. I know we need some years to develop care to this specific category as not everything is crystallized out yet for this specific group. We don't know exactly what is best for them at the moment. Therefore, I need to keep developing myself in this job as I feel partly responsible for their care (PA, neonatology department 04-02-2014).

This PA explains that she feels responsible for something bigger than her own work. Her job has become more meaningful to her as she now sees herself as part of a professional challenge to develop care for a very specific and highly fragile group of patients. She considers her work as more challenging now as she does more than just performing a list of tasks. This illustrates that in order to understand how individual PAs attach meaning to their work, one has to look beyond the performance of tasks. One PA in the emergency case explained that what mattered most to him in developing his role were not the tasks but the additional responsibilities he has as a PA.

> Everyone expects more of a PA. I believe a PA has some sort of management function as we need to be in charge of a team of nurses [. . .] We are concerned with stuff that exceeds the execution of clearly defined tasks. With this job comes an additional responsibility to keep developing the care as well as yourself [. . .] as a PA you are, more than a nurse, busy with issues that stay on your to-do list the entire day (PA, emergency department 31-03-2014).

This interview extract illustrates that meaning is something that individuals attach to what they do in their work. In this example, the PA derives meaning and value from his job as a PA through the additional clinical and management responsibilities he has obtained, not through a list of tasks. The additional responsibilities that come with the job and the fact that they are entrusted to take these up are making the work as a PA meaningful.

Hence, crafting a job is about changing tasks, creating new relations with others and about taking up additional responsibilities, act accordingly and attach meaning

[9] In this chapter job crafting is analysed from the perspective of the PA. As a consequence we analyse how PAs themselves attach meaning to and make sense of their work and occupational identity, we did not directly analyzed how others see the identity of the PA.

to it. This last step is a rather personal turn-around that individual practitioners need to make. The above has shown how individual PAs find meaning in their role and how they convince others that they are capable of acting according to these new responsibilities. However, job crafting is also about trusting yourself as a PA to take up new responsibilities. You have to change your work identity, i.e. to change how you see yourself and how others see you as an individual within a team. These shifts not only determine how PAs attach meaning to their own work, but also how their occupational identity is constituted. At the neonatology department, for example, seeing patients back after a few years together with their (seemingly) proud parents reminded the PAs of what their work really is about. It made PAs feel a vital part of the medical team that made this possible. However, PAs also articulated that it was not an easy endeavor to frame a new role and identity:

> What I believe is complex is that you have to know what is going on with all of the patients and be able to act immediately when required. You are responsible for 3 times 8 intensive care beds, 8 high-care patients, 15 medium care patients, and for the admission of new babies from the midwifery. It is complex to oversee that all and to make the right decisions on your own…I really felt this responsibility as a burden in the beginning; it takes a lot of your energy and it isn't about a procedure or technical skill. Those you can learn if you practice enough, dealing with the increased responsibility and making medical decisions about treatment plans is something you need to make part of your own…of yourself… [..]…The difficult cases remind me of this difficult responsibility (PA, neonatology department 28-01-2014).

Individual PAs find meaning in additional responsibilities and, as part of this process, create a new occupational identity. Creating this new identity at the workplace is not something PAs have to do all by themselves, as other PAs in the organization face similar challenges. We observed how carving out a place also involves collective work, although this causes new tensions to arise. Collective identity work done by a group of PAs may emphasize the need to clearly define what kind of tasks and responsibilities are being embraced and where responsibilities stop:

> One of the PAs describes a situation in which he discovered that what PAs do at his neonatology department is not generally accepted among PAs. In his role as a contact person for the parents of patients, he supervises situations in which babies pass away. During a meeting with PAs from other hospitals he asked a detailed question about one of the forms he has to fill out in such situations. The other PA were stunned by the question and responded immediately by advising him that that he, as a PA, should keep himself out of such situations because this is not something a PA should do (Observation notes, neonatology department, 04-02-2014).

This brief episode reflects two quite contrasting issues. First, it shows the variety in the ways the role of the PAs is enacted in organizations. Apparently, the exact role of a PA is situated and thus differs across hospital organizations. Second, it reveals that a professional place transcends the own work place as there is a common idea or belief what a PA should and should not do. This means that the professional identity exceeds the situated practice of a single department or hospital which becomes clear when PAs interact with others from other departments and organizations.

Carving out a place potentially exceeds the own organization, although the PAs in our study claimed they focus mainly on what they could achieve in their own work and at their own departments. We, however, did observe examples of collective job crafting as well. PAs indicated that collective action served their interest best. For example in discussions about reimbursement for additional vocational training and in salary negotiations with the hospital management, the PAs explained that they were only able to arrange this in their favor when they joined efforts with PAs from other departments. In neonatology, for example, PAs took the initiative in founding an internal professional association for PAs to support them in these efforts. The foundation was considered very useful, if not for the actual effects of changing salary and education, then for 'knowing that as a PA you are not alone in your struggles'. The advantages of collective job crafting on the one hand, and the individual privileges some PA experience on the other, reflect a certain tension between individual and collective forms of job crafting in practice.

As places are *endlessly made* (Creswell 2004) crafting a job does never come to a definite end. In both case studies it was fiercely debated how the PA's role should be developed further in the (near) future. It was for example discussed whether it would be a good idea to let the PAs specialize in a certain sub-field as a next step in their development. During the negotiations about further role development, another tension came to the fore: the tension between *pioneering* and *specifying*. On the one hand, PAs felt the desire to develop clear-cut descriptions of what their job is about so that their carefully carved out place cannot easily be disrupted. However, on the other hand they did not want to pinpoint their work and position themselves to allow for further development. PAs thus wanted to remain a pioneer while they also wished for more clarity and protection of their role. They argued that having a list of competences protected them from being pushed to their limits as the precisely defined qualifications and tasks gave them something to hold on to in negotiations about what (not) to do in practice.

Both the desire to protect the position of the PAs and the desire to develop this position further illustrate that carving out a place for new professionals involves *tinkering* with pioneering and specifying. Being flexible and creative enables to expand work space, yet specifying tasks, competences and qualifications enables protection of the carved out place from disruption and overload. PAs, as a new occupation, need to pursue both these, actually conflicting, purposes to establish certain boundaries but must also create flexibility within these boundaries to leave room for a more fluid or even *boundaryless* development.

5 Conclusions

Hospitals are staffed by an increasing variation of health care practitioners, and boundaries between them are fading. In this chapter we have demonstrated how a new occupation, the PA, carves out a place in a health care arena with vested professionals. In contrast to traditional literature on new professionals that stresses the battle for occupational domains and the obduracy of vested professional jurisdictions, we have shown how PAs carve out their place in practice through specializing themselves in, and contributing to, particular parts of health service provision. PAs develop their own expertise and routines in particular clinical tasks that are of added value to both the quality of care and to the existing skillsets of medical specialists and nurses. For example, according to our study, PAs in neonatology have developed themselves in carrying out specific medical procedures such as intubating infants, and gradually became more competent in this particular, yet crucial, procedure than the neonatologists. This made that they, rather than specialists, perform the intubations. The emergency PAs, in turn, focused on patients suffering from minor traumas and gradually became experts with newly developed routines in treating this group of patients, something that is also recognized and appreciated by the medical specialists.

As a new occupation the PAs thus had to position themselves in relation to other professionals and had to take on a new identity. We have shown that PAs had to let go of their former nurse identity in creating a new role as supervisor of the nurses. PAs moved in and out the nursing domain depending on their valuation of the situation at hand; they sometimes took over nurses' tasks to relief their work pressure while at other times they explicitly dissociated themselves from them by pointing out the differences in competence and hierarchy between them. In addition to these tasks and relations, PAs carved out a place through attaching new meanings to their expertise and acknowledged set of skills. Becoming an inherent part of the medical team made them feel more closely related to the care that was provided and PAs increasingly considered it as their personal responsibility to clinically contribute to the development of care for specific groups of patients. In this very process PAs make a personal turnaround as they need to believe that they are capable of contributing to clinical care and need to be acknowledged for this by other professionals. Carving out a place is thus also about relating oneself to others in a meaningful way and thereby creating and defining a new socially accepted work identity. It is this new identity that turns the PA into an intrinsic part of the medical team.

PAs not only craft their own job in these processes; they also carve out a place for the occupation of a PA in general. The first PAs acted as pioneers as their work also determined how professionals from other departments and organizations valued the PA's role. This entailed both individual and collective work. Sometimes PAs within a single organization joined efforts in negotiating about their work conditions such as salary or additional training opportunities. Yet, what we have described is just a snapshot of the place of the PA. The place of the PA as a new occupation is and never will be fixed as it is always becoming. In interaction with others, PAs will continue to develop this place further. We have shown here that it requires a lot of work to weave in a new occupation into the changing socio-fabric of daily life in health care practice.

Our analysis has revealed some interesting insights into the creation and role of professional boundaries, which—we believe—is also productive to the theoretical conceptualization of the notion of the boundaryless hospital. Carving out a place is both about creating and crossing boundaries. The boundaries of a place for a new occupation remain implicit, invisible or permeable most of the time and as such allow for easy collaboration and smooth processes of health care delivery in situated practices. At specific moments boundaries hamper the actual execution of tasks. Yet, at other times these boundaries become rather explicit, fixed and rigid and actually help to get the work done as they allow for smooth interdisciplinary work. At these instances boundaries seem to delineate a space that can be protected and that helps to present oneself as an authority. The moment that boundaries become explicit is, as our study has illustrated, not case-specific but rather situational. It depends on the (perceived) competences of a PA, the circumstances at hand (e.g. whether it is busy at the ward or not), the PA's eagerness and self-confidence, the willingness of an individual physician to leave a patient to a PA as well as on individual actions, ambitions and beliefs of and trust between those involved. The difference between individuals also accentuates the ambivalence of boundaries as there is a constant tension between what an individual PA and the group of PAs is allowed to do. This implies that it may be that one experienced PA is allowed in a specific situation to conduct a certain procedure while it is not incorporated in standard policy that is valid for all PAs. We argue that boundaries are the outcomes of mundane actions and interactions between professionals; they are blurred social objects that are malleable to some extent (Oldenhof et al. 2015). Always thought of as important to understand how professionals develop over time, professional boundaries are neither fixed nor clearly defined but highly situational and thus specific for a certain location, time and the present actors.

6 Discussion

The findings in this chapter add to both theory and practice. Our study contributes to theory on job crafting by providing descriptions of how PAs, as professionals who fulfil a new occupation, succeeded in carving out a place in particular health care settings. As the job of new professionals has not been settled yet, we were able to analyze not only how individuals actively *change* their job—suggesting that there is an established *job* already as is common in the majority of studies on job crafting, but also how they actively shape a new job and the meaning of it by creating boundaries.

We could have included the role and perceptions of other actors such as the residents, nurses and medical specialists, who also constantly craft their own job in relation to that of the PA. In this chapter we described the interactions with these professionals from the perspective of the PAs. However, as place making is a collective process, future research could focus on these interactions from the perspective of other actor's and their behavior. Another direction, which we touched upon but which could be used for further exploration, is the relationship between the micro job crafting processes in practice that we described and the macro, societal and institutional context in which these processes are embedded.

This may add additional insights to the possible contribution of new occupations to care delivery in general.

Our findings on how new professionals carve out a place have important implications for both policy and practice on the development of new occupations. First, continuously negotiated boundaries that are sometimes explicit and sometimes seemingly non-existent render it difficult to account for the outcomes of care provision as it is not always clear who is doing what exactly in the course of daily practice. Second, our results indicate that workforce or human resource management should be organized in a situated manner as we have demonstrated how professional occupations are enacted in practice. As both flexibility and rigidity are desirable and undesirable at the same time, new professional occupations are determined by the meaning people assign to it. This makes it relevant for managers to focus on the management of this meaning in a way that goes beyond influencing conditions that merely cultivate the diffusion of clear-cut roles. The way new professional roles arise out of the interweaving of multiple processes, as a result of the continuous work of developing, adapting, implementing and translating job boundaries, asks for a context-specific discussion about how individuals and groups of actors contribute to the development of their profession, especially in a general movement towards a more *boundaryless organization*.

References

Abbott A (1988) The system of professions: an essay on the division of expert labor. The University of Chicago Press, Chicago

Ainsworth S, Grant D, Iedema R (2009) 'Keeping things moving': space and the construction of middle management identity in a post-NPM organization. Discourse Commun 3:5

Allen D (1997) The nursing-medical boundary: a negotiated order? Sociol Health Illn 19 (4):498–520

Allen D (2015) The invisible work of nurses. Hospitals, organisation and healthcare. Routledge, London

Andrews GJ, Moon G (2005) Space, place, and the evidence base: part II—rereading nursing environment through geographical research. Worldviews Evid-Based Nurs 2(3):142–156

Ashforth BE, Mael F (1989) Social identity theory and organization. Acad Manag Rev 14:20–39

Barley SR, Kunda G (2001) Bringing work back in. Organ Sci 12(1):76–95

Berg JM, Wrzesniewski A, Dutton JE (2010) Perceiving and responding to challenges in job crafting at different ranks: when proactivity requires adaptivity. J Organ Behav 31:158–186

Blumer H (1966) Sociological implications of the thought of George Herbert Mead. Am J Sociol 71(5):535–544

Blumer H (1969) Symbolic interactionism: perspective and method. Prentice Hall, Englewood Cliffs, NJ

Campion MA, McClelland CL (1993) Follow-up and extension of the interdisciplinary costs and benefits of enlarged jobs. J Appl Psychol 78:339–351

Centellas KM, Smardon RE, Fifield S (2014) Calibrating translational cancer research: collaboration without consensus in interdisciplinary laboratory meetings. Sci Technol Hum Values 39 (3):311–333

Clegg S, Kornberger M, Pitsis T (2011) Managing and organizations: an introduction to theory and practice. Sage, London

Creswell T (2004) Place: a short introduction. Blackwell, Oxford
Currie G, Lockett A, Finn F et al (2012) Institutional work to maintain professional power: recreating the model of medical professionalism. Organ Stud 33:937–962
Dubois CA, Singh D (2009) From staff-mix to skill-mix and beyond: towards a systemic approach to health workforce management. Hum Resour Health 7(87):1–19
Gaakeer MI, Van den Brand CL, Bracey A, Van Lieshout JM, Patka P (2013) Emergency medicine training in the Netherlands, essential changes needed. Int J Emerg Med 6(19)
Geertz C (1973) The interpretation of cultures. Basic Books, New York
Gieryn TF (2000) A space for place in sociology. Annu Rev Sociol 26:463–496
Hackman JR, Lawler EE (1971) Employee reactions to job characteristics. J Appl Psychol 55 (3):259
Hackman JR, Oldham GR (1976) Motivation through the design of work: test of a theory. Organ Behav Human Perform 16(2):250–279
Hackman JR, Oldham GR (1980) Work redesign. Addison-Wesley, Reading, MA
Hughes EC (1971a) The sociological eye: selected papers. Transaction, Chicago
Hughes EC (1971b) Going concerns: the study of American institutions. Sociol Eye 1957:52–64
Ilgen DR, Hollenbeck JR (1992) The structure of work: job design and roles. In: Dunette M, Hough L (eds) Handbook of industrial and organizational psychology. Consulting Psychologists Press, Palo Alto, CA, pp 165–207
Leana C, Appelbaum E, Sheychuk I (2009) Work process and quality of care in early childhood education: the role of job crafting. Acad Manag J 52(6):1169–1192
Lipscomb M (2012) Abductive reasoning and qualitative research. Nurs Philos 13(4):244–256
Mesman J (2009) The geography of patient safety: a topical analysis of sterility. Soc Sci Med 69:1705–1712
Miner AS (1987) Idiosyncratic jobs in formalized organizations. Adm Sci Q 32:327–351
Oldenhof L, Postma J, Bal R (2015) Re-placing care: governing healthcare through spatial arrangements. In: Ferlie E, Montgomery K, Pedersen AR (eds) Oxford handbook of health care management. Oxford University Press, Oxford (in print)
Pratt M, Rockmann KW, Kaufmann JB (2006) Constructing professional identity: the work of role and identity learning cycles in the customization of identity among medical residents. Acad Manag J 49:235–262
Sanders T, Harrison S (2008) Professional legitimacy claims in the multidisciplinary workplace: the case of heart failure care. Sociol Health Illn 30(2):289–308
Schön DA (1983) The reflective practitioner: how professionals think in action, vol 5126. Basic Books, New York
Strauss AL (1993) Work and the division of labor. Sociol Q 26(1):1–19
Strauss AL, Fagerhaugh S, Suczek B, Wiener C (1985) Social organization of medical work. Transaction, New Brunswick
Suddaby R, Viale T (2011) Professional and field-level change: institutional work and the professional project. Curr Sociol 59:423
Tavory I, Timmermans S (2014) Abductive analysis. Theorizing qualitative research. The University of Chicago Press, Chicago
Tuan YF (1977) Space and place: the perspective of experience. University of Minnesota Press, Minneapolis
van Schothorst J, van den Brand CL, Gaakeer MI, Wallenburg I (2015) The role of emergency physicians in the institutionalization of emergency medicine. Eur J Emerg Med. doi:10.1097/MEJ.0000000000000346. http://journals.lww.com/euro-emergencymed/Abstract/publishahead/The_role_of_emergency_physicians_in_the.99360.aspx. Accessed 20 Dec 2015. Published online ahead of print November 2015
Wallenburg I, Tsiachristas A, De Bont A (2014a). New professional roles and health workforce skill mix in Europe. Deliverable 2.1 Munros Project. Erasmus University Rotterdam, January 2014

Wallenburg I, Janssen M, De Bont A (2014b) Taakherschikking in de zorg. Een praktijkonderzoek naar nieuwe professionele rollen in de Nederlandse gezondheidszorg. iBMG, Erasmus Universiteit Rotterdam, Rotterdam

Wrzesniewski A, Dutton JE (2001) Crafting a job: revisioning employees as active crafters of their work. Acad Manag Rev 26(2):179–201

Maarten Janssen holds a Master's degree in Science & Innovation management from Utrecht University. He is currently working as a Ph.D.-student at the institute of Health Policy & Management of the Erasmus University Rotterdam. His research combines different projects in which he focusses on the governance of health care innovation processes. Recent research projects include the work on new professional roles and the qualitative evaluation of innovation programs in long-term and secondary care.

Iris Wallenburg has a nursing background and studied health care sciences at the Erasmus University in Rotterdam. She finished her Ph.D. on medical training reform in 2012 at the VU University Amsterdam. Currently she works as Assistant Professor of Healthcare Governance at the institute of Health Policy & Management of the Erasmus University Rotterdam. Her research and teaching mainly focuses upon the development of professionals within health care organizations. Recent research projects include an international comparative analysis of new professional roles in Europe and the replacement of long-term care practices.

Antoinette de Bont studied health sciences at Maastricht University. She is an Associated Professor in Medical Sociology at the Erasmus University Rotterdam and worked as a Harkness fellow at Kaiser Permanente, an integrated care organization in the United States, in 2010. Her research focuses upon how health care professionals reshape their role in confrontation with new policy measures and new requirements set by their organizations. Other topics she studies include professional development, integrated care, patient safety and health care governance.

Personalized Medicine Challenges the Health Care System

Manfred Dietel

Abstract

Biomedicine has made incredible progress during the last decade offering totally new possibilities to treat various types of diseases, in particular cancer. Clinically relevant genomic analyses today are feasible within days and will be possible within hours in some years. While the costs of molecular diagnostics are decreasing the treatment procedures will remain extremely costly for years. Since the number of molecular-based intervention will increase dramatically the overall burden of the health care system will become a substantial challenge. All partners involved therein have to recognize the facts, discuss the challenges and find solutions by tearing down existing boundaries, otherwise a strain on or even a collapse of the system cannot be excluded. The reproach 'Only the rich survive' has to be avoided to ensure the balance and harmony of the social system.

Keywords

Health care insurances • Companion diagnostics • Oncology • Public institutions • Ministry of health • Personalized medicine • Cancer • Targeting drugs

1 Introduction

Under the heading of *personalized medicine* we understand the intention to diagnose and treat patients more precisely adapted to their individual needs. Among others this means that an intensive characterization of the patient, and often more

M. Dietel (✉)
Institute of Pathology, Charité Universitätsmedizin Berlin, Chariteplatz 1, 10117 Berlin, Germany

Humboldt Universität zu Berlin, Berlin, Germany
e-mail: manfred.dietel@charite.de

H. Albach et al. (eds.), *Boundaryless Hospital*, DOI 10.1007/978-3-662-49012-9_8

important of her/his specific disease becomes a key issue. Personalized medicine is relevant in radiology, radiation and nuclear medicine, cardiology, infectious diseases, diabetes, surgery, transplantation et cetera. The methods to do so vary and cover a broad spectrum of diagnostic measures, e.g. new imaging techniques; complex tissue based analyses, high through-put molecular assays etc., as well as a number of highly potent new treatment options. One of the various medical fields with great public relevance, fundamental clinical challenges and tremendous financial consequences is diagnostics and treatment of cancer (Dietel et al. 2013). This will be the major topic of this contribution.

2 Definition/Terminology

A prerequisite of personalized medicine is the capability to predict pre-therapeutically the response of individual tumors to certain (targeted) drugs. For this prediction reliable and reproducible biomarker and predictive assays are required (companion diagnostics).

Only for clarification, there are several terms around, which more or less mean similar issues, i.e. personalized medicine—individualized medicine—precision medicine—genomic medicine—stratifying medicine—P4 medicine (predictive, preventive, personalized, participatory) et cetera.

3 Oncology on Focus

A field of major importance in public health care systems and in particular in personalized medicine refers to oncology. Why oncology? Since decades the improvements in the diagnostic procedures to detect and characterize malignant tumors has been impressive, the improvements in the treatment of patients, however, was rather limited. Classical chemotherapy using more or less unspecific toxic agents was and is still a relevant column of cancer therapy; however, the possibility to develop new cytotoxic chemicals to gain more efficiency with less toxicity appears to be very limited. 2006 in a non-public hearing the Food and Drug Administration (FDA) stated that it will become very difficult in the future to get "new" anti-cancer drugs approved, which are based on the classical non-specific approach. This situation creates high pressure to intensify research activities with the aim to develop more specific and less toxic anti-cancer substances, so called targeted drugs. These drugs should be accompanied by a specific diagnostic procedure, so called predictive molecular pathology or companion diagnostics, to predict pre-therapeutically the efficacy and specifics of the drug-tumor interaction.

4 Companion Diagnostics

Molecular pathology is a rapidly growing field gaining center stage in the clinical management of tumors and the development of new anti-cancer drugs. To read a patients' tissue as "deeply" as possible and to obtain combined information on morphological, genetic, proteomic as well as epigenetic grounds has become the upcoming task of anatomic pathology. The aims are to provide

- clinicians with predictive information on the behavior of malignant tumors, e.g. drug response, prognosis and potential to metastasize and
- defined characteristics of a given tumor (over-expression of proteins, genetic alterations etc.) relevant for clinical drug selection regarding the individual patient.
- Future biomarker research on human tissue will define the basis for the development of new targeted drugs by research and the pharmacy industry.
- In addition, targeted therapy approaches based on molecular characteristics of the individual tumors are a central element for the structuring of national and international health care systems, balancing economical and medical needs.

During the last decade surgical pathology has adapted several molecular methods to scientific and diagnostic challenges, i.e. polymerase chain reaction and its multiple variants, comparative genomic hybridization, sequencing, DNA/RNA-array technology, methylation analyses etc. all on formalin-fixed paraffin-embedded tissue. This approach is capable of both identifying novel genes associated with disease development and clustering of genes predicting clinical outcome. All efforts are directed at improving tissue-based diagnoses and predictive relevance of molecular pathology of cancer.

5 Targeting Drugs

Application of new targeted compounds, e.g. therapeutic antibodies or kinase inhibitors, has revealed promising results in the clinics. However, the targeted drugs are active only in a limited number of tumors which express the target molecules. Classical examples are Her2/trastuzumab in breast cancer (BC), KRAS wild type colon/panitumumab (Vectibix®) or cetuximab (Erbitux®) and EGFR-mutated non-small cell lung cancer (NSCLC) being responsive to gefitinib (Tarceva®) and erlotinib (Iressa®), see the following list for details.

Predictive tissue-based biomarkers for targeted therapies—FDA/EMA-approved drugs associated with eligibility tests* (selection):

- Trastuzumab → metastatic breast cancer, overexpression/amplification of *HER-2*
- Cetuximab → metastatic colorectal cancer, overexpressing EGFR/wild-type *KRAS*
- Panitumumab → colorectal cancer with wild-type *KRAS* (mutation excluded)
- Gefitinib → non-small cell lung cancer with mutated *EGFR*
- Erlotinib → non-small cell lung cancer with mutated *EGFR*
- Crizotinib → non-small cell lung cancer with mutated EML4-ALK
- Nimotuzumab → metastatic colorectal cancer (still experimental)
- Lapatinib → metastatic breast cancer overexpression *HER-2/neu*
- Vemurafenib (PX4032) → malignant melanoma with mutated B-RAF
- Imatinib → CML, *bcr/abl*–positive (activated PK)
- Imatinib → GIST with activated c-kit receptor tyrosine kinase/CD117, exon 9 mut
- Rituximab (+CHOP), Y90-Ibritumomab, I131-Tositumomab → NHLymphoma with CD20
- Olaparib → platinum-sensitive, relapsed high grade serous epithelial ovarian, fallopian tube and primary peritoneal carcinomas with mutated BRCA1/2
- Gemtuzumab-Ozogamicin → AML with CD33 (>60 year.), mal. melanoma
- Tamoxifen ± chemo → ER+/HER2—breast cancer, mutation pattern—multigene assays

6 Four Clinical Examples

To exemplify and illustrate the potency and the problems in the field of personalized onco-therapy four examples of different tumor entities are given. This is of course only a selection; nevertheless it demonstrates the principles of the personalized medicine approach in oncology.

6.1 Colo-Rectal Cancer

Classical chemotherapy has certainly a great value in the treatment of Colo-Rectal Cancer (CRC). However, a substantial improvement will not be expected by the application of any kind of conventional chemotherapeutical drugs or their combinations. Thus, many researchers of universities, research labs and pharma industry jointly have been working very hard to develop and evaluate new strategies to fight CRC. Two therapeutic antibodies have been characterized to attack specifically surface proteins (receptors) of malignant CRC cells, i.e. Cetuximab and Panitumumab, both therapeutical antibodies. Under well-defined conditions both are now approved for metastatic colorectal cancer. A prerequisite to give the drugs is the characterization of the tumor regarding its so called RAS mutation status. This means due to clinical studies and to the pathophysiological mechanisms of action the tumors should not carry a RAS mutation but must wild-type RAS. The molecular analyses are exclusively tissue-based, shall be performed by an experienced molecular pathology laboratory and should be done under quality controlled conditions.

If a patient is suffering from CRC proven by molecular pathology as RAS wild type, only then the patient should receive one of the drugs. If this analysis is not performed health care insurances will not reimburse the cost of the treatment, which are indeed relatively high, approx. EUR 20–30,000.

6.2 Non-small Cell Lung Cancer

Lung cancer is one of the deadliest malignancies. In the status of a metastasized disease—approx. 70–80 % show metastases at time of diagnosis—the armamentarium of treatment was often limited to chemotherapy. Treatment approaches using tyrosine-kinase inhibitors (TKI) expanded the spectrum of anti-cancer measures and should be considered, if certain mutations can be proven for the individual case.

At present there are three TKIs approved by the FDA and the European Medical Agency. However, a prerequisite to treat patients with one of these drugs is to proof a mutation in the tumor-related EGFR gene or ALK gene, only then it is adequate to apply the drug to the patient (Fig. 1). The background of this decision lies in the scientifically proven connection that only if the EGFR gene shows an activating mutation or the ALK gene shows a translocation, e.g. an inversion, the drug will be effective.

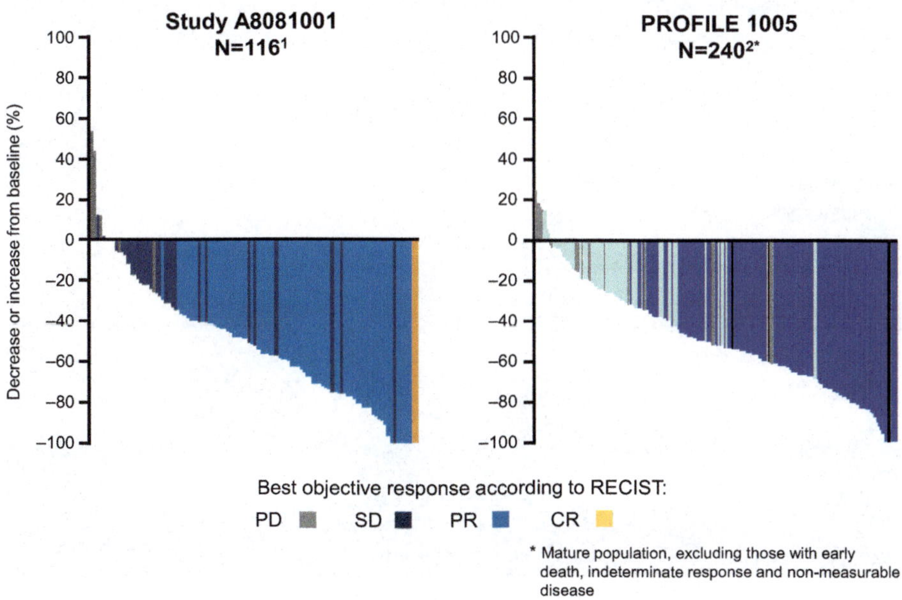

Fig. 1 Two clinical studies on the efficacy of an ALK inhibitor in ALK mutated non-small cell lung cancer showed an overwhelming reduction of tumor size and tumor burden as shown by the cases under the 0-line (This holds true only for ALK-mutated tumors) (Camidge et al. 2012; Kim et al. 2012)

6.3 Malignant Melanoma

Metastasized malignant melanomas represent a tumor type which can hardly be treated using classical approaches. Neither chemotherapy nor radiation or any other treatment have shown relevant efficacy. The introduction of new targeted drugs, i.e. tyrosine kinase inhibitors, has changed the scenario at least for a subgroup of patients showing up with a particular genetic alteration, i.e. a mutation in the BRAF gene.

50 % of all malignant melanomas exhibit a BRAF mutation, which has been shown to be druggable or actionable; this means there is a specific substance—the BRAF inhibitor vemurafenib—that appears to be very active in specifically attacking and inactivating mutated BRAF molecules in cells of a malignant melanoma (Fig. 2). Clinical studies presented by a number of research groups (Queirolo et al. 2015) have been very convincing, thus underlying the relevance of targeting drugs and personalized medicine in oncology.

In malignant melanoma we are facing a particular possibility, i.e. the combined application of targeting drugs. In addition to the BRAF inhibitor it makes sense to apply a MEK inhibitor which is active in the same pathway and which intensifies the efficacy of the treatment (Fig. 3) by almost doubling the overall survival of the patients treated.

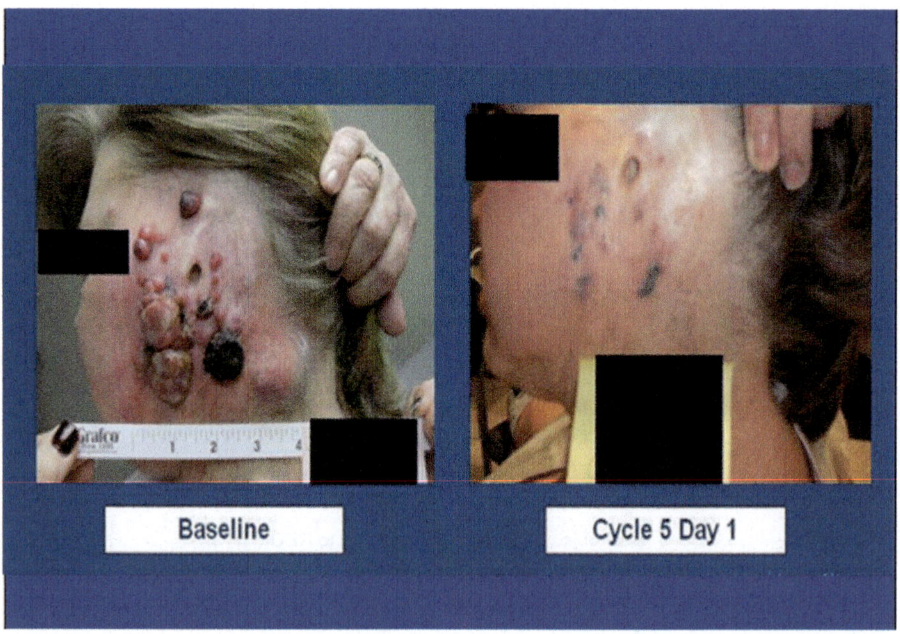

Fig. 2 Young woman suffering from metastasized malignant melanoma. The tumor showed a BRAF mutation detected in the tumor tissue by molecular pathology. Treatment with a BRAF inhibitor (Vemurafenib) leads to a dramatic reduction of tumor burden

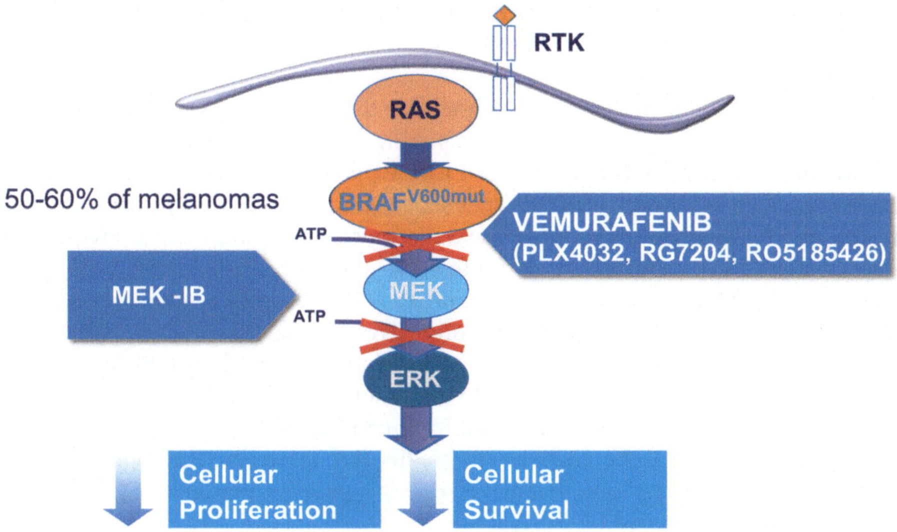

Fig. 3 In malignant melanoma a particular situation is given, i.e. the combined application of targeting drugs. In addition to the BRAF inhibitor Vemurafenib a MEK inhibitor can be applied which is active in the same pathway and intensifies the efficacy of the treatment; overall survival increased from 5.5 months with monotherapy to 9.9 months with combinational targeted therapy (Flaherty et al. 2012)

6.4 Breast Cancer

Malignant neoplasm of the breast is a frequent disease in elderly women. Since decades there have been efforts to develop personalized medicine for these patients. The first success was to detect the hormone status (estrogen receptor and progesterone receptor) in the tumor tissue and to treat BC patients accordingly with an anti-hormone drug, most often Tamoxifen. The next step was to analyze the tumor tissue also for a membrane bound receptor protein, i.e. HER-2. This was and still is the basis of a treatment with the therapeutical antibody Herceptin.

In recent years, multigene expression assays for cancer prognosis and partly prediction have become available providing additional information to standard histopathological and immunohistochemical techniques supporting clinicians in treatment decisions. The relevance of these assays is based on a particular clinical question: *Which patient with ER+ and Her2 neg. breast carcinoma will show a good prognosis when treated by endocrine therapy only?* This situation is important for ca. 60–70 % of all BC. Without going too much into details it can be summarized that multigene assays can answer the above stated question with a predictive accuracy and high clinical relevance. In particular the Europe-based EndoPredict® assay shows high predictive relevance and solid robustness in stratifying patients into low risk versus high risk of developing metastases within 10 years. This will help clinicians and patients to find the adequate way of individual treatment (Dubsky et al. 2013).

7 How and Why Personalized Medicine Challenges the Health Care System

After the disclosure of the human genome an intellectual and technical revolution took place. Since the matter is relatively complicated and does not suit very well to the lay-media it was not as much noticed by the public as it should have been. Due to the extraordinary progress in different sequencing techniques the understanding of genomic functions and interactions and the capability to analyze and investigate genetic alterations exploded in an up-to now unknown way. In the late 1990s sequencing the human genome cost approx. US$200 million and took several years. Today one can do this within some days for less than EUR 1000. This massive improvement opens the possibility to bring the technology and the increasing knowledge into daily clinical work to the benefit of the patients, for example by implementing targeting drugs in personalized medicine.

One does not have to be visionary to predict that these activities will certainly continue in order to perform intensive research on new personalized treatment options. This is underlined by the fact that the

- governmental support for universities and academic centers as well as several foundations is relatively intensive in US and Europe (the situation is totally different in underdeveloped countries of Africa and partly Asia) and
- Big Pharma spends billions in research and development of new drugs and clinical studies (ca. EUR 2 billion per substance) and marketing.

That this engagement is a rational investment is underlined by basic epidemiological data:

- On average the Western population will become older in the next decades due to better life conditions, more effective treatment options for cardio-vascular and infectious diseases as well as other protective influences, e.g. prevention programs, reduction of air pollution, et cetera.
- Following the WHO perspectives (World Health Organization 2015) in 2035 almost 50 % of the Western population will fall ill with cancer.
- Consequently, the demand for effective therapy will increase further.

The problematic consequences for national health care system is obvious since

- one cycle of target therapy (only the drugs) today costs approx. EUR 20–30,000 (e.g. at Charité Berlin there is a case which up to now costs EUR 350,000)
- a dramatic augmentation of expenditures will follow, thus
- personalized oncology may become a severe strain on financial resources.

Nevertheless intensive basic, translational and clinical research on new possibilities of fighting cancer will continue and will create organizational, intellectual and financial challenges to the currently health care system in Germany, which is far away of being flexible.

8 What Is Necessary to Implement Personalized Tumor Medicine?

The clinical examples demonstrate the necessity of pushing the field of personalized medicine forward. However, in the German health care system there are a number of boundaries, which currently hinder its adequate and fast implementation.

The boundaries actually existing today are

- *clinical* boundaries or competition between diagnostic institutions, clinical departments and research units within a hospital due to budget restrictions, loss or gain of importance, department-related egoism (figures matter) etc.
- *regional* boundaries between hospitals in a city or a region, in particular between university and non-university hospitals regarding patients due to financial reasons,
- *institutional* boundaries between clinical interests and administrative interests as well as insurances and the Ministry of Health.

8.1 How to Overcome Clinical Boundaries

To tear down clinical boundaries a careful analysis of the type of boundary and the aim of its reduction appears to be the crucial prerequisite. It must be consented by all participating sites that the aim above all others is better treatment with prolonged progression free survival and overall survival accompanied by less side effects. The second wanted goal is to enable better research in this field, which depends on transparent multidisciplinary interactions and is often linked to controlled access to high number of patients, reliable clinical follow-up data etc.

That means for introducing personalized medicine in daily practice it is essential to tear down classical boundaries between institutes, departments, clinics and hospitals and to establish fair and transparent interdisciplinary teams, which are constantly working together. A multidisciplinary unit to organize interdisciplinary cooperation in order to optimize complex cancer treatments is essential.

For this approach a new thinking must be initiated and in many places it is already on the way of being established, e.g. by creating competent interdisciplinary centers. The process of re-organization can be started as follows:

- The first step is to bring together the leading staff,
- to discuss and if possible to convince the leading staff of the expected win-win situation,
- to join the budgets and to clarify responsibilities,

- to announce investments in new technologies such as molecular analytics, tele-radiology, tele-pathology, video-conferencing, joint information systems etc. and
- to make this investment depending on the success of the team.
- In addition, new organizational structures and logistic improvements of hospitals are a prerequisite for personalized medicine, e.g. as it is the case with Comprehensive Cancer Centers (CCC). These tumor centers are necessary to thoroughly analyze the complex data related to each individual case. This is one of the strongly supported and meanwhile very successful programs of the German Cancer Society (DKG). However it has to be emphasized that neither the additional logistic efforts nor the additional activities performed by the physicians, nurses, IT personnel etc. are adequately reimbursed by the system. A point which needs to be clarified.

It is often helpful to use external advice for reshaping classical structures and for establishing novel decision trees.

8.2 How to Overcome Regional Boundaries

Competition between hospitals in a city or a region or between the responsible agencies is in general also in the health care system a necessary situation; however this situation becomes problematic, when financial aspects start to dominate clinical and organizational decisions. This fact gains relevance in personalized onco-medicine since the modern ways of treatment (examples see above) are of course more expensive and need much more medical staff and organizational efforts, e.g. for molecular pathologists, molecular biologists, bio-statisticians, oncologists experienced in targeted therapy. A major point is the adequate interpretation of the genetic data and results, which has to be done in a multidisciplinary tumor board (MDT board), which should be part of (comprehensive) cancer centers. Meanwhile there have been implemented clearly defined regulations—implemented by the German Cancer Society—how to organize and conduct MDT boards which are responsible for the final decision on the most appropriate treatment. All these activities have to be supplemented by a qualified administration.

8.3 How to Overcome Institutional/Social/Political Boundaries

On the mega level the players involved in modern personalized medicine are attending physicians, hospital administrations with local responsibilities, insurances as payers (at least in Germany) and the Ministry of Health responsible for regulating the system to the benefit of the patients. What are the divergent interests?

- Attending physicians are responsible providing an optimal treatment to their patient. This is the basis of their profession and almost always a personal intention as well. The costs for a treatment of course should be considered but cannot be the leading argument.
- The hospital administration has the duty to present a balanced budget to the responsible agency. Personalized onco-medicine with steadily increasing expenses is certainly not very welcome and creates a severe problem. This is in particular true for hospitals specialized in tumor medicine.
- Insurances face a really relevant problem since this type of treatment becomes an increasing factor in the overall budget and will certainly increase in the upcoming years and may become the driver of health care costs (see previous paragraph).
- Finally the German Ministry of Health has to organize and regulate the conflicting interests without increasing the fees for health care on one side and by avoiding the reproach of not doing everything for the patients on the other side—the Federal Chancellor of Germany Angela Merkel said "*... all cancer patients will get all they need ...*" (during a visit at the German Cancer Research Center Heidelberg, Apr 23, 2014).

It appears to be an urgent need to find solutions on the question how to implement the new anti-cancer measures without destroying the whole system. For this, a broad and open discussion between all partners, including health care insurances, politicians and other relevant groups of the society, e.g. the church and patient organizations, becomes an urgent need. Some ideas to approach these problems are:

- The first step is to critically analyze the situation. This should be done by the partners directly involved in the system. A working group should be initiated to collect the data and to develop a future scenario with regard to populations-based demography, predicted cancer rates, new targeting drugs, upcoming treatment options, e.g. based on proteomics, metabolomics etc. and several more.
- The upcoming financial burden presumably challenging the society in this or that way has to be calculated.
- As consequence for the daily cooperation between hospitals and health care providers a case by case discussion and decision should be considered. For this, a clear catalog of criteria has to be defined and publicly agreed.
- National authorities (government, health providers, insurances, the church etc.) have to inform the public to discuss different measures to be taken, e.g. to react by
  - cost adapted selection of patients, i.e. prognosis could play a crucial role
  - reimbursement only within a financial limit, i.e. rich survive, poor die
  - increase insurance fees,
  - cost cutting of other tasks of the health care system, e.g. health resorts etc.,
  - increase of self-participation regarding bagatelle diseases.

There are many ideas and possibilities the implementation and realization of which can be extremely difficult and unpopular to be implemented. Nonetheless, a neglect of the above mentioned topics may result in a difficult situation which can evolve in a couple of years.

9 Summary

The basic facts are:

- In oncology (and other fields of diseases) the way towards personalized therapy applying individual therapeutical measures to the patients, e.g. targeting drugs, is irreversible.
- Research and development will produce a steadily increasing number of new diagnostic procedures and targeting anti-cancer drugs what will accelerate the challenge.
- Personalized medicine is (slowly) being more and more recognized by politicians and health care financiers and it will be discussed and demanded more and more by the patients.
- However, public recognition of personalized medicine does not mean to realize its fundamental intrinsic problems and the willingness to approach the topic.
- The health care system has to adapt its structures but is not prepared.
- In particular the financial challenge is one important open question and is far from being solved.
- Hospitals have to adapt their internal structures and logistics but are not well prepared.
- Due to demography and further improvement of diagnostic high-through-put techniques and highly qualified treatment strategies overall market expectations are optimistic.

The partners involved in the care of cancer patients and patients with other diseases cannot ignore the scientifically driven progress of treatment options in biomedicine, thus the topic should be addressed and the foreseeable consequences must be discussed today and not tomorrow.

References

Camidge DR, Bang YJ, Kwak EL et al (2012) Activity and safety of crizotinib in patients with ALK-positive non-small-cell lung cancer: updated results from a phase 1 study. Lancet Oncol 13:1011–1019

Dietel M, Jöhrens K, Laffert M et al (2013) Predictive molecular pathology and its role in targeted cancer therapy: a review focussing on clinical relevance. Cancer Gene Ther 20(4):211–221

Dubsky P, Brase JC, Austrian Breast and Colorectal Cancer Study Group (ABCSG) et al (2013) The EndoPredict score provides prognostic information on late distant metastases in ER+/HER2-breast cancer patients. Br J Cancer 109:2959–2964

Flaherty KT, Infante JR, Daud A (2012) Combined BRAF and MEK inhibition in melanoma with BRAF V600 mutations. N Engl J Med 367(18):1694–1703

Kim DW et al (2012) Results of a global phase II study with crizotinib in advanced *ALK*-positive non-small cell lung cancer (NSCLC). Presented at the 2012 Annual Meeting of the American Society of Clinical Oncology (ASCO), Chicago, IL, 1–5 June 2012; Abstract 7533. http://meetinglibrary.asco.org/content/75135?media=vm&poster=1. Accessed 14 June 2015

Queirolo P, Picasso V, Spagnolo F (2015) Combined BRAF and MEK inhibition for the treatment of BRAF-mutated metastatic melanoma. Cancer Treat Rev 41(6):519–26. doi:10.1016/j.ctrv.2015.04.010 [Epub ahead of print]

World Health Organization (2015) World Health Statistics 2015. http://www.who.int/gho/publications/world_health_statistics/2015/en/. Accessed 6 June 2015

Manfred Dietel is currently Medical Director of the Institute of Pathology and former Head of the Board of Directors at the Charité University Hospital in Berlin, Germany. He previously served as Dean of the Medical Faculty at Charité. Before this, Professor Dietel was the Director of the Institute of Pathology at the University of Kiel, Germany. He received his medical education from the University of Hamburg, Germany, where he was promoted to Assistant Professor and also served as a full Professor of anatomical and surgical pathology.

In addition to routine diagnostic duties in clinical pathology Dietel's scientific interests include in-vitro cell growth of benign and malignant tumours of gastro-intestinal, ovarian and mesenchymal origin, prognosis of ovarian tumours, molecular mechanisms of drug resistance, molecular tumour pathology, telepathology, and predictive biomarkers. Methods of interest are cell culture, immunohistochemistry, in-situ hybridization, PCR, next generation sequencing (NGS) and telecommunication in diagnostic and scientific pathology.

Dietel is on the editorial board of several scientific journals and the WHO Classification of Tumours series: Pathology and Genetics of Gynaecological Tumours. He was President of the Congress of the European Society of Pathology (2001), Head of the Annual Meeting of the German Society of Senology (2001 and 2009) and Honorary President of its 2014 Congress.

He is a member of several national and international scientific societies including the American Association of Cancer Research, the European Society of Pathology and the German Society of Pathology.

Part III

Meeting the Challenges

Measuring Performance in Hospitals: The Development of an Operational Dashboard to Coordinate and Optimize Patient, Material and Information Flows

Kaat De Pourcq, Paul Gemmel, and Jeroen Trybou

Abstract

Currently, many Western countries are seeking ways to increase the efficiency and quality of health care. These efforts reflect stakeholders' expectations of improving performance in response to two important challenges. First, health care expenditures rise continuously and question the financial sustainability of current delivery systems. Secondly, health care systems suffer from unexplained variability and gaps in the quality of the patient-centered care. To make hospitals more patient-centered it is necessary to intervene on patient flow logistics. This assumes an integrated view on patient, material and information flows to align the different steps in the care process with the supporting processes and the required resources. Consequently, the development of process-oriented performance measurement systems is crucial. Most performance measures in hospitals are not process-oriented at the moment and cannot help a health care system to better synchronize the patient, material and information flows. This research describes a method to develop a reliable and valid set of both quality-focused and process-oriented key performance indicators and applies the findings to a case study on the process of hip replacement patients taking the opinion of internal stakeholders into account.

K. De Pourcq (✉) • P. Gemmel
Department of Innovation, Entrepreneurship and Service Management, Ghent University, Tweekerkenstraat 2, 9000 Ghent, Belgium
e-mail: kaat.depourcq@ugent.be; paul.gemmel@ugent.be

J. Trybou
Department of Public Health, University Hospital, Ghent University, De Pintelaan 185, 4K3, 9000 Ghent, Belgium
e-mail: jeroen.trybou@ugent.be

H. Albach et al. (eds.), *Boundaryless Hospital*, DOI 10.1007/978-3-662-49012-9_9

Keywords
Health care • Performance measurement • Process-orientation • Dashboard • Operating theater • Hip replacement • Key performance indicators • Quality of care • Patient flow

1 Introduction

To cope with financial, institutional and social, clinical and professional pressures, most hospitals are increasingly looking with interest at a new organizational paradigm, labeled as the *care-focused organization* (Villa et al. 2009). Hospitals can no longer support inefficient practices resulting from narrow functional areas and professional demarcations and from poor communication among departments and disciplines. Nor can they allow the high rate of delay and cancellation of clinical procedures, and the resulting waste of resources (Lega et al. 2013). These practices led to too many errors and inefficiencies in the past. The current processes in health care have to be modified in order to become better aligned and coordinated. This must lead to a more patient-centric workflow.

Consequently, the focus changes from *providing resources* over *managing capacity* to *managing flows* (Bohmer 2009). In this shift the flow of patients, materials and information should be integrated and synchronized (Rivard-Royer et al. 2003).

Understanding and controlling the different flows is one of the major challenges for hospitals in their quest for hospital accreditation. The current tendency towards accreditation and certification in the health care sector acknowledges the significance and benefits of process management (Smith et al. 2013). The finality of the accreditation procedure is that a third party such as the International Society for Quality in Health Care (ISQua) certifies in writing that the processes organized by the hospital comply with international standards related to quality, safety and patient satisfaction. This implies that hospitals need performance measures that tell them how adequate their processes are daily managed in order to meet the international standards.

Using the case of hip replacement in hospitals, we describe in this paper how a reliable and useful set of process-oriented performance indicators can be designed taking into account the views of multiple stakeholders. We first describe the evolution towards more process-oriented thinking. Secondly, the current state of performance measurement and dashboards in health care are outlined. Thereafter we illustrate a method to develop a reliable and valid set of process-oriented key performance indicators. Finally, managerial implications are discussed.

2 Process Thinking in Hospitals

From a historical point of view, hospitals are considered as a collection of professional functions, brought together to care for, and later cure, the patients. In this way it is not surprising that historically these hospitals were organized along functional departments. The further evolution of the hospital structure has been characterized by increasing specialization (within the functions) and centralization (to capture economies of scales). As a consequence, patients stay in small, specialized patient units supported by multiple ancillary and support departments. Such a hospital organization involves "multiple agents who have partial information, disparate (local) goals and limited communication capabilities" (Kumar et al. 1993).

The current culture in hospitals is still not sufficiently evolved towards a more integrated and holistic vision of the entire organization, mainly due to the absence of clear process thinking and the lack of knowledge about identifying and monitoring these processes with operational and strategic indicators (Gemmel et al. 2008).

A very important instrument used in the current hospital practice to become more process-oriented and to implement flow management are clinical pathways. Since the nineties, the development of clinical pathways or care maps introduced a new way of working in the hospital world. Clinical pathways can be seen as schedules of medical and nursing procedures, including diagnostic tests, medications and consultations designed to perform an efficient, coordinated program of treatment. The aim of a clinical pathway is "to enhance the quality of care by improving patient outcomes, promoting patient safety, increasing patient satisfaction and optimizing the use of resources" (Vanhaecht et al. 2007).

These clinical pathways were the start of the awareness that the treatment of a patient must be considered (as a time-based) sequence of activities that are performed by a team of different professional disciplines (input) to create a certain outcome (output). The development and implementation of clinical pathways are considered as a major step in the process orientation of a hospital (Gemmel et al. 2008).

Clinical pathways only map the patient flow in a very general way and are limited to the treatment processes and the clinical (supporting) resources. It can be considered as the clinical or care chain, i.e. "the chain of operations that need to be performed to produce a particular health service" (Vissers and Beech 2005). A more comprehensive process modelling technique must allow aligning and optimizing the clinical chain with the supply chain of materials and equipment as well with the information flow (see Fig. 1).

Supply chain management of *material flows* is a relatively new concept in health care that promotes the integration of activities such as the procurement, logistics, production and distribution of products to clients (Stadler 2008; Zanjirani et al. 2009). It represents the second largest expense for hospitals after labor costs on the provider side of the health care industry (Yang et al. 2007). However, hospital supply chains are unique and different from the typical industrial supply chains in many aspects (Baltacioglu et al. 2007). The structural difference of a service supply chain basically arises from the unique characteristics of services, which distinguish them from goods.

Health care services are complex and characterized by their highly specific nature. First, health care services are in their very nature physically intangible. The services cannot be touched or stored. Secondly, both the presence of the provider and the customer is needed and production and consumption are intertwined in a simultaneous way. Therefore the clinical, materials and information flows must come together in a Point-Of-Care (POC), where the patient and the

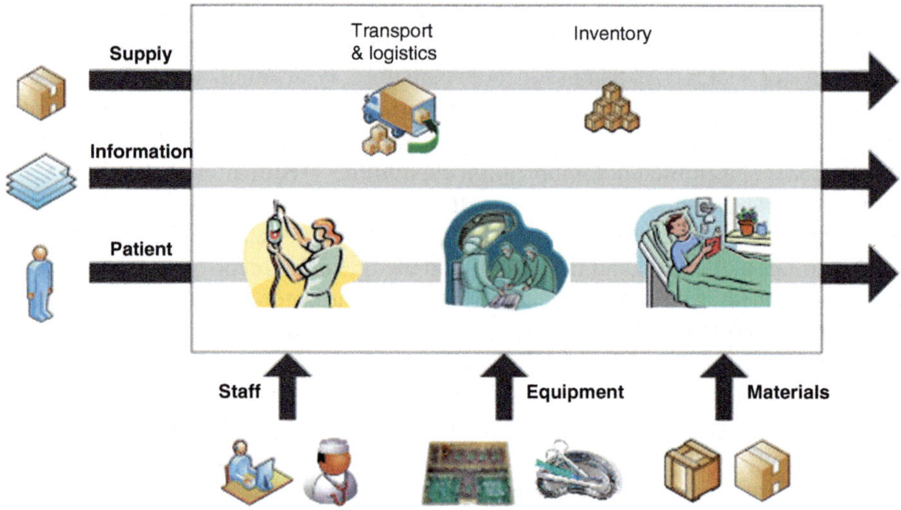

Fig. 1 An integrated view on patient, supply and information flows

health care professional interact. Thirdly, because of their intangible and simultaneous nature, health care services are perishable. The services cannot be buffered for a fluctuating demand. Timely delivery of the different components is therefore key to realize efficient processes. Fourthly, hospital processes are highly characterized by their heterogeneous nature. The fact that all flows interact at a certain point within the delivery process induces process variability. This makes it hard to predict the need of the several components and makes capacity management in terms of volume and timing a challenge. As such, hospital supply chain management is more complex and knowledge-intensive than traditional industry supply chain practices.

Three different types of supporting resources in supply chain practices can be identified (see Fig. 1):

(1) Materials: Common materials in hospitals are consumables e.g. prostheses, sterile goods and drugs. The materials flows within a single hospital are managed and supported in different ways. Often the end-to-end responsibility of the logistical processes are distributed over different departments and middle managers within the hospital.
(2) Equipment: The availability of equipment is crucial in order to ensure the interventions as planned. Consequently, capacity planning has to be aligned with the patient flow. Examples of equipment in health care are monitors, medical devices, surgical instruments and the operating room (OR).
(3) Staff: In hospital environments, the availability of skilled resources is crucial in order to ensure the interventions as planned. Physicians, nurses and logistic personnel interact with patients while delivering care.

In order to integrate the different flows, hospital information systems (HIS) such as electronic health records and computerized provider order entry, are critical

(Botta-Genoulaz and Millet 2006). Centralized communication engines exchange patient-related data of HIS such as administrative data, laboratory results, diagnostic results, health care images from one IT-system to another. However, the information in hospital IT systems is often limited to the treatment processes and the clinical (supporting) resources. It is a challenge in hospital management to integrate business functions and activities throughout supporting processes such as the supply chain. Synchronous information access and process integration between the company and its suppliers is regarded as a key strategic issue (Sadraoui and Mchirgui 2014).

The various departments involved in the different steps of a care process traditionally focus on their own, internal processes and costs. In general, they are not naturally inclined to coordinate their activities with other departments involved in the same care process. This coordination assumes an integrated view on patient, materials and information flows, to align the different steps in the care process with the supporting processes and the required resources. This requires attention for the development of process-oriented performance measurement systems (Gemmel et al. 2008).

3 Performance Measurement

The goal of performance measurement is to inform managers on the performance of their organization. As measuring all performance aspects within an organization is both unfeasible and irrelevant, most organizations select a number of performance indicators, based on the organization's objectives. According to Bauer (2004), "quantifiable metrics which reflect the performance of an organization in achieving its goals and objectives" can be considered as *key performance indicators (KPIs).* Shepherd et al. (2013) define key performance indicators as "a succinct measure that aims to describe as much about a system as possible in as few points as possible."

These performance indicators are not a goal in itself, but provide a basis for the organization's "management control system". It means that the data gathering system is applied in function of helping and coordinating the planning process and the control of decisions throughout the organization (Jorissen 1994). In general, performance measurement enables the organization's management to follow up, coordinate, control, and improve certain aspects of organizational activities (Kollberg et al. 2005).

In the profit sector, short-term financial indicators were dominant in the past, today non-financial indicators (such as quality and operational indicators) are of greater importance. This resulted in an extended range of performance indicators (Jorissen 1994). In the health care sector, ensuring quality has been an important issue for years, but financial measurement was the dominant mechanism of control until the 1990s (Aidemark 2001). The focus on financial performance, however, failed to provide a "big picture" assessment of the overall performance (Tarantino 2003).

In the last 10 years, performance measurement as a precondition with regard to quality improvement has become more important in the health care sector, caused by lapses in quality of care, safety issues, and low consumer satisfaction (Ten Asbroek et al. 2004; Becker et al. 2006), and as a result of medical progresses (Bothner et al. 2003; Ten Asbroek et al. 2004; OECD 2013) and changing delivery and environment in medicine (Becker et al. 2006). Wollersheim et al. (2006) even argue that the ultimate goal of performance measurement is to make the quality of health care more transparent, and to improve health care quality. Consequently, non-profit organizations have greater difficulties in developing performance indicators than profit organizations. In the health care sector, some performance aspects are difficult to measure, e.g. non-financial performance aspects (such as clinical outcomes and patient satisfaction) (Yang et al. 2005).

4 KPIs in Health Care

KPIs are developed for different purposes and at different levels depending on the specific goal of the indicator and the perspective of the user (see Fig. 2). In health care, three different levels of users' perspectives can be distinguished. More precisely, performance measurement is important to

(1) the individual (the micro-level) such as physicians, nurses and patients,
(2) health care organizations and its (sub)divisions (the meso-level) such as an emergency care department or an ambulatory care center and
(3) health care policy makers and authorities (macro-level) such as payers and licensing governments.

At the *micro-level* the principal target is the practitioner who treats individual patients and the purpose is to maximize the health benefit for that individual (Osoba 2002). On this level evidence-based medicine (EBM) and publicly available KPIs are increasingly used to improve the individual performance. Evidence-based medicine is defined as "the conscientious and judicious use of current best evidence from clinical care research in the management of individual patients" (Sackett et al. 1996). Health care professionals generally express positive attitudes towards EBM and acknowledge its significance in clinical performance (De Vito et al. 2009; Heselmans et al. 2009). Secondly, information obtained from publicly available KPIs can be used by patients or his or her relatives to know how a physician, unit or hospital is performing (Jha et al. 2008; Northcott and Harvey 2012). This becomes increasingly important in light of the emerging empowered patient and outcome measurement (Lux et al. 2011).

On the *meso-level* of organizational entities, performance measurement allows health care managers to make strategic decisions on hospital goals. Several performance objectives for hospitals have been identified. For instance, the Institute of Medicine (2001) makes a distinction between safe, effective, equitable, efficient, patient-centered and accessible care. In the PATH framework, satisfactory hospital

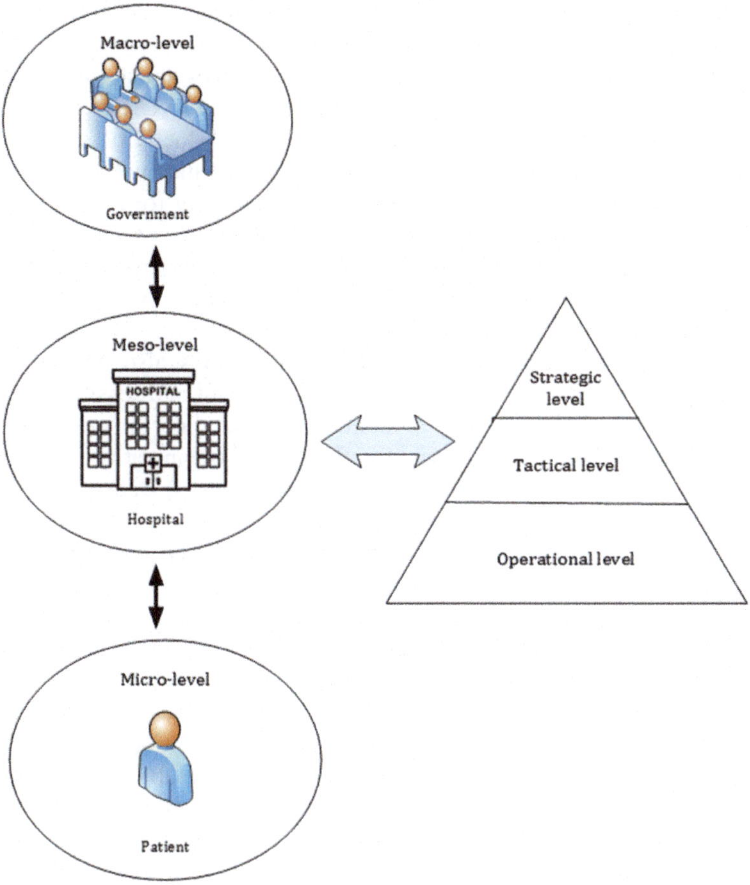

Fig. 2 Performance measurement in health care

performance is defined as "the maintenance of a state of functioning that corresponds to societal, patient, and professional norms". Six dimensions were identified for assessing hospital performance: clinical effectiveness, safety, patient centeredness, production efficiency, staff orientation and responsive governance (Veillard et al. 2005).

Within the *meso-level*, KPIs can be used on different management levels such as strategy, tactics and operations. KPIs can target the overall hospital level (Weerawat et al. 2013; Jacobs et al. 2005), only one department in a hospital e.g. ICU (Brown et al. 2014) or ER (Howell et al. 2014), a specific service line or clinical pathway (Gooch et al. 2009; Walters et al. 2012), or even a protocol or a procedure (Caughey et al. 2014; Panaretto et al. 2013).

At the *macro-level*, KPIs can play an important role in policy making (Hunter et al. 2014; Tashobya et al. 2014). On the one hand, the government can demonstrate accountability for operational and financial performance of the country's health systems by benchmarking specific performance indicators with other countries (Chukwuani et al. 2006; Mears et al. 2011). On the other hand, KPIs can be used to make strategic governmental decisions to establish future initiatives required for sound and sustainable national health systems (Greaves et al. 2012). Kaplan and Haas (2014) state that a physician's productivity should not be measured by inputs (number of patients seen) but by the quality of outcomes achieved. Public reporting of hospital quality data and pay for performance have emerged as two of the most widely advocated strategies for accelerating quality improvement. Hospitals engaged in both public reporting and pay for performance achieved modestly greater improvements in quality than did hospitals engaged only in public reporting (Lindenauer et al. 2007).

In order to avoid information overload, organizations also have to make a selection of performance indicators that are both relevant and feasible to measure and manage. Organizations are less inclined to adopt performance indicators without considering the added value for their own organization and base the selection of performance indicators on the organization's objectives, strategy and critical success factors to realize the objectives and strategy (Jorissen 1994). Moreover, following Kros and Brown (2012), there are several competitive performance dimensions of health care delivery e.g. cost, quality, speed and support after the service. Trade-offs exist between all of these competitive dimensions. Consequently, there is no consensus in literature which KPIs should be included, at which level they should be measured, and how precise they have to be.

Abo-Hamad and Arisha (2013) build a hierarchical structure, and break KPIs down into more precise indicators. In the research of Grigoroudis et al. (2012) the selection of 24 KPIs was based on hospital strategy and available data. They created a hierarchy applying the four perspectives of a balanced scorecard (BSC) at the top level. Parida and Chattopadhyay (2007) state that performance measures, formerly used for operational control only, should achieve vertical and horizontal integration of activities across hierarchical levels, e.g. operational, tactical and strategic levels within one organization. To achieve this, several performance measurement and management systems can be applied such as the balanced scorecard (see Fig. 3).

A balanced scorecard integrates different perspectives on hospital performance. It is a customized performance measurement system that looks beyond the traditional financial measures and is based on organizational strategies. The BSC is a performance measurement tool that can be customized for every organization and utilized as a strategic management framework to align an organization's strategies and objectives. Implementing BSC requires that executives develop coherent strategies in order to achieve the organization's mission and compile a set of KPIs to monitor the organization's performance and strategic alignment (Behrouzi et al. 2014).

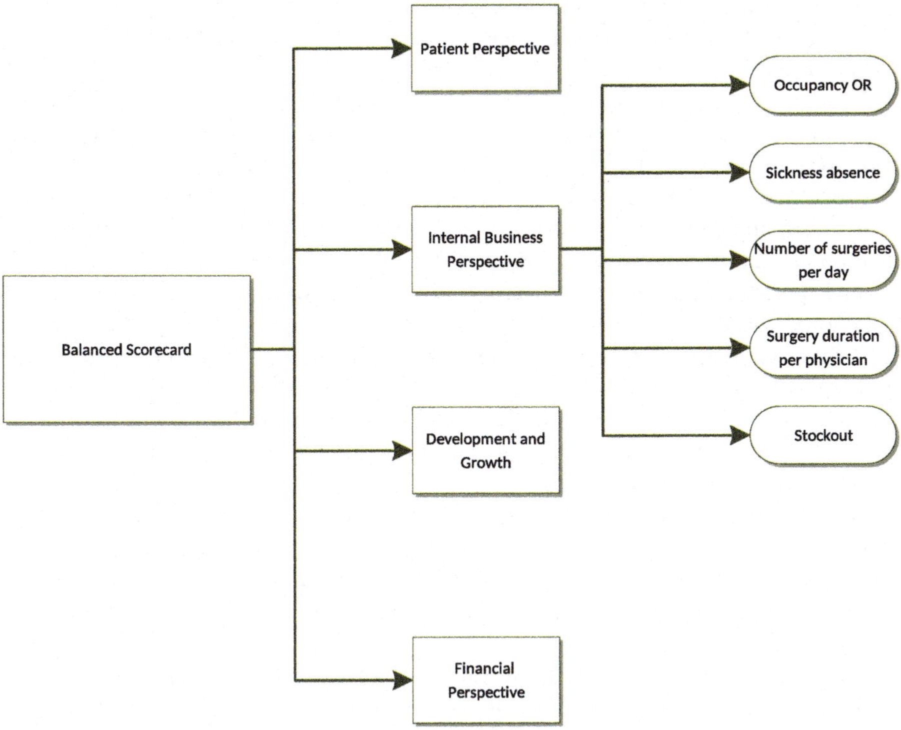

Fig. 3 Example of an hierarchical balanced scorecard

5 Developing a Dashboard

Organizations generate and deal with an ever growing amount of data (Yigitbasioglu and Velcu 2012), that make performance measurement a difficult assignment for managers and decision makers. Dashboards are expected to improve decision making by amplifying cognition and capitalizing on human perceptual capabilities (Yigitbasioglu and Velcu 2012).

The need to integrate large amounts of information across several levels or dimensions is not unique to health care decisions. Advances in cognitive science and computer technology have led to increasing interest in the use of interactive visual information displays to support decision making in these circumstances (Chen 2010). Information overload can be managed by implementing KPIs in a dashboard. A dashboard brings the firm's key metrics into a single display (Lapointe 2005). It displays the tip of an iceberg, i.e. what the user sees at first and if needed, gives the possibility to analyze and discover causes of poor performance. The terminology is borrowed from a vehicle dashboard, which reports the few metrics a driver needs to know. A dashboard is a relatively small collection of interconnected key performance metrics and underlying performance drivers that reflects both short- and long-term interests to be viewed in common throughout the organization.

However, putting performance measurement into practice is not always easy. There are a couple of challenges in the development of the performance measurement systems in hospitals:

Most performance measures in hospitals are not process-oriented (Gemmel et al. 2008) and cannot help a health care system to better synchronize the patients, materials and information flows. Many different stakeholders are having an impact on the performance of the different flows in a health care system. These stakeholders such as nurses, physicians, hospitals managers, suppliers, patients etc. all have their own view on performance and use different performance measures (Moore 2000). This leads to a large number of different potential performance indicators. Having a reliable method to selecting the *key* performance indicators which are really able to steer flows and processes in health care is therefore an important challenge.

As a result of insufficient powerful information systems and a lack of performance measurement tools within the health care sector, performance measures are not always complete and accurate (Eddy 1998). According to Smith (2005) uncritical reliance on performance data can lead to a number of unintended and adverse consequences.

To tackle these issues, in what follows, we describe a framework and an illustrative case showing how a reliable and valid set of process-oriented key performance indicators can be selected in the context of hip replacement patients including several stakeholders.

5.1 Framework

KPIs can be developed and monitored at different levels within a hospital, depending on the goal and needs of the specific user. Consequently, the level on which the dashboard should be implemented is determined by the selected KPIs. Nonetheless, even if a dashboard focuses more on the operational and tactical level, it is important that it is administered employing the vision and strategic goals of a hospital (Dumas et al. 2013). Parida and Chattopadhyay (2007) state that the strategic goals of an organization need to be broken down into objective targets for operating managers, which may act as performance drivers for this group. Pauwels et al. (2009) developed a conceptual framework to develop a dashboard that sustains this vision. They discuss the relations between demand for dashboards, supply of dashboards and the implementation process in driving adoption and use of dashboard systems (see Fig. 4).

5.1.1 Demand Side

Ambler (2003) identified two main approaches to metrics selection: the general and the tailored approach. The general approach limits the number of indicators to the

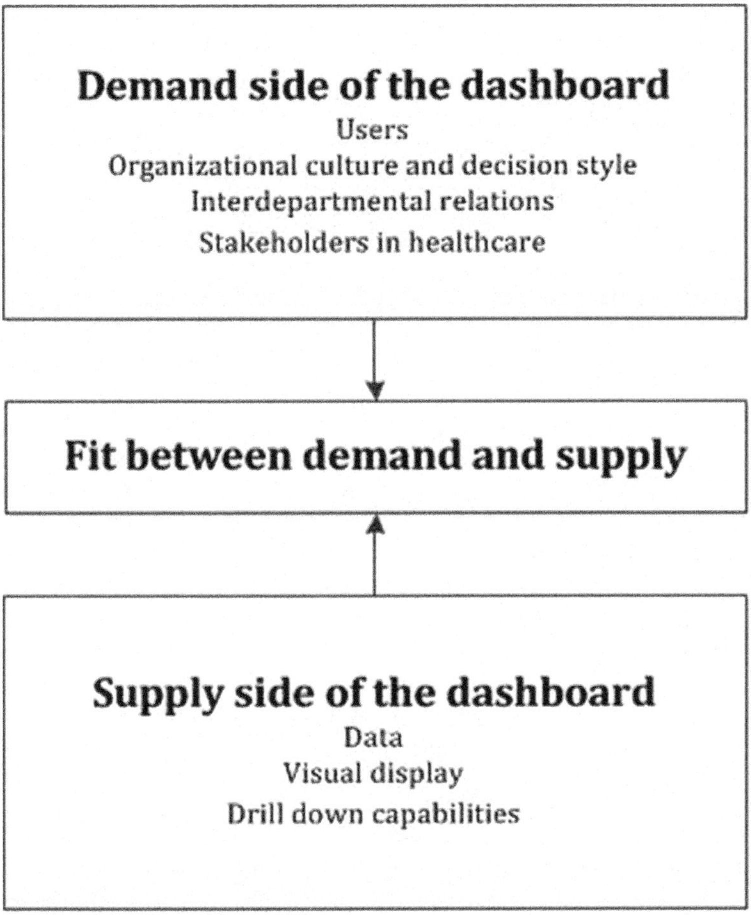

Fig. 4 The adjusted framework of Pauwels et al. (2009)

few that can be applied to all service organizations and has the advantage of comparability. The tailored approach argues that each business unit or company has its own strategy and requires differentiated metrics to track progress towards its specific objectives. This approach invites high-level communication throughout the organization of what is important to the business or hospital (Lapointe 2005). Since health care is a very a unique service setting, we use a tailored vision to select the KPIs (Ambler 2003).

Stelfox and Straus (2013) discuss that a concise and clear conceptual framework can be valuable in guiding development of performance indicators. A BSC is built on a four perspective design to identify what to measure and track for the implementation of strategy: (1) Financial perspective, (2) Customer perspective, (3) Internal business perspective and (4) Learning and growth perspective (Kaplan and Norton 2010). To avoid complexity of performance measurement, a BSC should not exceed five KPIs for each perspective within a medium-sized organization.

A good balanced scorecard should have a mix of outcome measures and performance drivers which steer performance (Berler et al. 2005). Moreover, outcome measures without performance drivers do not communicate how the outcomes are to be achieved (Kaplan and Norton 2010). This makes improvement a challenge because of the lack of insight into to root causes. The structure-process-outcome framework of Donabedian (1988) is used in this case to obtain this goal. *Structure* refers to the underpinning infrastructure and resources that an organization has in place to achieve its aims (staff, materials, policies and procedures). *Process* refers to what an organization actually does, and *outcome* refers to the results of what an organization did (Mant 2001).

Users

The demand side represents the side of the users who will employ the dashboard. This includes hospital senior management, but also representatives of other levels such as process owners and process participants e.g. the coordinating physician; head of department, head nurse (Dumas et al. 2013). Paine (2004) recommends that those who will (a) use the system, (b) be measured by it, and (c) make decisions based on it, should be involved. Consequently, different key stakeholders including physicians, nurses, and hospital middle and top management should be consulted.

Organizational Culture

Naturally, the approach of making decisions has fit the decision style of the hospital. An organization has a prevailing attitude and a certain standard approach of doing things and making decisions (Gale et al. 2014). Organizational culture varies across hospitals and over time. This variation is associated with a variety of organizational characteristics and routine measures of performance (Jacobs et al. 2013). Undoubtedly a one-size fits all solution (a universal dashboard) cannot be applied due to different cultures in health care organizations. A more in-depth understanding of the views on the decision style of the hospital and the organization culture will be required. Essential involvement of leadership at multiple levels is essential according to Render et al. (2011).

Interdepartmental Relations

Interdepartmental relations should be taken into account. The goals of a department need to be aligned with the goals of the hospital. If there is a situation of rivalry and mistrust among departments, there exists a risk that the dashboard will be (mis)used for the interests of individuals at the cost of the organization's goals (Dumas et al. 2013). For example, a dashboard in the case of hip surgery has to ensure that it does not evoke undesired trade-offs where other processes within the operating theater interact with the process of hip surgery outside the operating theater such as the nursing ward or the recovery room. Moreover, there might occur a trade-off with other clinical processes within the OR such as abdominal surgery. To prevent this issue, administrative managers are involved in the development of the KPIs.

Stakeholders in Health Care

Health care services face a variety of stakeholders with different demands and constraints. Five groups of stakeholders can be identified: patients, employers, providers, payers and manufacturers (Institute of Medicine 2010). Therefore, the dashboard has to include measures to integrate specific views of the different stakeholders.

5.1.2 Supply Side

In a later stage it is important to link data of information systems to the KPIs using a bottom-up approach. In our framework this is represented by the supply side. The fit between demand and supply is critical for dashboard success (Lim and Benbasat 2000; Goodhue and Thompson 1995). The type of information provided should match with the decision responsibilities of the users and the metrics in the dashboard should be those that are crucial for a hospital.

Metrics

The use of metrics currently available in the hospital speeds up the process of implementing a dashboard at a minimal cost. However developing new measures for better metrics may be worthwhile in the long run. A great challenge is "the choice among using indicators for which there is data available versus developing new indicators" (Kelley et al. 2006). Miller and Cioffi (2004) found that consumer-based measures give more actionable insight in a service dashboard. Consequently, measures that include the patient perspective will give a better overview of performance within the patient process. Populating the dashboard with data is anything but trivial. HIS have enormous quantities of data. Some of the data may be collected daily (e.g. the duration of a surgery), whereas other data is collected annually or even less frequently (e.g. job satisfaction). It is crucial for hospital managers and IT innovators to select the right data and link them to the key performance metrics.

Visual Display

A performance dashboard visualizing the selected KPIs offers a remedy to the information overload problem and makes the information of IT systems manageable. Good information visualization can help to process complex information more efficiently (Yigitbasioglu and Velcu 2012).

Drill-Down Capabilities

Hospital managers have to be able to interpret important data from IT systems, however too much information makes it hard to keep the right focus (Yigitbasioglu and Velcu 2012). A dashboard presents information for performance management in a structured and efficient way. The drill-down capabilities of the dashboard give the opportunity to track the underlying causes of a problem and structure the information. Drilling-down means that one goes from a more general to a more detailed level of information.

6 Illustrative Case Study

In this exploratory case study we verify a method to investigate which key performance indicators should be measured, monitored and implemented in a health-care service operations dashboard. To this end, case study research is a particular approach (Yin 2013). Hence, our study took an in-depth case study approach. The process of hip surgery is selected as the use case. Many hospitals have already developed a clinical pathway for hip replacement. The procedure is relatively standardized, which makes it a good candidate for an in-depth analysis in terms of the utilization of materials, information and other resources (Gemmel et al. 2008).

The case study focuses on the process within the operation room (OR). The OR department is a key hospital resource, as 60–70 % all hospital admissions are induced by pathology requiring a surgical intervention (Denton et al. 2007). Denton et al. (2007) state that operating rooms are the largest cost center and greatest source of revenues for most hospitals. Approximately 1/3rd of all surgeries are for orthopedic reasons, of which 10–15 % are related to hip surgery. Consequently, this orthopedic case study is a very relevant study within the setting of health care. The study was done in two different hospitals. The first hospital has a capacity of 822 beds, employs 2300 people and 220 physicians. The second hospital has a capacity of 554 beds, has more than 1600 employees and 170 physicians.

6.1 Selection of KPIs

First, an exhaustive overview of frequently applied KPIs was developed based on a systematic literature review. More precisely, we updated the results of the systematic review of Liu and Itoh (2013) who had analyzed articles in PubMed and PubMed Central published until 2012. Liu and Itoh (2013) compiled a list of 66 indicators. We applied the same selection criteria and searched PubMed from June 2012 to April 2014. Since the focus of this study is the operation room and the process of hip surgery, we included the following terms: "THP OR total hip replacement or hip arthroplasty or hip surgery" and "Operating room OR Operation room OR OR". Based on the results of our systematic review, 72 additional indicators were added. Thereafter, the list was revised by two experts and a pilot interview with a surgeon was carried out.

The indicators were structured and presented in a tree hierarchy. Level 1 represented the four variables of the balanced scorecard. Level 2 clustered 24 indicators. In level three these clustering variables are broken down into 138 KPIs resulting from the literature review.

To select the most relevant key performance indicators different stakeholders involved in the hip surgery process were interviewed. An interview consisted of two main parts:

Part 1: A Semi-Structured Interview
The interviewees were asked which performance indicators were measured in the hospital. They also judged the usefulness and importance of the performance indicators.

Part 2: A Structured Interview
This part was based on the results of the literature review and consisted of three phases: The exhaustive list of 138 indicators was shown to the interviewee by presenting them on cards. In the first phase participants could select all indicators they found important and should explain why they are important (1). Next they had to select 20 KPIs they found most important to measure and follow up (2). Finally, they had to eliminate another ten KPIs (3).

Kaplan and Norton (2010) states that each perspective should not be measured by more than five KPIs. The number of indicators monitored by a dashboard has to be manageable. In the health care literature the number of KPIs ranges from 10 to 30. Liu and Itoh (2013) created a list of 27 outcomes. Twenty-four KPIs were measured in the research of Harris et al. (2011). However, Shohet (2006) used only 11 KPIs. In our case we decided to retain 20 KPIs.

6.2 Practical Issues in the Selection Process of KPIs

Following the framework of Pauwels et al. (2009), we investigated the perspectives of different users and stakeholders. The case study showed discrepancies in perspectives between professionals practicing at the hospital (i.e. physicians and head nurses) and the hospital management. Physicians, head nurses and the medical operating room managers tend to focus dominantly on the patient perspective contrary to administrative and nursing operating room management, who focused more on internal processes. Moreover, the perspectives of professionals changed as the restrictions with respect to the number of indicators that they were allowed to select became smaller. The patient perspective became also more important for administrative and nursing operating room management.

Furthermore, the staff of the hospitals tends to have a different focus on the four perspectives of the balanced scorecard. Comparing the results of the two hospitals, we found that in the first two phases hospital one focused more on internal processes than hospital two. This indicates that each hospital should develop their own tailored dashboard. However, we decided in this illustrative case study to incorporate both visions in one list.

The list of 20 KPIs in Table 1 shows that the selected indicators are not equally divided over the four domains of the balanced scorecard. Only a few KPIs within the developed list are focusing on development and growth and financial perspective. The priority of the participants in the study was the patient's perspective. Most indicators within this category focus on patient safety and satisfaction. However, waiting time between admission and surgery (17) is shown to be important too. This indicates that the interviewees value the patient flow. Eight of the twenty indicators

Table 1 List of 20 KPIs and BSC domain

No.	Key performance indicator	BSC
1	Surgery safety checklist	1
2	Occupancy OR	2
3	Patient satisfaction with care/service	1
4	Acute pain management	1
5	Performance evaluation of employees	3
6	Cost/surgery	4
7	Percentage of patients that recommends the hospital to family and friends	1
8	Post-operative evaluation of functional status	1
9	Nosocomial infections	1
10	Number of hospitalization days	1
11	Material cost/surgery	4
12	Sickness absence	2
13	Duration of operating time per physician	2
14	Mortality/morbidity	1
15	Lost or expired products	2
16	Job satisfaction survey	2
17	Waiting time for operation/surgery	1
18	Number of times a surgeon proceeds hip surgery	3
19	Unplanned readmission	1
20	% of material missing at the start of the operation	2

1—Patient Perspective, 2—Internal Business Process, 3—Learning and Growth, 4—Financial Perspective

selected are measures that monitor performance of the patient, materials and information flows. Patient and resource flow-oriented KPIs are indicated in Table 1.

In this study we categorized three types of resources: skills, equipment and materials (see Fig. 1). There are four KPIs that focus on skills (5, 12, 13, 18). Specialization and performance of health-care workers proved to be very important. Occupancy of the OR (2) is positioned as an equipment-focused KPI on the second place in the list. Further the availability (20) and losses of materials (15) were very important KPIs linked to materials. Consequently, participants selected indicators that also measure down-stream value added processes next to quality indicators.

In the next stage, managers will have to supply the dashboard with data from the HIS. The performance of the IT systems in this case will not be measured by a specific KPI but the performance of IT systems will influence the measurement of the selected KPIs indirectly because of the integration of the demand and supply side.

7 Practical Implications

Looking at the changing health care environment, performance measurement should include the performance of processes. To analyze process flows in health care it is important to evaluate the "full picture" of processes in health care. Downstream value-added processes have to be evaluated taking performance of the upstream surgery-relevant process into account. KPIs of downstream value-added processes in health care have already been investigated in the field of supply chain and information technology.

The current tendency towards accreditation and certification in the health care sector has also led to a lot of research in performance measurement of quality in the upstream processes. However, there is still a gap in performance measurement research where both types of processes are integrated in a performance measurement system. In this study we analyzed a method to incorporate KPIs of the upstream surgery-relevant process as well as KPIs of the downstream value-added processes. Subsequently, it is important for hospital managers to combine key performance metrics of all processes.

KPIs in health care are developed for different purposes and at different levels depending on the goal and the perspective of the user. This makes performance measurement a complicated and difficult task. It is important to clearly define the goal of the performance measurement (Pauwels et al. 2009). This way, the KPIs can be selected on the right level with the right purpose. Parida and Chattopadhyay (2007) state that performance measures, formerly used for operational control only, should achieve vertical and horizontal integration of activities across hierarchical levels e.g. operational, tactical and strategic levels within an organization. The key performance metrics need to reflect the vision and strategic goals of a hospital (Dumas et al. 2013). Institutional theory argues that the institutional environment in which organizations operate drives the choices they make (Covaleski et al. 2003; Cardinaels and Soderstrom 2013). In the hospital setting, both internal actors (i.e. different professional groups) and external stakeholders (i.e. government, patients, and insurers) define the institutional environment. In this paper we explored the opinion of the internal actors. We used the balanced scorecard as a framework to investigate the strategy choices made by the internal actors. Liu and Itoh (2013) used a framework combining stakeholders' perspectives, health care outcomes and performance shaping factors. It depends on the preferences of hospital managers and the culture of an organization which framework should be applied.

Different professional groups have their own incentives, and conflicts among these groups can result in the continuation of suboptimal accounting and performance systems (Meyer and Rowan 1977; Covaleski et al. 2003). An understanding of the perspective of the internal actors can guide future efforts to improve health care efficiency. Paine (2004) recommends that opinions of those who use the system and are measured by it should be included in the development of the dashboard. Hospital managers have to make sure that all opinions are taken into consideration. They should involve patients and nurses as well. In this study we interviewed physicians, nurses in middle and the top management. Each stakeholder uses a set of diverse criteria and standards to evaluate the legitimacy of the organization (Cardinaels and Soderstrom 2013). The results of the case study confirmed this. Physicians, head nurses and the medical operating room managers tended to focus more on the patient perspective contrary to the administrative and nursing operating room management, who focused more on internal processes. Naranjo-Gil and Hartmann (2007) show that CEOs with medical backgrounds put stronger emphasis on the use of non-financial measures and the interactive use of management control systems, whereas CEOs with financial backgrounds focus more on financial measures and diagnostic forms of control.

The hospital as an institution relies heavily on the physician, who employs the resources of a hospital to treat patients (Eldenburg 1994). Physicians often have little accountability to hospital management. However, hospitals tend to be more efficient when they receive institutional support from their stakeholders (Meyer and Rowan 1977; Dimaggio and Powell 1983; Scott 2001). In this study some physicians expressed that hospital management did not consider their opinion to the extent they had expected. Since improved management accounting systems for influencing decision making (e.g. more detailed cost systems and better performance indicators to monitor quality) may only work if hospital boards consider performance evaluation systems that align the incentives of various internal stakeholders towards a common goal (Pizzini 2006). Hospitals must carefully balance the opinions of different groups of internal stakeholders.

It is a challenge in hospital management to integrate business functions and follow-up processes and relevant KPIs. A dashboard supplied with relevant data improves the visibility and manageability of the KPIs. Consequently, the integration of the HIS at the supply side of the dashboard is crucial. Managers assisted by users of the dashboard and IT-innovators have to decide which available data should be captured from the HIS and which new data has to be collected. Donabedian (1988) states that structure, process and outcome indicators should be included. Participants of the study selected indicators out of the three categories. However, some of the outcome indicators are qualitative and hard to measure e.g. patient and employee satisfaction (Brien and Ghali 2008). These qualitative KPIs are very important and should be monitored. The interviews stated that it is the extra effort worth to measure them. The results of the illustrative case study show that it is important to incorporate qualitative patient-oriented measures in a service-oriented dashboard.

In conclusion, process thinking in health care is gaining importance. The different steps within the care process have to be aligned with the supporting processes and the required resources. Hospitals that better monitor patient inflows, capacity constraints, and service quality might be more successful in surviving as premium providers of care (Hsu 2011). This indicates that process-orientation requires attention for the development of process-oriented performance measurement systems. The proposed framework (Pauwels et al. 2009) is a good manual for hospital managers to develop a dashboard to manage these processes. Moreover, the study presented offers a good approach to investigate which key performance indicators should be measured, monitored and implemented in a health care service operations dashboard.

References

Abo-Hamad W, Arisha A (2013) Simulation-based framework to improve patient experience in an emergency department. Eur J Oper Res 224(1):154–166. doi:10.1016/j.ejor.2012.07.028

Aidemark L-G (2001) The meaning of balanced scorecards in the health care organisation. Financ Account Manag 17(1):23–40

Ambler T (2003) Marketing and the bottom line, 2nd edn. Financial Times Prentice Hall, London

Baltacioglu T, Ada E, Kaplan MD et al (2007) A new framework for service supply chains. Serv Ind J 27(2):105–124. doi:10.1080/02642060601122629

Bauer K (2004) KPIs—the metrics that drive performance management. DM Rev 14(9):63

Becker B, Formisano A, Roger MD (2006) Strategic planning for departmental divisions in an academic health care centre. Am J Med 199(4):357–365

Behrouzi FP, Shaharoun AMP, Ma'aram AP (2014) Applications of the balanced scorecard for strategic management and performance measurement in the health sector. Aust Health Rev 38 (2):208–217. doi:10.1071/AH06017410.1108

Berler A, Pavlopoulos S, Koutsouris D (2005) Using key performance indicators as knowledge-management tools at a regional health-care authority level. IEEE Trans Inf Technol Biomed 9 (2):184–192. doi:10.1109/TITB.2005.847196

Bohmer RMJ (2009) Designing care: aligning the nature and management of health care. Harvard Business Press, Boston

Bothner U, Brinkman A, Gebhard F et al (2003) Balanced scorecard. "Tool or toy" im Krankenhaus? Anaesthesist 52:947–956

Botta-Genoulaz V, Millet P-A (2006) An investigation into the use of ERP systems in the service sector. Int J Prod Econ 99(1–2):202–221. doi:10.1016/j.ijpe.2004.12.015

Brien SE, Ghali WA (2008) Public reporting of the hospital standardized mortality ratio (HSMR): implications for the Canadian approach to safety and quality in health care. Open Med 2 (3):70–73

Brown SE, Ratcliffe SJ, Halpern SD (2014) An empirical comparison of key statistical attributes among potential ICU quality indicators. Crit Care Med 42(8):1821–1831. doi:10.1097/CCM.0000000000000334

Cardinaels E, Soderstrom N (2013) Managing in a complex world: accounting and governance choices in hospitals. Eur Account Rev 22(4):647–684

Caughey GE, Ellett LMK, Wong TY (2014) Development of evidence-based Australian medication-related indicators of potentially preventable hospitalisations: a modified RAND appropriateness method. BMJ Open 4(4):e004625

Chen C (2010) Information visualization. Wiley Interdiscip Rev Comput Stat 2(4):387–403. doi:10.1002/wics.89

Chukwuani CM, Olugboji A, Akuto EE et al (2006) A baseline survey of the primary healthcare system in South Eastern Nigeria. Health Policy 77(2):182–201. doi:10.1016/j.healthpol.2005.07.006

Covaleski MA, Dirsmith MW, Samuel S (2003) Changes in the institutional environment and the institutions of Governance: extending the contributions of transaction cost economics within the management control literature, Accounting. Organ Soc 28(5):417–441

De Vito C, Nobile CG, Furnari G et al (2009) Physicians' knowledge, attitudes and professional use of RCTs and meta-analyses: a cross-sectional survey. Eur J Public Health 19(3):297–302

Denton B, Viapiano J, Vogl A (2007) Optimization of surgery sequencing and scheduling decisions under uncertainty. Health Care Manag Sci 10(1):13–24

DiMaggio PJ, Powell WW (1983) The iron cage revisited: institutional isomorphism and collective rationality in organizational fields. Am Sociol Rev 48(2):147–160
Donabedian A (1988) The quality of care: how can it be assessed? JAMA 121(11):1145–1150
Dumas M, La Rosa M, Mendling J et al (2013) Fundamentals of business process management. Springer, Berlin
Eddy DM (1998) Performance measurement: problems and solutions. Health Aff 17(4):7–25. doi:10.1377/hlthaff.17.4.7
Eldenburg L (1994) The use of information in total cost management. Account Rev 69(1):96–121
Gale NK, Shapiro J, McLeod HST et al (2014) Patients-people-place: developing a framework for researching organizational culture during health service redesign and change. Implement Sci 9 (1):106. doi:10.1186/s13012-014-0106-z
Gemmel P, Vandaele D, Tambeur W (2008) Hospital Process Orientation (HPO): the development of a measurement tool. Total Qual Manag 19(12):1207–1217
Gooch KL, Smith D, Wasylak T et al (2009) The Alberta Hip and Knee replacement project: a model for health technology assessment based on comparative effectiveness of clinical pathways. Int J Technol Assess Health Care 25(2):113–123. doi:10.1017/S0266462309090163
Goodhue DL, Thompson RL (1995) Task-technology fit and individual performance. MIS Q 19 (2):213–236. doi:10.2307/249689
Greaves F, Millett C, Pape UJ et al (2012) Association between primary care organisation population size and quality of commissioning in England: an observational study. Br J Gen Pract 62(594):e46–e54. doi:10.3399/bjgp12X616364
Grigoroudis E, Orfanoudaki E, Zopounidis C (2012) Strategic performance measurement in a health care organisation: a multiple criteria approach based on balanced scorecard. Omega 40 (1):104–119. doi:10.1016/j.omega.2011.04.001
Harris R, Bridgman C, Ahmad M et al (2011) Introducing care pathway commissioning to primary dental care: measuring performance. Br Dent J 211(11):E22. doi:10.1038/sj.bdj.2011.1005
Heselmans A, Donceel P, Aertgeerts B et al (2009) The attitude of Belgian social insurance physicians towards evidence-based practice and clinical practice guidelines. BMC Fam Pract 10(1):64
Howell SC, Wills RA, Johnston TC (2014) Should diagnosis codes from emergency department data be used for case selection for emergency department key performance indicators? Aust Health Rev 38(1):38–43
Hsu SH (2011) Cost information and pricing: empirical evidence. Contemp Account Res 28 (2):554–579
Hunter BM, Requejo JH, Pope I, Daelmans B, Murray SF (2014) National health policy-makers' views on the clarity and utility of Countdown to 2015 country profiles and reports: findings from two exploratory qualitative studies. Health Res Policy Syst 12:40. doi:10.1186/1478-4505-12-40
Institute of Medicine (2001) Committee on the quality of health care in America. Crossing the quality chasm: a new health system for the 21st century. National Academy Press, Washington, DC
Institute of Medicine (2010) Roundtable on value & science-driven health care. In: Yong P, Olsen L, McGinnis J (eds) Value in health care: accounting for cost, quality, safety, outcomes, and innovation. National Academies Press, Washington, DC
Jacobs R, Goddard M, Smith PC (2005) How robust are hospital ranks based on composite performance measures. Med Care 43(12):1177–1184
Jacobs R, Mannion R, Davies HTO et al (2013) The relationship between organizational culture and performance in acute hospitals. Soc Sci Med 76:115–125. doi:10.1016/j.socscimed.2012.10.014
Jha AK, Orav EJ, Zheng J et al (2008) Patients' perception of hospital care in the United States. N Engl J Med 359:1921–1931. doi:10.1056/NEJMsa0804116
Jorissen A (1994) Prestatiemeting. Naar een betere beheersing van bedrijfsactiviteiten. MAKLU Uitgevers, Antwerpen

Kaplan RS, Haas DA (2014) How not to cut health care costs. Harv Bus Rev 64(11):116–122
Kaplan RS, Norton DP (2010) The balanced scorecard—measures that drive performance. Harv Bus Rev 1:134–142
Kelley ET, Arispe I, Holmes J (2006) Beyond the initial indicators: lessons from the OECD Health Care Quality Indicators Project and the US National Health care quality report. Int J Qual Health Care 18(September):50
Kollberg B, Elg M, Lindmark J (2005) Design and implementation of a performance measurement system in Swedish health care services: a multiple case study of 6 development teams. Qual Manag Health Care 14(2):95–111
Kros JF, Brown E (2012) Health care operations and supply chain management: strategy, operations, planning, and control. Wiley, San Francisco, CA
Kumar A, Ow PS, Prietula MJ (1993) Organizational simulation and information systems design: an operations level example. Manag Sci 39(2):218–240
Lapointe P (2005) Timken rolls out a marketing dashboard for industrial bearing group. Market NPV 3(1):3–6
Lega F, Marsilio M, Villa S (2013) An evaluation framework for measuring supply chain performance in the public health care sector: evidence from the Italian NHS. Prod Plan Control 24(10/11):931–947
Lim KH, Benbasat I (2000) The effect of multimedia on perceived equivocality and perceived usefulness of information systems. MIS Q 24(3):449–471
Lindenauer PK, Remus D, Roman S et al (2007) Public reporting and pay for performance in hospital quality improvement. N Engl J Med 356(5):486–496. doi:10.1056/NEJMsa064964
Liu HC, Itoh K (2013) Conceptual framework for holistic dialysis management based on key performance indicators. Ther Apher Dial 17(5):532–550. doi:10.1111/1744-9987.12019
Lux MP, Fasching P, Schrauder M et al (2011) The era of centers: the influence of establishing specialized centers on patients' choice of hospital. Arch Gynecol Obstet 283(3):559–568
Mant J (2001) Process versus outcome indicators in the assessment of quality of health care. Int J Qual Health Care 13(6):475–480. doi:10.1093/intqhc/13.6.475
Mears A, Vesseur J, Hamblin R et al (2011) Classifying indicators of quality: a collaboration between Dutch and English regulators. Int J Qual Health Care 23(6):637–644
Meyer JW, Rowan B (1977) Institutionalized organizations: formal structure as myth and ceremony. Am J Sociol 83(2):340–363
Miller A, Cioffi J (2004) Measuring marketing effectiveness and value: the Unisys marketing dashboard. J Advert Res 44(3):237–243. doi:10.1017/S0021849904040334
Moore MH (2000) Managing for value: organizational strategy in for-profit, nonprofit, and governmental organizations. Nonprofit Volunt Sect Q 29(suppl 1):183–208
Naranjo-Gil D, Hartmann F (2007) How CEOs use management information systems for strategy implementation in hospitals. Health Policy 81(1):29–41
Northcott HC, Harvey MD (2012) Public perceptions of key performance: Alberta Canada. Int J Qual Health Care 24(3):214–223
OECD (2013) Health at a glance: OECD indicators. OECD, Paris. doi:10.1787/health_glance-2013-en
Osoba D (2002) A taxonomy of the uses of health-related quality-of-life instruments in cancer care and the clinical meaningfulness of the results. Med Care 40(6):III31–III38
Paine KD (2004) Using dashboard metrics to track communication. Strateg Commun Manag 8 (5):30–33
Panaretto KS, Gardner KL, Button S et al (2013) Prevention and management of chronic disease in Aboriginal and Islander community controlled health services in Queensland: a quality improvement study assessing change in selected clinical performance indicators over time in a cohort of services. BMJ Open 3(4):e002083. doi:10.1136/bmjopen-2012-002083
Parida A, Chattopadhyay G (2007) Development of a multi-criteria hierarchical framework for maintenance performance measurement (MPM). J Qual Maint Eng 13(3):241–258. doi:10.1108/13552510710780276

Pauwels K, Ambler T, Clark BH et al (2009) Dashboards as a service: why, what, how, and what research is needed? J Serv Res 12(2):175–189. doi:10.1177/1094670509344213

Pizzini MJ (2006) The relation between cost-system design, managers' evaluations of the relevance and usefulness of cost data and financial performance: an empirical study of US hospitals. Account Organ Soc 31(2):179–210

Render M, Freyberg R, Hasselbeck R et al (2011) Infrastructure for quality transformation: measurement and reporting in veterans administration intensive care units. BMJ Qual Saf 20 (6):498–507

Rivard-Royer H, Beaulieu M, Friel T, HEC Montréal (2003) Groupe de recherche Chaîne. HEC Montréal, p 10

Sackett DL, Rosenberg W, Gray J et al (1996) Evidence based medicine: what it is and what it isn't. BMJ 312(7023):71

Sadraoui T, Mchirgui N (2014) Supply chain management optimization within information system development. Int J Econ Financ Manag 2(2):59–71

Scott WR (2001) Institutions and organizations. Sage, Thousand Oaks, CA

Shepherd KD, Farrow A, Ringler C, Gassner A, Jarvis D (2013) Review of the evidence on indicators, metrics and monitoring systems. World Agroforestry Centre (ICRAF), Nairobi, p 6

Shohet IM (2006) Key performance indicators for strategic healthcare facilities maintenance. J Constr Eng Manag 132(4):345–352, http://dx.doi.org/10.1061/

Smith PC (2005) Performance measurement in health care: history, challenges and prospects. Public Money Manag 25(4):213–220

Smith M, Saunders R, Stuckhardt L et al (2013) Best care at lower cost: the path to continuously learning, health care in America. The National Academies Press, Washington, DC

Stadler H (2008) Supply chain management—an overview. In: Stadler H, Kilger C (eds) Supply chain management and advanced planning: concepts, models, software and case studies. Springer, Berlin, pp 9–33

Stelfox HT, Straus SE (2013) Measuring quality of care: considering measurement frameworks and needs assessment to guide quality indicator development. J Clin Epidemiol 66 (12):1320–1327

Tarantino DP (2003) Using the balanced scorecard as a performance management tool. Physician Exec 29(5):69–72

Tashobya CK, Da Silveira VC, Ssengooba F et al (2014) Health systems performance assessment in low-income countries: learning from international experiences. Global Health 10(5):5. doi:10.1186/1744-8603-10-5

Ten Asbroek AHA, Arah OA, Geelhoed J et al (2004) Developing a national performance indicator framework for the Dutch health system. Int J Qual Health Care 16(S1):i65–i71

Vanhaecht K, De Witte K, Sermeus W (2007) The care process organisation triangle: a framework to better understand how clinical pathways work. J Integr Care Pathw 11(2):54–61. doi:10.1258/j.jicp.2007.169

Veillard J, Champagne F, Klazinga N et al (2005) A performance assessment framework for hospitals: the WHO regional office for Europe PATH project. Int J Qual Health Care 17(6):488

Villa S, Barbieri M, Lega F (2009) Restructuring patient flow logistics around patient care needs: implications and practicalities from three critical cases. Health Care Manag Sci 12(2):155–165

Vissers J, Beech R (2005) Health operations management: basic concepts and approaches. In: Vissers J, Beech R (eds) Health operations management: patient flow logistics in health care. Routledge, New York, p 344

Walters JL, Mackintosh S, Sheppard L (2012) The journey to total hip or knee replacement. Aust Health Rev 36(2):130–135. doi:10.1071/AH11050

Weerawat W, Pichitlamken J, Subsombat P (2013) A generic discrete-event simulation model for outpatient clinics in a large public hospital. J Health Care Eng 4(2):285–305

Wollersheim H, Faber MJ, Grol RPTM et al (2006) Vertrouwen in verantwoorde zorg? effecten van en morele vragen bij het gebruik van prestatie-indicatoren. Centrum voor Ethiek en Gezondheid, Den Haag

Yang C-C, Cheng L-Y, Yang C-W (2005) A study of implementing Balanced Scorecard (BSC) in non-profit organizations: a case study of private hospital. Hum Syst Manag 24(4):285–300

Yang SL, Su SI, Chien CW et al (2007) Logistics innovation process model and its application—a case study of a Medical Center in Taiwan. Hosp Health Serv Adm 40(4):72–85

Yigitbasioglu OM, Velcu O (2012) A review of dashboards in performance management: implications for design and research. Int J Account Inf Syst 13(1):41–59. doi:10.1016/j.accinf.2011.08.002

Yin RK (2013) Case study research: design and methods. Sage, London

Zanjirani R, Farahani N, Davarzani H (2009) Supply chain and logistics in national, international and government environment. Springer, Heidelberg

Kaat De Pourcq is a Ph.D. researcher at Ghent University, Belgium, Department of Innovation, Entrepreneurship and Service Management. Her research focuses on health operations management and more particularly on the patient experience. She is a member of the Curama Healthcare Management Research Center and the Center for Service Intelligence at Ghent University, and has experience as a hospital nurse.

Her current research is part of a multidisciplinary project. The ultimate goal of this study is to develop a method and toolbox for the coordination, alignment and optimization of the patient, supply and information flows taking into account various resources (such as materials, staff and equipment) and the introduction of innovative IT systems such as RFID. To simultaneously increase the efficiency and quality of their operations, hospitals invest in process management and process optimization from an organizational and patient perspective. This assumes an integrated view on the flows of patient, materials and information. However, integrating the perspectives of the industry into health care is challenging. The findings in this study have led to the writing of this book chapter.

Paul Gemmel is a Professor of Service and Healthcare Management at the Faculty of Economics and Business Administration at Ghent University and Senior Research Fellow at the Vlerick Business School, both located in Belgium. He is co-founder of the Curama Healthcare Management Research Center, the Center of Service Intelligence (CSI) at Ghent University and of the MINOZ Research Center for Hospital Management at the Vlerick Business School. His research is in the area of service operations management and health care operations management. His current research focuses on how process changes in hospitals have an effect on operational efficiency, service quality and the patient experience. He has been involved in several process improvement projects with health care managers in emergency departments, chemotherapy day units, diabetic clinics etc. He has participated in projects on hospital management for the Flemish and Belgian government. He is (co-)author of several articles in peer reviewed health care and service management journals and of several management books.

Jeroen Trybou combines an economic and clinical background. He is Assistant Professor of Healthcare Management and Policy at Ghent University, Belgium, and acts as a Senior Advisor Finance & Strategy of health care organizations (Probis Consulting). He is also visiting professor at University College Odisee in Ghent, member of the board of an elderly care organization (VZW Ter Kimme) and the Dutch Society of Health Economics. Currently he is lead author of about 15 international peer-reviewed articles. He presents his research frequently at conferences and participates as a reviewer for several journals.

The Boundaryless Hospital Through Risk Management Approach: A Case Study of the A&E Unit of a Tertiary-Care Hospital in Malta

Sandra C. Buttigieg, Dorothy Gauci, and Prasanta K. Dey

Abstract

Over the years, several scholars and policy makers have attempted to provide solutions to minimize risk in health care, and consequently improve patient safety. Possible solutions are to have parts of the health services better integrated, as well as to optimize resources safely through risk management principles. Twenty years ago, Braithwaite and colleagues discussed the future of the hospital and coined the term *boundaryless hospital* (Braithwaite et al., Aust NZ J Med 24(5):565–571, 1994). The authors foretell a radical change in the nature of the modern hospital with the advent of state-of-the-art information technology and innovative clinical equipment. Similarly, over the past two decades, risk management principles have been applied to health care (Dey et al., Manag Serv Qual 16(2):203–222, 2006; Liberatore and Nydick, Eur J Oper Res 189(1):194–207, 2008). Health care organizations are being tasked with doing more with less while still striving to safeguard patient safety as well as to operate at lowest levels of risk. The main aim of this research is to improve the quality of care in the accident and emergency (A&E) unit of a Maltese tertiary-level hospital through the assessment of risk and the concept of a *boundaryless hospital*. This study adopts a risk management framework to identify risk factors that affect the quality of care, analyze their likelihood and impact, and develop responses to mitigate those risks. Through assessment of the risks at the system level, innovative solutions can be applied to reduce boundaries in the patient care pathway.

S.C. Buttigieg (✉) • D. Gauci
Faculty of Health Sciences, Department of Health Services Management, University of Malta, Room 7, Block A, Level 1, Mater Dei Hospital, 2090 Msida, Malta
e-mail: Sandra.buttigieg@um.edu.mt

P.K. Dey
Aston Business School, Aston University, Birmingham, UK

H. Albach et al. (eds.), *Boundaryless Hospital*, DOI 10.1007/978-3-662-49012-9_10

Keywords
A&E Unit • Boundaryless hospital • Risk analysis • Risk map • Cause and effect diagram • Malta • Quality of care

1 Introduction

Among the top priorities of any health care system, the most costly, and with the highest risk, is the accident and emergency (A&E) department. This remains the first port of call to the ever technologically advancing secondary and tertiary care. In many countries, there is a wide gap between what community and primary services can offer and what is available in secondary and tertiary care (Genet et al. 2013). It is no surprise that the frequency of use of emergency services is on the increase, both in the U.S., as well as in Europe, as patients' expectations of receiving the best evidence-based and most technologically sophisticated management is on the rise (Schuur and Venkatesh 2012). In the UK, for example, this increase was 3.6 % annually over a 10-year period, after adjusting for age. The reasons for this being mainly "complex and inter-related and include rising community expectations" (Lowthian et al. 2012). One commonly hypothesized reason is associated with service reduction in the primary health sector, which may push more people to use A&E as their 'primary' service. Additionally, a reduction of primary health care services and curtailment of the social care budget may affect more vulnerable key groups like the frail and the elderly, leading to more severe clinical conditions, thereby requiring more emergency care and hospitalization (Schuur and Venkatesh 2012). Additionally, Dixon et al. (2011) provide a comprehensive assessment on whether or not the UK population accesses the health services appropriately, and found lower utilization of primary care services by the lower socio-economic groups that are then more likely to experience emergency admissions. Several scholars and policy makers have attempted to provide solutions as to how the various parts of the health services can be better integrated, as well as how to optimize resources safely through risk management principles. Twenty years ago, Braithwaite and colleagues discussed the future of the hospital and coined the term *boundaryless hospital*. The authors foretell a radical change in the nature of the modern hospital with the advent of state-of-the-art information technology and innovative clinical equipment (Braithwaite et al. 1994). Similarly, over the past two decades, risk management principles are being applied widely across sectors, not the least of which is health care (Dey et al. 2006; Liberatore and Nydick 2008). The quest for doing more with less, while striving to operate at maximum levels of safety and at lowest levels of risk has become an absolute necessity in health care.

The main aim of this research is to improve quality of care in the accident and emergency (A&E) unit of a Maltese tertiary-level hospital through the assessment of risk and the concept of a *boundaryless hospital*. This study adopts a risk management framework to identify risk factors that affect the quality of care, analyze their likelihood and impact, and develop responses to mitigate these risks. This analysis will primarily look at the operational systems in place at the A&E and what aspects of this system lead to added risk. Through assessment of the risks at the system level, innovative solutions can be applied to reduce boundaries in the patient-care pathway.

2 A&E in a Boundaryless Hospital

The concept of a *boundaryless hospital* depicts hospital services that are not limited by boundaries of space, expertise or sectors. The integrated concept of care would envision maximized system efficiency through the use of IT services and technological innovations that reduce boundaries that may be barriers for the delivery of services (Braithwaite et al. 1994). The concept of boundaryless organizations is not a new one. Indeed, its chief architect is GE's CEO Jack Welch, who famously spoke of the need to "knock down the walls that separate us from each other on the inside and from our key constituents on the outside" (Hirschhorn and Gilmore 1992, p. 104). Nevertheless, its application to health services, and in particular to emergency services, brings with it many challenges. The acute and emergency nature of the A&E service often pushes physicians and nurses to function as if in a silo service. The A&E is the entry point for most patients reaching the hospital but may find itself cut off from both primary care services, as well as from other hospital departments, namely because of its gatekeeping role. Internally, professionals in the A&E deal with a large volume of "boundary work" as patients move through the service—from initial entrance, stabilization, diagnosis and treatment (Nugus et al. 2010). The hectic, fast-paced A&E department, in which professionals must make quick decisions while dealing with different service providers and technologies, is therefore a complex system characterized by dynamic interactions between services and individuals along the patient trajectory. With every boundary encountered in the A&E, the risks of lowering efficiency and quality decrease as interactions with other services bring the possibility of miscommunication, misunderstandings and conflicts (Duckett and Nijssen-Jordan 2012).

3 Why Focus on Risk Management?

As patients are facilitated through the A&E department, the boundaries, which are often characterized by bottlenecks, waiting, misinformation and crisis management bring with them risks that may impact on the efficiency and quality in the delivery of care. As professionals seek to integrate clinical services across disciplines and departments, risks arise as a product of the operational processes within the system. The more complex the system is, the greater the possibility that system failures occur. This makes risk management an important tool to be applied where the topmost priority is for management to fully understand the boundary points in the system and the risks that may arise at these boundaries. Risk management covers the process of identifying, analyzing, and responding to risk (Hopkin 2014). Through this, it aims to maximize the results of positive events and minimize the consequences of adverse events. Risk management can therefore be applied effectively to any system if the operational processes within the system are clearly outlined, thus allowing for identification of the key features in the system that may be a source of risk. In 2009, the International Organization for Standardization (ISO) published the ISO 31000 family of standards that specifically relate to risk management. The aim is to supply a standardized universal framework that can be used widely and that is available to practitioners and companies, thus allowing for a standard method in the application of risk management in organizations (Purdy 2010).

Risk can be defined as any possible event that can negatively affect the operability of a system. In the context of the complexity of health care systems, health care risk management addresses five categories of possible risk in the system: (a) patient-care related (care and clinical management of patients); (b) medical-staff related (medical staff conduct, training, licensing etc.); (c) employee related (occupational health and safety); (d) property related (repair, maintenance of equipment and buildings) and (e) financial (American Society for Healthcare Risk Management 2010).

The risk management methodology applies four key phases (American Society for Healthcare Risk Management 2010):

(1) **Risk identification**—the process by which risks in the system environment that constitute potential losses are identified. Loses may be financial, physical human or intangible.
(2) **Risk analysis**—determining the potential severity of the loss which is linked to the risk and the probability of such a loss occurring. This stage of the process establishes the seriousness of the risk and provides guidance on the type of strategy required to address the risk.
(3) **Risk response development**—responses to the risk are developed. They can relate to controlling the risk through preventing losses or mitigating the loss or financing the risk which involves pay off for the losses that occur.
(4) **Control and documentation**—risk management strategy is documented, controlled and evaluated to assess the adequateness and appropriateness of the strategies employed.

4 Risk Management in the Health Care Setting

Health care risk management was born as a sub-discipline of management in the U. S., primarily due to increases in malpractice cases in the 1970s that led to financial pressures on hospitals with a surge in patient claims and consequently demands on medical professional insurers. Out of this was born, what is now known as the American Society for Healthcare Risk Management. At the time, health care risk management focused primarily on the risks associated with financial loss at health care organization level. However, following the publication of a report from the Institute of Medicine showing the widespread consequences of medical error in hospitals, focus shifted toward patient safety. The report "To err is human: Building a safer health system" highlighted the toll that medical errors have on patients, as well as on health care organizations. In the U.S., in terms of total national cost of preventable adverse medical events (loss of income, disability, health care costs and loss of production), it is estimated that between US$17 and 29 billion are lost annually with over half being attributed to health care cost (Kohn et al. 2000). Furthermore, this movement toward patient safety highlights the parallel, and sometimes overlapping, work undertaken by quality managers and risk managers. All disciplines involved in risk management work to analyze adverse events and to specifically find root causes of these events (ECRI 2009). The stakeholders that have a vested interest in risk management are patients, health insurers, medical indemnity insurers, hospital systems and federal agencies (American Society for Healthcare Risk Management 2010).

A systematic review by De Vries et al. (2008) found that nearly one out of every ten patients can expect to experience an adverse event upon admission to a hospital. Nearly half of these were classified as preventable adverse events. Similarly, in a study by Smits et al. (2010) they found 61 % of all adverse events were related to human error and that interventions related to adverse events should be directed primarily to human causes. However, in recent years there has been a paradigm shift in focus, namely that rather than targeting interventions to address errors by personnel, organizations are being asked to audit their operating systems to determine failures that in the first place can lead to these human errors. While it may be difficult to change the human component that leads to mistakes, system-level changes can help prevent, detect and mitigate any errors (Nolan 2000). This makes risk management an ideal management tool that can be applied widely across health care settings, since its primary goal is to outline and assess the operational processes within any system that may lead to error.

5 Risks in the Accident and Emergency Department

The A&E department is a unique system and presents a complex network of processes due to the nature of the services offered. Patient-doctor contacts in the A&E are different than in other settings within hospitals as they are not usually linked to prior relationships between doctors and patients, contacts are brief, and patients' assessments often take place within fast-paced and hectic environments (Cydulka et al. 2011). Moreover, overcrowding at A&E departments remains one of the key drivers affecting quality of care and adds to increased risk within the system (McCusker et al. 2014; Roberge et al. 2010). Epstein et al. (2012) identified a clear association between high levels of emergency room crowding and risk of preventable medical errors. Overcrowding in the A&E department is affected by input, throughput and output factors along patient care pathways as patients move into, within and out of the department. Non-urgent visits and a large amount of visitors lead to a high volume of patient traffic and congestion within the department. This, coupled with inadequate staffing and communication failures, creates gridlocks in the speedy movement of patients within and out of the department. Bed shortages create the final bottleneck delaying admission of patients for inpatient care and further adding to the frequently and globally reported problems of overcrowding, confusion and crisis management of A&E departments (Hoot and Aronsky 2008).

Against this background, it comes as no surprise that a commonly cited root cause of error at A&E is miscommunication between staff members, which is therefore a point of risk in particular during transition of care or handoff of patients across different health care professionals (Cheung et al. 2010). Another primary concern of patients at A&E relates to missed diagnoses or diagnostic errors, failure to reach correct diagnoses or misdiagnoses, all of which can lead to serious harm and even death (Kachalia et al. 2007). White et al. (2004) found that 45 % of malpractice suits are due to failure to diagnose. More recently and providing more objective evidence, Tehrani et al. (2011) revealed that diagnostic errors are the most frequent and most costly of all medical mistakes in a 20-year summary of U.S. malpractice claims for diagnostic errors from 1985 to 2005. In this review, the authors discovered that 54 % were due to failure to diagnose, 19 % were due to delay in diagnosis, and 10 % were due to the wrong diagnosis. The literature provides ample evidence that the A&E department brings with it inherent levels of risk at multiple points in its operating systems, which warrant detailed assessments to prevent errors and to ensure improved quality of care. One way of keeping vigilant on avoiding risks is to conduct frequent risk identification in health care data (Ryan et al. 2012) and audits of near misses (Tunçalp and Souza 2014), while adopting 'learning' organization strategies (Dahlgaard et al. 2011). Specifically within the A&E, newer triage systems have been developed and validated so as to minimize risk and improve emergency medical decision-making. For example, a new five-level protocol, Medical Emergency Triage and Treatment System (METTS), in primary triage and secondary priority decisions in emergency medicine, combines vital signs, symptoms, and signs in the triage decision and is a reliable triage method and a sensitive tool for secondary re-evaluation of patients in A&E (Widgren and Jourak 2011). Moreover, it is clear that the A&E department should not operate in silos within its confines, but must function beyond its boundaries in coordinated activities with stakeholders both within the health sector, as well as across sectors. This calls for examining risk management principles within the concept of the *boundaryless hospital* and applying these principles to the A&E department.

The salient risks within the A&E identified earlier, namely miscommunication, crisis management, chaotic environment and problems with diagnoses can be mitigated through virtual means by capitalizing on the benefits of a fully integrated information technology system across health services (Buntin et al. 2011; Waterson 2014), and physically by establishing clear pathways of communication with stakeholders outside the hospital (e.g. GPs, rehabilitation, social care, police etc.) and those in other departments within hospitals for expertise and consultations. An analogous networking systems being employed in larger countries with multiple emergency service providers are trauma networks. Trauma networks are primarily employed to ensure that all patients suffering an injury are treated at the time and place that benefits them most, regardless of the place of injury. The network consists of a group of services and professionals who offer an integrated trauma service across multiple professionals and organizations. A number of studies across different countries have shown the benefits in service delivery and quality of trauma and critical care. In Florida, the advent of trauma networks has shown reductions in mortality and length of stay among geriatric patients in areas serviced by trauma networks primarily due to better accessibility of services (Ang et al. 2014). Another study in the U.S. assessed the use of the Internet for image transfer across centers in a trauma network during patient transfers. The study showed that with the implementation of an Internet-based transfer system there was a reduction in the repeat of CT scans leading to savings of US$84.65 per patient and reduction in radiation exposure associated with the trauma (Flanagan et al. 2012). Similar studies in Europe have shown the improvements in health outcomes for trauma patients and better allocation of services with the introduction of trauma networks in the UK (McQueen et al. 2014) and Germany (Ruchholtz et al. 2014).

6 Case Study

6.1 Setting

This study was conducted within the A&E department of Mater Dei Hospital—the main acute public tertiary hospital in Malta. Mater Dei Hospital was opened in 2007 and offers state-of-the-art services across a number of specialties. While many stand-alone IT packages are available in the hospital and state-of-the-art diagnostic technologies are used, these services lack integration across systems. The A&E department caters to almost 300 patients per day; the bulk of emergency care in Malta is delivered here since it is the only department offering critical care services on the island. Due to this, the A&E department has felt the strain leading to long waiting hours and overcrowding (Muscat et al. 2014). Studies have found that the service suffers a major bottleneck due to waiting time for admission into in-patient services while over 80 % of patients who do not fit the highest priority criterion can expect to wait a minimum of 1 h before first assessment and 4 h before admission to hospital or discharge (Azzopardi et al. 2011).

6.2 Method

This study used a case study method at the A&E department at Mater Dei Hospital. Following a review of the literature, a risk management framework for the A&E department was formulated and risk factors were identified with respect to processes, human and materials resources, and infrastructures using a cause and effect

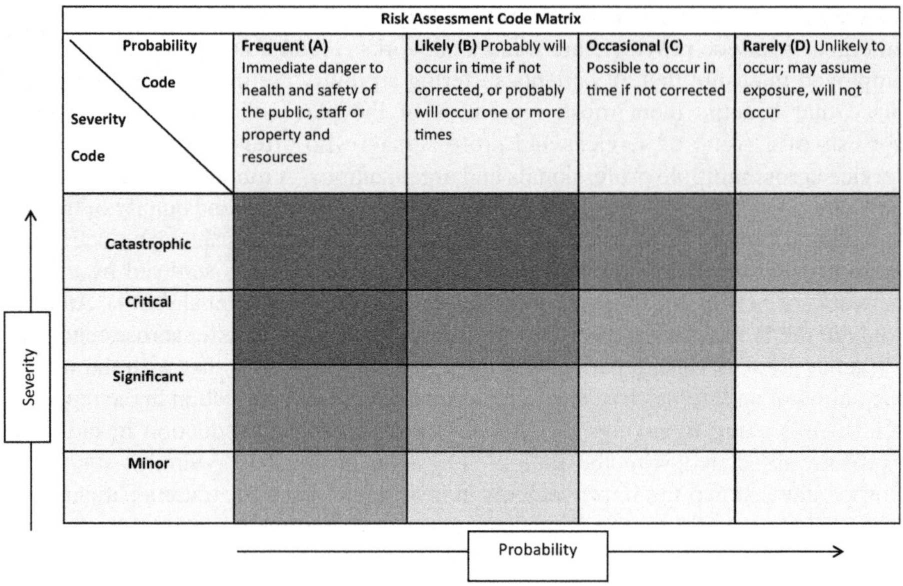

Fig. 1 Risk assessment grid for severity and probability of risk

diagram. To ensure that the framework developed was representative of the system within A&E at Mater Dei Hospital, a 3-h observational session was held. Once the framework was finalized, a focus group session was held with seven A&E staff members: a consultant emergency medicine, a junior doctor, a practice development nurse, a newly graduated nurse undergoing a specialized training, a radiologist, a porter and a receptionist.

The focus group session was structured into two parts. The first part consisted of an expert review of the risk model developed, with emphasis on outlining general and specific risks inherent within the system. The second part of the session addressed the likelihood and impact of risks, which were determined using a risk severity grid. Figure 1 shows the grading of the probability of risk versus the severity. The focus groups were also tasked with suggesting/were asked to suggest mitigating measures for these risks.

Apart from the data gathered in the focus group, time-motion data were collected over an hour during the observational study to assess the doctor-patient contact time while reviewing patients in the A&E. This analysis looked at the time allocated to patient care and time used up due to unrelated interruptions.

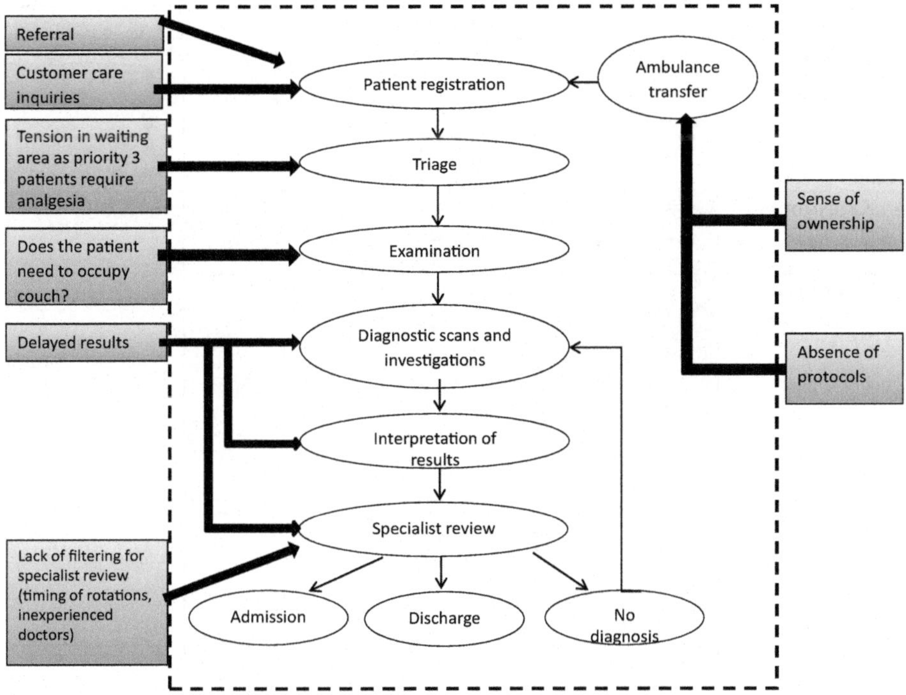

Fig. 2 Risk identification in Maltese A&E along patients' pathways

6.3 Results

6.3.1 Focus Group

Figure 2 describes the patient pathway (enclosed in dash box) within the A&E department as conceptualized during the focus group session. The risks (gray boxes) outlined at different points along the pathway within the system are attached to the respective boundary points in the pathway.

It is clear that at every point, from when the patient is transported to the A&E by ambulance or is referred by other health care professionals into the A&E, risks arise due to interactions with patients and staff, as well as interactions between staff. This clearly highlights the border work occurring along the patient pathway as patients move between different services and as members of the staff negotiate the dynamic relationships within these services.

The focus group was asked to assess the risk probability and severity for each risk highlighted using the risk matrix described previously. Figure 3 outlines the risk severity and probability as assigned by the A&E staff members.

One notes that none of the risks were listed as minor by the staff and no risk was given a probability of 'rarely'. Miscommunication and limited IT services were highlighted as likely and catastrophic risks in the A&E department. In addition to acute shortage of beds, limited staff and bottlenecks, which are all linked to

Risk Assessment Code Matrix				
Probability Code / Severity Code	**Frequent (A)** Immediate danger to health and safety of the public, staff or property and resources	**Likely (B)** Probably will occur in time if not corrected, or probably will occur one or more times	**Occasional (C)** Possible to occur in time if not corrected	**Rarely (D)** Unlikely to occur; may assume exposure, will not occur
Catastrophic		Communication, HR, Staff levels, IT, bottle necks, bed shortage		
Critical	Delayed CT-Scan	Stress in waiting areas, Lack of Filtering to specialists, absence of protocols for porters, teamwork, resource capacity, prioritisation, stress, multitasking, lack of experience		
Significant		Referrals, Customer care enquiries, Lack of sense of ownership, finances, media, lack of training,	Does the patient really need the couch?	
Minor				

Fig. 3 Severity of risks and probability of risks in the A&E, as outlined by focus group

increased waiting time and overcrowding, delay in performing CT scans was categorized as critical and frequent. The other risks were seen as likely with the degree of severity varying from critical to significant. This risk matrix helps prioritize the areas in the system that require most attention based on the level of severity and the probability of the risk occurring.

Table 1 shows the risk themes categorized as general or specific risks under the headings of risk type highlighted by the American Society for Healthcare Risk Management (2010).

Most of the risks highlighted by staff members at the A&E were patient-related risks outlining the focus on risks specifically within the process of patient-care management. This may indicate that the health care service providers focus on quality of care rather than on elements of risk that may influence financial or property losses.

After outlining the risks and their severity/probability, members of the focus group were asked to outline mitigating measures to address the risks. The following recommendations were put forward:

- Implement quality assurance frameworks to be able to assess quality of care at the A&E
- Increase space in the department by providing alternatives that make health centers more attractive, thus reducing the number of individuals seeking care at the A&E who do not require such emergency care
- Facilitate the referral mechanisms, especially the ones from primary health services and mental health services, to avoid unnecessary referral of non-urgent cases
- Implement the use of key performance indicators (KPIs) specific to the department, such as timing of the duration for the patient to meet health care professionals that are monitored and fed back into the system on a regular basis
- Provide for a floor manager who can co-ordinate and filter patients though the system to reduce unnecessary reviews by consultants, thus reducing delay and burden on specialists.
- Enable the IT system to provide timely and correct data to be able to implement the quality assurance measures. In addition, implement a dashboard system focused on A&E activities to help managers prioritize time and human resources
- Allow specific diagnostic tests, such as CT scans and ECGs, to be aligned operationally with the whole system because barriers to access are primarily due to the fact that these systems are run by separate departments in Mater Dei Hospital outside of the Emergency Department
- Use point-of-care testing at A&E that can save time in reaching critical decision making and save lives

6.3.2 Time-Motion Analysis

During the 1-h observation session, time-motion analysis for one consultant's review of a patient was conducted. The consultant was tasked with reviewing the case of a child injured in a bike accident. The total amount of patient-doctor contact time for this case was 26.5 min from the beginning to the end of the review; however as illustrated in Table 2, the actual time taken to review the patient was 33.5 min because of multiple interruptions for consultation on three other cases

Table 1 General and specific risks identified by focus group, by risk category

	Patient-related	Medical staff-related	Employee-related
General risks	Patients waiting in A&E corridors Irritated patients and relatives Increase in human error due to long shifts	Multitasking of A&E consultants (frequent interruptions) Varying quality in training across A&E professional groups Lack of experience of young professionals	Stress, particularly when A&E is overcrowded Lack of psychological support to staff
Specific risks	Delayed results of investigations Delayed CT scans Absence of protocols IT system	Lack of sense of ownership by staff	Customer care inquiries

Table 2 Time motion analysis of review of Case 1, with outline of points were review was interrupted

	Case 1	Case 2	Case 3	Case 4
T	Start of review			
T + 1		1 min interruption		
T + 3.5			2 min interruption	
T + 8.5		30 s interruption		
T + 9.5			1 min interruption	
T + 15.5				1 min interruption
T + 23.5		30 s interruption	30 s interruption	
T + 31		30 s interruption		
T + 33.5	End of review			

which increased the time needed to complete the review of this particular patient by 7 min.

This time-motion analysis shows that multi-tasking and multiple interruptions reduce the efficiency of the examination and review of patients in the A&E department as person-to-person contact is required for information purposes. But above all, the interruptions might be potential sources of medical error as the physician is highly likely to lose concentration or become distracted.

7 Discussion

This study helps shows how risk management can be affectively applied to identify risk factors, analyze them and develop risks responses with the involvement of health care professionals active in the field. This helps the health professionals develop a sense of ownership and make decisions on implementing quality improvement projects through appropriate analysis of service level efficiency. Additionally, this allows for the practicing of preventive approaches in quality of care. This approach is relevant in the context of boundary work assessment because the boundaries in health service delivery—cross sectorial, cross-professional and cross-entity—are all points in the service delivery pathway that may bring risk of exposure to loss.

To avoid constraint by inertia, any organization or department, like the A&E, should constantly evaluate itself with performance measurements and risk assessment. This helps to keep the momentum to improve the value drivers of the organization toward a fully efficient and 'no risk state'. This is a goal that we aspire to but are unable to fully achieve due to the very nature and dynamics of health care. Health care organizations, including the A&E, are considered as professional complex adaptive systems (Chassin and Loeb 2013), leading to insights for improving the service from within. In this study, participants outlined a number of risks that arise along the patient pathway in the A&E. Focus group participants highlighted how risks arise as patients transition from one service to the other—

be it from initial registration into triage or examination to consultant review. This shows clearly that a lack of integration in services and limited seamlessness in the boundary negotiations between professionals and services during multiple stages of patient handoff reduces efficiency and, worse still, quality of care. The symptoms of these boundaries are a silo nature of services and professionals and the characteristic features of A&E departments today—overcrowding, miscommunication, bed shortages, stress, errors and overworked staff.

The boundaryless hospital services envisioned by Braithwaite and colleagues 20 years ago suggest that reducing or limiting these boundaries is achievable through the use of technological and IT advances (Braithwaite et al. 1994). Indeed, participants in this study highlighted the need for specific IT systems that can provide timely and correct data to staff, thus reducing the person-to-person contact time required to make decisions on the course of action taken for the care of patients. A study by Frisse et al. (2012) assessed the financial impact of health information exchange in the emergency department. The study evaluated the financial implication of having a comprehensive set of clinical and administrative data available through a single health information system. The web-based system was available in 11 emergency departments. The approximate annual savings made through the availability of the single access data system was US$1.07 million with the majority of the costs being saved through reduction in admissions. Indeed "ehealth" and the use of Internet are pushing the traditional boundaries within health service delivery. A number of examples are available where transfer of patient information is possible across a large network that is not restricted to a specific building, sector or profession (Rusu et al. 2011). In Malta, a number of ehealth related services were made available in 2006 that facilitate access to services by professionals such as online referrals. A novel ehealth application launched in Malta 2012 is the "myhealth" platform. This system enables patients and doctors to access electronic health records over the Internet through a unique e-id (Muscat et al. 2014). While as yet, the Internet and IT integrated services are not readily used in the A&E in Malta, the appearance of ehealth platforms applied in the health sector may indicate an impetus to implement more innovative IT solutions to improve access to services and create smoother service delivery.

This study found that a major risk in the A&E is the overcrowding due to unnecessary referrals—either self-referral or from other services. Indeed, better networking between primary and other care services such as mental health and rehabilitation would serve to reduce overcrowding of emergency services and ensure that those requiring the most critical care are served quickly and efficiently. Due to the limitation of size and service providers in Malta, trauma networks may not be a plausible system as applied in larger countries with greater issues of accessibility due to distance. However, an innovative solution being employed in the A&E to also address the boundary issues in accessing services in other departments is the use of point-of-care testing (POCT). POCT is often simple tests that incorporate user-friendly technologies (Pai et al. 2012). An important aspect of POCTs is that they can be conducted by non-specialized health care staff for in the emergency department, thus removing the boundary developed between the A&E and other external departments. Indeed, POCT helps health care professionals obtain results right at the patient's bedside, which ensures that results are faster and can be assessed quicker reducing the risks seen because of unnecessary delay. In 2013 the A&E department at Mater Dei Hospital introduced a stand-alone blood analyzer machine, to analyze blood gases (arterial or venous and include pH, HCO_3 and base excess), lactate, urea, electrolytes, blood glucose and others as POCT. The aim of the POCT services is to reduce delay in obtaining definite diagnoses that can save lives.

8 Conclusion

A&E is the point of a patient's entry in many secondary- and tertiary-level care hospitals. Therefore, quality of care in A&E has a strong impact on overall quality of care of hospitals and health systems. Emergency service can indeed be referred to as the heart of a health system and, therefore, the malfunction of the A&E would result in a snowballing negative effect on other parts of the system. If the risks of non-achievement of quality in an A&E are studied and appropriate mitigating measures are undertaken, not only can one improve A&E performance but this improvement will cascade to the rest of the hospital and health system so that the overall performance would be substantially enhanced. Although quality of care in an A&E has been studied at length in health care literature, very little has been discussed about the use of risk management principles and, in particular, within the context of a *boundaryless hospital* in dealing with quality management issues and challenges within an A&E. Indeed, the removal of unnecessary boundaries and application of the proposed framework could be adopted in any health care system for achieving superior quality of care through risk management principles.

References

American Society for Healthcare Risk Management (2010) Risk management handbook for health care organizations. Wiley, San Francisco

Ang D, Norwood S, Barquist E, McKenney M, Kurek S, Kimbrell B, Garcia A, Walsh CB, Liu H, Ziglar M, Hurst J (2014) Geriatric outcomes for trauma patients in the state of Florida after the advent of a large trauma network. J Trauma Acute Care Surg 77(1):155–160

Azzopardi M, Cauchi M, Cutajar K, Ellul R, Mallia-Azzopardi C, Grech V (2011) A time and motion study of patients presenting at the accident and emergency department at mater dei hospital. BMC Res Notes 4(1):421

Braithwaite J, Vining R, Lazarus L (1994) The boundaryless hospital. Aust NZ J Med 24 (5):565–571

Buntin MB, Burke MF, Hoaglin MC, Blumenthal D (2011) The benefits of health information technology: a review of the recent literature shows predominantly positive results. Health Aff 30(3):464–471. doi:10.1377/hlthaff.2011.0178

Chassin MR, Loeb JM (2013) High-reliability health care: getting there from here. Milbank Q 91 (3):459–490

Cheung DS, Kelly JJ, Beach C, Berkeley RP, Bitterman RA, Broida RI, Dalsey WC, Farley HL, Fuller DC, Garvey DJ, Klauer KM, McCullough LB, Patterson ES, Pham JC, Phelan MP, Pines JM, Schenkel SM, Tomolo A, Turbiak TW, Vozenilek JA, Wears RL, White ML, Section of Quality Improvement and Patient Safety, American College of Emergency Physicians (2010) Improving handoffs in the emergency department. Ann Emerg Med 55(2):171–180

Cydulka RK, Tamayo-Sarver J, Gage A, Bagnoli D (2011) Association of patient satisfaction with complaints and risk management among emergency physicians. J Emerg Med 41(4):405–411

Dahlgaard JJ, Pettersen J, Dahlgaard-Park SM (2011) Quality and lean health care: a system for assessing and improving the health of healthcare organisations. Total Qual Manag Bus Excell 22(6):673–689

De Vries EN, Ramrattan MA, Smorenburg SM, Gouma DJ, Boermeester MA (2008) The incidence and nature of in-hospital adverse events: a systematic review. Qual Saf Health Care 17 (3):216–223

Dey PK, Hariharan S, Brookes N (2006) Managing healthcare quality using logical framework analysis. Manag Serv Qual 16(2):203–222

Dixon A, Le Grand J, Henderson J, Murray R, Poteliakhoff E (2011) Is the NHS equitable?: a review of the evidence. LSE Health and Social Care, London School of Economics and Political Science, London

Duckett S, Nijssen-Jordan C (2012) Using quality improvement methods at the system level to improve hospital emergency department treatment times. Qual Manag Health Care 21 (1):29–33. doi:10.1097/QMH.0b013e31824180f6

ECRI (2009) Risk management, quality improvement, and patient safety. Risk Qual Manag Strateg 2(4)

Epstein SK, Huckins DS, Liu SW, Pallin DJ, Sullivan AF, Lipton RI, Camargo CA Jr (2012) Emergency department crowding and risk of preventable medical errors. Intern Emerg Med 7 (2):173–180

Flanagan PT, Relyea-Chew A, Gross JA, Gunn ML (2012) Using the internet for image transfer in a regional trauma network: effect on CT repeat rate, cost, and radiation exposure. J Am Coll Radiol 9(9):648–656

Frisse ME, Johnson KB, Nian H, Davison CL, Gadd CS, Unertl KM, Turri PA, Chen Q (2012) The financial impact of health information exchange on emergency department care. J Am Med Inform Assoc 19(3):328–333. doi:10.1136/amiajnl-2011-000394

Genet N, Boerma W, Kroneman M, Hutchinson A, Saltman RB (2013) Home care across europe. European Observatory on Health Systems and Policies, London

Hirschhorn L, Gilmore T (1992) The new boundaries of the "boundaryless" company. Harv Bus Rev 70(3):104–115

Hoot NR, Aronsky D (2008) Systematic review of emergency department crowding: causes, effects, and solutions. Ann Emerg Med 52(2):126–136

Hopkin P (2014) Fundamentals of risk management: understanding, evaluating and implementing effective risk management. Kogan Page, London

Kachalia A, Gandhi TK, Puopolo AL, Yoon C, Thomas EJ, Griffey R, Brennan TA, Studdert DM (2007) Missed and delayed diagnoses in the emergency department: a study of closed malpractice claims from 4 liability insurers. Ann Emerg Med 49(2):196–205

Kohn LT, Corrigan JM, Donaldson MS (2000) To err is human: building a safer health system. National Academies Press, Washington, DC

Liberatore MJ, Nydick RL (2008) The analytic hierarchy process in medical and health care decision making: a literature review. Eur J Oper Res 189(1):194–207

Lowthian JA, Curtis AJ, Jolley DJ, Stoelwinder JU, McNeil JJ, Cameron PA (2012) Demand at the emergency department front door: 10-year trends in presentations. Med J Aust 196(2):128–132

McCusker J, Vadeboncoeur A, Lévesque J, Ciampi A, Belzile E (2014) Increases in emergency department occupancy are associated with adverse 30-day outcomes. Acad Emerg Med 21 (10):1092–1100

McQueen C, Crombie N, Perkins GD, Wheaton S (2014) Impact of introducing a major trauma network on a regional helicopter emergency medicine service in the UK. Emerg Med J 31 (10):844–850. doi:10.1136/emermed-2013-202756

Muscat NA, Calleja N, Calleja A, Cylus J (2014) Malta: a health system review. WHO, Copenhagen, 2014. Health Syst Transit 16(1)

Nolan TW (2000) System changes to improve patient safety. BMJ 320(7237):771–773

Nugus P, Carroll K, Hewett DG, Short A, Forero R, Braithwaite J (2010) Integrated care in the emergency department: a complex adaptive systems perspective. Soc Sci Med 71 (11):1997–2004

Pai NP, Vadnais C, Denkinger C, Engel N, Pai M (2012) Point-of-care testing for infectious diseases: diversity, complexity, and barriers in low-and middle-income countries. PLoS Med 9 (9):e1001306

Purdy G (2010) ISO 31000: 2009—setting a new standard for risk management. Risk Anal 30 (6):881–886

Roberge D, Pineault R, Larouche D, Poirier LR (2010) The continuing saga of emergency room overcrowding: are we aiming at the right target? Healthc Policy 5(3):27–39

Ruchholtz S, Lefering R, Lewan U, Debus F, Mand C, Siebert H, Kuhne CA (2014) Implementation of a nationwide trauma network for the care of severely injured patients. J Trauma Acute Care Surg 76(6):1456–1461. doi:10.1097/TA.0000000000000245

Rusu M, Saplacan G, Sebestyen G, Todor N, Krucz L, Lelutiu C (2011) eHealth: towards a healthcare service-oriented boundary-less infrastructure. Appl Med Inform 27(3):1–14

Ryan PB, Madigan D, Stang PE, Marc Overhage J, Racoosin JA, Hartzema AG (2012) Empirical assessment of methods for risk identification in healthcare data: results from the experiments of the observational medical outcomes partnership. Stat Med 31(30):4401–4415

Schuur JD, Venkatesh AK (2012) The growing role of emergency departments in hospital admissions. N Engl J Med 367(5):391–393

Smits M, Zegers M, Groenewegen PP, Timmermans DR, Zwaan L, van der Wal G, Wagner C (2010) Exploring the causes of adverse events in hospitals and potential prevention strategies. Qual Saf Health Care 19(5):e5. doi:10.1136/qshc.2008.030726

Tehrani AS, Lee H, Mathews S, Shore A, Frick K, Makary M (2011) 20-year summary of US malpractice claims for diagnostic errors from 1985–2005. In: 33rd Annual Meeting of the Society for Medical Decision Making, Chicago, IL, pp. 22–26

Tunçalp Ö, Souza J (2014) Maternal near-miss audits to improve quality of care. BJOG 121 (s4):102–104

Waterson P (2014) Health information technology and sociotechnical systems: a progress report on recent developments within the UK national health service (NHS). Appl Ergon 45 (2):150–161

White AA, Wright SW, Blanco R, Lemonds B, Sisco J, Bledsoe S, Irwin C, Isenhour J, Pichert JW (2004) Cause-and-effect analysis of risk management files to assess patient care in the emergency department. Acad Emerg Med 11(10):1035–1041

Widgren BR, Jourak M (2011) Medical emergency triage and treatment system (METTS): a new protocol in primary triage and secondary priority decision in emergency medicine. J Emerg Med 40(6):623–628

Sandra C. Buttigieg is Associate Professor and Head of the Department of Health Services Management at the Faculty of Health Sciences at the University of Malta. She lectures in health services management, public health, and family medicine. Dr Buttigieg graduated MD (University of Malta in 1987), M.Sc. in Public Health Medicine (1997), and MBA (Executive) (2002). In 2007, she obtained her Ph.D. in Management from Aston University, UK, and in 2009, was elected Fellow of the Faculty of Public Health of the Royal Colleges of Physicians of the UK. In 2008, Dr Buttigieg was appointed Honorary Research Fellow at Aston University, UK, and in 2013, Honorary Senior Research Fellow at the University of Birmingham, UK. Dr Buttigieg is Visiting Scholar at James Madison University, Virginia, US, and at the Kuwait University, Kuwait. She is also a fellow of two programs of the Salzburg Global Seminar related to health care. Her research is mainly in health management, public health and organizational psychology. She has published articles in management and health journals, and is currently on the Editorial Advisory Board of the Journal of Health Organization and Management. She is a member of the research committee of the Health Care Management Division, American Academy of Management.

Dorothy Gauci holds a Master's degree in Epidemiology from the London School of Hygiene and Tropical Medicine. In 2013 she joined the Department of Health Services Management, University of Malta. Her Master's thesis analyzed survival and statistical cure for colorectal cancer in Malta. Since 2008 she has been working within the Ministry for Energy and Health, Malta, being primarily responsible for the implementation and analysis of national health surveys. She is also the representative for Malta within the morbidity and health interview survey technical groups set up by EUROSTAT. 2012–2013 she undertook an 8-month traineeship within the European Monitoring Centre for Drugs and Drug Addiction (EMCDDA) in Lisbon and worked primarily on data management and statistical support.

Prasanta K. Dey is a Professor of Operations Management at Aston Business School, UK. Prior to joining Aston University in 2004, he worked for five years in the University of the West Indies in Barbados as a Director of the graduate project management program and 13 years in Indian Oil Corporation Limited, India, as a project executive. He specializes in supply chain management and project management. He has published more than a hundred research papers in leading international refereed journals. He has accomplished several research projects in supply chain optimization and project management maturity studies in manufacturing, services and construction globally covering both small- and medium-sized enterprises (SMEs) and large sectors. He has received funding from Ford Foundation, Research Council UK, British Council, West Midlands Manufacturing Advisory Services, EU and ERDF. He has delivered several research projects in health care in Barbados, Malta and the UK. He is the Editor-in-Chief of the International Journal of Energy Sector Management.

Leveraging the Value for Health Care Providers Using Clinical Workflow Analytics

Eva Gattnar, Okan Ekinci, and Jens Schneider

Abstract

Improving the effectiveness and efficiency of health care is very important nowadays. Optimization of clinical workflows regarding quality, time and costs is one of the current key management strategies. Applying clinical workflow analytics, the whole hospital's workflows can be assessed. The assessment results provide the possibility to identify process strengths, weaknesses and risks, which can be used for further risk analysis and process optimization in health care. Besides that, clinical decision support can be provided based on the analytics results. Both lead to an improved quality of clinical processes and workflows. Especially for hospitals it can directly enhance the clinical, operational and financial outcome and the quality of care while leveraging the *value* in health care.

Keywords

Clinical workflow • Workflow analytics • Clinical process optimization • Clinical process quality • Value

1 Introduction

Driving clinical information technology (IT) has been a priority for many large health care organizations like hospitals, partly due to IT's capability as a powerful tool for not only monitoring patient safety in the care delivery settings, but also in helping organizations rapidly achieve clinical, operational and financial efficiency.

E. Gattnar (✉) • O. Ekinci • J. Schneider
Siemens Healthcare GmbH, Healthcare Consulting, Allee am Röthelheimpark 3a, 91052 Erlangen, Germany
e-mail: eva.gattnar@siemens.com

H. Albach et al. (eds.), *Boundaryless Hospital*, DOI 10.1007/978-3-662-49012-9_11

For a number of organizations, IT investments have been primarily focused on infrastructure developments such as implementing transactional systems, either for back office operations including finance and billing, or on direct patient care in hospital departments (Jackson and Chequeta 2009) like radiology.

Often clinical processes are supported by the clinical IT systems but lacking at the same time process quality focus. Extracting additional data from involved clinical IT systems for process and workflow improvements build tremendous possibilities for process improvements based on workflow analysis and lead to new applications for health care consulting business enabling leveraging the *value* for health care providers.

In this contribution, first the relevant terms like process quality, process quality improvement and workflow are introduced. Based on this, nowadays' challenges in health care are presented leading to the explanation of *value* in health care. Finally, clinical IT systems are described as providers of necessary data for workflow analytics applications within health care organizations like hospitals.

2 Processes and Process Quality

2.1 Process Quality

Processes are significant components within an organization. Process orientation and process management are among others the most important management methods to support customer-oriented strategies and products. Thereby, the economic benefit of mature processes is approvable. Following the international Detecon study (DETECON 2009; Gattnar and Ekinci 2011), a higher operational performance of an organization's processes results directly in an improved return on equity (ROE) as well as in an improved return on assets and return on investment (ROI). The resulting positive financial effects are exactly measurable. To be successful, companies have to apply optimization approaches aiming a higher process maturity and improved process performance (Gattnar and Ekinci 2011). However, there is a high amount/number of IT implementations in hospitals, which do not fulfill the expectancy regarding the ROI.

Organizational processes are affected by quality, costs and time aspects. According to the traditional quality-cost model, achieving a higher process quality requires higher conformance expenditure. However, according to a modified model, in a dynamic learning environment, quality-based learning allows the reduction of the conformance expenditures. Process quality improvements also correlate with the time dimension depending on the organization in question. Considering time-critical processes, time has a more important role as it has in a non-critical environment. Process quality itself is constrained by the risks, which an organization is willing to accept (Gattnar and Ekinci 2011; Ekinci and Gattnar 2011). Process-oriented risks are risks associated with "incomplete, incorrect or poorly-managed implementation of processes" (Van Loon 2004). Thereby, not all aspects of risks are addressed. They may additionally include "strategic, organizational, financial, personnel and product related risks" (Van Loon 2004). Following

Van Loon (2004), especially process-oriented risks are often caused by inappropriate process management. Examples are not deployed best practices or inappropriate management practices (Van Loon 2004). Furthermore, appropriate process quality always requires process quality assurance. Thereby, defined processes have to be assessed regarding the compliance with specific organizational guidelines as well as internal and external standards (Gattnar and Ekinci 2011; Kneuper and Wallmüller 2009).

2.2 Process Quality Improvement and Optimization

Quality of services and products correlates often directly with process quality. Therefore, processes should not be reduced to simple task descriptions. In fact, they should be applied as an important basis for service or product quality improvement (Gattnar and Ekinci 2011).

Process quality can be affected through process improvement itself and an increased process performance. Process assessments can be performed to evaluate the organizational processes and assure a high quality (Gattnar and Ekinci 2011). The assessment results should be used for guiding the initiation of potential process improvements and enhance process performance and outcome (Freidinger 2008). The objectives include also the organizational establishment of baseline tools supporting improvement efforts and the measurement of the improvement activities' progress (Ahern et al. 2004).

Clinical process optimization for increased efficiency and effectiveness through breaking down departmental barriers is an important goal for health care providers. Working directly with physicians across departmental boundaries is the prerequisite to develop organizational and structural workflow improvements. To achieve that, appropriate measures and responsibilities have to be defined to support a process improvement implementation.

3 Healthcare Environment

3.1 Challenges in Health Care

Improving the effectiveness and efficiency of health care is very important nowadays. Optimization of clinical pathways regarding quality, time and costs is one of the current key management strategies. Although they are highly standardized, the diagnostics and treatment processes can be more or less time-consuming depending on the workflow bottlenecks in a particular hospital. To identify workflow bottlenecks and reduce risks in clinical workflows it requires a thorough understanding about both the clinical IT systems and clinical workflows (Gattnar et al. 2011; Ekinci et al. 2011; Detschew et al. 2011).

Risks in health care often lead to quality problems and reduce the quality of care. Reducing the risk means less time is spent fixing problems and more time is spent efficiently and effectively treating patients. Therefore, health care organizations have to systematically evaluate and improve their process quality and have to address all relevant quality dimensions in health care: the structure, the process and the outcome dimension (Gattnar and Ekinci 2011; Ekinci and Gattnar 2011).

Besides that, a process focus within health care organizations complements the emphasis the organization places on both its people and its technology. Thereby, health care organizations are today typically faced with the following three critical dimensions (Gattnar and Ekinci 2011):

(1) people with skills, training, and motivation, who improve processes and use equipment and tools,
(2) procedures and methods defining the relationship of tasks, which help to perform the processes,
(3) tools and equipment used in the organization, which can be used to simplify and automate processes and make work more efficient and effective.

Clinical workflows are therefore strongly influenced by the closed interaction between people, procedures, tools and equipment. The synergies and interactions of these three dimensions create competitive advantages leading to organizational success within health care.

3.2 "Value" in Health Care

The objective of health care organizations—providing best quality of care to patients—is reached by the medical services provided by the hospital. Theoretically, these services are described in a "medical production function" with labor and capital as its inputs. The inputs are efficient in the sense that no input is wasted at any level of quality. Efficiency of treatment is measured as cost per unit of output at any level of quality of the hospital (Healthknowledge 2013).

Even though not all hospitals and health systems have made the switch from fee-for-service to a pay-for-value model, the time is ripe for organizations to begin experimenting with performance and quality of care incentives (Punke 2013). Following that, *value* in health care can be described as a ratio between the outcomes that matter to patients in terms of quality and the cost per patient (Porter and Lee 2013).

4 Clinical IT Systems

Health care processes are nowadays heavily dependent on information technology (IT). With the enormous impact and rapid evolvement of IT, there is a major demand for standardization in health care IT (Gattnar et al. 2011; Ekinci et al. 2011; Detschew et al. 2011; Wirsz 2000). DICOM (Digital Imaging and Communications in Medicine) as one of the clinical standards defines the format and mechanism for exchange and storage of information in radiological environment (NEMA 2013). DICOM includes a large number of specific services and the producers are committed to their implementation because of so-called conformance statements. By comparing the declarations of different systems, basically it is possible to determine, whether they can interact with each other (NEMA 2009). Manufacturers have at least a minimum level of general conformance requirements to meet, in order to demonstrate general conformity to the DICOM standard. Conformance statements are an integral part of the DICOM standard (Gattnar et al. 2011; Ekinci et al. 2011; Detschew et al. 2011).

So-called DICOM worklists are generated by the Radiology Information System (RIS). They contain patient data, details of the examination orders, the procedure parameters and appointments and can be accessed by image acquisition devices (modalities) for planning examinations. In return, a modality is able to generate so-called Modality Performed Procedure Steps (MPPS), a structured information (such as start time, end time, status, dose, material consumption etc.), which can be sent to the RIS at the beginning ("MPPS in progress") and the end ("MPPS completed") of an examination (Gattnar et al. 2011; Ekinci et al. 2011; Detschew et al. 2011; Noumeir 2005).

Outside the radiology department of a hospital the second important clinical standard, Health Level 7 (HL7), standardizes the transfer of patient information between IT systems (HL7 2011). The communication in HL7 follows the message-based communication principle. Accordingly, the various systems interact with each other via messages. Data exchange is initiated between two or more systems through an event from the real world (trigger event) such as the admission of a patient (Gattnar et al. 2011; Ekinci et al. 2011; Detschew et al. 2011). This event implies the exchange of data between the various systems, distinguishing between specific and general requests. The patient's master data request initiated by a laboratory information system (LIS) would correspond to a specific request. General requests are on the contrary usually caused by short-term events in the real world. If such a trigger event is registered in a system, a transaction is started, which in turn causes an event and respectively a transaction on the target system (Gattnar et al. 2011; Ekinci et al. 2011; Detschew et al. 2011). While DICOM is a standard for image transmission in radiology, HL7 is a standard for electronic data exchange outside of radiology in the catchment area of the hospital information system (HIS). A HIS is an IT-based management system. It supports medical and clinical patient care and documentation, organization, administration and communication in a hospital (Haas and Kuhn 2007; Huang 2010). Another important task of the HIS is the evaluation of the costs and the efficiency of hospital organization for a longer period of time (Huang 2010).

The RIS is one of the IT systems in the field of radiology, which controls the daily tasks of one or more radiological departments. It is responsible for both—the administrative and clinical support—in the radiology to relieve the staff from administrative tasks. On the other hand, it improves the quality of radiological examinations (Huang 2010). Picture Archiving and Communications Systems (PACS) as another component represent the technological core of a modern, digital radiology department (Ralston and Coleman 2009). The main task of PACS is to store, distribute and display medical images for interpretation and evaluation. Further IT systems in radiology departments are so-called modalities. Modalities are known as imaging systems in the medical industry (Gattnar et al. 2011; Ekinci et al. 2011; Detschew et al. 2011). Modalities represent combined with PACS the technological core of a modern, digital radiology department (Gattnar et al. 2011; Ekinci et al. 2011; Detschew et al. 2011; Ralston and Coleman 2009).

5 Workflow Analytics in Health Care

Health care organizations perform services in the field of patient care, diagnostics, treatment etc. Patient care and treatment entail certain risks. Risks that occur become problems that can reduce the quality of care and may even cause business failures. Reducing the risk means less time is spent fixing problems and more time is spent efficiently and effectively treating patients (Gattnar and Ekinci 2011; Ekinci and Gattnar 2011). Analyzing the data generated and stored by the clinical IT systems can help health care organizations to systematically evaluate and improve their process quality and to address all relevant quality dimensions in health care: the structure, the process and the outcome dimension (Gattnar and Ekinci 2011).

Clinical workflows are characterized as people-intensive and patient-centered processes where physicians and clinical staff work closely together use materials, devices and methods to attend and treat the patient (Gattnar and Ekinci 2011). Clinical workflow analytics can be used for clinical workflow capability and maturity measurement taking the synergies and interactions between people, procedures, tools and equipment into account (Gattnar and Ekinci 2011).

Many quality improvement initiatives in health care focus either on improved efficiency or on improved patient satisfaction. According to Carman et al. (1996)

> Reengineering may produce process improvements without producing change in work culture. Such gains may or may not be held and may or may not have a positive effect on customer satisfaction. All of the elements of continuous quality improvement taken together are designed to achieve a change in the workforce culture that will produce process improvements, facilitate holding the gains from process improvements, and impact favorably on customer satisfaction as well as increase economic efficiency.

Distilling data from clinical IT systems is essential for performing clinical workflow capability and maturity measurements as described above. Following Ahern et al. (2004), process capability is “the inherent ability of a process to produce planned results”. In particular, process capability is essential regarding the predictability and measurement of clinical workflows. Furthermore, measuring the process capability and maturity helps to identify quality and productivity issues and provides solutions to control and eliminate them. Finally, a continuous improvement of process capability increases also an organization’s whole process maturity.

Besides that, clinical IT systems have enormous potential to enhance the *value* in today's challenging health care environment. Analyzing additional data from clinical IT systems like HIS, RIS, PACS, LIS and modalities, the return on investment can be enhanced while delivering the best possible outcomes for patients. Thereby, clinical workflow analytics can help to identify the potential fields, where process improvements should be performed within health care organizations. Aiming that, it is necessary to investigate how these improvements can be effectively disseminated and implemented across the health care organization.

On that account, the long-term challenge in health care organizations requires focusing on additional available data and the way in which it can be used. A practical example is the management of time-critical diseases such as heart attack or stroke. Clinical workflow analytics used for instance for clinical decision support in such time-constrained care situations can save time while increasing quality of care and therewith improving the care process. Furthermore, clinical workflow analytics within the health care IT environment enables the usage of new process optimization approaches and solutions. Using techniques supported by clinical workflow analytics leads additionally to an automated and standardized patient monitoring, process mining and workflow management. Based on that, the implementation of innovative care pathways to ensure sustainable quality of care is supported. In addition, the IT systems in health care can be used at the same time in an efficient and effective manner accounting value-oriented aspects in health care.

6 Conclusion

For cost reduction and quality enhancement reasons, the use of IT analytics technologies to manage clinical workflows is currently a top priority for the majority of hospitals. Using clinical workflow analytics, the whole hospital's workflows can be assessed. The assessment results provide the possibility to identify process strengths, weaknesses and risks, which can be used for further risk analysis and process optimization in health care. Besides that, clinical decision support can be provided based on the analytics results. Both lead to an improved quality of clinical processes and workflows. Especially in hospitals it can directly enhance the clinical, operational and financial outcome and the quality of care while leveraging the *value* in health care.

However, devising a successful strategy for implementing new IT analytics infrastructure in hospitals is not always easy with tight budgetary margins and high expectations from the management. The majority of hospitals is therefore first developing an infrastructure that focuses on improving data collection, storage and processing to reduce the challenges during the IT implementation (Bresnick 2015). 37 % of hospitals implementing IT analytics have problems with managing volumes of data effectively (Caraher and Tobin 2015). In addition, interoperability issues, cultural resistance, and difficulties defining what data needed to be collected affect more than a third of organizations. To reduce these challenges, the IT efforts should stay focused on providing a solid foundation of data capture and storage capabilities (Bresnick 2015).

References

Ahern D, Clouse A, Turner R (2004) CMMI distilled—a practical introduction to integrated process improvement, 2nd edn. Addison-Wesley, Boston

Bresnick J (2015) How successful hospitals start to tackle Big Data analytics. http://healthitanalytics.com. Accessed 1 Dec 2014

Caraher K, Tobin M (2015) Analytics in healthcare, CDW Survey, CDW Healthcare. http://www.cdwnewsroom.com. Accessed 1 Dec 2014

Carman J, Shortell S, Foster R et al (1996) Keys for successful implementation of TQM in hospitals. Health Care Manag Rev 21(1):48–60

DETECON (2009) Der Einfluss der Prozessreife auf den Erfolg von Telekommunikationsunternehmen. Detecon Study. www.detecon.com/bpm. Accessed 1 Dec 2014

Detschew V, Gattnar E, Ekinci O (2011) A novel way of standardized and automized retrieval of timing information along clinical pathways. In: Proceedings of the 23th international conference of the European Federation for Medical Informatics (MIE 2011). IOS Press, Amsterdam, The Netherlands, pp 507–211

Ekinci O, Gattnar E (2011) Qualitätsmanagement im Krankenhaus—Konzepte, Rahmenbedingungen und Standards. In: Podium der Wirtschaft, Recht & Soziales, vol 21, VHK. Altdorf b. Nbg, pp 67–130

Ekinci O, Gattnar E, Detschew V (2011) Interoperable process monitoring using clinical IT-standards and healthcare information systems. In: Informatics 2011 (I2011)—Proceedings of the IADIS Multi Conference on Computer Science and Information Systems (MCCSIS 2011), IADIS Press, pp 59–66

Freidinger R (2008) Geschäftsprozessmodellierung. University of Cooperative Education, Stuttgart

Gattnar E, Ekinci O (2011) Process assessment and improvement using capability maturity models. In: Podium der Wirtschaft, Recht & Soziales, vol 22, VHK, Altdorf bei Nürnberg, pp 121–148

Gattnar E, Ekinci O, Detschew V (2011) An integrated approach to standardized and automated extraction of clinical process cycle times. In: e-Health 2011 (eH2011)—Proceedings of the IADIS Multi Conference on Computer Science and Information Systems (MCCSIS 2011). IADIS Press, pp 128–136

Haas P, Kuhn K (2007) Krankenhausinformationssysteme—Ziele, Nutzen, Topologie, Auswahl. In: Kramme R (ed) Medizintechnik: Verfahren, Systeme, Informationsverarbeitung, 3rd edn. Springer, Berlin, pp 733–755

Healthknowledge (2013) Principles of health economics. Health Knowledge, Public Health Textbook. http://www.healthknowledge.org.uk/public-health-textbook. Accessed 1 Dec 2014

HL7 (2011) Health Level 7. http://www.hl7.org. Accessed 1 Dec 2014

Huang H (2010) PACS and imaging informatics, 2nd edn. Wiley, Hoboken, NJ

Jackson L, Chequeta A (2009) Leveraging business intelligence for healthcare, Oracle White Paper. Oracle Corporation, Redwood Shores, CA

Kneuper R, Wallmüller E (2009) CMMI in der Praxis—Fallstudien zur Verbesserung der Entwicklungsprozesse mit CMMI, dpunkt.verlag, Heidelberg

NEMA (2009) Part 2: Conformance. National Electrical Manufacturers Association, Rosslyn, VA

NEMA (2013) Digital imaging and communications in medicine. http://medical.nema.org. Accessed 1 Dec 2014

Noumeir R (2005) Benefits of the DICOM modality performed procedure step. J Digit Imaging 18 (4):260–269
Porter M, Lee T (2013) The strategy that will fix health care. Harv Bus Rev 91(10):50–70
Punke H (2013) Top 10 strategic initiatives for hospitals in 2013. Becker's Hosp Rev. http://www.beckershospitalreview.com/strategic-planning/top-10-strategic-initiatives-for-hospitals-in-2013.html. Accessed 1 Dec 2014
Ralston M, Coleman R (2009) Introduction to PACS. In: Branstetter BF (ed) Practical imaging informatics: foundations and applications for PACS professionals. Springer, New York, pp 33–48
Van Loon H (2004) Process assessment and improvement—a practical guide for managers, quality professionals and assessors, 2nd edn. Springer, New York
Wirsz N (2000) Overview of IT-standards in healthcare. Electromedica 68(1):21–24

Eva Gattnar holds a Diploma and a Master's degree in Computer Science. For her doctoral degree she has done research in the field of medical informatics with focus on clinical process modelling, monitoring, workflow analysis and optimization as well as clinical decision support systems. Before joining Siemens Healthcare Enterprise Solutions she worked for the Siemens Healthcare Competence Center Business Intelligence (BI), where she was responsible for the development of new BI-applications as a BI consultant and project manager. As a Business Development Manager she is focusing on new business models for hospitals. Besides that, she is lecturer for e-health at the Technical University Nuremberg, Germany.

Okan Ekinci joined Siemens Healthcare 2006 as Global Marketing Manager, Cardiovascular MRI, and became Chief Medical Officer, Cardiology, in 2008, Global Head of Cardiology in 2009 and Vice President Healthcare Consulting & Clinical Affairs in 2013.

Before joining Siemens Healthcare he worked as Section Chief Cardiovascular MRI & CT at the German Clinic for Diagnostics (DKD) in Wiesbaden, Germany. Before that he had done his residency/fellowship in cardiology at Kerckhoff Heart Center in Bad Nauheim and DKD Wiesbaden, Germany. He still practices medicine part-time as an instructor for advanced cardiac imaging and serves the European Commission as an expert for the same topic.

Okan Ekinci studied medicine in Izmir, Mainz and Houston, and graduated in 1998 from the University of Mainz, Germany. He holds an MBA from the European School of Management and Technology (Berlin) and is senior lecturer for cardiac imaging at the University College Dublin.

Jens Schneider holds a German degree in business administration and is since more than 10 years successful as a consultant and in other leading roles in hospitals. He specialized in strategy, organization development, process consulting, controlling and green hospital for hospitals globally as well as projects for C-suite of Siemens Healthcare. He gained work experience in stationary and ambulatory health care facilities in several countries, in health care politics, commercial banking and consulting. Since 2008 he has been working within Siemens Healthcare Consulting and he is leading the department.

Role and Function of the Emergency Department in a Boundaryless Hospital: Optimizing the Process Flow

Maximilian C. von Eiff and Wilfried von Eiff

Abstract

Over the last years an increase of patient demand in hospital emergency departments (ED) by at least 7–10 % per year has been observed.

In a *boundaryless hospital* the ED plays a pivotal role as a gatekeeper and has a hub function because 30–50 % of all inpatients are admitted as emergency patients first. The ED is challenged to overcome four typical boundaries: the management boundary of being forced to enhance medical quality and contain costs simultaneously, the primary-acute care boundary, the boundary between ED management and hospital management (management level) and the boundary between ED patient service and acute care service (clinical level). Tearing down these boundaries by optimizing the process of ED patient flow can contribute to shorten average length of stay in the ED, to lower patient risks and to reduce treatment costs. In two independent randomized, prospective two-center cohort studies (with 184 and 260 patients) evidence could be verified that process optimization for the treatment of patients suffering from acute coronary syndrome (ACS) contributes significantly to both cost savings and enhanced medical quality. Moreover, point-of-care testing (POCT) technology leads to speeded up turn-around times for lab test results of critical parameters. As a consequence, crowding effects could be reduced and an exoneration of ED capacity could be stated.

Keywords

POCT • Emergency department • Process optimization • Laboratory • ACS • Acute coronary syndrome • Troponin • Thoracic pain • Patient flow

M.C. von Eiff
Faculty of Medicine, University of Pécs, Pécs, Hungary

W. von Eiff (✉)
Center for Health Care Management and Regulation, HHL Leipzig Graduate School of Management, Jahnallee 59, 04109 Leipzig, Germany
e-mail: wilfried.von.eiff@hhl.de

H. Albach et al. (eds.), *Boundaryless Hospital*, DOI 10.1007/978-3-662-49012-9_12

1 Context: The Boundaryless Hospital and the Role of Emergency Departments

Most of the developed health care systems (especially the German health care system) are divided in more or less independently acting service sectors: the primary care sector (containing general practitioners, family doctors, imaging centers), the secondary care sector (determined by acute care hospitals and specialized clinics), the rehabilitation sector (outpatient rehab facilities and rehab clinics) and the sector for elderly care (nursing homes, elderly homes, meals on wheels, community service/nurse/physician). Furthermore, these four sectors of care provision are financed by different services and steering regulations are set by different parties.

1.1 The Value Chain in Health Care

The management approach of the *boundaryless hospital* aims to overcome these sectoral borders as well as interfaces in hospital workflows and especially to reduce handover situations, which are typical sources for failures and waste of resources. This approach orientates business models of medical care close to the management concept of the value chain: best performing internal and external organizational units get an integrated part of patient service processes in order to secure outstanding levels of medical quality, safety and patient-centeredness (Fig. 1).

The value chain approach, originally developed for industrial branches (Porter 1998) and successfully transformed for health care (Eiff 2013b), intends to align the core business processes strictly to the customers' needs and leads to a process-driven organization that is characterized by overcoming the classical management approach "Only doing by yourself is doing best".

1.2 Purpose of the Emergency Department

With 40–50 % of all inpatients admitted as emergency patients first (DGINA 2010), the question for the strategic, medical and economic functionality of an emergency organization gets a particular meaning. The interdisciplinary emergency care unit is a gatekeeper and has a hub function between primary care sector and inpatient care. Additionally, it is the first focal point for patients with different medical condition symptoms and disease entities: patients with minor wounds such as not dangerous cuts as well as poly-traumatized patients, people with life-threatening diseases (stroke, AMI, embolisms etc.) and abuse patients (alcohol, medicaments, drugs etc.). The emergency department quickly

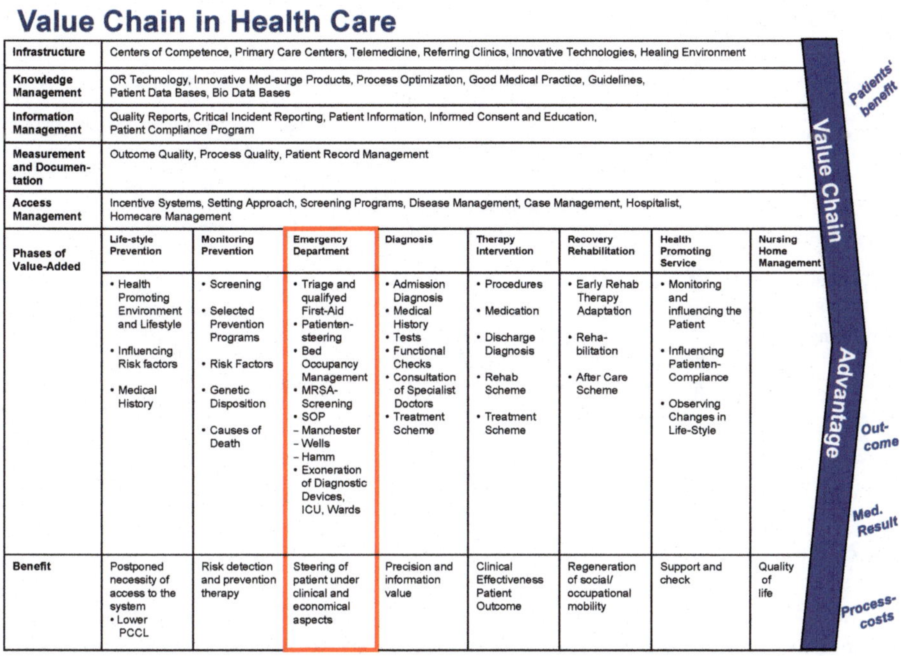

Fig. 1 The pivotal role of the emergency department as liaison institution between primary and secondary care sectors

- provides for a qualified diagnosis adapted to the relevant subject areas,
- initiates the primary therapy, and
- decides on further patient treatment (release from hospital/referral to the GP, observation in the reception ward or chest pain unit, transfer to the responsible and most capable medical department).

In that sense, the emergency department plays a pivotal role in the care process for patients in critical life-threatening conditions and is a linking pin between the primary and the secondary care sector.

The ED is challenged to overcome four typical boundaries (Fig. 2)

- The *Management Boundary* (1) is typical for the situation in German hospitals especially because administrative decision-makers prefer to base procurement decisions (medical devices, surgical products,. . .) rather on purchasing prices than oriented to life-cycle costs of an investment. An investment in POCT technology in order to shorten the therapeutic turn-around time for a troponin-I marker from 112 to 20 min contributes to reducing "crowding effects" and resource blockades in the emergency department. A quick measurement of troponin-I has clinical relevance for ED patients with "non-specific thoracic pain" and especially for high-risk patients with a low suspicion of ACS ("late responders").

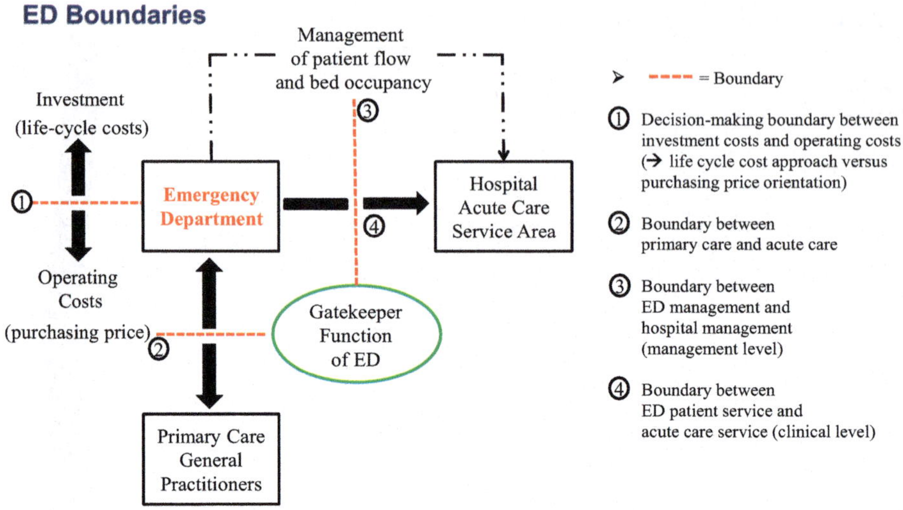

Fig. 2 Typical boundaries an emergency department has to overcome

- The *Boundary between primary care and acute care* (2) forces the ED management to integrate the preclinic emergency care into the care process inside the ED. The transmission of the result of a 12-channel ECG to the ED before the patient with suspicion of ACS arrives in the clinic could be life-saving and leads to a controlled medical process. On the other hand between 50 and 70 % of the patients showing up in the ED do not really need emergency treatment. These patients contribute to increasing waiting times and resources blockade in the ED and should better be served in the primary care sector.
- The *Boundary between emergency care and acute care area* (cath lab, ICU, IMC, ward) is characterized by two levels: The *management level* (3) copes with the common problem that beds and treatment resources are not available on time. In consequence, the ED management is encumbered with bed management and other time consuming activities of coordinating the patient flow. On the *clinical level* (4) the emergency physicians have to manage continuum services from acute care specialists (e.g. neurology in case of stroke; specialists for ophthalmology, pediatrics, obstetrics, etc.).

In these four areas of conflicting boundaries the ED plays the role of a gatekeeper.

1.3 Process Optimization

In many German hospitals the emergency departments suffer from crowding effects caused by an extended average length of stay (LOS) and due to the phenomenon that between 30 and 70 % of the patients entering the ED do not deserve an emergency status. The waiting times for troponin test results of patients with non-specific thoracic pain (12–18 % of ED patients) are one reason for non-acceptable length of stay in the ED. In addition the variation in the turn-around time (TAT) between taking the blood and the availability of the test results is fluctuating between 42 and 121 min (average TAT = 73 min): a non-controlled process with high variance and cost intensive blockades of ED resources. These figures result from scientific analyses carried out by the Center for Hospital Management, University of Münster, in three German teaching hospitals.

Taking this background into account it seems to be worth looking for opportunities to optimize the process of caring for patients with "non-specific thoracic pain" and especially for high risk patients with a low suspicion of ACS. The critical success factor for efficient and effective treatment of ACS patients is the availability of the results of a troponin check. In other words, a short time between taking the blood sample from an ACS patient and the therapeutic decision of the physician (=therapeutic turn-around time) contributes to lowering risks for patients and to a shortened length of stay in the emergency department.

Basically, troponin tests can be processed in two alternative resource settings:

- Performing troponin measurement in a central laboratory setting leads to a minimum LOS of 174 min in the ED.
- A point-of-care-testing technology is said to carry out troponin test results within 15 min after taking the blood sample and so has the potential to reduce crowding effects.

2 POCT as an Investment Object

The achievement potential of clinical processes is determined by means of performance criteria

- Throughput/waiting time
- Medical quality (complications, infections, relocations ...)
- Consumption of resources
- Patient outcome
- Costs (direct costs, indirect costs, opportunity costs, intangible costs)
- Error rate/proneness to error
- Risks (probability of loss, discovery probability, consequences for the patient in case of appearance)

Medical decision structures—critical in terms of time and with economical relevance—are typically found in the area of the central emergency department. The application of POCT in the ED raises the following questions:

- Can POCT devices help to eliminate quality disturbing variances from clinical processes?
- Is there a connection between stability and projectability of a diagnostic process on the one hand and medical treatment quality and patient outcome on the other hand?
- Can staff, medical devices and functional diagnostic areas in the ED and in the wards be supported by prompt availability of certain lab parameters so that the costs of patient care processes can be decreased in total?
- Is it clinically relevant that certain lab parameters (e. g. D-dimer for diagnostic of venous thromboembolism; TSH for quick clarification regarding contrast agent tolerance; NT-pro BNP for risk stratification of ACS and congestive heart failure; troponin I/T for diagnostic clarification of patients with acute coronary syndrome: NON-STEMI patients) are available in the quickest possible turn-around time?
- Do certain lab parameters (e.g. TSH) have the character of a time limiting factor for the complete diagnostic and therapeutic process, and will transfers of the patient to a non-appropriate ward area be avoided?

The application of POCT technologies in the ED therefore requires an investment decision, in which the investment returns and the amortization of financially determined investment of the POCT technology are to be compared to the economical, strategic and clinical benefit effects.

From the controlling point of view it is to clarify:

Why a hospital should invest EUR 30,000 (plus continuous costs for consumables, e.g. diagnostic assays for the determination of selected lab parameters) for a POCT diagnostic technology, the performance of which could be less expensively covered by the own central lab?

Due to initial investment of the pay-off risk and due to limited reversibility of the decision, every investment plan has to be linked strategically and to be evaluated based on facts throughout a structural decision process.

In the area of medically embossed processes, the evaluation of investment alternatives are especially demanding. Investments are to be considered with regard to ethical maxim for acting:

- increased risks for patients and personnel
- process costs for the medical organization/hospital
- medical quality
- patient outcome and
- aspects of economy

As method of assessment, the concept of "risk-weighted process analysis" (Eiff 2012) proved effective in several pilot experiments with so-called "medical products critical in handling". Figure 3 demonstrates that the investment in POCT technologies for patient-near acute diagnosis of NON-STEMI patients in addition to the existing laboratory nevertheless is worthwhile, as by this investment process

Investment Decisions

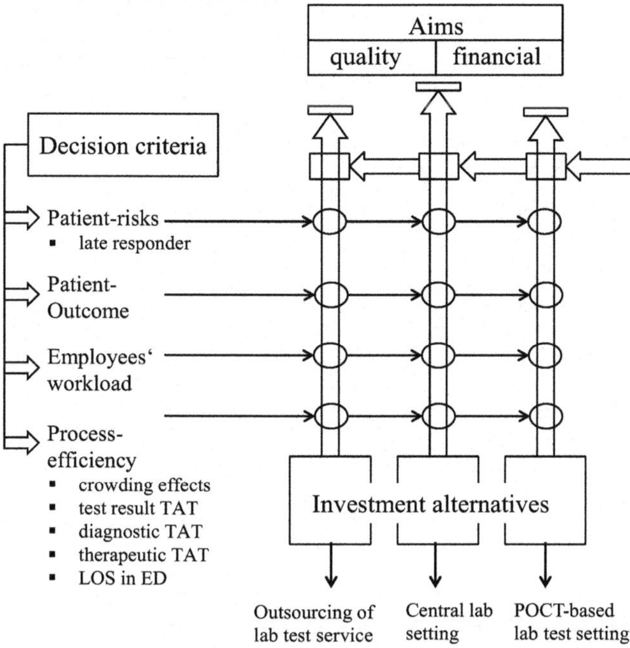

Fig. 3 Investment decisions must be compatible with ethical and guiding principles

costs are decreased, patient outcome is improved, medical result quality is increased, and patient risk is reduced. Investment decisions must be evaluated with regard to clinical risks and compatibility with ethical and guiding principles.

Of major importance in the investment decision process is the decision dimension *risk*. Aim of the medical sector and at the same time ethical standard is the maxim to provide the patient with the treatment he requires in the specific situation. That bears the lowest avoidable risk. The costs arising from this treatment then are dependent variables that may only be questioned with regard to value analysis (cheapening without loss of functionality). If investment decisions in the medical environment only depended on costs and returns or on the amount of a (capped) budget, the medical performance possible with these economic resources wouldn't be appropriate anymore and the patient risk of an adverse event and a damage resulting therefrom would increase. In this situation of the "magical triangle" (Fig. 4) the assessment of an investment optimum is impossible. Ultimately, we aim at finding a medical economic consensus, in which all parties are convinced that all three decision dimensions have been considered adequately: patient care on an appropriate quality level (evaluated by the existing structure quality and the medical performance) with affordable costs and acceptable risk.

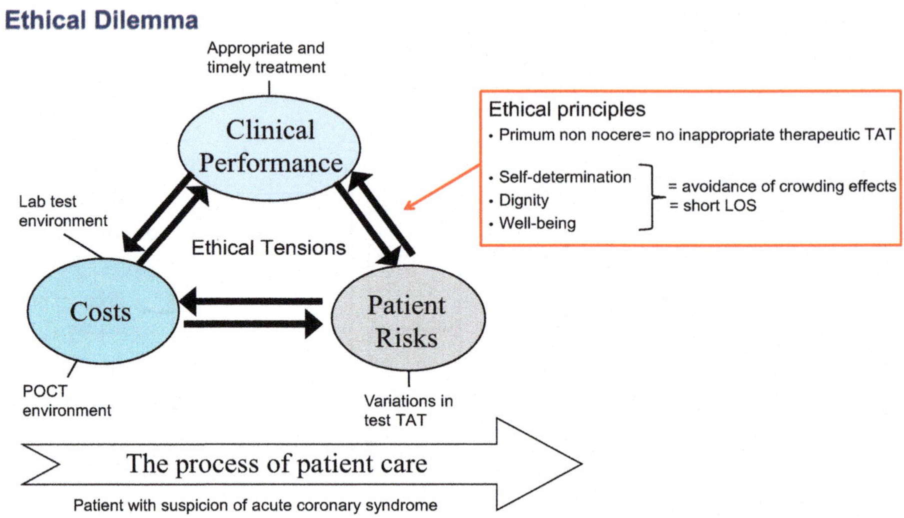

Fig. 4 The typical decision dilemma between appropriate medicine, investment costs patient risks

3 Empirical Study in the Emergency Department of a Maximum Provider Hospital

In the ED assessed in our first study about 36,000 patients are admitted per year of which 20,000 patients are discharged after treatment and 16,000 patients are transferred to the acute care area of the hospital for additional diagnosis and treatment. On a normal weekly day in average 121 patients show up in the ED (Fig. 5). About 12,000 patients need to be diagnosed by troponin (I/T) detection.

Due to the high number of emergency patients crowding effects occur and waiting times for patients rose up to 6 h and more. This is especially the case in peak situations in combination with limited resources which lead to delays in treatment. As a consequence, patients reacted dissatisfied and the costs of treatment arose because of increasing length of stay in the ED.

3.1 Aim of the Study, Setting and Methodology

Due to the fact that especially patients with unclear ACS contribute to the crowding effects, the study was focused on such patients. Because all these patients are diagnosed on troponin (I/T) lab parameter it is fair to say that the turn-around time for troponin lab test results determines the length of stay of the patient in the ED and contributes to higher patient outcome and enables to state a faster diagnosis.

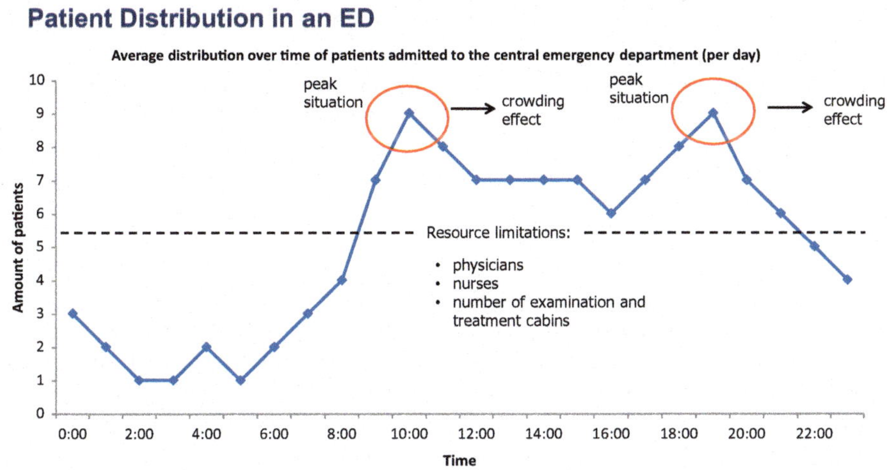

Fig. 5 Daily patient distribution in an ED

The study design was based on the comparison of two different settings: a central lab testing setting and a POCT setting. The patients included in the study were those where it was necessary to clarify an infarct event (NON-STEMI patient).

In every setting the turn-around times of 92 troponin tests were compared (time span between taking the blood sample from the patient to bedside availability of the troponin test result).

The comparison of the two different settings was based on Six Sigma methodology. The basic idea of the Six Sigma approach is built on is the phenomenon of variation. Disruptions in quality and efficiency of the medical treatment process can usually be retraced to the phenomenon of variation, which can be found in all parts of living and working processes. The phenomenon of variation especially in service processes has been named the most important cause for errors, unnecessary costs and client satisfaction. Variation is a sign of not properly controlled services. Once time pressure is added to this lack of service control, the risk of error rises exponentially. Variation needs to be in balance with the quality demand of the client who pays for the service (e.g. an airline traveler) or the demand of a to-be-operated patient for receiving a state-of-the-art medical treatment oriented to ethical standards in medicine.

The knowledge of variation is a much more meaningful indicator for the productivity (client orientation, fair prices, quality) than the use of averages: average waiting time of a patient for an x-ray-diagnosis, average costs of a surgical procedure etc. An average recovery time of 20 days does not say very much about the quality of the entire care process. This value can only be achieved by adding up some patients' 28 day recovery times and others' 12 day recovery time. According to ethical and economic reasons, it is best to keep variance as low as possible and declare a cumulative goal of 14 days (instead of the average 20 days).

Table 1 99 % perfection is not enough for the health care system (Matthews 2004)

99 % perfection = 2.8 Sigma	99.9997 % perfection = 6 Sigma
5000 not correctly performed surgical procedures per week	1.7 not correctly performed surgical procedures per week
200,000 wrong prescriptions a year	68 wrong prescriptions a year
48,000–98,000 avoidable deaths in hospitals per year	17–34 avoidable deaths in hospitals a year

To make the phenomenon of variation transparent, the Six Sigma concept has proven itself in the industry as well as in American and Singaporean hospitals (Matthews 2004). Six Sigma defines quality as a measure of variance from a given performance standard or promise of quality (Eiff 2007). It was derived from a measuring index that is used in quality management: Defects per million opportunities (DPMO) = actually occurred defects in one million error possibilities.

Every DPMO value corresponds to a Sigma value. A DPMO shows the frequency in which the error will possibly occur. An error possibility (opportunity) is every chance that a given request (promise of quality) is not or not correctly exercised. Especially in health care, even a 99 % degree of perfection is ethically and economically not acceptable: Patients and hospital workers are highly endangered in the scenario, and on the other hand, squandering resources also lead to prevention of future investments (Table 1).

Every process, every error phenomenon, every variance of a determined quality standard in a hospital could generally be improved with the help of Six Sigma. For example: Reduction of patient falls, avoidance of medication mistakes, shortening of circulation time for pharmaceutical goods, shortening of billing cycles for private patients as well as those with health insurance, shortening of waiting periods for heart attack patient at the heart catheter lab, etc.

For the first step in detecting Six Sigma value, following definitions need to be established:

- *unit of performance* (object/product/service) to be delivered to the patient
- *requirements* or the main parts that make up the performance that will satisfy or anger the patient
- Number of *requirements* for every performance category (*unit*) in which the number of "requirements" equals the number of error possibilities

3.2 Fictitious Example: Emergency Department

The most important demands on the ED from the patient's point of view are:

- Maximum amount of time spent waiting for a doctor (first sight) is 15 min;
- Turn-around time for troponin (cTnI) not longer than 60 min;
- Length of stay in the ED not longer than 2 h

These three demands are equal to three error possibilities for every patient visit. Let's take e.g. the data of 500 patients, among which 83 patients had to wait more than 15 min to be seen by the doctors, the troponin results of 25 patients were available after more than 60 min and 54 patients stayed inside the ED more than 2 h.

Thus, the Sigma value would compute:

$$\frac{(83 + 25 + 54)}{500x3} = \frac{162}{1.500} = 0.108 \ = \text{Defects per opportunity}$$

With a (generally assumed) base of 1 million error possibilities, this means 108,000 mistakes in a million (=DPMO). This corresponds to a Sigma value of about 2.75—hardly a satisfactory situation.

In accordance to the kind of project, Six Sigma provides two approaches to solve a problem (DeFeo 2004; Eckes 2001; Eiff 2013a; Pande and Holpp 2002):

a) The DMAIC Cycle method is used, if an existing service process with regards to client orientation, higher quality and lower costs (elimination of existing wastefulness in the "hidden factory") needs to be optimized and reorganized.
b) The DFSS Method (Design for Six Sigma) is used, if a completely new concept is to be established and realized. For instance, the construction of a new hospital, functionally designed, will comply with the demands of patient care and patient triage with regard to innovative care methods and financial restrictions of the DRG system (shorter stays, tendency towards outpatient or pre-inpatient care).

Six Sigma is process-oriented, thus four categories of measurements are generally taken (Fig. 6):

- Output (=direct process results)
- Outcome (=the process results as felt by the patient with long-term effect)
- Process variables (process efficiency, use of resources, complications)
- Input (=objects that are added into the process to be changed with regards to goals, e.g. patient demands, factors or pieces that are needed to create output and outcome considering the process goals/patient demands)

Typical input for medical service processes are, e.g. quality of prediagnosis, quality of a pretreatment, health status of the patient (multi-morbidity) etc. Pertaining to the performance measurement and quality of processes in an ED, see Buttigieg et al. (2015).

3.3 Results

The Six Sigma ANOVA analysis demonstrated that the stability of the POCT-based process is much higher (Fig. 7) compared to the lab test process (Fig. 8).

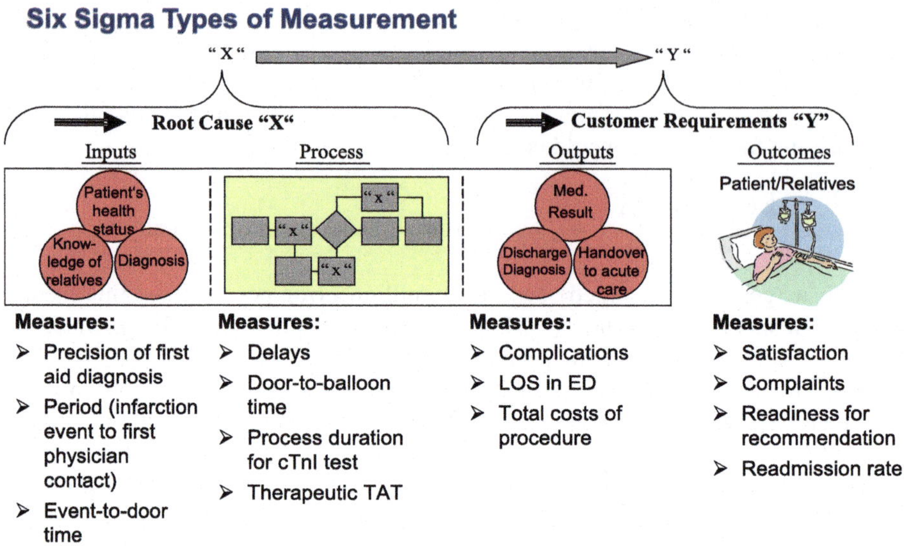

Fig. 6 Six Sigma types of measurement reflect input and process figures as well as output and patient outcome results

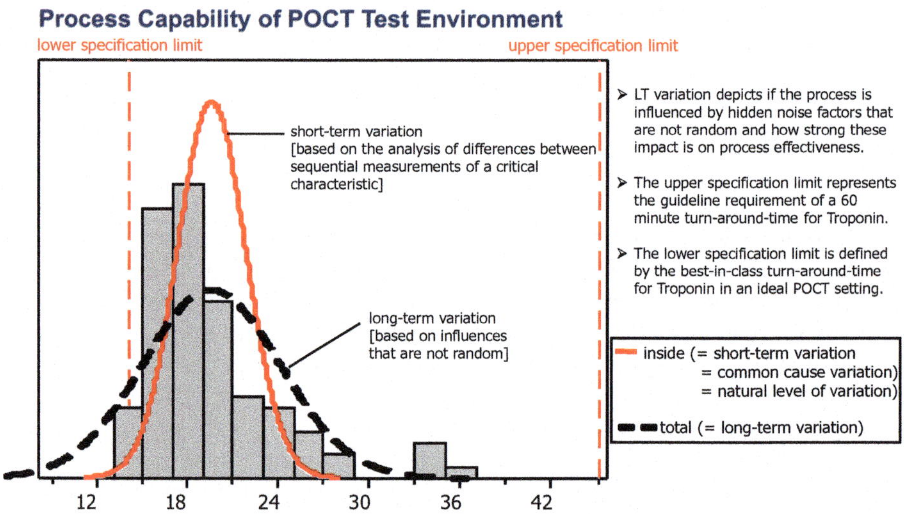

Fig. 7 The POCT test environment ensures a robust and controlled diagnostic process and contributes to a short length of stay for patients in the ED

In the lab test environment only 21 (out of 92) tests met the requirement of a 60 min TAT, while 100 % of POCT tests did. Obviously, there is high evidence that clinical decision-making is faster in a POCT setting compared to a central lab test environment. As cTnI obtained to be a precise predictor for patient mortality and

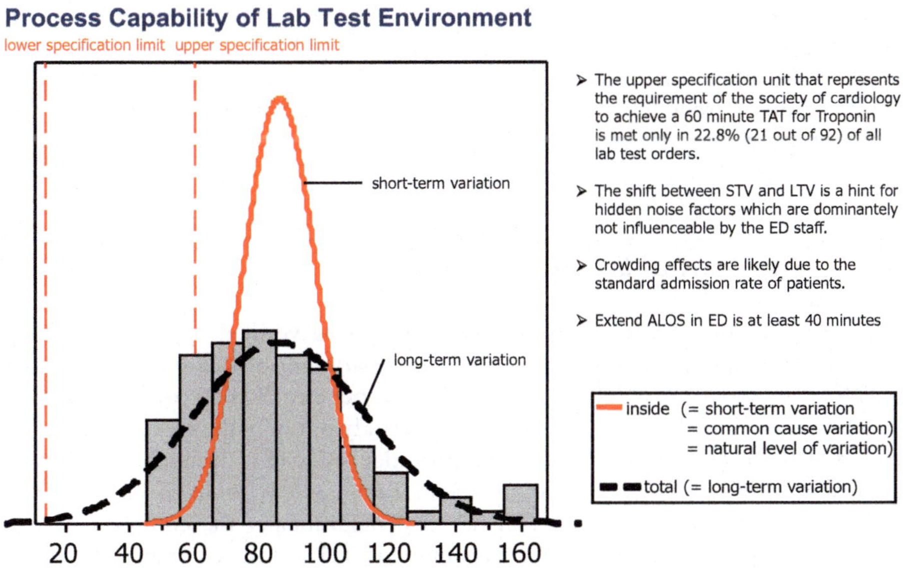

Fig. 8 The process capability of the lab test environment does not meet the clinical requirements (troponin availability within 60 min as international standard)

contributes to reducing length of stay in the ED clinical and economic effects can be expected by fastening the TAT of lab test results.

3.4 Findings

- The average turn-around time of troponin tests critical for the success of treatment of NON-STEMI patients and the avoidance of costs (opportunity costs of crowding effects) is about 18 min by using POCT and nearly 80 min in case of the lab test setting.
- The reduction of treatment time and length of stay in the ED leads to less crowding effects, so at the end of the day less treatment capacity is needed to meet the patients' requirements.
- Using a Rolled Throughput Yield as a measure of process stability and process output it is stated that the opportunity to produce a correct and timeliness diagnosis for unclear ACS patients is only 52 %.

Troponin is a significant indicator for diagnostic and therapeutic quality of unclear ACS patients (NON-STEMI patients). The troponin test helps to find or deny alternative pathways of treatment (cath lab interventions, ECG,...). This indicator information contributes to a significant reduction of needless stressing if cost intensive resources e.g. intensive care beds and to avoid opportunity costs as well as direct costs of treatment. Another finding is that 10–20 % of transmural myocardial infarction events are not identified by using a 12-channel ECG. High sensitive troponin, available in 18–25 min can help to overcome this diagnostic gap.

4 The Control Study

The results of the POCT emergency study could be verified by a second study carried out by the authors in an emergency department of a maximum provider which has to serve about 220 emergency patients per day (80,000 patients per year) of which 12–18 % shine up with ACS. In this study not only the turn-around times of lab test parameters critical to therapeutic decisions (e.g. troponin) have been compared in different service settings (central lab test environment versus POCT technology based on iSTAT system devices); additionally the complete change management process from central lab testing to POCT testing has been secured and analyzed pertaining to employee acceptance, learning curve effects and cost savings. 169 patients were included in the study.

In this second study the TAT between blood withdrawal and availability of the troponin test result in a central lab test environment varies between 42 and 121 min (mean = 73). The therapeutic TAT which characterizes the point of time when the doctor's decision is made in this setting varies between 44 min and 4 h and 51 min. This extreme variation is a significant sign for a non-controlled process with a high prone to error probability. This process leads to a capacity blockage in terms of examination and therapy cabins and in consequence to a non-appropriate extended LOS in the ED. The organizational change from central lab testing to a POCT setting contributes to a more efficient capacity utilization (Fig. 9) due to a significantly reduced therapeutic TAT (Fig. 10).

As troponin is said to be a relevant predictor for patient mortality, time savings pertaining to the treatment time of ACS patients are not only crucial in terms of economic categories like costs, use of capacity and work burden, but also relevant referring to medical risks for the patient.

As an additional finding it could be pointed out that employees' satisfaction with the process organization increased because the POCT setting was considered to be more beneficial: self-controlled process, reduced TAT, shorter LOS for the patient, less stress for the staff. 72 % of the employees assessed the POCT setting as efficient and effective in terms of resource use and burden of work. Compared with this, only 30 % rated the central lab setting as satisfactorily.

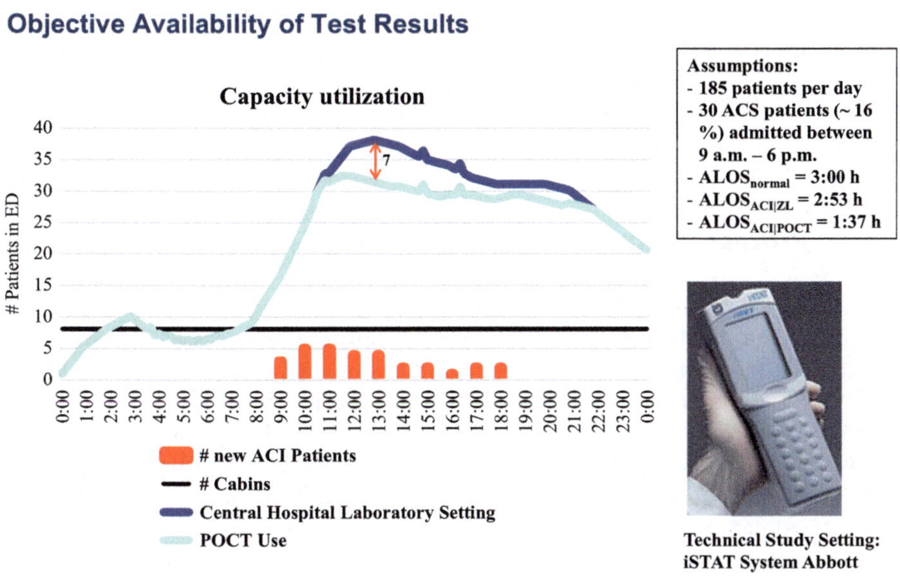

Fig. 9 POCT technology contributes to a smelting of crowding effects in the ED

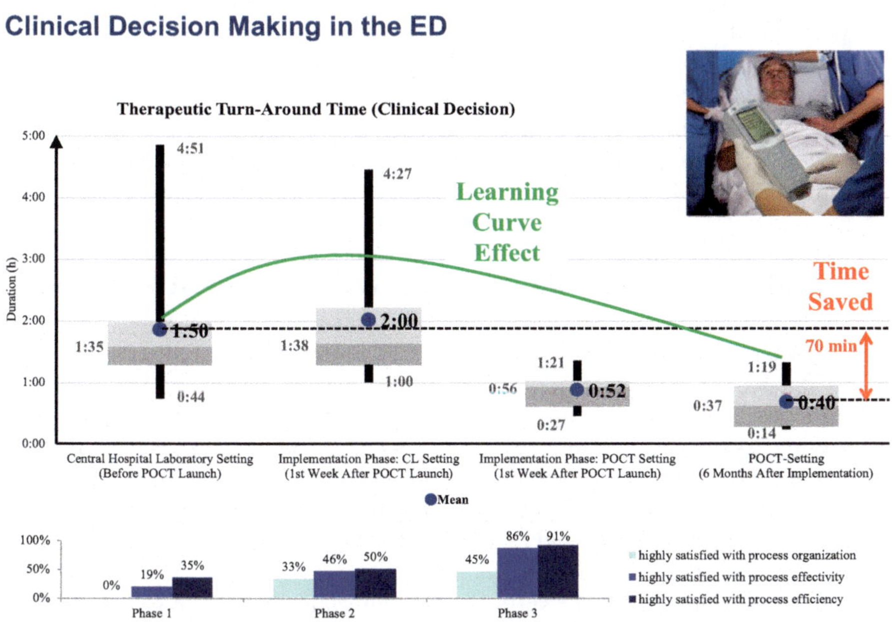

Fig. 10 POCT technology enables ED physicians to speed up the therapeutic turn-around time

5 Organizational and Technological Keys to Success in the ED

The needs-based, economical treatment of emergency patients is linked to three but critical keys to success.

5.1 Process Integration and Networking

The ED is the focal point for coordination between emergency first aid rescue operations and inpatient further treatment. Therefore, it is necessary to adjust the providers in the acute care chain with regard to time and contents to each other so that the patient is taken care of on high quality medical level in every phase and without delay. Thus, an important success factor for an ED is the professionally intensive and immediate communication with ED clinicians in preclinical acute care. The more qualified the ambulance team is able to treat stroke, AMI or traumatized patients, the earlier and the more precise the relevant information can be transmitted to the ED—even before admission of the patient to the ED.

Experiences from the AMI Kerckhoff Clinic network Bad Nauheim show that the time between first medical contact after infarction event and vessel openings in the cardiac catheterization laboratory (Contact-to-Balloon Time) is under 3 h and the Door-to-Balloon Time is under 70 min, if the emergency doctors on the transport already

- take blood samples
- analyze the 12-channel ECG, and
- announce the patient's arrival to the catheterization laboratory via the "red telephone" (Fig. 11)

5.2 Admission/Short Stay Patients' Ward and Chest Pain Unit

These institutions avoid the following problems in the treatment process:

- Erroneous allocation to medical disciplines due to imprecise diagnostics resulting from time pressure (e. g. approx. 25 % of angina pectoris patients suspect to acute coronary syndrome get an extra-cardiac diagnosis)
- Unnecessary interclinical secondary transports
- Time-delay in diagnostics and therapy due to lack of availability of technology (MRT, CT etc.) or medical consultants
- Lack of capacity puffer for short-time monitoring; thereby blocking of U-B-places or too early return to ward
- Stationary hospitalization in night hours with considerable disturbances of other patients
- Use of stationary intensive care beds instead of early minimum invasive ventilation (additional costs: EUR 1200–1500/day).

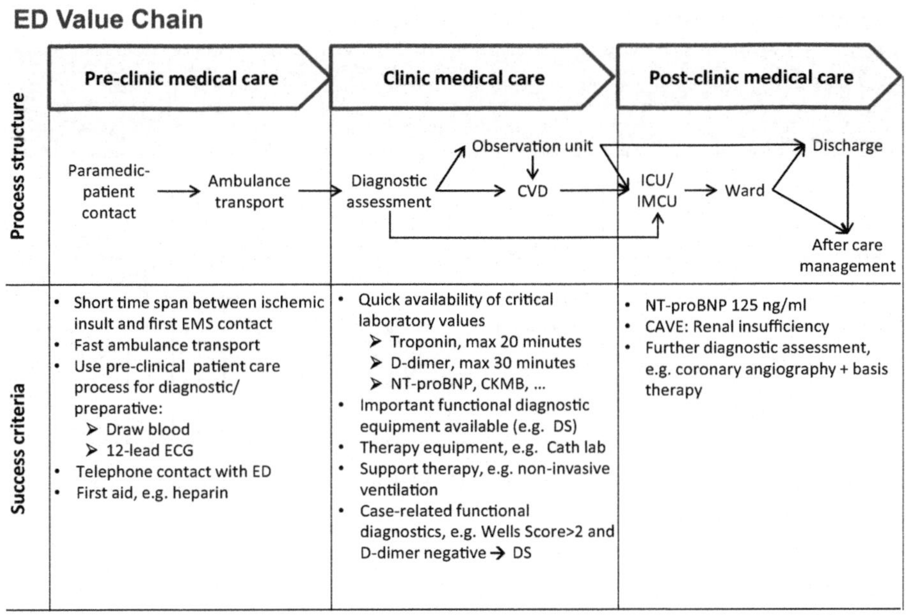

Fig. 11 Close linking of preclinical, clinical and post-acute emergency management as key to success for quality and economy

5.3 POCT Technologies in the ED

Risk versus cost analysis of alternative organization forms of EDs as well as of different concepts of process management for emergency patients show that a fast availability of clinically critical lab parameters (troponin I/T; beta-humane choriongonadotropine; D-dimer; Procalcitonin; NT-proBNP; ...) contributes to securing medical quality (treatment result), to improving patient condition (outcome) and to reduce patient care costs (see the analysis of error possibility and effect analysis carried out in an ED for patients with acute coronary syndrome; Fig. 12).

Considering the generic process of acute care (Fig. 13), it becomes clear that quality (reliability of measuring values) and duration (turn-around time) of the partial process of lab diagnostics are critical success factors for clinical quality, patient satisfaction and costs of the clinical acute care management and post emergency care.

It must be stated that by lab diagnostic services based on POCT technologies, patient safety is being increased, diagnosis and therapy processes are accelerated, and contingency and process costs are being decreased; that applies particularly when—in case of fast availability of lab parameters—the function diagnostics is being avoided or relieved or due to the specific situation used for necessary early diagnosis declaration.

Failure Mode and Effect Analysis (FMEA)

Process	Potential			Current controls	Rating			RPN	Recommended actions
	Error	Cause(s)	Effects		Occurrence	Detection	Severity		
Test TAT	Troponin value first available after 60-120 minutes	• Huge variation in time of testing in the central laboratory (CL) • Peak times in CL	• Crowding/long waiting times • Resource overstrained • Unneeded admissions to ICU • Suboptimal outcome	• Call to laboratory for results • Call for expert evaluation, e.g. a cardiologist.	8	9	7	504	POCT in ED
Analysis			Assessment						Optimization
Diagnose with lab-parameter	False negative Troponin	• No high sensitive Troponin • Wrong cut off (too high: 30 ng/L) • CAVE: assay specific cut offs	• Undetected AMI	• Evaluation of delta value for troponin according to guidelines • Guideline recommended evaluation of 99th percentile	8	6	6	288	• High sensitive Troponin test • POCT diagnostic • Lower cut off (99th percentile) • CAVE: guidelines

Fig. 12 Risk analysis and risk stratification by FMEA gives the opportunity to analyze the robustness of a clinical process

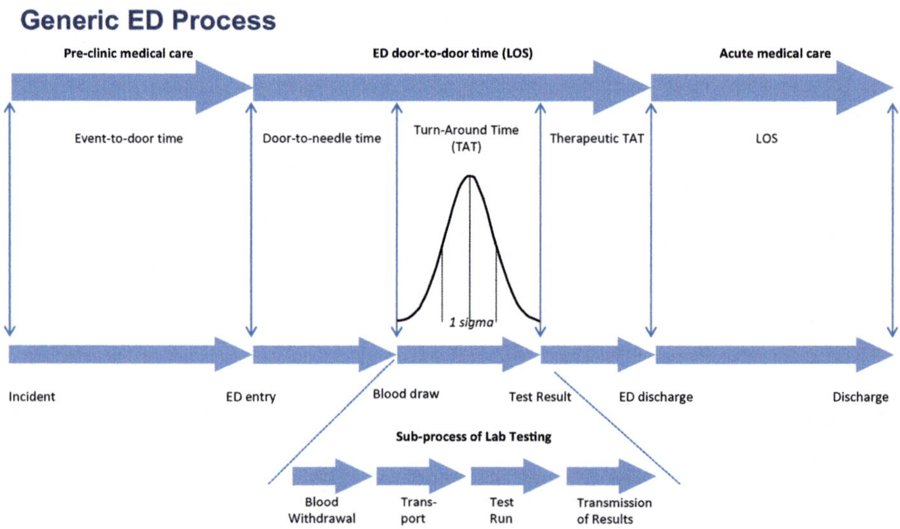

Fig. 13 Turn-around time and variance of the availability of critical lab parameters determine the clinical and economic success of the ED

POCT enables the fastest possible availability especially of the parameters relevant to the decision-making, troponin I/T, BNP/NT-proBNP, D-dimer and lactate, where troponin I/T and lactate are indicative predictors of increased morbidity.

- BNP/NT-proBNP values are available after 35 min and enable an early clarification of pulmonary or cardiac causes and indicate a cardiac insufficiency. The classical functional diagnostics (X-Ray) is remarkably slower.

- BNP/NT-proBNP values are available via POCT after 20 min and enable an early cardiac decompensation and a CHE differentiation in case of difficulty breathing or pulmonary embolism.

This POCT risk evaluation (BNP/NT-proBNP) replaces the more time-consuming ECG (ideally: 10 min; reality: 2–3 h) and supports the decision of a fast discharge from the registered practitioners.

- TSH is a further time-limiting factor because the TSH values decide on when which imaging method can be used. Via central lab diagnostics, the TSH value is only available after 60–90 min. Therefore, it would be eligible to have the TSH value qualified via POCT technology in the emergency department within 20 min. For clarification of the kidney functions and thus also for additional clarification of a contrast agent incompatibility are available via POCT in a qualified way after 2 m.

If the D-dimer values are available for a patient with leg pain (suspicion of thrombosis) after 20 min, we can—in combination with a WELLS Score examination—immediately decide if the patient can be discharged home or has to be classified as high-risk patient; in this case, a Doppler examination must follow subsequently whereby the function diagnostics can be avoided. The thereby gained time of 1–2 h increases patient satisfaction and avoids crowding effect in the ED.

Related to the above mentioned database the turn-around times of clinically critical lab parameters (particularly troponin I) in different technical settings:

- POCT measurement in the ED (equipment: Radiometer AQT90 FLEX),
- measurement in the hospital central lab and
- measurement by external lab

have been compared.

For the care of patients with acute coronary syndrome (NON-STEMI), it is of clinical and economical relevance to have troponin I values available after 18–20 min. On the one hand, by use of high-sensitive troponins the risk of unidentified AMIs (EVA syndrome) is decreased; on the other hand, the total patient stay in the ED per acute coronary syndrome is reduced from 05/05:30 h (central lab) to 04:20/04:30 h (POCT diagnostics).

Consequences of this point-of-care solution:

- Significantly shorter patient stay of patients with acute coronary syndrome (40–60 min shorter)
- Avoidance of UIB position blocking
- Avoidance of early relocation due to capacity deficiency in the ER to the "wrong" ward (e. g. ICU with daily costs of EUR 1000–1200)
- Qualified, targeted subsequent treatment
- Avoidance of "crowding effects".

This analysis also shows that POCT technologies in the ER—from the point of view of ER clinicians—enable a controlled and projectable diagnostic process: The variances in the turn-around time by now lie between 40 and 160 min for central lab solutions and between 13 and 34 min for POCT supported organization (technical setting: AQT90 FLEX).

High-sensitive POCT diagnostics also supports in cases in which not all patients that need treatment are identified by other (earlier) diagnostic methods: the rate of AMIs not identified in the 12-channel ECG is between 10 and 20 %.

Furthermore, in this study it becomes clear that the consequent use of POCT in acute care testing alone is not sufficient to exploit all rationalization potentials. On analyzing the work of Renaud et al. (2008) regarding "confounding factors" you realize that POCT benefits can be (over)compensated by other structural or organizational disadvantages (Fig. 14). The POCT solution on average is 71 min faster compared to the central lab solution. The fact that patient stay in the ED is in both technical settings (central lab test vs. POCT environment) approximately identical, possibly result from a short stay ward/chest pain unit being integrated in the central lab setting. Ultimately, it can be assumed that the capacity need in the ER can be reduced by 25–28 % by POCT combined with other structure and process optimizing measurements.

The question for the economic appropriateness of an investment in POCT technologies (in the present setting approx. EUR 28,000 for a POCT equipment) doesn't amount to a mere cost per sample comparison with the central lab. Crucial is that this investment decision can also be safeguarded by taking into consideration the criteria "precise, reliable and timely diagnosis", "process follow-on costs" and "patient risk" (see risk-weighted process cost analysis Fig. 15).

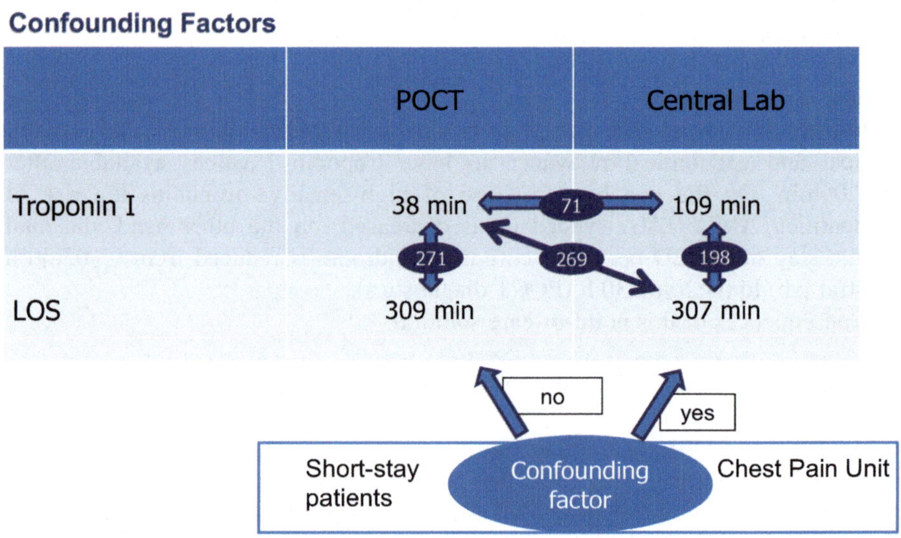

Fig. 14 POCT and short stay wards/chest pain units contribute to reducing necessary ER resources (U/B places) up to 28 % (Renaud et al. 2008)

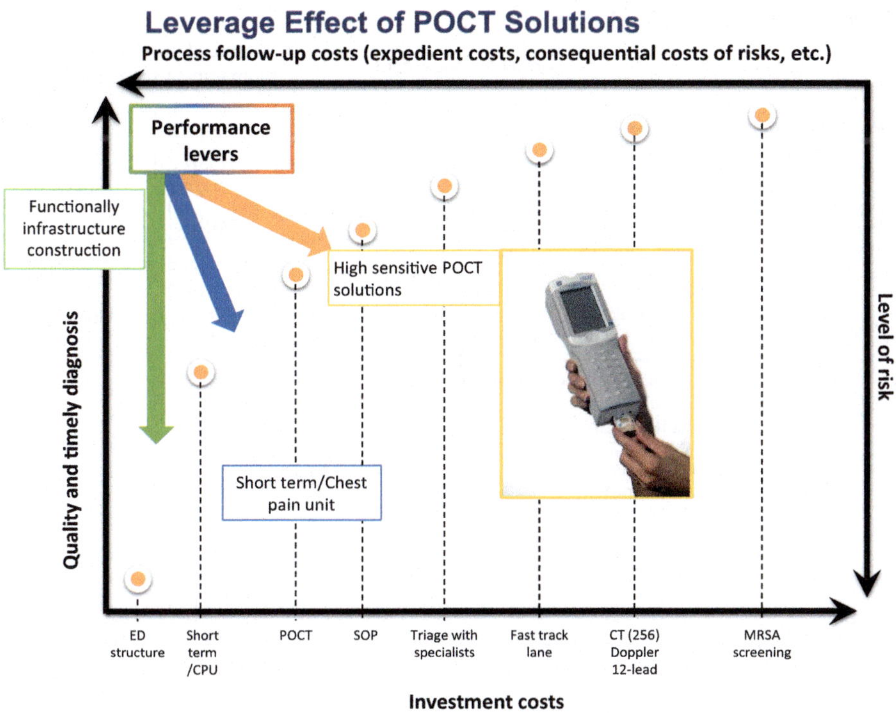

Fig. 15 POCT is a significant key to success: It is organizationally easier and less cost intensive to establish a POCT equipment instead of activating other performance levels

6 Conclusion

The emergency department plays a pivotal role as a gatekeeper in a boundaryless hospital. The ED is a linking pin between the primary care sector, the preclinic medical emergency care and the acute care area of a hospital. The challenge for every ED is to steer patients with life-threatening conditions, e.g. patients with acute coronary syndrome, without any delay through a controlled emergency diagnosis and treatment process. As it turned out, an early detection of the ACS root causes determines the outcome prognosis of patients and contributes to a more efficient resource scheduling as well as to cost savings. Here, POCT technology used for classification of critical lab test parameters like high-sensitive troponin as a marker to exclude or verify a myocardial infarction is accepted to be a beneficial investment to support the ED management.

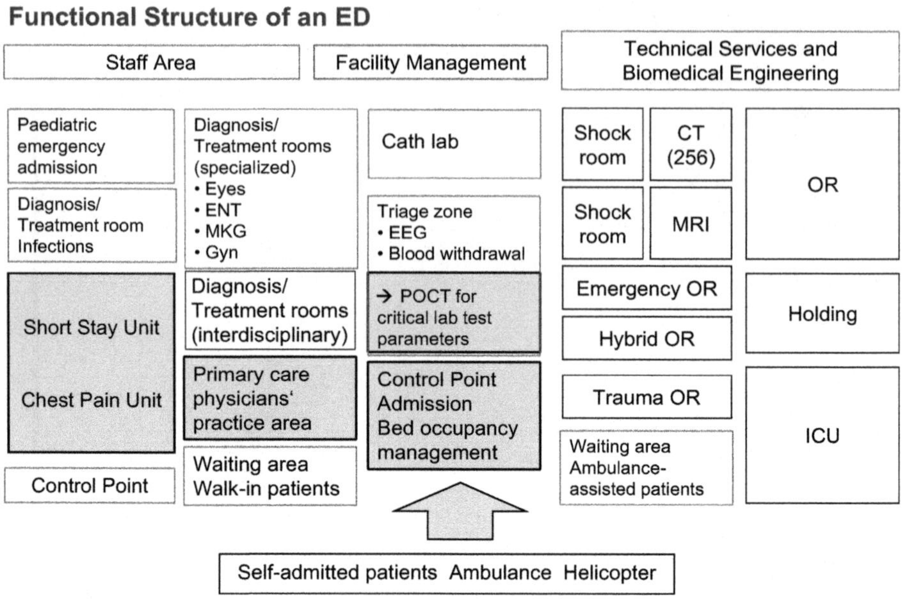

Fig. 16 An ED encloses "boundaryless functions": chest pain unit/short stay unit, primary care physician practice area, triage zone with POCT technology, admission control point/bed occupancy management

Quality and economy of the acute care depend directly on a timely diagnostic lab medicine: the lab medicine takes up to 70 % of the time of the total diagnostic process and its results. In order to reduce the turn-around time, parameters critical with regard to time and therapy are determined with advantage against POCT devices. Effects:

- reduced waiting time for the patient,
- treatment starts earliest possible,
- the therapeutic prognosis is improved,
- monitoring capacity in the ED is relieved, and
- qualified discharging diagnosis or qualified treatment decision relieves intensive medicine and intermediate care.

From the perspective of ED, POCT is a self-determined process for determination of diagnosis-relevant and time-critical lab parameters (e. g. troponin I/T; CK-MB; D-dimer). It can be recognized that patient risks, patient satisfaction, medical results and process costs can be positively influenced by POCT in the ED.

Further critical success factors in the clinical emergency care facilitating the pivotal role of an ED in a boundaryless hospital are:

- process integration and networking of preclinical, clinical and post-acute care (integration with primary care emergency institutions, fire brigades, ambulances) and
- establishment of short stay wards and chest pain units.

In that sense, the ED is a turntable critical to the success of a boundaryless hospital and encloses *boundaryless functions* like chest pain unit, primary care physician examination area, control point and occupancy management. These functions fulfil the role of a linking pin in a boundaryless hospital (Fig. 16).

References

Buttigieg SC, von Eiff W, Farrugia P, von Eiff MC (2015) Process optimization in the emergency department by the use of point-of-care-testing (POCT) in life-threatening conditions: comparative best practice examples from Germany and Malta. In: Buttigieg SC, Rathert C, von Eiff W (eds) International best practices in health care management. Advances in health care management, vol 17. Emerald, Bingley, pp 195–219

DeFeo JA (2004) Why are employees prodding health-care providers to adopt new management systems? Reducing the cost of health care. Clin Leadersh Manag Rev 2:80–85

DGINA (2010) Zahl der Patienten in Notaufnahmen steigt weiter. http://www.dgina.de/media/download_gallery/pressemitteilungen/20100929_Pressemitteilug_DGINA.pdf. Accessed 28 Sept 2015

Eckes G (2001) The Six Sigma revolution. How general electric and others turned process into profits. Wiley, New York

Matthews MR (2004) A legacy for leaders: opportunities in Six Sigma for healthcare providers. Creative Healthcare USA, Scottsdale

Pande PS, Holpp L (2002) What is Six Sigma? McGraw-Hill Education, New York

Porter ME (1998) On competition. Harvard Business Review Press, Boston

Renaud B, Maison P, Ngako A, Cunin P, Santin A, Hervé J, Salloum M, Calmettes MJ, Boraud C, Lemiale V, Grégo JC, Debacker M, Hémery F, Roupoie E (2008) Impact of point-of-care testing in the emergency department evaluation and treatment of patients with suspected acute coronary syndrome. Acad Emerg Med 15(3):216–224

von Eiff MC (2007) Patient risks and avoidable costs. Hospital 9(5):22–24

von Eiff W (2012) POCT in the ED—relevant clinical and economic advantages. http://www.acutecaretesting.org. Accessed 24 June 2015

von Eiff MC (2013a) Six Sigma im Labor: Beherrschte Diagnostikprozesse als Ziel. In: von Eiff W (ed) POCT-management. Klinische und ökonomische Effekte. medhochzwei Verlag, Heidelberg, pp 379–398

von Eiff W (2013b) Wettbewerbsstrategie. Bedeutung des Porter-Ansatzes für Kliniken. Health Care Manag 5(2013):14–17

Maximilian C. von Eiff is a doctoral student at the University of Pécs (Hungary), Faculty of Medicine. His research is focused on diagnosis and treatment of epilepsy, especially alternative treatment approaches for attack prophylaxis. Furthermore, he is member of the workgroup "Economy in Medicine" at Kerckhoff Clinic, Bad Nauheim, Germany, where he is working on the prevention of post-operative surgical site infections (including the analysis of economical and clinical effects). Another area of his research is the impact of a "healing environment approach" on medical quality, patient outcome, length of stay and the financial status of a hospital. He finished a Six Sigma training at ISSSP (Scotsdale, Arizona, U.S.) and in this field he supported process improvement studies on glucose monitoring of diabetes patients and emergency management of patients with life-threatening conditions.

Wilfried von Eiff is Professor of Health Care Management at the HHL Leipzig Graduate School of Management and is the Director of the Center for Hospital Management, a research institute linked to the University of Münster, Germany. Both institutions are well-known for international and national research, consulting and government advisory activities in the fields of cost–benefit analysis of medical technology and clinical procedures, strategic management and mergers and acquisitions in the health care sector, business ethics in medicine, risk management and health service research. Prof. von Eiff is a founding member of the initiative Best Practice Management in Healthcare and Hospital Management, which is part of the European Hospital Management Association (EHMA). He is member of various boards of directors in health care and industry. Before, he was Director and Member of the Board of the University Clinic of Giessen, Germany, and also Managing Director of an international automotive company overseeing the fields of organization, process, logistics and IT management. He holds a doctoral degree from the Faculty of Business Administration, University of Tübingen, Germany, as well as a doctoral degree from the Faculty of Medicine, University of Giessen.

Stakeholder Involvement Transcends Boundaries in University Hospitals

Evelyn Plamper and Edgar Schömig

Abstract

The view of a university hospital on its stakeholders and its reputation through the lenses of stakeholders are important factors for its position in highly competitive health care fields. Knowledge and emotions of stakeholders influence trust and confidence in a hospital. The values, a university hospital is convincingly cherished for, are mirrored in its reputation. Cologne University Hospital differentiates 12 stakeholder groups as co-creators of values - among them patients, employees, referrers, the science community, politicians and the broader public. All stakeholders need to be involved by a university hospital in a systematic way, and profound knowledge about the determinants of reputation is useful.

Keywords

Stakeholder involvement • Determinants of reputation • University hospital • Referrer relations • Hospital-patient relations • Patient satisfaction • Hospital-stakeholder relations • Employee engagement • Cologne University Hospital • Reputation management

E. Plamper, MD, MPH (✉)
Corporate Development, University Hospital Cologne, Kerpener Str. 62, 50937 Cologne, Germany
e-mail: evelyn.plamper@uk-koeln.de

E. Schömig, MD
University Hospital Cologne, Kerpener Str. 62, 50937 Cologne, Germany
e-mail: edgar.schoemig@uk-koeln.de

H. Albach et al. (eds.), *Boundaryless Hospital*, DOI 10.1007/978-3-662-49012-9_13

1 Mission and Challenges of University Hospitals

University hospitals and their medical faculties are challenged by the rapid shift of medicine due to new insights into molecular basics of life. Closely intertwined with high-ranked research institutions, some of the university hospitals have proven to be drivers for innovation by pursuing a fast translation of fundamental research into new effective and more agreeable diagnostics and treatments.

Due to demographic trends, university hospitals are treating a rising number of elderly and multimorbid patients allowing them longer and more agreeable lives despite their complex diseases. Some university hospitals—Cologne University Hospital is among them—are also specialized in the prevention and the treatment of underweight premature infants in perinatal centers, where many special disciplines cooperate hand in hand. Also patients with rare diseases may find bundled expertise in a university hospital.

Meeting the challenges to create value for the society in highly specialized individual medicine and to increase public health, a university hospital has to cope with many, often divergent and conflicting interests of its stakeholders. Hospital services have to be targeted towards individual patients' needs and high-quality standards. To supply an attractive work environment, stable platforms for interaction of medical specialties and scientific networks are fundamental.

Internal boundaries exist mainly in financial restrictions due to rising costs allotted for labor and for energy consumption, also due to increasing investment in safety compliance and in the safety and quality of technical devices, in addition, due to a sometimes unforeseen complexity of regulatory framework conditions and health policy demands. Another important internal boundary is the division of labor in a usual organizational structure along disciplines and sub-disciplines. Most of the time they are beneficial, albeit this is not always the case. A special matter is the dichotomy of administration (human resources, finance, procurement, maintenance etc.) and medicine in its breadth of research, teaching and patient care. Clinical centers are an internal answer in boundary crossing.

Institutional boundaries are to be regarded as external boundaries. These boundaries have become more and more manifest and from the patients' points of view more irking. Especially in long-term care in complicated chronic diseases cooperation with other hospitals, with rehab centers, with private doctors is necessary. They are only possible with agreed-upon financial arrangements and agreed-upon rules for cooperation. Networking becomes imminent.

Boundaries have to be crossed, especially if the university hospital commits itself to being a hub in translational networks and to be trusted as competent partner in internal and external cooperation.

Cologne University Hospital has put some effort into expert dialogs in order to gain better knowledge of public and private preferences, for reflections on inputs, costs, outputs and outcomes and intends to focus its strategy on stakeholder involvement, to create a platform of legitimation and to build and foster a strong coalition of support.

2 Reputation-Related Factors

The values, a university hospital is living up to, are reflected by its reputation. Stakeholders base their judgement not only on facts, but also on opinions of themselves or of others. On the one hand reputation means prestige in view of the public, on the other hand reputation, including competence, engagement, integrity and trustworthiness, results from the perception and the appraisal or valuation of the stakeholders—in words of Zyglidopoulos (2001) '*a set of knowledge and emotions held by various groups of stakeholders, concerning aspects and activities*' of the university hospital. Thus reputation combines a public and an individual dimension.

Both, the public and the individual dimension, are influenced by the internal and external boundaries of the university hospital and also by the efforts to transcend these boundaries.

Reputation relies on trust and confidence. Our understanding follows the view of trust as being future-oriented—trust as choice or risk following good image regardless of prior experiences—, while confidence is based on prior good experiences, thus is past-oriented and accordingly reputation is a record of past actions. Confidence must be "earned" (e.g. by excellent treatment of a family member), while an image can be built by good communication (e.g. around famous or at least well-known researchers hired by the university hospital).

If a university hospital does not live up to the expectations of its various stakeholders, it may even loose its autonomy due to the stakeholders' verdict. Such a loss would not be compatible with the academic self-image.

3 Relevance, Importance and Influential Power of University Hospitals' Stakeholder Groups

Reputation from the point of view of stakeholder groups is a critical factor for a university hospital, especially in a highly competitive market. In our views the management of the university hospital has the (important!) task to identify early-on reputation risks, conflicting stakeholder interests and expectations. The knowledge base on factors shaping the reputation of university hospitals is scarce, as well as the knowledge about the effects of different means to improve reputation (Geurtsen et al. 2012).

Bennington and Moore (2010) have shown *that* '*public value is created, when the organization adds value to society and when stakeholders value the actions of the organization*'. Expectations of stakeholders regarding the organization determine '*what is valued by stakeholders and what adds value to society*' [ibid].

In an initial approach towards systematic stakeholder management stakeholder analyses shed light on the relevance of different stakeholders measured by the degree of their influential power. However, the difficulty to cover all aspects especially those transcending the boundaries of the university hospital, be they internal or external, has to be kept in mind.

To *assess the importance* of stakeholder groups we asked members of the board and heads of clinical departments to rank the importance of single stakeholder groups according to the stakeholders' level of interest, power, support mechanisms, available sanctions, dependency and risk (see Chap. 4). The list below gives an overview of the most relevant groups. To gain better awareness on stakeholders' preferences and to tailor our stakeholder approach—who should how and when be involved—12 groups of main stakeholders were distinguished along the trajectories of research, teaching and medical care with emphasis on local, regional and international aspects.

Stakeholder/Interest Groups of a University Hospital

- Patients/relatives (extremely important)
- Employees (extremely important)
- Scientific community (extremely important)
- Students (extremely important)
- Referrers (extremely important)
- Health insurers/purchasers (extremely important)
- Strategic/cooperating partners (science/industry) (important)
- Society/public/citizens/media (important)
- Competitors (important)
- Politicians (city/district/regional government/federal government) (important)
- Supervisory board (important)
- University (Management Board) (important)

4 Stakeholders' Importance

The importance of stakeholders depends on their influential power on the hospital, see list below. Which stakeholder should be involved depends on the power the stakeholder has, on the interests the stakeholder has in the organization, if the stakeholder can support the organization, whether sanctions are available, how far the organization is depending on the stakeholder, and on the risk the organization experiences towards the stakeholder (Bryson 2003).

Criteria for the Influential Power of Stakeholders

- Interest
- Power
- Support mechanisms
- Available sanctions
- Dependency
- Risks

Professionals have great influential power due to their identification (high interest) with the university hospital, depending on the competitive and recruiting situation.

Within its current strategic process *University Medicine 2025* Cologne University Hospital has readjusted its vision and mission and has evaluated how corporate values are lived. Using an approach of broad involvement of employees Cologne University Hospital is developing the strategy 2025 and is defining goals for hospital care, research and training. A focused approach and broad *involvement of personnel* with regard to challenges and opportunities provided ample reward on employee satisfaction in the university hospital. This targeted process has to be supported and lived by many (clinicians, nurses, researchers, board members and others).

Patients and referrers have great influential power due to free choice of hospitals for elective care, while financing infrastructure and research and teaching gives the regional government of the federal state of Germany North Rhine-Westphalia major influential power.

5 Determinants of Reputation

Stakeholders actually judge a hospital in relation to others, and can withhold their support, if they are not convinced that a hospital is living up to standards. Depending on the region and on the demand university hospitals are also faced with intensive competition with other hospitals. So stakeholders can prefer another hospital or retract their support. Patients, employees, the scientific community and students can be regarded as co-producers of individual or public value. In a broader view other hospitals and other service providers also have to be regarded as co-producers.

Every single patient may judge, whether diagnostics and treatment are delivered in a trustworthy manner, whereas an employee may judge the attractivity of the employer according to work conditions and work-life balance. A politician—also the financiers—may judge the hospital according to an increase of ***public value*** (e.g. saved lives at the boundaries of life, progress in combating rare diseases, augmenting public health) in relation to investments in the university hospital and in the medical faculty, while the purchasers may judge, whether the hospital's view of quality is outcome-oriented and whether it is still viable with reduced costs.

The way stakeholders form an opinion about an organization is not as structured as we expect. The setting in which the university hospital is located also influences opinions. Stakeholders use a plethora of sources to reach a verdict. Furthermore, stakeholders (patients or students) are not only recipients but may influence other stakeholders by giving their opinions through e.g. social media, printed media, broadcast, television or in person.

To increase our knowledge on reputation and on how stakeholders form an opinion we investigated relevant aspects of reputation as described by Davies et al. (2004), who distinguished the following aspects of reputation:

- Agreeableness
  Agreeableness means that the organization/hospital can be characterized as friendly, open, pleasant and straightforward. Such a hospital is concerned, empathic and reassuring, supportive, honest, sincere and trustworthy.
- Enterprise
  An enterprising organization or hospital can be characterized as modern, cool, trendy and young, up-to-date and innovative, also daring.
- Competence
  A competent organization or hospital can be characterized as reliable, hard-working and secure, also ambitious and wanting to achieve good results.
- Chic
  Chic stands for a charming, stylish and elegant, but also prestigious and exclusive organization or hospital. It may be snobby and elitist.
- Ruthlessness
  Ruthlessness correlates negative with reputation and such an organization/hospital appears rather arrogant, selfish, dominant and aggressive. It may also be authoritarian, inward-oriented and controlling.

Since it is almost impossible to assess, whether an organization is performing the way it should, and whether the medical indications for diagnostics and procedures are the best to get, more qualitative concepts related to the service delivery process should be used for the evaluation of reputation. Therefore the mentioned generic elements of reputation were entered into the discussions in the university hospital.

5.1 The Value of Patient Satisfaction

The *hospital-patient relations* seem to rely not only on medical competence and respectful and empathetic care but also on the awareness the hospital personnel shows for patient preferences. For strengthening the awareness for reputation determinants we want to assess what leading persons of the university hospital (board members and heads of clinical departments) think about stakeholders preferences. A pilot test indicated that the leading persons imagine that patients see 'agreeableness', 'enterprising' and 'competence' as extremely important and 'chic' as important attributes, while 'ruthlessness' is not relevant in the view of patients. The consequences are to be further discussed.

Corporate reputation depends on the right strategies aiming at high competence and special expertise on all hierarchical levels, aiming at the propensity towards innovation, at attractivity for patients and personnel and at financial stability and profitability. It is clear that the organization needs to be agreeable, has to implement structures and processes to best embed agreeableness in the organization. Examples can be 'individual guidance of patients', 'support nets in many disciplines' or 'spiritual support in intensive care'.

Regarding innovativeness, Cologne University Hospital has introduced platforms for research and skills labs for training purposes.

Further reflection on the impact of those findings is necessary. Without doubt, stakeholders' preferences of hospital attributes have to be included in concepts of reputation management.

5.2 Patient Questionnaires

Just mentioned here, though not further discussed, is the future relevance of quality indicators for hospital care, which are again under broad political discussion in Germany.

Reputation in the views of patients is most important. They have the power, in case of non-emergency cases, to choose the hospital that adhers best to their expected standards.

For the last 6 years we regularly drew a 2-month sample of inpatients and asked them to fill in questionnaires. The patients' answers allow a clear view on patient experiences with quality of services, treatment, communication or attractivity of buildings. It is valued as an important tool for organizational and procedural improvement. Benchmarking is a helpful tool to raise awareness for differences between departments and to provide incentives for exchanges of good ideas for solutions. Figure 1 shows in an exemplary manner our internal benchmarking of patients' satisfaction in clinical departments.

'Recommendation of the hospital' is evaluated as a critical indicator for reputation of the hospital. Additional instruments like evaluation of complaints, certifications of medical units (e.g. cancer centers), risk-assessments and critical incidence reports support reputation management according to patients' interests and their evaluation of output and outcome.

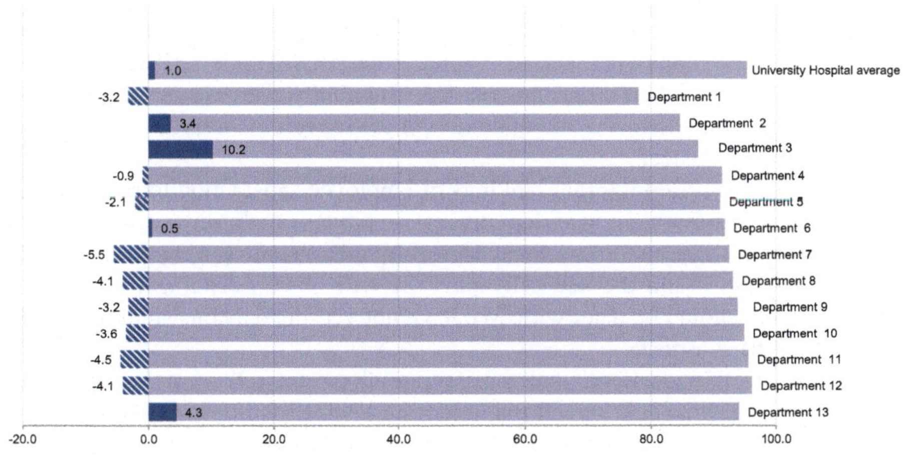

Fig. 1 Patients' recommendation rate in 13 clinical departments (in percent) 2013 vs. 2012, indicating improvement (*dark*) or deterioration (*dashed*) (based on data of Cologne University Hospital, Corporate Development Unit)

6 Interaction with Patients

Interaction with stakeholders according to Bryson (2003) is based on different participation categories 'inform', 'consult', 'involve', 'collaborate with' or 'empower'.

All instruments used for interaction need to be aligned to most heterogenic patient groups and need to be offered in different grades of intensity according to the states of health and to the needs related to specific diseases.

The purpose of this paper does not allow us to dig deeply into these important aspects. Here we see a deficit that is difficult to overcome when transcending external boundaries.

In a highly competitive region like Cologne matters of branding are also important. It is under discussion, whether patients are mainly attracted by an umbrella brand or if sub-brands based on medical specialties—reaching out for different disease-related heterogenic groups of patients—are more useful and should be promoted more intensely.

7 From Employee Satisfaction to Employee Engagement

An organization can develop a very positive reputation based on outcome-oriented internal human resources strategies. In a university hospital 'change for excellence' requires systematic analysis of person-, team- and organization-related perspectives. At the end of change projects they are rarely evaluated. Many enterprises—also university hospitals—continue to evaluate employee satisfaction.

Our own research on employee satisfaction with the employer showed (in a regression analysis) that two factors have a strong influence (Table 1).

The *odds ratio* (OR) as a measure of effect size showed that the probability to be satisfied with the employer rises 4.71-fold, if an employee is satisfied with the opportunity for individual development. The probability rises almost sevenfold, if the employee is satisfied with the reputation of the university hospital. The p-value shows high significance.

Furthermore we used internal rankings of employee satisfaction to raise awareness among the different clinical departments, institutes or administrative divisions and to involve them in discussions. Here, organizational aspects dealing with internal boundaries and the necessity plus the will of transcending them rise to the surface and should be dealt with. We have not yet found a consistent way, how to deal with these aspects.

But it is well understood that satisfaction does not tell us anything about engagement, and it is well agreed that adorning oneself with results about overall satisfaction of the enterprise does not support improvement or change, while a university hospital's interest in employees' *commitment* and *engagement* seems to

Table 1 Influence on employee overall satisfaction with the employer (Cologne University Hospital, Corporate Development Unit 2014, internal paper)

Independent variable	Odds ratio (OR)	95 % confidence interval	p-value
Opportunity for individual development in the view of employees	4.71	3.62–6.14	≤ 0.01
Reputation of Cologne University Hospital in the view of employees	6.94	5.42–8.89	≤ 0.01

provide a more valuable approach to improve services in health care, research and training.

We see missing satisfaction as a mere indicator for the need to change, while employees' organizational commitment—which describes the intensity of connectedness of employees with the enterprise—can be regarded as a stronger indicator for engagement, productivity and innovation. It is also important for recruitment strategies and the development of talented people.

An effective communication and internal process of involvement imbedded in the corporate strategy seems to improve the university hospital's ability to attract, retain and develop talented employees.

The continuous dialog on the mission statement also helped to strengthen the reputation of the organization in the view of employees, be it scientists, lab workers or physicians, nurses or administrative staff. Engaged employees, keen to "go the extra mile", may strongly influence the success of the university hospital. As they are important multipliers, spreading their stories internally and externally is a continuous task of communication.

8 Referrers' Relations

An opinion-leading group of external stakeholders are referrers, be it basic-care hospitals or physicians (e.g. general practitioners and private specialists). About 70–80 % of elective patients choose a hospital following the advice of their physicians (Bienert 2012).

For positioning, expanding and networking activities of the university hospital its relations with the referrers are crucial. Their *influential power* stems from their high interest in the university hospital and their possibility of imposing sanctions such as non-referral and spreading news on reputation.

The university hospitals' interest in good relations with referrers aims at

- high utilization rate of beds,
- ensuring the quality of patient treatment across inpatient-outpatient borders by using interdisciplinary, bundled expertise and early access to innovative medical treatment,
- getting high reputation rates from referrers and

- living up to the promised guideline 'leading a good dialog with cooperating partners'.

The referrers' interest in the university hospital may be
- high-end treatment for their patients and
- efficient hospital stays on the basis of reliable cooperation processes.

Referrers choose a hospital out of good experience. Especially former specialist staff members who are now in charge of chief positions in (referrer) hospitals or outpatient care judge the structures and organization they have experienced themselves during their time at the university hospital and eventually compare them with every new referral. Furthermore, their referrals depend on the stability of networks with physicians of the hospital community, which promise easy access to second opinions.

Although referrers are influenced by a good reputation in the public and the media, patient feedback after hospital stay, the service portfolio, and high-end medical equipment, these factors become less important if referrers have bad experiences with the attitudes and interactions of the staff of the university hospital.

Referrers may also be under pressure of other stakeholders with conflicting interests, be it their physicians associations or the health insurances or changing expectations of their patients, see Fig. 2.

8.1 Referrer Questionnaires

It is the responsibility of the specialized clinical departments to survey their referrers. Organ Cancer Centers are obliged to view every 3 years the referrer satisfaction as one condition for recertification. Established topics of the questionnaire are satisfaction with

- accessibility of center or department/availability of medical colleagues
- appointments for patients and waiting times
- velocity and quality of providing medical records (or other important information)
- type of therapeutic concepts and involvement of the referrer in treatment process
- patient satisfaction and
- interest in participation at tumor boards.

Recent referrer satisfaction results of Cologne University Hospital show that referrers see scope for improvement in barrier-free appointments (some show interest in web-based solutions), direct phone access to specialist colleagues at defined times, updated information in case of organizational changes and on-time information in case of problems (e.g. postponed surgery, result of clinical procedures). The surveyed referrers also confirmed the importance of a loyal communication with patients in accordance with referrers' interests, including concerted follow-up ambulatory care and medication.

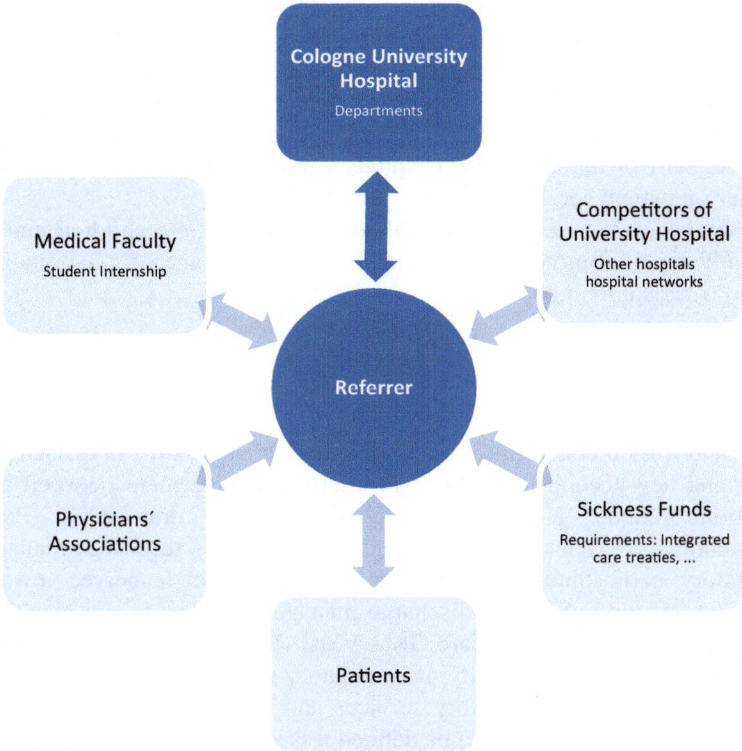

Fig. 2 Stakeholders of Cologne University Hospital's referrers

The main referral reasons stated were 'service portfolio', 'proximity of hospital' and 'own experience with center or department', followed by 'good reputation' and 'medical expertise', 'patient preference'. 'Option to inscribe to clinical studies' and 'certified quality standards' were mentioned less often.

8.2 Conclusions for a Targeted Referrer Involvement

According to the results of satisfaction questionnaires the involvement of referrers should be based on their expectations in a way that the different specialized departments can offer special and targeted forms of involvement, be it 'information', 'consulting', 'participation' or 'empowerment'. We give some examples:

Continuing education and information about the special expertise of a department, be it the potential of innovative medical treatment or the quality of services, enables referrers to deliver evidence-based treatment. A recent 'update on internal medical treatment' offered by the internal departments was followed by 200 practitioners and private specialists.

Advanced training is offered for a limited number of medical staff of teaching hospitals.

Integrated care contracts overcome borders between in- and outpatient treatment. One example: patients of the department of psychiatry diagnosed with psychosis and in need of continuous low care services receive home care services by medical staff of the university hospital in close cooperation and coordination with other outpatient services.

Another integrated care contract called 'On Feet' offers children and young adults with impaired motoric abilities a fine-tuned package of rehabilitation and 'high end' medical treatment.

9 Outlook

Efficient and trusted communication requires reliable standards in discharge management and new technical solutions in interface management between hospital information systems and outpatients offices. The draft Care Provision Strengthening Act (Deutscher Bundestag 2015) provides discharge management as obligatory in hospital treatment. This concretization is geared towards an improvement of the liability of discharge management. The Social Health Insurance Act to Structure Medical Care GKV-VStG (Bundesgesetzblatt 2012) aims at further improvement of the quality of ambulatory specialized care, the differentiation between high and low quality services and reduction of double structures. Though the specification is still to be defined it is already obvious that competition and rivalry between hospitals and ambulatory medical specialists with regard to certain services will further increase.

10 Implications for Governance

The Cologne University Hospital is a nationally and internationally renowned institution with great innovative strength. Solutions for major medical problems, outcomes and outputs of hospital care, research and education depend on an established and functioning interdisciplinarity among specialists on different levels and across different clinical or administrative departments. Especially in times of increasing financial pressure on hospitals it is useful to include the views of stakeholders into strategy, solution finding and concepts of change.

A consistent *reputation management* helps to attract stakeholder attention and continuously focus on *hospital-stakeholder relations*. Some core principles linked to governance should be implemented:

- *Communicate values* and principles of the university hospital internally and externally.
- Develop a *mission statement* and initiate a continuous dialog on values throughout the enterprise to confirm authenticity and visible governance.

- Develop the corporate strategy with broad *participation* of leaders and staff.
- Involve *stakeholders as multipliers* in the daily routine according to needs in different aspects and evaluate the results.
- Be proactive and prepare the correct handling of critical situations and establish a respectful and professional management with errors. Sober judgement and *self-assessment* help stakeholders and the public to continue a trustful relationship.
- Recent error cases in hospitals have demonstrated how proactive communication and *crisis management* decide on trustworthiness and reputation.
- Support and *manage actively* a positive reputation. Promote a trustworthy personalization of the enterprise by communicating (oral statements, interviews) proper reception of services and experiences with the university hospital. It should be a constant source for journalists.
- Give examples of individual values and special expertise to increase the potential for employee identification with the enterprise especially in aspects of societal relevance.
- With *corporate design* establish a general brand plus concurring special brands of the university hospital providing a distinctive and characteristic image that combines health care, research and medical education in a unique and positive way (strategic corporate communication).

The *external perception* of the enterprise requires an unbiased *self-perception*. Power and influence of the identified stakeholders and their potential impact need to be analyzed. Based on those results the university hospital will be able to develop appropriate strategies, meet the interests of stakeholders and make use of them for the hospital's legitimate interests.

To increase its reputation Cologne University Hospital needs to invest in buildings and infrastructure according to changing demands of the diverse groups of patients and personnel with often diverging, even conflicting interests. Organizational improvement for patient and process safety in highly technical work environments of a university hospital is a continuous task. Further research is required to explore and to better understand stakeholder interaction of university hospitals and to identify means for improvement with high impact on reputation.

More efficiency and a superb *reputation* will help to cope with the hospital's challenges. If an enterprise is keeping, loosing, or gaining reputation, this is connected with the inner and outer *boundaries* of any university hospital.

References

Bennington J, Moore MH (2010) Public value: theory and practice. Palgrave Macmillan, London

Bienert ML (2012) Professionelles Zuweisermarketing. In: Korff U (ed) Patient Krankenhaus. Springer Gabler, Wiesbaden, pp 161–175

Bryson JM (2003) What to do when stakeholders matter: a guide to stakeholder identification and analysis techniques. Seminar paper, LSE 2003, http://cep.lse.ac.uk/seminarpapers/10-02-03-bry.pdf. Accessed 21 Jan 2015

Bundesgesetzblatt (2012) GKV-Versorgungsstrukturgesetz. www.bgbl.de. Accessed 3 July 2015

Davies G, Chun R, da Silva R, Roper S (2004) A corporate character scale to assess. Employee and customer views of organization reputation. Corp Reput Rev 7(2):125–146

Deutscher Bundestag (2015) Entwurf eines Gesetzes zur Stärkung der Versorgung in der gesetzlichen Krankenversicherung (GKV-Versorgungsstärkungsgesetz GKV-VSG). http://dip21.bundestag.de/dip21/btd/18/040/1804095.pdf

Geurtsen A, Plamper E, Laeven AWM (2012) When and how are stakeholders (to be) involved? Reputation of university hospitals as critical factor for involvement. Paper presented at the EGPA 2012, Bergen, 5–8 Sept 2012

Zyglidopoulos SC (2001) The impact of accidents on firms' reputation for social performance. Bus Soc 40:416–441. http://bas.sagepub.com/content/40/4/416.full.pdf+html. Accessed 22 Jan 2015

Evelyn Plamper is Head of Corporate Development of Cologne University Hospital, Germany. She was awarded her medical degree from Tübingen University in 1982. She worked as medical assistant in Nuremberg City Hospital and with a general practitioner. After her postgraduate degree in public health she was research assistant in the Institute of Health Economics and Epidemiology at the University of Cologne. Main research areas were evaluation of early prevention programs, tobacco use prevention strategies, hospital benchmarking projects accompanying the introduction of the DRG-financing system. In 2007, Evelyn Plamper joined the management of Cologne University Hospital and is responsible for strategic management, inhouse consulting in reorganization processes and project and process portfolio management. Her fields of engagement include stakeholder management, quality of hospital services, patient satisfaction with service delivery and aspects of corporate culture, mission and strategic personnel development. In corporate strategy internal and external boundaries are important development aspects.

Edgar Schömig is Chief Physician as well as Chief Executive Officer of the Cologne University Hospital. He was awarded his medical degree from Würzburg University in 1986. From 1986 until 1994 he was a postdoctoral fellow and lecturer at the Department of Pharmacology at the University Hospital Würzburg. In 1994 he was awarded a full professorship of pharmacology and toxicology at the Medical Faculty of the University of Heidelberg. Since 2001 he has been Director of the Department of Pharmacology at the University Hospital Cologne and from 2004 until 2006 elected Dean of the Medical Faculty, University of Cologne. Since 2006 Professor Schömig is CEO of Cologne University Hospital.

Cologne University Hospital is a dynamic and science-oriented clinic with more than 10,000 employees. It belongs to the fastest growing hospitals in Germany. From 2005 to 2014 the number of inpatients increased by 33 %. Medical progress, patient expectations and a competitive health market are major challenges to be met by modern hospital management.

The Hospital Situation for Diseases Requiring Sophisticated Examinations Using Epilepsy as an Example

Christian E. Elger

Abstract

Epilepsy is one of the most common neurological diseases and at least one-third of the patients who are diagnosed require highly specialized treatment. Since the number of specialized centers is limited due to cost considerations, a complex selection process must be in place in order to provide specialized treatment for these patients, and a *boundaryless hospital* is the only organizational structure offering the necessary environment. Modern electronic media provide a basis for communication among different partners. At the moment, however, communication and collaboration obstacles appear to be almost insurmountable due to reimbursement problems coupled with the vanity of single players. In addition to costs being reduced, treatment continues to improve, research is developing rapidly, and therefore this structure should be of general interest to the public. However, politics must provide the framework. This is the case in Switzerland where certified, specialized centers have been established that represent the growing success of the boundaryless hospital concept.

Keywords

Epilepsy • Specialized epilepsy centers • Antiepileptic drugs • Drug resistant • EEG • MRI • Epilepsy genetics • Seizures • Early referral • Research • Data collection • Highly specialized medicine • Germany • Switzerland

C.E. Elger (✉)
Department of Epileptology, University of Bonn, Sigmund-Freud-Str. 25, 53105 Bonn, Germany
e-mail: christian.elger@ukb.uni-bonn.de

H. Albach et al. (eds.), *Boundaryless Hospital*, DOI 10.1007/978-3-662-49012-9_14

1 Introduction

Epilepsy is one of the most common neurological diseases affecting more than 600,000 patients in Germany (Hamer et al. 2012) and approximately 70 million people worldwide (Ngugi et al. 2011). Despite its singular name, epilepsy is not a "stand-alone" disease. Instead, it is comprised of a large group of brain diseases that have different causes, different diagnostic requirements and, thus, different treatment regimens. These diseases share only one common characteristic: the epileptic seizure. Since the causes of epilepsy range from large, easy-to-detect brain lesions to subtle functional alterations of the brain, the detection of which is a challenge even in specialized centers, the diagnostic depth necessary for effective treatment can be considerable. This variety of diagnostic and therapeutic procedures cannot be offered by every neurological department. Additionally, epileptological expertise for evaluating the findings and placing them into the proper therapeutic context is often lacking. However, epilepsy centers in Germany have been designed to fill this gap and are set up in order to meet these specific requirements.

In general, epilepsy patients can be divided into two groups: those who are easy-to-treat (two-thirds of patients) and those who are difficult-to-treat (one-third of patients). Normally, the latter group can be identified 3–5 years after the initial epilepsy diagnosis, as their response to drug therapy is limited. Estimates show that only a very small portion of the 200,000 difficult-to-treat patients (most of whom are therapy-resistant to antiepileptic drugs) are referred to specialized epilepsy centers (Kobau et al. 2008). This is primarily due to the limited number of patients who can be admitted for treatment in epilepsy centers (due to space constraints and long waiting lists of up to 6 months or more). In order to solve the treatment gap, European countries have established networks and triage systems amongst centers and neurological departments/neurologists. Because the amount of technical data in epilepsy is limited and easily transferable via digital media, the use of electronic media and telemedicine in epilepsy diagnosis and treatment could serve as a model for other similarly complex diseases (Sheanon and Pitkanen 2013).

2 Epilepsy: Causes and Methods of Confirmation

The causes for epilepsy can be genetic, metabolic, immunological or structural. The respective diagnostic requirement depends on the suspected cause derived from anamnestic data.

2.1 Genetically Determined Epilepsies

Despite its name, the term "genetically determined" is misleading because an exact determination of which specific gene is involved has only been found in a very small number of epilepsies. Laboratories can confirm this diagnosis. Special institutions help determine the diagnosis of epileptic encephalopathy for limited costs. For all other genetically determined epilepsies (idiopathic-generalized epilepsies) and also idiopathic-focal epilepsies of childhood, the decisive diagnostic tool is the electroencephalogram (EEG), see Sect. 3.1. Mobile long-term EEG is used most often.

2.2 Metabolically Determined Epilepsies

The metabolic causes of epilepsy, specifically in children, are multi-faceted. Certain institutions specialize in these types of epilepsy diagnoses. However, the diagnostic procedures utilized for examining patients with these diseases are not performed by any one single institution and sometimes it is difficult to determine which institution performed a specific procedure. Thus, a databank which uses an organized work flow system could help identify and document which samples were sent by which (specific) institution (i.e., blood samples, muscle samples, cerebrospinal fluid, etc.). With the help of such an organizational system, the necessary diagnostic procedures could be easily performed and the patient would not need to be transferred to a specialized hospital.

2.3 Immunologically Determined Epilepsies

The cause for newly diagnosed epilepsies in adult patients who are middle-aged or older can often be traced to autoimmune diseases. Antibody detection is a fast growing field in epilepsy, and the underlying diseases are probably still underestimated in terms of incidence. Those few institutions possessing both the necessary tools for antibody detection and state-of-the-art technology should be utilized in order to detect these diseases. Once diagnosed, patients should then be referred to a specialized center for treatment.

2.4 Structurally Determined Epilepsies

The human brain is a complicated structure comprising approximately 100 billion neurons. The cerebral cortex is the area in which higher functions are processed. Since an epileptic seizure is a non-specific reaction of disturbances of the homeostasis of the brain, most of the structural abnormalities within the cortex serve as triggers for epileptic events. They are defined as being epileptogenic. The epileptogenic lesion is the central biomarker when considering surgical proceedures are being considered. Its localization, nature and dimension determine whether or not a patient can be treated with an epilepsy surgical procedure (Bien et al. 2013). The primary investigation procedure for detecting lesions is magnetic resonance imaging (MRI).

3 Highly Specialized Methods in Epilepsy

3.1 Electroencephalogram Recordings

In epilepsy, the electroencephalogram (EEG) is the only tool which reflects the epileptogenic process in the brain by specific potential fluctuations which are obtained via electrodes attached to the head. Thus, an EEG recording is mandatory for proving an epilepsy diagnosis or, in other cases, determining the area of the brain in which the activity is generated (as with focal epilepsy). The so-called routine EEG is performed by neurologists and neuropediatricians in private practices and in all neurological/neuropediatric departments. However, many patients require more sophisticated diagnostic procedures such as a long-term EEG (the patient is mobile), a multi-channel EEG (up to 256 channels), or video monitoring (here, the patient is usually placed in a fixed position). In addition to the EEG, the behavior of the patient is also simultaneously recorded on video. Because of the nature of the latter investigations, the patient must be physically present during the recordings. Due to the complexity of the EEG signal, an analysis can only be performed by an expert within the field. Since the indicator for more complex EEG recordings is also based on the level of expertise, a simple EEG service in a non-specialized hospital with non-specialized staff is counterproductive as it would add up to a misuse of resources.

3.2 Magnetic Resonance Imaging

MRI in epilepsy patients is very challenging since the cerebral alterations which cause epilepsy are subtle and require not only special investigative protocols, but also a high level of expertise in order to be detected. By using the correct protocol and following the guidelines set forth by neurological societies within specific countries, radiologists should be able to obtain scans from patients with epilepsy. However, the evaluation must be conducted by an expert in both epilepsy and neuroradiology, because only a combination of these two fields will lead to relevant and significant results (Oertzen et al. 2002). In the case of epilepsy, this means identifying suitable candidates for surgery and estimating the level of difficulty of the operation, if required.

4 Virtual Cooperation in Epilepsy Treatment

As previously mentioned, epilepsy is a disease which, as a model, provides two promising approaches for less cost-intensive and higher quality treatment by applying telemedicine methods.

4.1 Expert Review of Data

First, specimens can be transferred to specific centers. Prerequisites for this are clearly stated protocols which can be realized even under non-specialized hospital conditions and the appropriate infrastructure in those highly specialized centers which are handling the specimen. A similar approach could be performed with MRI scans as a cloud computing structure could permit several specialists access to an image. Using a given protocol, the images can be stored anywhere. A video conference meeting can then be set up during which everyone can view the scans simultaneously and thus a conclusive diagnosis and a constructive concept can be generated for the patient.

4.2 Optimized Patient Transferral to Specialized Centers

The second method essentially requires the physical presence of the patient in a highly specialized center. However, for the approximately 200,000 patients in Germany who are potential candidates, there are not nearly enough specialized centers for thorough work-up examinations. Therefore, the boundaries between neurologists in private practices, neurologists in non-specialized hospitals, and those in highly specialized centers must be overcome via digital means. In order to do so, a "triage system" must be generated which enables the identification of patients having a good treatment perspective and then assigning them to a specialized center. Thus, the total number of difficult-to-treat patients referred to a specialized center would be considerably reduced.

5 Research Aspects

The advantage of centralizing difficult-to-treat patients in highly specialized hospitals is that disease-related data are concentrated within these institutions. If algorithms exist, then the collection of data becomes so systematic that the evaluation of diagnostic and therapeutic procedures becomes more and more valuable. In addition, the increase in patient numbers enables systematic research and thus progress in diagnosis and treatment. This is already the case in those institutions which analyze specimens such as antibodies, and serve as centers for specialized diagnoses. The Neuroimmunology Center (Nuffield Department of Clinical Neurosciences) at the University of Oxford compiled an overview of patients with limbic encephalitis. This overview was so extensive that their work was published in leading scientific journals within the field (Vincent et al. 2011; Carvajal-González et al. 2014). The comprehensive research was accomplished despite the fact that the patients with this disease were spread throughout the UK. Had all the patients been treated in only one or two centers, the scientific yield would have been much better. Another example is the National Hospital of Neurology in London which is specialized in neurology and neurosurgery and has specialists for all types of diseases affecting the nervous system. Their success in the diagnosis and treatment of patients not only generates a constant referral from other hospitals, but also attracts scientists from all over the world who support the evaluation (University College London Hospitals 2014).

6 Obstacles and New Ways

Apart from the vanity of the physicians involved, a major obstacle for a boundaryless hospital in Germany is the current payment system which punishes collaboration and rewards solo attempts (e.g. repeating expensive diagnostic procedures or performing such procedures despite lacking required expertise). This is unfortunately true for most hospital systems worldwide.

Switzerland, however, has started to move in a direction which has generated some progress. A law was launched which addresses the coordination and concentration of highly specialized medicine by regulating the number of highly specialized hospitals and the procedures performed there (Bundesversammlung der Schweizerischen Eidgenossenschaft 1996; Schweizerische Sanitärdirektorenkonferenz 2003). This law guarantees adequate payment for the maintenance of highly specialized medicine. Whereas previously the planning for highly specialized medicine varied from canton to canton, this process is now centralized for all of Switzerland. The accreditation of a center for a specific disease is related to the center's responsibility towards providing diagnoses and medical treatment at the highest level. The future will show whether or not this concept fulfills expectations and if successive *boundaryless hospitals* with adequate financial compensation become a reality (Schweizerische Konferenz der kantonalen Gesundheitsdirektorinnen und -direktoren 2008).

In the case of epilepsy, a *boundaryless hospital* could save money, improve and accelerate appropriate diagnosis and treatment, contribute to scientific progress (especially with regard to rare conditions) and could possibly even serve as an educational center. An important requirement for progress in this direction is a change in the principles of the health economic system and a stronger reinforcement of expertise for the benefit of difficult-to-treat patients.

References

Bien CG, Raabe AL, Schramm J, Becker A, Urbach H, Elger CE (2013) Trends in presurgical evaluation and surgical treatment of epilepsy at one centre from 1988–2009. J Neurol Neurosurg Psychiatry 84(1):54–61. doi:10.1136/jnnp-2011-301763

Bundesversammlung der Schweizerischen Eidgenossenschaft (1996) Bundesgesetz 832.10 über die Krankenversicherung (KVG). https://www.admin.ch/opc/de/classified-compilation/19940073/index.html. Accessed 15 June 2015

Carvajal-González A, Leite MI, Waters P, Woodhall M, Coutinho E, Balint B, Lang B, Pettingill P, Carr A, Sheerin U, Press R, Press R, Lunn MP, Lim M, Maddison P, Meinck H, Vandenberghe W, Vincent A (2014) Glycine receptor antibodies in PERM and related syndromes: characteristics, clinical features and outcomes. Brain 137(Pt 8):2178–2192. doi:10.1093/brain/awu142

Hamer HM, Dodel R, Strzelczyk A, Balzer-Geldsetzer M, Reese J, Schoffski O, Graf W, Schwab S, Knake S, Oertel WH, Rosenow F, Kostev K (2012) Prevalence, utilization, and costs of antiepileptic drugs for epilepsy in Germany—a nationwide population-based study in children and adults. J Neurol 259(11):2376–2384. doi:10.1007/s00415-012-6509-3

Kobau R, Zahran H, Thurman DJ, Zack MM, Henry TR, Schachter SC, Price PH (2008) Epilepsy surveillance among adults—19 States, Behavioral Risk Factor Surveillance System, 2005. MMWR Surveill Summ 57(6):1–20

Ngugi AK, Kariuki SM, Bottomley C, Kleinschmidt I, Sander JW, Newton CR (2011) Incidence of epilepsy: a systematic review and meta-analysis. Neurology 77(10):1005–1012. doi:10.1212/WNL.0b013e31822cfc90

Schweizerische Konferenz der kantonalen Gesundheitsdirektorinnen und -direktoren (2008) Interkantonale Vereinbarung über die hochspezialisierte Medizin. http://www.gdk-cds.ch/index.php?id=822. Accessed 18 Dec 2014

Schweizerische Sanitärdirektorenkonferenz (2003) Koordination und Konzentration der hochspezialisierten Medizin: Schlussbericht der Arbeitsgruppe "Spitzenmedizin" zuhanden des Vorstandes der Schweizerischen Sanitätsdirektorenkonferenz (SDK). https://www.santesuisse.ch/de/dyn_output.html?&content.void=12395. Accessed 15 June 2015

Sheanon E, Pitkanen A (2013) Epilepsy on the horizon: Dublin forum focused on epilepsy care and research in Europe. Epilepsia 54(10):1713–1714. doi:10.1111/epi.12346

University College London Hospitals (2014) Annual report and accounts 2013/2014. www.uclh.nhs.uk/aboutus. Accessed 15 June 2015

Vincent A, Bien CG, Irani SR, Waters P (2011) Autoantibodies associated with diseases of the CNS: new developments and future challenges. Lancet Neurol 10(8):759–772. doi:10.1016/S1474-4422(11)70096-5

von Oertzen J, Urbach H, Jungbluth S, Kurthen M, Reuber M, Fernandez G, Elger CE (2002) Standard magnetic resonance imaging is inadequate for patients with refractory focal epilepsy. J Neurol Neurosurg Psychiatry 73(6):643–647

Christian E. Elger is the Director of the Department of Epileptology at the University of Bonn, Germany. From 2006 through early 2015, he served as the Medical Director for Life & Brain Ltd., a strategy development company also located at the University of Bonn.

He studied physiology and neurology at the University of Münster and later became a Professor of Epileptology at the University of Bonn.

Christian E. Elger has served as President of the German Society of Clinical Neurophysiology and Chairman of the German division of the International League Against Epilepsy (ILAE), where he has been a member of the Committee of European Affairs. From 2004 to 2008, he served as an Associate Editor for the journal *Brain*. Currently, he is an Associate Editor for *Epilepsy and Behavior* and has published numerous articles on experimental and clinical epileptology, as well as on cognitive research.

Identifying the Adoption Process for Electronic Health Services: A Qualitative Study

Isabel Ramtohul

Abstract

The implementation of information and communication technology in the health care sector is of considerable interest, since it has been proved that it leads to benefits like improved health care quality, patient safety and satisfaction as well as favorable cost-effectiveness compared to traditional services.

However, the implementation of electronic health services (e-health services) as innovative interventions or tools into routine care is a slow and unpredictable process. To speed up this development and to attain a wide dissemination, this study aims at identifying the decision-making process of the first use (adoption process) of an e-health service from the user's respectively patient's perspective. Fifty seven conducted semi-structured problem-centered interviews reveal that the typical adoption process consists of the following six phases: (1) latency phase, (2) initiative phase, (3) information phase, (4) decision phase, (5) trial phase and (6) confirmation phase. These insights contribute to the adoption theory.

In order to guarantee a comprehensive analysis of the adoption process for e-health services, the paper has the following structure: A definition and a classification of e-health (services) as well as the theoretical concepts and a literature overview of the adoption process lay the foundation for the conducted study. In the following, the study description and the results of the qualitative e-health user interviews are presented. The paper ends with implications on theory and practice and a short outlook.

Keywords

e-health services • Adoption • Adoption process • Innovation-decision process • Health care • Decision-making

I. Ramtohul (✉)
Institute of Health Care Management and Health Sciences, University of Bayreuth, Prieserstraße 2, 95444 Bayreuth, Germany
e-mail: isabel.ramtohul@uni-bayreuth.de

H. Albach et al. (eds.), *Boundaryless Hospital*, DOI 10.1007/978-3-662-49012-9_15

1 Introduction

The implementation of information and communication technology in the health care sector is of considerable international interest (Black et al. 2011). In large part this is attributed to the challenges of a growing and aging population. This development increases the need for more efficiency and effectiveness in health care. In this context, electronic health services (e-health services) are expected to improve health care quality, patient safety as well as satisfaction and have a positive impact on cost-effectiveness as they are able to overcome critical boundaries in health care through new structures and solutions like continuous monitoring, prompt interventions in the case of emergency, communication between relevant stakeholders or facilitation of labor-intensive health services. To prove these assumptions, a multitude of studies has been conducted for all kinds of e-health services until now.

Numerous study results support the postulated use of e-health services. The analysis of telemonitoring for chronic obstructive pulmonary disease (COPD) as a means of continuous monitoring shows a trend towards a reduced number of exacerbations (Pedone et al. 2013) and hospital admissions (Trappenburg et al. 2008). In the case of heart failure, the assessment of the cost-effectiveness identifies the remote patient monitoring as the dominant technology over existing standard care as cost savings are combined with a gain of quality-adjusted life years (Klersy et al. 2011). As an example for telephone-based e-health services, telephone counseling for smoking cessation compared with self-help materials or no intervention has a positive impact on smoking cessation as it increases continuous abstinence for both actively and passively recruited smokers based on an intensified communication (Tzelepis et al. 2011). Furthermore, the use of interactive asynchronous communication channels, like email or online discussion boards, specifically tailored for patients with chronic illnesses leads to improved health behavior as well as health outcomes (De Jong et al. 2014).

Despite these promising results, the implementation of e-health services as new interventions or tools into routine care is a slow and unpredictable process (Berwick 2003). To speed up this development and to realize a wide dissemination, the acceptance of these services is a fundamental prerequisite. Therefore, current research focuses on the identification of factors that positively influence the acceptance and in consequence the decision to use an e-health service. A multitude of studies exists which analyzes different e-health services from the patient's, the health care professional's or the organization's perspective. With regard to the perspective of the individual patient, adoption determinants like trust in the service provider, perceived ease of use and usefulness, health need or anonymity are identified for technology-based self-diagnosis tools, telecare services for elderly persons or comprehensively for a broad range of e-health services (Lanseng and Andreassen 2007; Sintonen and Immonen 2013; Ramtohul 2015). Focusing on health care professionals, a review of Gagnon et al. (2012) on influencing factors of information and communication technologies reveals among others design, technical concerns, perceived usefulness, complexity or familiarity. Concerning organizations like hospitals, the question of relevant adoption factors is e.g., investigated for health information technology (HIT) applications like e-health radiology, emailing or patient scheduling. In this context, the size of the hospital or its urban location is crucial for the adoption decision (Zhang et al. 2013).

In contrast to this primary research objective, the analysis of the decision-making process with the result to adopt or to reject an e-health service as a possible second research aim in this context is often neglected. There exist fundamental theoretical and conceptual approaches of this process (see especially Nabih et al. (1997) and Rogers (2003a) or Kollmann (2013) for the field of online marketing and the corresponding detailed explanations in Sect. 3), but recent empirical investigations in a specific practical context, like the health care sector, are scarce[1]. But not only is the knowledge about relevant adoption factors essential for the success of an innovation but also the knowledge about the process, about how this decision is made (Wee 2003). Therefore, it is the main objective of this study to reveal this adoption process for e-health services from a patient's perspective. The results facilitate the deduction of concrete implications for service providers and health care professionals to support this individual adoption process.

The structure of the paper is as follows: Sect. 2 gives a definition and a classification scheme for e-health services. The explanation of the fundamentals of the innovation-decision process follows in Sect. 3. Section 4 contains the study description and the results of the qualitative e-health user interviews. The final Sect. 5 consists of implications for theory and practice as well as a short outlook.

2 Definition and Classification of e-Health Services

The use of the term e-health emerged with the application of information and communication technologies in the health care sector (Pagliari et al. 2005). Their spread during the last decades was accompanied by numerous attempts to formulate a definition for this phenomenon (Eysenbach 2001; Oh et al. 2005; Pagliari et al. 2005; Showell and Nøhr 2012; Cunningham et al. 2014). Due to an evolving variety of e-health applications with respect to solutions, structures, stakeholders, outcomes, contexts, perspectives and theoretical issues targeted (Oh et al. 2005; Pagliari et al. 2005), the existing definitions show differentiating aspects in the understanding of e-health (applications). As to e.g., the facet of technologies applied, some encompass a broad scope covering electronic and digital processes, while others focus solely on the use of the Internet (Meier et al. 2013). Additionally, a differentiation of applications for all stakeholder groups compared to specific

[1] Kyratis et al. (2012) focus e.g., on the adoption and implementation of technology in primary and acute care organizations in England.

target populations like health care professionals or patients is frequently conducted in the definitions (Pagliari et al. 2005). More recently, against the background of the demographic and epidemiological change, the facets of meeting the needs of the different stakeholders, increasing patient engagement, focusing on patient-centric services and consequently moving towards a more personalized health care have been added to the understanding of e-health (Ball and Lillis 2001; Geissbühler 2012).

Taking the dynamic environment of e-health applications into account, a broad definition is needed to cover the already existing applications and the future developments (Eysenbach 2001; Pagliari et al. 2005). This was Eysenbach's (2001) intention, when he defined e-health as

> [...] an emerging field in the intersection of medical informatics, public health and business, referring to health services and information delivered or enhanced through the Internet and related technologies. In a broader sense, the term characterizes not only a technical development, but also a state-of-mind, a way of thinking, an attitude, and a commitment for networked, global thinking beyond boundaries, to improve health care locally, regionally, and worldwide by using information and communication technology.

Consequently, this is the most cited definition (at least until the year 2005, as revealed by Oh et al. 2005). As it mentions the terms "state-of-mind", "way of thinking" and "attitude", it implicitly covers the recently emerging aspects of need satisfaction and patient focus with the aim of personalizing health care. Therefore, Eysenbach's definition is also applied for this study.

In accordance with this understanding, an approach for the classification of currently existing e-health areas and services is described in the following in order to provide an overview from a more problem solving practical perspective. There, applications of e-health services are divided into three comprehensive fields focusing on solutions for health care professionals and patients respectively as well as for health care business management (Pagliari et al. 2005):

1. E-health services with a focus on health care professionals: e.g., decision aids for practitioners like reminders or care pathways, clinical management tools like electronic health records, educational tools, electronic clinical communication tools, electronic networks, discipline- and disease-specific tools or telemedicine applications
2. E-health services with a focus on consumers or patients respectively: e.g., decision aids for patients, information and educational tools on the web, clinician-patient communication tools like clinical email and web-based messaging systems for consultation, disease monitoring or service-oriented tasks like appointment booking, online screening tools or virtual health communities

3. Health care business management: e.g., billing and tracking systems or audit and quality assessment systems

As the research objective is the innovation-decision process from the user's perspective, e-health-services being of interest within this study stem from the second field.

The following section deals with the fundamentals of the innovation-decision process and the results of a literature review on this process in the context of technology-based services, health services as well as technology-based health services of individuals.

3 Fundamentals of the Innovation-Decision Process

Before elaborating on the literature review, the theoretical concepts are described in order to create a fundamental understanding.

3.1 Theoretical Background

The innovation-decision process constitutes the core of the decision of either adopting or rejecting an innovation. Therefore, the name adoption process is used synonymously in the literature. It is based on Rogers (2003b), who originated the diffusion of innovations theory in the context of social sciences and elaborated a fundamental concept of this process. In his widely accepted understanding, this adoption process "[...] is the process through which an individual (or other decision-making unit) passes from first knowledge of an innovation to the formation of an attitude toward the innovation, to a decision to adopt or reject, to implementation and use of the new idea, and to confirmation of this decision." This definition expresses the understanding that the decision about the use of an innovation is not taken instantaneously but rather consists of different characteristic stages (Ryan and Gross 1943). In general, the following five phases can be identified (Rogers 2003c):

1. Knowledge stage: The decision-making unit first gains knowledge about an innovation's existence and understands how it works. This can be based on random information or active search for the solution to an existing problem. In this context, it is assumed that individuals are especially susceptible for information which is in accordance with their attitude, beliefs and needs (Hassinger 1959).
2. Persuasion stage: The decision-making unit forms a favorable or unfavorable attitude towards the innovation based on a consciously conducted specific information search about costs and benefits of the innovation. During this stage, the involvement of the potential adopter is required.

3. Decision stage: The decision-making unit chooses to adopt or to reject the innovation. In this context, "adoption is a decision to make full use of an innovation as the best course of action available, [whereas] rejection is a decision not to adopt an innovation" (Rogers 2003e).
4. Implementation stage: Up to this stage, the adoption process implies only thinking and mentally deciding. Now however, the decision-making unit uses the innovation in practice for the first time. In general, this stage follows the preceding one rather directly, unless some logistical problems, like temporary unavailability of the innovation, occur.
5. Confirmation stage: The decision-making unit wishes to reassure the decision made about the innovation. However, it might be possible that the adopter changes his mind when the innovation did not meet his expectations.

In conclusion, the adoption process is characterized by information seeking and processing activities. The general aim is to reduce uncertainties about advantages and disadvantages of the innovation (Rogers 2003d).

Nevertheless, this fundamental concept of different and clearly separable stages has evoked criticism due to an assumed high involvement and consequently purposeful actions and cognitive processes of the potential user (Robertson 1971; Gatignon and Robertson 1991). Therefore, extended concepts of the innovation-decision process consider different levels of involvement. Consequently, awareness leads not only to an active information seeking behavior but also to passive acceptance or passive resistance (Nabih et al. 1997). These two fundamental concepts of five different stages in the adoption process and the consideration of different levels of involvement leading to passive or active decisions are combined and visualized in Fig. 1. They constitute the theoretical foundation of the innovation-decision process in this study.

3.2 Literature Review on the Adoption Process in the Context of Technology-Based Services, Health Services and Technology-Based Health Services of Individuals

Although Rogers' (2003a) fundamental innovation-decision process is applicable both to individuals and other decision-making units, this literature review focused on individual adoption processes as the single user, respectively patient, is the interesting subject in this study. Furthermore, the search strategy included technology-based services, health services as well as technology-based health services in order to cover all related investigations. Consequently, studies on adoption processes in other areas or strategic decision-making processes in organizations were excluded.

In the field of technology-based services, only a limited number of studies explored the individual adoption process. Kollmann (2013) dealt with the marketing of Internet-based services like electronic marketplaces and mobile services. For their usefulness, it is not only crucial to adopt a service in the first place but also to

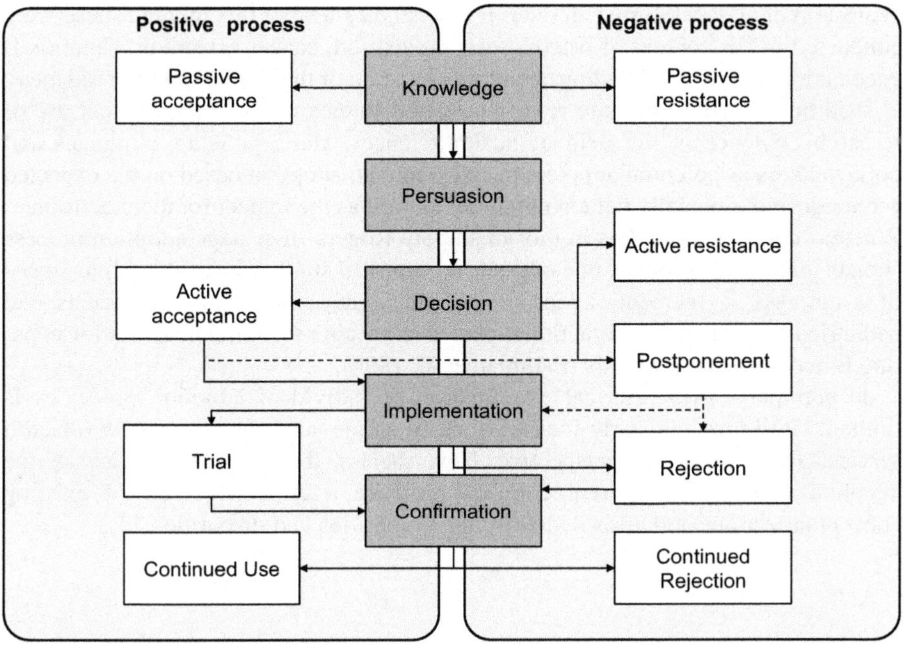

Fig. 1 Comprehensive innovation-decision process adapted from Rogers (2003a) and Nabih et al. (1997)

apply it frequently afterwards. Therefore, the basic adoption process is expanded by the construct of acceptance, which signifies in this context the variable use of the service in terms of intensity and frequency after the initial adoption. As a consequence, this process consists of the following seven phases: (1) awareness, (2) interest, (3) expectation/evaluation, (4) trial/experience, (5) implementation, (6) determination of application and (7) use. In a study of Nabih et al. (1997) the interviewed persons were asked to describe the adoption process for a product, which they assessed innovative for themselves (At that time, portable telephones or the Internet were seen as technology-based innovative services.). As result, most participants showed a behavior of passive resistance. Other observed stages were adoption, trial, adoption and trial postponement, rejection, active resistance as well as active and passive acceptance thus confirming the existence of these different phases.

In the field of health services, the decision-making process is often investigated in the context of precautions aiming at reducing the threat of an illness or injury or of increasing the prospects for recovery. Here, the Precaution Adoption Process Model tries to explain all phases leading to a health-protective behavior (Weinstein et al. 2008). It was originally proposed by Janis and Mann (1977) and consists of the following seven stages: (1) unaware of the health issue, (2) unengaged by issue, (3) undecided about acting, (4) decided not to act (this constitutes a separate phase for the rejection), (5) decided to act, (6) acting and finally (7) maintenance.

Weinstein et al. (2008) give an overview of studies testing this model. These were conducted in the context of osteoporosis prevention, cancer screening, hepatitis B vaccination, home radon testing, smoking cessation or the consumption of red meat.

Additionally, the literature review revealed studies on the adoption and use of research evidence in the field of health sciences. Here, patients, clinicians and policymakers as potential adopters decide about an adoption based on the expected economic and especially patient outcomes as well as the impact for the practitioner. Whereas conceptual studies in this area apply Rogers' five stage adoption process (Logan and Graham 1998), one of the few empirical studies determined four stages of awareness, agreement, adoption and adherence for family physicians and pediatricians evaluating the national pediatric vaccine recommendations for hepatitis B and acellular pertussis (Pathman et al. 1996).

In summary, the empirical examination of individual adoption processes is limited. Until now, no study focuses directly on the adoption process for e-health services from the user's perspective. Nevertheless, the conducted review of the adoption process in different contexts provides a good overview of existing conceptualizations and allows identifying similarities and disparities.

4 Study Description and Main Findings

In the following, the research design of the study, the data collection and the data analysis are described. Subsequently, the findings from the interviews are presented in detail.

4.1 Research Design

The literature review reasons that the empirical investigation of the innovation-decision process in different contexts is limited (e.g., Pathman et al. 1996; Nabih et al. 1997) or, as it is the case for e-health services, (even) missing. Furthermore, this process may constitute a complex phenomenon of a considerable time span as the existence of several definable stages is widely accepted. In order to reveal the actual "why", "how" and "what" of the decision-making (Hesse-Biber and Leavy 2011a) and to reproduce a picture of this potentially complex process as close to reality as possible, a descriptive qualitative research approach is adequate (Hesse-Biber and Leavy 2011b). This procedure enables to inductively conclude the innovation-decision process for e-health services from the user's perspective and consequently contribute to a theoretical concept of this process in the field of e-health services (Flick 2014).

In order to achieve the research objectives, qualitative semi-structured interviews as the most widely used interviewing format for qualitative research are chosen as the appropriate methodical approach (DiCicco-Bloom and Crabtree 2006). To assure the focus on e-health services and their innovation-decision process, the problem-centered interview is employed (Witzel 2000). Nevertheless, this procedure also allows new viewpoints.

The applied interview guideline for the semi-structured problem-centered interviews consists of three parts. The first introductory part aims at generating a common understanding of the concept of e-health services as the object of investigation. The second part focuses on the detailed analysis of all aspects having an influence on the adoption decision and process of the user of the e-health service. During this part, the interviewer visualizes all these factors and events on a chart which symbolizes the decision-making process. In the third part, these handwritten notes are presented to the interviewed person and are orally summarized by the interviewer. This approach aims at communicatively validating the interview as it allows to accurately record the time of the single events on the x-axis of the chart and to clarify ambiguities and inconsistencies. The y-axis indicates the probability of adopting the concerned e-health service. For the single events, the interviewed person has to express how likely it was at that time to adopt the e-health service. All generated charts constitute the basis for the identification of one or more typical innovation-decision processes for e-health services. The critical incidence technique supports this process. This technique as a qualitative methodology collects observed incidents having a special significance for a specific question (Flanagan 1954). Following the approach of a content analysis, it involves the classification of critical incidents within the adoption process, like the information sources used, with the intent of uncovering patterns within the innovation-decision process. Therefore, it is necessary that the interviewed persons describe a specific situation of adoption in part two of the interview in as much detail as possible in order to identify common patterns (Bitner et al. 1990).

4.2 Study Population

The above described semi-structured problem-centered interviews were conducted with 57 persons. The participants were all contacted in person. The selection of the interviewees aimed at achieving representativeness with regard to contents, as this is characteristic for qualitative research. Therefore, a key criterion was that all participants have used one of the e-health services of interest at least once. Additionally, both frequent and infrequent users were included. Furthermore, the aim was to have a diverse sample with regard to the different e-health services, age and socioeconomic factors. Of the interviewed e-health users 38 were female and 19 were male and their age ranged from 20 to 68 years. All interviews were conducted by the same researcher. Apart from the three-part interview guideline, additional standardized questions were used to investigate the participants' attitude towards technology-based services and their health consciousness. In general, the participants showed a positive attitude towards the use of technology because of its potential advantages like convenience or saving time and money (mean = 4.0 based on the answers of a 5-point Likert scale with 1 = "I totally disagree" and 5 = "I totally agree"). In terms of knowledge about one's own health problems, the interviewed persons indicated a high level of knowledge (mean = 3.7). The experience with e-health services in general reached an average of 2.6.

The participants related their adoption processes to the following different e-health services: 36 persons referred to various online information platforms, searching either for general information (n = 20) or for answers to specific questions (n = 16). 14 persons stated different communication tools. Among these, 11 used synchronous communication with a health professional via telephone, while three persons applied asynchronous communication tools like e-mail (n = 2) and the exchange of messages on a discussion board (n = 1). Furthermore, four participants utilized mail-order pharmacy options, two telemonitoring and one interviewed person applications for mobile devices (apps).

The appropriateness of the sample size was evaluated by referring to recommendations for comparable research questions. A literature review of studies using qualitative interviews revealed a range from 1 to 95 participants with the mean sample size of 31 (Mason 2010). This is in accordance with general guidelines in qualitative research, where 15 participants are seen as the smallest acceptable sample (Bertaux 1981). For qualitative problem-centered interviews in particular, 20–30 interviews of 1 h are proposed to cover about 90–95% of all relevant aspects of the research question (Griffin and Hauser 1993). Taking these recommendations into account, the sample size of 57 participants seemed appropriate to reach the aim of the study. On average one interview took about 30 min.

The whole data collection process followed a stepwise approach with several consecutive stages of conducted interviews. This guaranteed the generation of an inductive-deductive reciprocal relationship between the previous knowledge and the new empirical data both for the survey and the evaluation process (Witzel 2000).

4.3 Data Analysis

Before each interview, consent for participation and tape recording was obtained. All interviews were transcribed verbatim. Regarding data analysis, the software MAXQDA 10 was used to identify process patterns based on the principles of the critical incident technique. The multiple-stage interview and evaluation process contributed to the development of these patterns through the stepwise consideration of new aspects and the affirmation of existing findings. For the initial analysis a scheme of conceptual codes was used which was developed during the literature research. It covered possible characterizing factors on the adoption of e-health services like starting point, trigger of the process, initial awareness of the service, evaluation, information sources, emotions, intention to use again or measures of adoption support. In the ensuing steps of the analysis, this preliminary scheme of codes was modified and extended.

The identified process patterns were then combined with the adoption process charts stemming from the interviews. These comprehensive data constituted the basis for the analysis of the adoption process. In this step, the processes on the whole as well as single phases within—separable by incisive events—were compared until clear similarities and differences were identified. The author, who also conducted the interviews, coded all the data and analyzed the process charts.

In order to achieve an adequate measurement quality, the validity of the study as well as the reliability of the results were taken into account. Concerning the validity of the study, the communicative validation ensured the content validity of the interviews. Process validity was provided by the use of computer assisted qualitative data analysis software. The sufficient sample size finally contributed to the result validity. The reliability of the results was enhanced by their reproducibility. For this purpose, the whole empirical research process was thoroughly documented.

4.4 Findings from the Patient Interviews

The results of the interviews provide insights into the decision-making process for e-health services from the user's perspective. In the following section, the identified ideal phases of the adoption process in the context of e-health services will be presented and illustrated with an example. Nevertheless, it has to be taken into account that variations may occur, especially when considering the person's level of involvement (see Sect. 3). Suffering from an acute health condition leads to a more active and systematic search for information about a potentially helpful e-health service than the need for more general health-related information (e.g., required vaccination for long-distance travels).

The results are based on the content analysis of the transcribed interviews and the structural analysis of the generated individual process charts throughout the interviews. In general, the innovation-decision process for e-health services from the patient's perspective consists of the following six phases: (1) latency phase, (2) initiative phase, (3) information phase, (4) decision phase, (5) trial phase and (6) confirmation phase. In the following, these phases are described in more detail:

(1) Latency phase

The moment when a person gains knowledge about the existence of an e-health service constitutes the beginning of the adoption process. In the special context of Internet-based e-health services, this often happens by chance. Service providers normally undertake active information and marketing measures, whereas physicians rarely appear as communicators in this phase. In most cases, the e-health service falls into oblivion after this first gain of knowledge, as the person normally does not have an urgent health need. Concrete statements about the adoption probability are not possible. The term "latency" stems from the situation that the first information about a health service falls apart with the incidence of actual need. This is characteristic in the context of health care, when the general public is e.g., informed about new therapy options for different illnesses.

The following example describes the respective phases of an ideal adoption process and presents the content of one typical interview. Although this example refers to the infrequently mentioned service of mail-order pharmacy ($n = 4$), it is also applicable to all other stated e-health services.

Example: A healthy woman aged 38 years coincidentally notices the advertisement of a mail-order pharmacy while she is searching for different items on a general retail website. As the advertisement of the mail-order pharmacy is replaced by the advertisement of another online company after a few seconds, the woman pays no particular attention to the mail-order pharmacy. Additionally, she does not feel a need for concrete pharmaceuticals.

(2) Initiative phase

The appearance of the trigger of the core adoption process characterizes this phase. In the majority of the cases investigated, this is an arising health need. But also the general need for information in a health-related context or the wish to save money through the use of an e-health service triggers the adoption process. Depending on the length of the latency phase, the person remembers the e-health service in more or less detail. The trigger of the process leads to an increasing adoption probability, as the person connects the e-health service with the satisfaction of the existing needs. In general, the initiative phase can be characterized as punctual.

Example: After a while, the woman suffers from various mild flu symptoms. As the treatment with different household remedies does not relieve the symptoms, she decides to take some medicine to get rid of the flu more quickly. In this situation she remembers the advertisement of the mail-order pharmacy again as she is not motivated to leave the flat because of the flu.

(3) Information phase

To improve the knowledge about the particular e-health service, the person searches for specific information about this service. Depending on the degree of uncertainty about the advantages and disadvantages of the e-health service, the information search lasts from only a few minutes to several weeks, thus determining the length of the information phase. Here, different information sources like the Internet, magazines, journals, scientific literature or information material of the service provider are used. Additionally, the exchange of experiences with family, friends or the family doctor may take place. Therefore, an intrapersonal and an interpersonal evaluation occur. In the course of this phase, the uncertainty about the e-health service is reduced. Consequently, the probability of rejection decreases.

Example: To gain information about mail-order pharmacies and their range of products, the woman searches the Internet for different providers. She compares them in terms of available flu remedies, special offers, conditions of delivery, evaluation of previous customers as well as structure and ease of use of the website. [In this example, the interviewee did not contact friends or family. Consequently, only an intrapersonal evaluation took place.]

(4) Decision phase

Based on the information gained in the previous phase, the person decides now about trying or rejecting the e-health service. This normally is a notional event without visible actions. Additionally, it can be characterized as punctual.

Example: After the woman has compared different mail-order pharmacies, she is convinced of giving this way of buying pharmaceuticals a try. Her final decision is then based on the price for one particular flu remedy. She decides to order at the mail-order pharmacy with the lowest price.

(5) Trial phase

Depending on the decision, the first trial takes place. After the first use, the person evaluates the e-health service in terms of quality of the service components, of the service result as well as the perceived usefulness. The result of this evaluation determines the probability of a future reuse. In the absence of external restrictions like limited availability or missing access the decision and the first use directly succeed. Therefore, this phase—comparable to the initiative phase and the decision phase—can be characterized as punctual.

Example: The woman selects the chosen flu remedy at the mail-order pharmacy with the lowest price. After entering her personal data like address and way of payment she finally orders. She is very surprised that she receives the ordered remedy the very next day. After taking it for several days as prescribed, the flu symptoms disappear.

(6) Confirmation phase

In this final phase of the adoption process the reuse of the e-health service takes place. When a health need is the trigger of the adoption process, it is difficult to predict the date of the reuse and consequently the length of the confirmation phase. Depending on this, the probability of the reuse might decrease in this phase, as the memory of the satisfying result and the perceived usefulness may fade over time.

Example: Several months after suffering from the flu symptoms, the woman decides to travel to Africa because she has dreamt since childhood to participate in a safari. In her travel guide it is highly recommended to take a first-aid kit as the provision of remedies and other medical equipment might be restricted. As she has been very satisfied with the handling of her first order and also with the reasonable price, she decides to order the missing items for the first-aid kit from the mail-order pharmacy.

Figure 2 visualizes the described adoption process for e-health services. The underlying boxes for each phase indicate the average duration. The indefinite time units on the x-axis account for different lengths of the whole adoption process (durations between a few minutes and several weeks were observed), but consider the same course of the process. The narrow boxes for the initiative phase, the decision phase and the trial phase symbolize their punctual character (as described

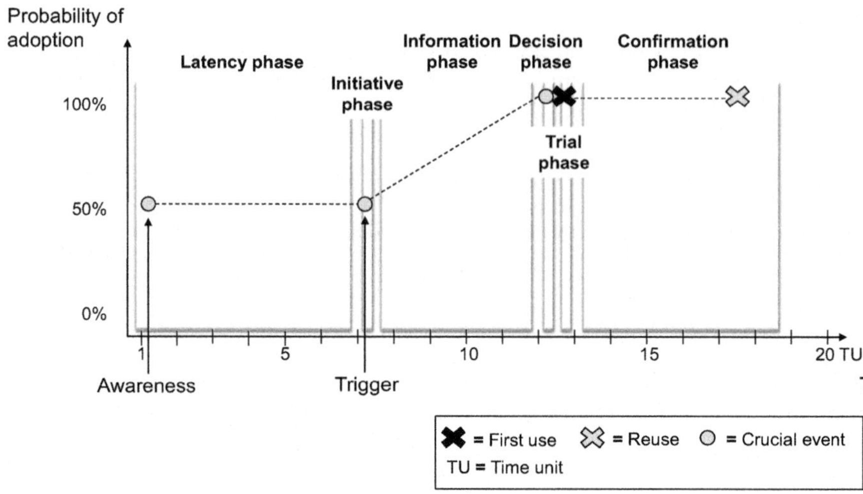

Fig. 2 Typical adoption process for e-health services as discovered in the interviews

above). The probability values indicate the mean of all participants in the separate phases.

5 Implications for Theory and Practice, Conclusions

This study was the first to investigate the decision-making process for e-health services from the user's perspective. Therefore, these findings have important implications for the theory and practice in the field of e-health services thus contributing to solutions for the major challenges of the health care sector stemming from an aging population.

With regard to theory, this study did not focus on the often investigated relevant adoption factors based on a quantitative data analysis but on the whole decision-making process to first use an e-health service. As this procedure is based on qualitative semi-structured problem-centered interviews, it covers the potential complex decision-making with a variety of relevant influencing factors, possibly changing during the chronological sequence of the adoption process. Consequently, it contributes to the theoretical knowledge about the adoption process. It is consistent with Rogers' (2003a) widely accepted and applied innovation-decision process, but adds knowledge to the specific context of e-health services. In this field, the typical process consists of the following six stages: (1) latency phase, (2) initiative phase, (3) information phase, (4) decision phase, (5) trial phase and (6) confirmation phase.

Based on this general process, the next step comprises more research with regard to different types of e-health services. In this study, the e-health services of online health information platforms used for searching either general or specific information, various communication tools like telephone, e-mail or exchanging messages on a discussion board, mail-order pharmacies, telemonitoring devices and apps have not been covered in equal parts. This has to be taken into account in future research as the findings suggest that specific adoption processes exist for specific e-health services. The following example supports this assumption: Whereas the adoption process for health-related information sources in the Internet passes through the identified single phases rather quickly and straightforward, processes for other e-health services like telemonitoring devices or specific communication tools reveal more influencing factors and difficult decision situations.

Additionally, the age of the interviewed persons has to be considered. Therefore, future research needs to expand the sample beyond the realized age range from 20 to 68 years. On the one hand, the elderly have a greater need for e-health services as their health status is impaired by various age-associated illnesses. On the other hand, they are often still characterized as averse to technology. The identification of specific adoption processes according to different age groups, e.g., with a focus on the elderly, helps to tailor supporting measures to particular needs.

Furthermore, the theoretical concept of the decision-making process has to be constantly verified for innovations in the rapidly developing environment of information and communication technologies. This can be illustrated through the representation of apps within the interviews. Although more than 80 % of the current 21 million smart phone owners in Germany have installed apps (BITKOM 2013), only one interviewed person refers to the decision of using a health-related app. This suggests that the general degree of dissemination is not yet reached in the health-related context. Besides, the individual adoption process is always influenced by the time in different ways (Rogers 2003a). Therefore, it is likely that the surveyed adoption processes differ from those which would be investigated at another point in time. In order to consider the influence of time on these processes, it would be necessary to conduct this research on a regular basis.

Finally, the applied study design is not only applicable for revealing the adoption process of e-health services but also of any other innovative service. Furthermore, the procedure is also suitable for focusing on the health care professional's perspective or on the service provider's perspective.

In addition to the implications for the adoption theory, the results also provide contributions for several entities in the public health sector. The knowledge about the decision-making process of the single user helps health care professionals and service providers to positively influence and support the adoption decision. In this context, the examination of the whole adoption process provides deeper insights than the identification of relevant adoption factors alone.

First of all, the adoption process of e-health services starts with a latency phase. This implies that the general awareness for a specific e-health service has to be raised by different players in the health care system in order to increase the adoption probability in the case of actual need. Firstly, health policy makers have to create the necessary conditions to integrate e-health services as equivalent services within the health care sector. In this context, especially the question of eligibility for reimbursement has to be answered. Additionally, service providers need to intensify marketing measures to highlight the advantages of the corresponding e-health service like an improved communication between health care professional and patient, an intensified support of the patient, tailored information for the patient, reduced health care costs for the patient or a round-the-clock monitoring of the patient which allows him or her to stay in the familiar home environment. Finally, health care professionals are able to inform patients selectively about advantageous e-health services based on their comprehensive knowledge about the patient's preferences and needs.

Additionally, a positive adoption decision depends heavily on the quality of the available information in the preceding information phase. Consequently, trustful information about the corresponding e-health service has to be promoted. As the existing information about e-health services in the Internet—as one of the mostly used sources—often lacks objectivity, reliability and an appropriate level of quality, official institutions or organizations within the health care sector have to be responsible for offering neutral and scientifically-based information about the benefits and costs of e-health services for specific patient groups.

Finally, the innovation-decision process has to go along with the possibility of giving feedback on it. The implementation of a feedback tool provides deeper insights not only into the features of the e-health service but also into existing helpful information and support throughout the decision-making from the new user's perspective. This information is essential for facilitating the decision of future users. Furthermore, the feedback of health care professionals is of equal importance as their opinion about an e-health service is crucial for the user's adoption decision.

With regard to future development, this study offers several perspectives. Like outlined above, the study has to be replicated for those e-health services which have been underrepresented in the study like apps, telemonitoring, mail-order pharmacies or asynchronous communication tools. Additionally, different e-health services should be investigated aiming at specific target groups which might benefit most from their usage (e.g., How do youngsters adopt apps which focus on preventive measures against tobacco or alcohol abuse, unhealthy eating habits or sedentary lifestyle? or How do elderly adopt telemonitoring devices?). Besides, the chronological order within the adoption process warrants further investigation in order to identify relevant patterns for a positive adoption decision. Furthermore, as care providers like physicians or pharmacists function as multipliers or opinion-leaders, their adoption process has to be investigated in the same way.

While the undertaken qualitative approach constitutes a necessary first step, the current results need to be confirmed by further quantitative studies. This could follow the procedure of Pathman et al. (1996) to quantify the distribution of (potential) e-health users to the different adoption stages and their underlying characteristics like beliefs, level of agreement or information sources used. In addition to this quantitative confirmation of the adoption process, appropriate measures to support adoption for the different types of processes need further elaboration. A first step comprises the identification and collection of a variety of possibly effective measures. In a next step, they should be tested in practice and evaluated by the e-health users in terms of their level of acceptance and effectiveness.

In summary, the study results improve the understanding of the innovation-decision process in the health care sector thus helping to address the adoption challenges in order to facilitate the initial implementation of e-health services. The experiences gained for the e-health services under investigation will also be (at least partly) transferable to other e-health services and to future developments in this context.

References

Ball MJ, Lillis J (2001) E-health: transforming the physician/patient relationship. Int J Med Inform 61(1):1–10

Bertaux D (1981) From the life-history approach to the transformation of sociological practice. In: Bertaux D (ed) Biography and society: the life history approach in the social sciences. Sage, London, pp 29–45

Berwick DM (2003) Disseminating innovations in health care. JAMA 289(15):1969–1975

BITKOM (2013) BITKOM-Umfrage: Zahlungsbereitschaft für Apps steigt. http://www.marktforschung.de/nachrichten/marktforschung/bitkom-umfrage-zahlungsbereitschaft-fuer-apps-steigt. Accessed 06 Aug 2015

Bitner MJ, Booms BH, Tetreault MS (1990) The service encounter: diagnosing favorable and unfavorable incidents. J Mar 54(1):71–84

Black AD, Car J, Pagliari C et al (2011) The impact of eHealth on the quality and safety of health care: a systematic overview. PLoS One 8(1), e1000387

Cunningham SG, Wake DJ, Waller A et al (2014) Definitions of eHealth. In: Gaddi A, Capello F, Manca M (eds) eHealth, care and quality of life. Springer, Milano, pp 15–30

De Jong CC, Ros WJG, Schrijvers G (2014) The effects on health behavior and health outcomes of Internet-based asynchronous communication between health providers and patients with a chronic condition: a systematic review. J Med Internet Res 16(1), e19

DiCicco-Bloom B, Crabtree BF (2006) The qualitative research interview. Med Educ 40 (4):314–321

Eysenbach G (2001) What is eHealth? J Med Internet Res 3(2), e20

Flanagan JC (1954) The critical incident technique. Psychol Bull 51(4):327–358

Flick U (2014) An introduction to qualitative research. Sage, Los Angeles

Gagnon MP, Desmartis M, Labrecque M et al (2012) Systematic review of factors influencing the adoption of information and communication technologies by healthcare professionals. J Med Syst 36(1):241–277

Gatignon H, Robertson TS (1991) Innovative decision processes. In: Robertson TS, Kassarjian HH (eds) Handbook of consumer behavior. Prentice-Hall, Englewood Cliffs, pp 316–348

Geissbühler A (2012) eHealth: easing the transitions in healthcare. Swiss Med Wkly 142:w13599

Griffin A, Hauser JR (1993) The voice of the customer. Mark Sci 12(1):1–27

Hassinger E (1959) Stages in the adoption process. Rural Sociol 24(1):52–53

Hesse-Biber SN, Leavy P (2011a) The practice of qualitative research. Sage, Thousand Oaks, p 3

Hesse-Biber SN, Leavy P (2011b) The practice of qualitative research. Sage, Thousand Oaks, p 10

Janis IL, Mann L (1977) Decision making: a psychological analysis of conflict, choice, and commitment. Free Press, New York

Klersy C, De Silvestri A, Gabutti G et al (2011) Economic impact of remote patient monitoring: an integrated economic model derived from a meta-analysis of randomized controlled trials in heart failure. Eur J Heart Fail 13(4):450–459

Kollmann T (2013) Online-Marketing. Grundlagen der Absatzpolitik in der Net Economy. Verlag W Kohlhammer, Stuttgart
Kyratis Y, Ahmad R, Holmes A (2012) Technology adoption and implementation in organisations: comparative case studies of 12 English NHS Trusts. BMJ Open 2, e000872
Lanseng EJ, Andreassen TW (2007) Electronic healthcare: a study of people's readiness and attitude toward performing self-diagnosis. Int J Serv Ind Manag 18(4):394–417
Logan J, Graham ID (1998) Toward a comprehensive interdisciplinary model of health care research use. Sci Commun 20(2):227–246
Mason M (2010) Sample size and saturation in PhD studies using qualitative interviews. Forum Qualitative Soc Res 11(3), 8
Meier CA, Fitzgerald MC, Smith JM (2013) eHealth: extending, enhancing, and evolving health care. Annu Rev Biomed Eng 15:359–382
Nabih MI, Bloem G, Poiesz TBC (1997) Conceptual issues in the study of innovation adoption behavior. Adv Consum Res 24(1):190–196
Oh H, Rizo C, Enkin M, Jadad A (2005) What is eHealth (3): a systematic review of published definitions. J Med Internet Res 7(1), e1
Pagliari C, Sloan D, Gregor P et al (2005) What is eHealth (4): a scoping exercise to map the field. J Med Internet Res 7(1), e9
Pathman DE, Konrad TR, Freed GL et al (1996) The awareness-to-adherence model of the steps to clinical guideline compliance. Med Care 34(9):873–889
Pedone C, Chiurco D, Scarlata S et al (2013) Efficacy of multiparametric telemonitoring on respiratory outcomes in elderly people with COPD: a randomized controlled trial. BMC Health Serv Res 13:82
Ramtohul I (2015) The adoption of e-health services: comprehensive analysis of the adoption setting from the user's perspective. Health Policy Technol 4(3):286–293. doi:10.1016/j.hlpt.2015.04.007
Robertson TS (1971) Innovative behavior and communication. Holt, Rinehard and Winston, New York
Rogers EM (2003a) Diffusion of innovations. Free Press, New York
Rogers EM (2003b) Diffusion of innovations. Free Press, New York, p 20
Rogers EM (2003c) Diffusion of innovations. Free Press, New York, pp 168–194
Rogers EM (2003d) Diffusion of innovations. Free Press, New York, p 172
Rogers EM (2003e) Diffusion of innovations. Free Press, New York, p 177
Ryan B, Gross NC (1943) The diffusion of hybrid seed corn in two Iowa communities. Rural Sociol 8(1):15–24
Showell C, Nøhr C (2012) How should we define eHealth, and does the definition matter? Stud Health Technol Inform 180:881–884
Sintonen S, Immonen M (2013) Telecare services for aging people: assessment of critical factors influencing the adoption intention. Comput Hum Behav 29(4):1307–1317
Trappenburg J, Niesink A, de Weert-van Oene G et al (2008) Effects of telemonitoring in patients with chronic obstructive pulmonary disease. Telemed e-Health 14(2):138–146
Tzelepis F, Paul CL, Walsh RA et al (2011) Proactive telephone counseling for smoking cessation: meta-analyses by recruitment channel and methodological quality. J Natl Cancer Inst 103 (12):922–941
Wee TTT (2003) Factors affecting new product adoption in the consumer electronics industry. Singap Manag Rev 25(2):51–71
Weinstein ND, Sandman PM, Blalock SJ (2008) The precaution adoption process model. In: Glanz K, Rimer BK, Viswanath K (eds) Health behavior and health education. Theory, research, and practice, 4th edn. San Francisco, Jossey-Bass, pp 123–148
Witzel A (2000) The problem-centered interview. Forum Qualitative Soc Res 1(1):1–9
Zhang NJ, Seblega B, Wan T et al (2013) Health information technology adoption in U.S. acute care hospitals. J Med Syst 37(2):9907

Isabel Ramtohul Since 2011, Dr. rer. pol. Isabel Ramtohul is a postdoctoral research assistant at the Institute of Health Care Management and Health Sciences at the University of Bayreuth, Germany. She teaches health services research and health care marketing. Furthermore, she works on different research projects, e.g., on adoption and diffusion of health care services, on unmet health care needs and on regional health services research structures. Between 2007 and 2011 she was a research assistant at the Department of Marketing and Strategic Management at the University of Basel, Switzerland. There, she did her doctorate on the topic of "Adoption of technology-based health services", laying the cornerstone for her analysis of the boundaryless hospital concept. She holds a Diploma in Sports, Business & Law from the University of Bayreuth, Germany.

Infection Prevention Networks and the Role of the Boundaryless Hospital

Dennis Haking

Abstract

Annually, there are approximately 900,000 nosocomial infections in Germany. These infections are often caused by multi-resistant bacteria like MRSA. The spread of these bacteria is fostered by the inappropriate and unnecessary use of antibiotics in the inpatient and outpatient, and also agricultural sector. In order to prevent the spread of multi-resistant organisms, cross-sectoral, concerted actions of health facilities and the community have to be forced. Therefore structures have to be implemented that motivate the players in a health care system to make efforts in infection prevention and patient safety. For countries with a relatively high MRSA rate as it is the case in Germany, it is necessary to have a benchmark with regions or countries like the Netherlands which show a significantly lower MRSA rate. The factors which determine the success of the Dutch prevention strategy have to be clearly evaluated and constructively adopted according to the requirements of the German health care system. The superior aim is to connect the service sectors in the health care system to establish concerted actions in terms of infection prevention. Established regional infection prevention networks show successfully how to overcome sector boundaries as well as internal boundaries, e.g. in hospitals.

Keywords

Infection prevention • Networks • Hygiene management • MRSA • Antibiotics • EurSafety Health-Net • Germany • The Netherlands

D. Haking (✉)
CKM—Center for Hospital Management, University of Muenster, Scharnhorststrasse 110, 48151 Muenster, Germany

Center for Health Care Management and Regulation, HHL Leipzig Graduate School of Management, Jahnallee 59, 04109 Leipzig, Germany
e-mail: dennis.haking@wiwi.uni-muenster.de

H. Albach et al. (eds.), *Boundaryless Hospital*, DOI 10.1007/978-3-662-49012-9_16

1 Introduction

Most of the hospital infections are caused by the bacterium Methicillin-resistant Staphylococcus aureus (MRSA). MRSA is responsible for several difficult-to-treat infections in humans, because of the limited antimicrobial therapy options. The multi-resistant pathogen developed from Staphylococcus aureus bacteria, went through the process of natural selection. Resistance to beta-lactam antibiotics, which include the penicillins and cephalosporins was the evolutional result.

Especially in health care institutions like hospitals, nursing homes and rehab clinics, MRSA can lead to troublesome complications, because here we find many risk factors for a MRSA infection like the use of invasive devices, and patients with open wounds, or a weakened immune system.

Staphylococcus aureus most commonly colonizes the anterior nares. But it can also be found in the rest of the respiratory tract, open wounds, intravenous catheters, and the urinary tract. MRSA can be detected by screening the patients. Therefore swabs from the nostrils, throat, wounds, axilla, perineum, and/or the inguinal region are taken.

MRSA leads to prolonged and severe courses of disease, which is leading to labor-intensive and expensive consequences for the hospital due to complex hygienic measures and expensive antibiotics. In the case of an MRSA outbreak even entire wards might be closed.

Table 1 shows the additional costs per MRSA (infection) case. The costs are caused by blocked beds (because of the isolation of MRSA infected patients), by the high costs for antibiotics, by costs for increased nursing care and the costs for the prolonged stay in the hospital.

It is obvious that the costs highly depend on the setting. The setting is influenced by the kind of infection, but also by the region.

Like the costs, also the MRSA rate, defined as the share of MRSA isolates in the Staphylococcus aureus isolated from blood cultures, differs from region to region. Figure 1 shows the MRSA rates determined by the European Center for Disease Prevention and Control. It clearly shows that the Netherlands and the Scandinavian countries have relatively low MRSA rates compared to countries from Southern Europe like Portugal, Italy, Greece or Malta. Germany is located in the mid-level with a MRSA-rate of 21 %.

First, we try to discover, why the MRSA rate in Germany is 20 times higher compared to the Netherlands, then the role of the boundaryless hospital in infection prevention networks is depicted and finally the current outcomes and boundaries of such networks are demonstrated.

2 Historical Background

The penicillin Methicillin was introduced in 1959. The first resistance against this antibiotic was reported in Great Britain in 1961 (Jevons 1961). Similar cases were reported from the United States, Australia and Japan. In these countries, the

Table 1 Additional costs per MRSA case converted in Euro (25 June 2015) (Huebner et al. 2009; Wernitz et al. 2005)

Author	Setting	Additional costs per MRSA case
Abramson and Sexton (1999)	Bloodstream infections caused by MSSA	EUR 8630
	Bloodstream infections caused by MRSA	EUR 24,193
Geldner et al. (1999)	MRSA-patients on Intensive Care Unit	per day EUR 1622
Rubin et al. (1999)	MRSA vs. MSSA in a hospital in New York	EUR 2233–3304
Kim et al. (2001)	MRSA-infections in a hospital in Toronto	EUR 10,380
Engemann et al. (2003)	Postoperative wound infections with MRSA	EUR 12,417
Herr et al. (2003)	MRSA-patients on a surgical ward	EUR 9261.65
Reed et al. (2005)	MSSA-Bacteraemia	EUR 15,513
	MRSA-Bacteraemia	EUR 31,270
Wernitz et al. (2005)	Postoperative wound infections	EUR 11,354.59
	Pneumonia	EUR 29,277.25
	Bloodstream infection	EUR 13,536.52
	Urinary tract infection	EUR 4656.82
	Other infections	EUR 5299.12
Shorr et al. (2006)	Pneumonia	EUR 6904
Greiner et al. (2007)	Bloodstream infections caused by MSSA	EUR 10,573
	Bloodstream infections caused by MRSA	EUR 24,931
Resch et al. (2009)	MRSA-infections in 11 German hospitals	EUR 8198

resistance against Methicillin has become an increasing problem. The Dutch hospitals had and still have a significantly low MRSA rate. Since the start of the surveillance of MRSA in 1989, the prevalence of MRSA stayed more or less constant at 1 % in the Netherlands.

One reason for the good MRSA management in the Netherlands is the early recognition of the rising MRSA problem. As one of the first countries, the Netherlands introduced national guidelines for the prevention of MRSA in 1980 (Fig. 2). Nearly all countries which implemented national guidelines considerably later nowadays have significantly higher MRSA rates.

By early developing measures to prevent the spread of MRSA, the Netherlands were able to keep the rate on a very low level. Especially the optimized use of antibiotics and the so called search-and-destroy policy are critical factors of their success.

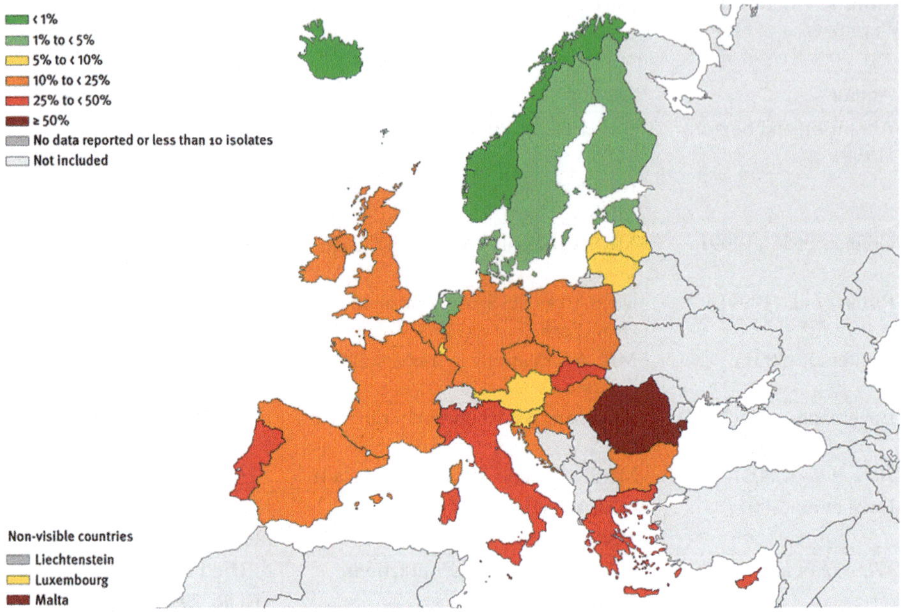

Fig. 1 MRSA rates in Europe (European Centre for Disease Prevention and Control 2014)

3 Antibiotic Stewardship in Hospitals

Another crucial reason for the fact that the Netherlands have one of the lowest MRSA prevalence in the world is the culturally determined limited use of antibiotics (Dekker and van den Broek 2010). Antibiotics make once lethal infections treatable. But often the use of antibiotics is unnecessary or inappropriate. This leads to the growing problem of antibiotic resistance and additional threats for patients who are unnecessarily exposed to risks due to side effects of the antibiotics. The misuse of antibiotics has become one of the most serious and growing threats to public health. As Fig. 3 shows, it is not only a threat to health but has also a tremendous economic impact. Threats are compared due to their impact and their likelihood.

In order to reduce the misuse of antibiotics, hospitals implement so called Antibiotic Stewardship Programs (ASPs). Again, Dutch hospitals were pioneers in doing so. Aims of the ASPs are to optimize the treatment of infections and to reduce adverse events associated with antibiotic use as well as antibiotic resistance. Due to these aims quality of care and patient safety is improved. There is no blueprint for ASPs. The programs differ according to the size and types of care due to a wide variety of hospitals. But there are seven core elements which give an orientation (Centers for Disease Prevention and Control 2014).

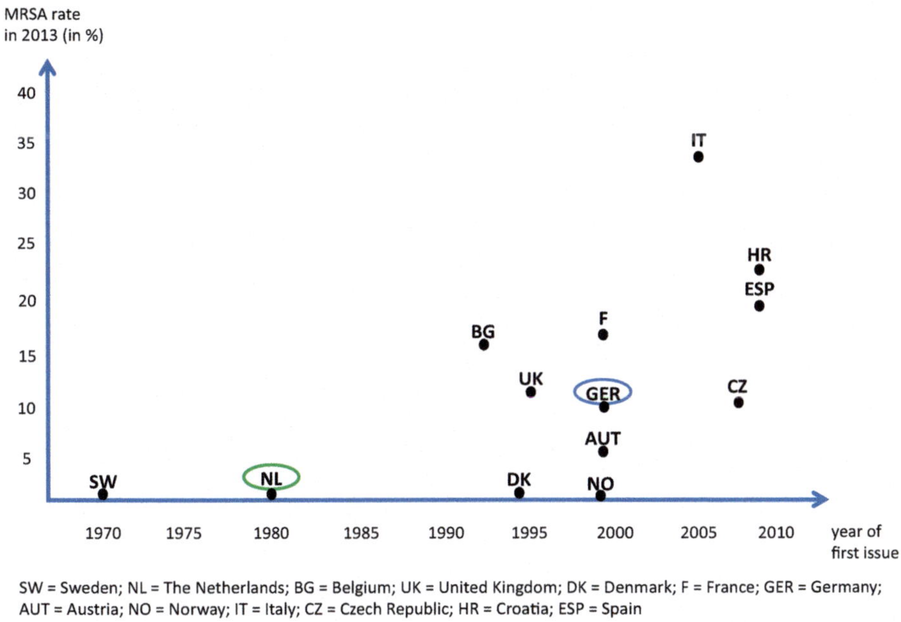

Fig. 2 The first issue of national guidelines for prevention and control of MRSA in different European countries and the MRSA rate in 2013 [data from Kalenic et al. (2010) and European Centre for Disease Prevention and Control (2014)]

Leadership Commitment The ASP has to be supported by the hospital leaders by providing human, financial and technical resources. Especially in case of human resources, the leaders have to ensure to give sufficient time to the staff, support them with training and education and enable an interdisciplinary team work.

Accountability One ASP leader has to be appointed, who is responsible for the outcomes. It is recommended to appoint a physician in this case. As a co-leader a pharmacist should be appointed. The leaders should undergo a formal training in infectious diseases and/or antibiotic stewardship.

Key Support An ASP is only successful if the key support groups are constructively involved in the program. Depending on the setting of the hospital the key supporters are:

- Clinicians and department heads as prescribers of antibiotics
- Infection preventionists and hospital epidemiologists as coordinators of the facility-wide monitoring and prevention of health care-associated infections
- Quality management staff, who cares for treatment quality and patient safety issues
- Laboratory staff, who accounts for the proper use of tests and the flow of results

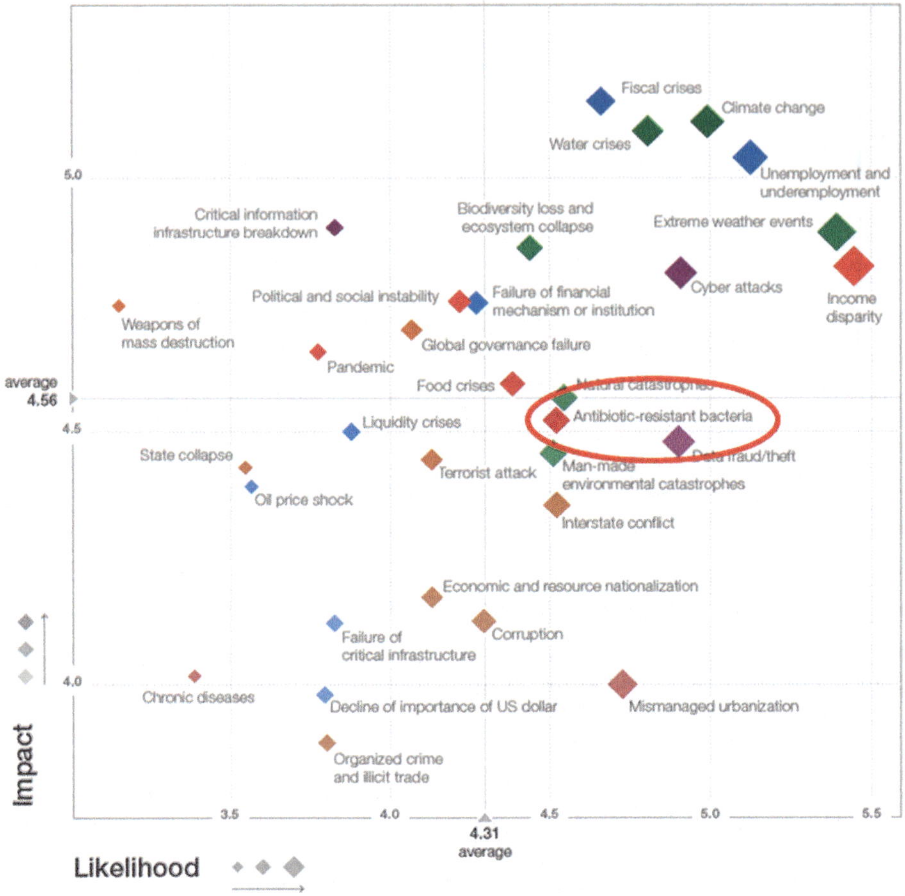

Fig. 3 Economic impact of antibiotic-resistant bacteria (World Economic Forum 2014)

- Information technology staff, who is critical for the integration of stewardship protocols into existing workflows.
- Nurses, who can assure that bacterial cultures are performed before starting antibiotics and who review medications as part of their routines.

Implementation of Policies and Interventions Policies concern the documentation of the dose, duration and indication for an antibiotic use in order to have an accessible data base for further treatments and to develop facility specific treatment recommendations based on national and international guidelines and local circumstances. Interventions are classified as broad (e.g. antibiotic time-outs, prior authorization, prospective audit and feedback), pharmacy-driven (e.g. automatic changes from intravenous to oral antibiotic therapy, dose adjustments, dose optimization, automatic alerts, etc.) and infection and syndrome specific interventions (e.g. community-acquired pneumonia, urinary tract infections, skin and soft tissue infections, MRSA etc.)

Tracking and Monitoring Antibiotic Use and Outcomes Without measurement, it is not possible to find improvement opportunities. Therefore antibiotic use process measures and antibiotic use measure (defined daily dose; DDD) and outcome measures should be evaluated.

Education ASPs should provide regular updates on antibiotic prescribing, antibiotic resistance and infectious disease management, e.g. by didactic presentations, posters, flyers, newsletters and case reviews.

Emerging Developments in Antibiotic Stewardship There will be many developments concerning antibiotic stewardship in the future, e.g. the wider integration of IT (using clinical data) or the role of new diagnostic laboratory testing technology like new rapid diagnostic tests for detecting antimicrobial resistance.

But it has to be stated that hospitals are not the only institution in a health care system where antibiotics are administered. In Germany, especially the outpatient sector and the agricultural sector are the biggest users of antibiotics. The problems that stem from these two sectors are discussed in Sect. 6.

4 Role of the Staff

Another reason why the Netherlands' infection prevention efforts are superior to Germany is the high density of qualified personnel in terms of microbiology, epidemiology, hygiene and infection prevention. There are three microbiologists/hospital hygienists (physicians) per 1000 beds in the Netherlands, in Germany the number is 0.3 per 1000 beds. In Germany education in the above mentioned subject areas is neglected, e.g. there are only few universities which educate microbiologists. With regard to nurses Germany has a similar lack of hygiene specialists. With the adjustment of the "infection prevention law" (Infektionsschutzgesetz; IfSG 2000) the German government responded to this lack of specialists and obliged the hospitals to fulfil a given quota of hygiene specialists until the end of 2016 [section 23(8), point 3 IfSG]. Due to the general lack of physicians and especially nurses in the German health care system this quota is viewed critically by the expert associations. It is proven that a low nurses-to-patient ratio correlates with a higher number of failures (e.g. infections) in the treatment process. As the hands are the main vector for the transmission of germs, the use of hand disinfectants and gloves are the simplest measures to prevent infections. But the compliance to these measures is determined by structural preconditions and the cultural embedding of hygiene awareness. Hygiene needs time and a lack of time due to a lack of personnel especially leads to a low compliance to hand hygiene.

Furthermore, the cost pressure in the German health care system fosters the trend of outsourcing. Many hospitals hire their cleaning staff externally to save expenses. Often this external cleaning staff has utopian time standards for cleaning patient rooms/wards. The resulting time pressure leads to a poor quality of cleaning which fosters the spread of germs.

The economy-driven medicine, triggered by the introduction of the DRG (diagnosis related groups) system, leads to cost struggles which are often solved by reducing staff, because 60–70 % of the hospital costs are personnel expenses (Statistisches Bundesamt 2014). The proven result of staff reduction in hospitals is the loss of quality in patient care and health problems of the overworked staff (e.g. Aiken et al. 2014). The structural preconditions have to be improved: the profession of nursing should be more attractive (better working conditions, better payment), the education of specialists (especially in terms of hygiene) has to be extended and high levels of quality in care should be rewarded (pay-for-performance).

5 The Search-and-Destroy Policy in the Netherlands

In order to prevent the transmission of MRSA, a stringent Search and Destroy policy was applied in the Netherlands. This policy considers the screening and isolation of patients with an increased risk for the carriage of MRSA. This mainly affects patients which have been treated in a hospital abroad. The group of patients exposed to pigs or veal calves was added in 2006. Typical for this strategy is the rigorous isolation regime. The isolation is performed in a room with an anteroom where the staff has to put on their personal protective equipment (mask, hat, gown and gloves). A special airflow gradient has to be installed to prevent airflow from the room to the corridor. The treatment with antibiotics of MRSA carriers (both patients and staff) is described in guidelines. The eradication of MRSA is performed in the hospital, so that the patient can be discharged MRSA-free (Van Rijen and Kluytmans 2009).

In Germany, it is not possible to implement this strategy because of lacking capacities and the sectoral separation of treatment. The eradication of MRSA takes approximately 2 weeks. Usually the treatment is started in the hospital and continued in the outpatient sector. Thus, the Dutch strategy was adjusted to the so called "Search and Follow" strategy (Friedrich 2009; Fig. 4).

Like in the Dutch strategy, first of all, MRSA carriers should be identified by screenings according to risk factors. To prevent antibiotic resistance, guidelines for the restrictive use of antibiotics are implemented (Antibiotic Stewardship). Identified MRSA carriers who are discharged from hospital are finally followed in outpatient treatment which means the communication with other health care institutions concerning the therapy of the patients and the MRSA carrier status. To

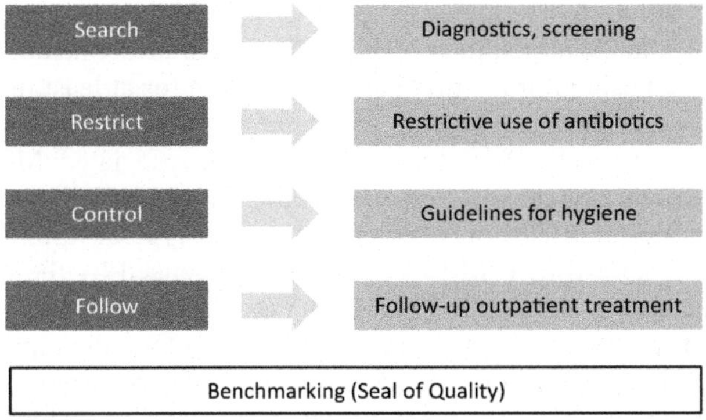

Fig. 4 The search and follow strategy

generate a sustainable effect, participating institutions in infection prevention networks are rewarded with a seal of quality (characteristic for the EurSafety Health-Net which is presented in Sect. 7).

6 Boundaries Affecting Infection Prevention and the Role of the Hospital

As mentioned before, there are boundaries to overcome to implement a successful MRSA prevention strategy. In addition to the boundary separating the inpatient from the outpatient sector, there are many more internal and external boundaries which negatively affect infection prevention and foster the spread and transmission of multi-resistant bacteria in the health care system. In the following these boundaries are revealed and the resulting challenges for the German health care system, especially for German hospitals, are pointed out. It will be shown that the sectoral separation in the German health care system has a tremendous impact on infection prevention. The complex German system is illustrated by using the example of MRSA spread. At first the focus is put on the different types of MRSA, which is important when speaking about sectors and sector boundaries. If there is no Methicillin resistance, the type of Staphylococcus aureus is called Methicillin-sensible Staphylococcus aureus (MSSA). If there is an MRSA-infected/colonized patient, the types of MRSA are differentiated by the place of infection/colonization. The different forms can exactly be genotyped. The best-known type is the hospital-acquired MRSA (H-MRSA) and is bound to hospitals or comparable institutions in the health care system (nosocomial infections). There are mainly four causes for getting a nosocomial infection: patient factors (e.g. multi-morbidity, weakened immune system), environmental factors (contamination of medical devices, contact to other patients, contaminated water, etc.), technical factors (e.g. new methods of invasive medicine) and the human factor (e.g. working conditions, lacking time for hygiene). Overall, there are up to 900,000 nosocomial infections annually in Germany (Walger et al. 2013). The second type is the community-acquired MRSA (C-MRSA). The MRSA is community-acquired if the MRSA-positive specimen was obtained outside the hospital (Salmenlinna et al. 2002). It can affect healthy people who had not been in a hospital or another health institution for at least one year. C-MRSA is mainly found were many people are at the same place, e.g. in sport clubs, in the army, in jail, etc. The third type, the livestock-associated MRSA (L-MRSA) is mainly acquired by people who are working in intensive livestock farming (pigs, chicken, cattle). It affects only regions where this type of farming is performed intensively. The spread of L-MRSA is heavily influenced by the misuse of antibiotics in the veterinary medicine. Considering these three types of MRSA it is obvious that the MRSA types are associated with three sectors: the inpatient, the outpatient and the agricultural sector. As a consequence the boundaries separating these sectors are the most important factors influencing the effective and efficient infection prevention. In the following, the focus is put on Fig. 5 to show the internal (no. 3–5) and external (no. 1–2, 6–8) boundaries which influence the infection prevention from the view of a German hospital.

1. Boundary inpatient/outpatient sector (external boundary): The hospital is not able to influence the treatment of MRSA carriers in the outpatient sector. Due to financial restrictions there is rare incentive to conduct MRSA eradications in order to keep away multi-resistant bacteria from the hospital. Another problem is

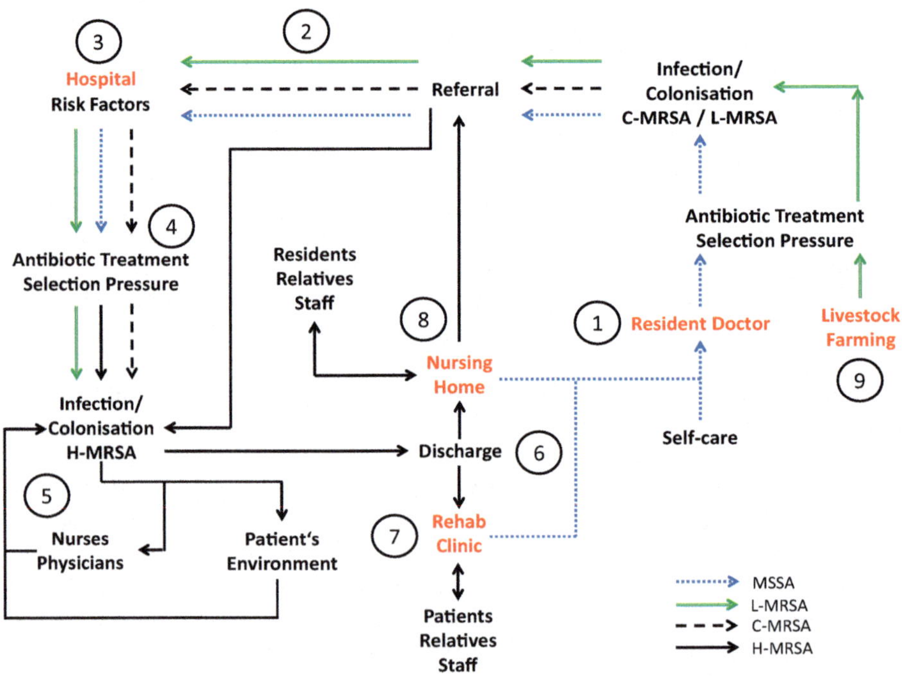

Fig. 5 Boundaries affecting infection prevention [own representation based on Heizmann et al. (2005)]

the misuse of antibiotics in the outpatient sector. 85 % of all antibiotics used for humans are consumed in the outpatient sector (Bundesamt für Verbraucherschutz und Lebensmittelsicherheit 2014).
2. Ambulance/patient transport: Here, the outpatient sector is connected with the inpatient sector. It is essential for the ambulance staff to know the MRSA status of the patient to make the right preparations and cooperate with the hospital.
3. Hospital admission: At admission it is very important to classify the patient according to the MRSA risk factors and conduct a screening and/or an isolation of the patient. Efficient admission processes are one of the success factors in terms of intra-hospital infection prevention.
4. Antibiotic treatment: Like in the outpatient sector, the misuse of antibiotics has to be avoided. Antibiotic Stewardship programs lead to the reduction of resistances, not only in hospital but in the entire health care system.
5. Hygiene management puts emphasis on interrupting infection chains. Standard precautions, hand hygiene compliance and isolation are the driving factors for a successful hygiene management. It should be understood as an internal boundary which positively affects the infection prevention. The hygiene management affects all internal processes like the treatment process or logistic processes, e.g. internal patient transports, as well as the education—in terms of infections prevention—of relatives and visitors who come into the hospital.
6. Discharge management: The discharge management affects the spread of MRSA between the hospital and other health care institutions (rehab clinics, nursing homes, etc.) as well as the outpatient sector. A good communication and cooperation between the sectors and institutions is crucial for avoiding the spread of MRSA and other germs.
7. Rehabilitation clinics: Knowing the MRSA status of a patient is important for rehab clinics, too. MRSA-positive patients are in contact with other patients, relatives and the staff. To avoid the spread in and out of the rehab clinics hygiene measures have to be established. A coordinated treatment with other institutions (private doctors, hospitals, nursing homes, etc.) is very important, because the readmission to hospital or discharge to a nursing home is common.
8. Nursing homes: Especially the residents of nursing homes are at a high risk for getting an infection, because of their age- and disease-related weakened immune system. Special hygiene measures are essential and knowing the MRSA status is crucial to prevent the spread among other residents, relatives and staff. Furthermore, residents of nursing homes are often so called "revolving door patients", that means they often alternate between treatment in hospitals and living in their nursing home. A coordinated treatment is very important to keep away multi-resistant bacteria from the hospital and the nursing home.
9. Livestock Farming: 2/3 of all antibiotics are used in the veterinary medicine (Polke-Majewski 2014). In many cases they are used to prevent diseases and not to treat them (original purpose of antibiotics). Thereby the spread of resistances is fostered. The pathogens are not only found in the live animals but also in slaughterhouses and on the meat sold in the stores. People working in intensive

animal farming with direct contact to the animals are often colonized with L-MRSA.

The demonstrated boundaries, sectors and institutions are not exhaustive. There are many other important institutions in the outpatient sector like outpatient dialysis, which have to be mentioned. Personal hygiene in the daily life, e.g. when cooking meat, is not to be underestimated with regard to infection prevention.

The inner boundaries and external boundaries of the hospital need a coordinated process concerning colonized and infected patients. Otherwise a powerful infection prevention system is not practicable. Therefore, the health policy has to enact laws and give incentives to the health care institutions which support and reward efforts in infection prevention.

7 Infection Prevention Networks

Network structures are essential to connect all sectors and players in a health care system to reach an effective and efficient infection prevention and patient safety. The first infection prevention network was the MRSA-net, which was founded in the Dutch-German border region in 2005. The aim was to determine the MRSA rate on the German side and lower it to a Dutch level. On the Dutch side the inflow of MRSA from Germany to the Netherlands should be controlled and the spread of C-MRSA be prevented. The overall goal was to optimize the cross-border medical care and to increase patient safety. Cooperation and the share of information were the key success factors. The network was renamed and extended in 2009. Now it is called the EurSafety-Health-Net. Efforts were extended along the entire German-Dutch border. New participants have been acquired. The network has developed into a powerful cross-border quality association for patient safety and infection prevention. The network consists of hospitals, nursing homes, rehab clinics, residential doctors, public health departments, laboratories, insurance companies, universities and other health-related institutions. In order to measure the success of the network activities many studies were conducted. One of them dealt with the development of MRSA in 40 German hospitals, taking part in the network (Jurke et al. 2013). Therefore items like the MRSA screening rate, MRSA burden, MRSA incidence and MRSA cases were evaluated in the period 2007–2011. The screening rate (share of admitted patients screened) increased from 4.38 to 34.4 %. As a result, more MRSA carriers were identified (2007: 2351; 2011: 4512). This is the so-called "screening paradox". There are efforts (like the screening) made to prevent infections, but the absolute number of MRSA cases initially increases. Nevertheless, if you do not look for them, you cannot find them. And if you do not find them, you cannot fight them. The essential result from increasing the screening rate is that the share of nosocomial MRSA cases significantly decreased from 21 % in 2007 to 8 % in 2011. That means that the implementation of the search & follow policy was really successful. If hospitals (also nursing homes) implement this strategy successfully they are rewarded with a quality seal which stands for a sustainable commitment in terms of increasing patient safety and infection prevention. The seal is valid for 2 years and then is audited again. For hospitals, five levels with different goals are achievable. The best hospitals currently gained seal number three. As the German health care policy currently puts the focus on quality and pay-for-performance, such a seal could be a quality indicator for participating hospitals. There is a similar seal for nursing homes and a quality seal for rehabilitation clinics is currently being developed.

The implementation of area-wide regional infection prevention networks is a sustainably pursued objective of the German government (Gesundheitsministerkonferenz 2006).

8 Conclusion

The spread of multi-resistant bacteria is not a matter of single institutions (e.g. hospitals) in a health care system. It is a dynamic system which is influenced by many players and factors. Occurring problems are mainly prescribed by the system, e.g. by its sectoral separation. It is a normal phenomenon that boundaries create silo thinking and opportunistic behavior. To overcome these barriers, structures have to be implemented that encourage cooperation, information sharing and concerted actions. Infection prevention networks have the potential to bring all parties to the table in order to collectively prevent infections and to improve the quality of patient care. But it is necessary to clearly show the benefits of a participation in such a network, because additional efforts (human resources, financial resources, time, etc.) are associated with such an engagement. The networks have to be promoted and supported by the government. Laws, guidelines and recommendations that encourage health care or healthcare-related institutions to participate in regional infection prevention networks have to be addressed. Otherwise the many inter- and extra-sectoral boundaries cannot be pulled down and the growing resistance to last-line antibiotics will progress rapidly.

References

Abramson M, Sexton D (1999) Nosocomial methicillin-resistant and methicillin-susceptible staphylococcus aureus primary bacteremia: at what costs? Infect Control Hosp Epidemiol 20:408–411

Aiken LH, Sloane DM, Bruyneel L, Van den Heede K, Griffiths P, Busse R, Diomidous M, Kinnunen J, Kózka M, Lesaffre E, McHugh MD, Moreno-Casbas MT, Rafferty AM, Schwendlimann R, Scott PA, Tishelman C, van Achterberg T, Sermeus W (2014) Nurse staffing and education and hospital mortality in nine European countries: a retrospective observational study. Lancet 383:1824–1830

Bundesamt für Verbraucherschutz und Lebensmittelsicherheit (2014) GERMAP 2012. Antibiotika-Resistenz und -Verbrauch. Bericht über den Antibiotikaverbrauch und die Verbreitung von Antibiotikaresistenzen in der Human- und Veterinärmedizin in Deutschland. Antiinfectives Intelligence. Gesellschaft für klinisch-mikrobiologische Forschung und Kommunikation mbh, Rheinbach

Centers for Disease Prevention and Control (2014) Core elements of hospital antibiotic stewardship programs. US Department of Health and Human Services, Atlanta. http://www.cdc.gov/getsmart/healthcare/pdfs/core-elements.pdf. Accessed 7 Jul 2015

Dekker T, van den Broek P (2010) Successful control of MRSA spread in Dutch hospitals. Int J Infect Control 6(1):i1

Engemann J, Carmeli Y, Sogrove SE, Fowler VG, Bronstein MZ, Trivette SL, Briggs JP, Sexton DJ, Kave KS (2003) Adverse clinical and economic outcomes attributable to Methicillin resistance among patients with staphylococcus aureus surgical site infection. Clin Infect Dis 56:592–598

European Centre for Disease Prevention and Control (2014) Antimicrobial resistance surveillance in Europe 2013. Annual report of the European Antimicrobial Resistance Surveillance Network (EARS-net). ECDC, Stockholm

Friedrich AW (2009) EUREGIO MRSA-net Twente/Münsterland: search & follow durch euregionale Netzwerkbildung. Gesundheitswesen 71:766–770

Geldner G, Ruoff M, Hoffmann HJ, Georgieff M, Wiedeck H (1999) Eine Kostenanalyse von MRSA-Infektionen auf einer operativen Intensivstation. Anasthesiol Intensivmed Notfallmed Schmerzther 34:409–413

Gesundheitsministerkonferenz (2006) Ergebnisniederschrift der 79. Konferenz der für das Gesundheitswesen zuständigen Ministerinnen, Minister, Senatorinnen und Senatoren der Länder am 29. und 30. Juni in Dessau. https://www.rki.de/DE/Content/Infekt/Krankenhaushygiene/Erreger_ausgewaehlt/MRSA/MRSA_GMK.pdf. Accessed 7 Jul 2015

Greiner W, Rasch A, Köhler D, Salzberger B, Fätkenheier G, Leidig M (2007) Clinical outcome and costs of nosocomial and community-acquired Staphylococcus aureus bloodstream infection in haemodialysis patients. Clin Microbiol Infect 13:264–268

Heizmann P, Heizmann WR, Hetzer R (2005) MRSA: Reizmechanismen, Epidemiologie, Risikofaktoren, Prophylaxe, Therapie. Z Herz- Thorax Gefäßchir 19:78–88

Herr CE, Heckrodt TH, Hofmann FA, Schnettler R, Eikmann TF (2003) Additional costs for preventing the spread of Methicilin-resistant staphylococcus aureus and a strategy for reducing these costs on a surgical ward. Infect Control Hosp Epidemiol 24:673–678

Huebner NO, Huebner C, Kramer A (2009) Ökonomische Aspekte des Hygienemanagements von MRSA. Gesundheitswesen 71(11):771–776

IfSG (2000) Gesetz zur Verhütung und Bekämpfung von Infektionskrankheiten beim Menschen. http://www.gesetze-im-internet.de/ifsg/. Accessed 2 Jul 2015

Jevons MP (1961) Celbenin-resistant staphylococci. BMJ 1:124–125

Jurke A, Köck R, Thole S, Hendrix R, Rossen J, Daniels-Haardt, I, Friedrich AW (2013) Reduction of the nosocomial meticillin-resistant Staphylococcus aureus incidence density by a region-wide search and follow-strategy in forty German hospitals of the EUREGIO, 2009 to 2011. Euro Surveill 18(36). pii=20579

Kalenic S, Cookson B, Gallagher R, Popp W et al (2010) Comparison of recommendations in national/regional guidelines for prevention and control of MRSA in thirteen European countries. Int J Infect Control 6(2):i1

Kim T, Oh P, Simor A (2001) The economic impact of methicillin-resistant staphylococcus aureus in Canadian hospitals. Infect Control Hosp Epidemiol 22:99–104

Polke-Majewski K (2014) Das Wundermittel wirkt nicht mehr. http://www.zeit.de/wissen/gesundheit/2014-11/antibiotika-keime-resistenz-bakterien/komplettansicht. Accessed 1 Jul 2015

Reed SD, Friedman JY, Engemann JJ, Griffiths RI, Anstrom JK, Kave KS, Styjewksi ME, Szcech LA, Reller LB, Corey GR, Schulman KA, Fowler VG Jr (2005) Costs and outcomes among hemodialysisdependent patients with methicillin-resistant or methicillin-susceptible staphylococcus aureus bacteremia. Infect Control Hosp Epidemiol 26:175–183

Resch A, Wilke M, Fink C (2009) The cost of resistance: incremental cost of methicillin-resistant staphylococcus aureus (MRSA) in German hospitals. Eur J Health Econ 10:287–297

Rubin RJ, Harrington CA, Poon A, Dietrich K, Greene JA, Moiduddin A (1999) The economic impact of staphylococcus aureus infection in New York City hospitals. Emerg Infect Dis 5 (1):9–17

Salmenlinna S, Lyytikäinen O, Vuopio-Varkila J (2002) Community-acquired methicillin-resistant staphylococcus aureus. Emerg Infect Dis 6(8):602–607
Shorr AF, Tabak YP, Gupta V, Johannes RS, Liu LZ, Kollef MH (2006) Morbidity and cost burden of methicillin-resistant staphylococcus aureus in early onset ventilator-associated pneumonia. Crit Care 10(3):97–103
Statistisches Bundesamt (2014) Kostennachweis der Krankenhäuser. Statistisches Bundesamt, Fachserie 12, Reihe 6.3, 2013. Wiesbaden
Van Rijen MM, Kluytmans JAJW (2009) Costs and benefits of the MRSA search and destroy policy in a Dutch hospital. Eur J Clin Microbiol Infect Dis 28:1245–1252
Walger P, Popp W, Exner M (2013) Stellungnahme der DGKH zu Prävalenz, Letalität und Präventionspotenzial nosokomialer Infektionen in Deutschland 2013. Hyg Med 38 (7/8):329–338
Wernitz MH, Keck S, Swidsinski S, Schulz S, Veit SK (2005) Cost analysis of a hospital-wide selective screening programme for methicillin-resistant staphylococcus aureus (MRSA) carriers in the context of diagnosis related groups (DRG) payment. Clin Microbiol Infect 11:466–471
World Economic Forum (2014) Global risks 2014, 9th edn. World Economic Forum, Switzerland

Dennis Haking graduated in the field of business administration at the University of Muenster, Germany in 2011 and holds a Master of Science (M.Sc.) degree. He focused his studies on the fields of hospital management and management. At present he works for the Center for Hospital Management (CKM; University of Muenster) and the HHL Leipzig Graduate School of Management as a research associate and doctoral student. His research focuses on the systemic, economic and medical effects of infection prevention networks and the spread of multi-resistant pathogens. He is member of the EurSafety Health-Net, a cross-border infection prevention network acting along the Dutch-German border. He is also a lecturer for hospital management.

Part IV

The Boundaryless Hospital from the Patients' Perspective

From Community Analysis to Prototype: Creating an Online Matchmaker for Inflammatory Bowel Disease Patients

Jermain Kaminski

Abstract

Since about five years, the MIT Center for Collective Intelligence, Cambridge, U.S., and the Chronic Collaborative Care Network (C3N) at Cincinnati Children's Hospital, Cincinnati, U.S., have been working together to improve care for inflammatory bowel disease (IBD) patients by harnessing methods of computational social science. The goal of this contribution is (1) to present an approach in measuring communication patterns and sentiments within online communities of IBD patients, (2) to analyze the enablers for a better connectedness of community members, and (3) to introduce a prototype application of a collective intelligent online network for IBD patients, named "YouMeIBD". The mobile application, developed within an interdisciplinary student class at MIT and four other universities, aims to improve the connectedness, well-being and diffusion of innovations in a community of IBD patients.

Keywords

Social network analysis • Sentiment analysis • Coolhunting • Patient community • Collaborative innovation network • Inflammatory bowel disease (IBD)

J. Kaminski (✉)
Witten/Herdecke University, Alfred-Herrhausen-Straße 50, 58448 Witten, Germany

MIT Center for Collective Intelligence, Massachusetts Institute of Technology, 245 First Street, Cambridge, MA 02142, USA
e-mail: jermain@media.mit.edu

H. Albach et al. (eds.), *Boundaryless Hospital*, DOI 10.1007/978-3-662-49012-9_17

1 Introduction

Innovation and care for patients become increasingly decentralized and digitalized in the medical system of the future. In fact, disease discovery, treatment and social support are already taking place online, mediated through an increasing number of self-tracking platforms and mobile applications. With more and more patients providing their data and proposing new ideas in a collaborative system, health innovation becomes a bottom-up process, reframing the current top-down logic of health innovation. This article presents an example analysis on the inner workings of a patient online community and shows how data analysis can contribute to the development of a new online patient platform aiming to improve the diffusion of innovation.

In their remarkable book "Connected", Christakis and Fowler point out: "*For thousands of years, social interactions were build solely on face-to-face communication. But technology changed this with the [...] ways of communicating person-to-person at a distance.*" Christakis and Fowler (2011)

Truly, new technologies enabled individuals to peer beyond an individual's social horizon and to create new connections independently from physical distances; this holds true for patients communicating online. As Wagner's Chronic Care Model (Wagner 2001) further suggests, the best outcomes in health care depend on decision support, effective delivery systems, information systems and active communication among health care teams and patients (cf. Gloor et al. 2011). Virtual communities may support knowledge about a disease and can improve the self-management process through a number of mechanisms such as enhanced self-care, the support of patient–physician interactions, structured information, the improvement of emotional well-being and individually perceived disease control (cf. Wellman 1992; Gallant 2003; Eysenbach et al. 2004; Elliott et al. 2007).

The analysis shown in this article concentrates on an online community of inflammatory bowel disease (IBD) patients. IBD is a chronic disease further explained in Sect. 2), affecting more than 3.8 million people in the U.S. and Europe combined. The patients, mostly diagnosed at an age between 15 and 35 (Loftus 2007; Economou and Pappas 2008; CCFA 2015), are particularly interested in encouragement through online social networks and finding health information online (Wicks et al. 2010, 2011). Indeed, the young age and Internet connectivity of the patient group provides a key asset both for the community analysis and prototype development.

The key methods described in this article emerge from the field of *computational social science* (Lazer et al. 2009). Computational social science became a foundation in the understanding of community dynamics and their inherent economics, which also counts for health related networks (Valente 2010; Christakis and Fowler 2011). It is a relatively new research discipline that serves to measure and understand social behavior and phenomena with the help of analyzing digital traces. The research field emerges with the increasing capacity to collect and analyze big data. One underlying core belief of computational social science is that social and economic behaviors can be found in data patterns.

Social network analysis, a sub-discipline of computational social science, focuses on measuring and visualizing the connections among people within social organizations and contributes toward understanding their communication patterns, structures and sentiments (Wellman 1988; Wasserman and Faust 1994; Portier et al. 2013). Revealing the *social physics* (Pentland 2014) behind transactions in health networks can be a key success factor in identifying levers that "make or break" a successful network, in particular with regard to the diffusion of innovations (Rogers 2003[1962]). In a sense, like the eye is said to be a window to the soul, network patterns might be a window to the soul of a community.

The empirical foundation of the IBD online community analysis presented in Sect. 3 is an anonymized and subsampled dataset of five public IBD-related Facebook groups, covering data from 2006 to 2011. Analyzing an online group on IBD is valuable, because it might not only mirror real-world friendship networks but also helps to identify key discussion topics. While Facebook groups might be the first stop for most patients seeking online connections, they are also alternatives to patient-oriented websites such as *PatientsLikeMe* (http://patientslikeme.com) or the IBD-focused *Crohnology* (http://crohnology.com), both providing excellent information on self-tracking and medication effects. That being said, no online platform can be a jack-of-all-trades. For instance, platforms with a focus on self-tracking and data may not simultaneously fulfill a patient's desire of social interaction and personal connectedness. Admittedly, it is a big challenge to unify all of a chronic patient's needs in just one platform.

Section 4 presents an analysis on the diffusion of innovation for the case of *whipworm* therapy, a potentially effective medication for IBD patients. Since 2005, experimental and clinical data sustain the idea that helminths like the whipworm might provide protection against the disease. By means of coolhunting (Gloor and Cooper 2007) the term "whipworm", it was possible to investigate the presence and connotation of the term both in the World Wide Web and in public Facebook group discussions. The analysis was highly contributory, because it demonstrated both how the external information (www) on whipworm therapy transfers into the network (Facebook) and how the network structure within Facebook groups affected the diffusion of information.

Section 5 presents a prototype mobile application, targeting the identified issues in the diffusion of innovations within the IBD online community (Baebler et al. 2011; Fuehres et al. 2011; Kaminski et al. 2012). The mobile application "YouMeIBD" applies matching algorithms known from dating websites to improve the connectedness of patients both virtually and locally. The ultimate goal of the application is to support a better diffusion of innovation and to enable a collaborative innovation network (COIN) (Gloor and Cooper 2007).

After all, the main purpose of this contribution is to provide practitioners with information on how the analysis of an existing community can contribute towards the development of a new platform. That being said, the content focuses intentionally more on the bigger picture than the small details and metrics of our analysis.

2 About Inflammatory Bowel Disease

In 1981, IBD researcher Cooke states "*Despite a view that Crohn's disease is a frightening diagnosis for both doctor and patient* (Gazzard et al. 1978), *the long term prognosis is good*" (Cooke 1981). In 2015—more than three decades of research later—it can be stated that this finding did not lose its expressiveness. The understanding of IBD is still incomplete, but advances in medical therapies and surgical techniques stepwise improved the patients' quality of life.

Inflammatory bowel diseases encompass the two main classifications of *Crohn's disease* (also known as regional enteritis or Morbus Crohn's, named after American gastroenterologist Burrill Bernard Crohn, cf. Crohn et al. 1984) and *ulcerative colitis*. Both diseases are characterized by chronic intestinal inflammation of the digestive system (Isaacs et al. 2005; Ruyssers et al. 2008) and are associated with high morbidity and reduced quality of life (McLeod et al. 1991; Cohen 2002; Longobardi et al. 2003; Kappelman et al. 2007). Pathophysiological, Crohn's disease can affect any part of the digestive system, while the most common site is the colon. Compared to ulcerative colitis, Crohn's disease is often segmental and the rectum is commonly spared. Patients with IBD often suffer from limited gastrointestinal motility leading to symptoms such as abdominal pain, fatigue, gastro-intestinal obstruction, bleeding and weight loss, concomitant with changes in the enteric nervous system (Geboes and Collins 1998; Ruyssers et al. 2010).

An IBD like Crohn's disease seems to run in some families. While males and females seem equally affected, Crohn's disease may occur in people of all ages, but it is predominantly a disease of adolescents and young adults, mainly in the age between 15 and 35 (Loftus 2007; Economou and Pappas 2008; Sonnenberg 2009; Thukkani et al. 2011; CCFA 2015). In fact, 10 % of those affected are less than 18 years old (CCFA 2015). While some patients have long periods of remission, i.e. periods when they are free of symptoms, the chronic nature of the disease can induce a permanent psychological pressure for the patient (Ruyssers et al. 2010; Sajadinejad et al. 2012).

Although the causes of the disease are still subject to research, the current hypothesis claims that IBD results from an uncontrolled (auto-) immune response to the normal gut flora (Xavier and Podolsky 2007; Ruyssers et al. 2008, 2010). Both genetic and environmental factors may contribute to the damaging mucosal immune response (Fiocchi 1998; Ruyssers et al. 2008). For the etiology of the disease, it is suggested that the lack of exposure to intestinal parasites like helminths, as a result of enhanced living standards and medical conditions, modulates the development of the immune system and thereby increases the risk of immune diseases in certain populations (Weinstock et al. 2002; Lashner and Loftus 2006; Garn and Renz 2007; Ruyssers et al. 2008; Strachan 2000). This assumption is supported by epidemiological studies that show an inverse relation between the frequency of helminth colonization and the prevalence of IBD (Weinstock et al. 2002; Elliott and Weinstock 2012). Correspondingly, while the incidence of IBD has steadily been increasing in the developed world since 1950 (Lakatos 2006; Ruyssers et al. 2008; Burisch and Munkholm 2013), it has a geographic trend, repeatedly been reported in northern regions, especially in North America and Europe (Loftus 2004; Probert and Brown 2008; Thukkani et al. 2011). While Alic (2000) and Bernstein et al. (2001) find that the incidence of Crohn's disease is highest in well-developed countries, the hygiene hypothesis states this is directly related to higher hygienic standards in respective countries (Strachan 2000; Ruyssers et al. 2008).

In terms of frequency, it is estimated that about 1.6 million U.S. Americans suffer from IBD. Compared to the U.S. population, it means that 1 out of 200 people suffer from IBD (Loftus 2004; Isaacs et al. 2005; Kappelman et al. 2007; CDC 2014). Approximately 70,000 new cases are diagnosed each year (Loftus 2007; CCFA 2015). For Europe, the number of people with IBD is estimated to be about 2.2 million (Burisch et al. 2013; Loftus 2004).

The treatment of the disease usually includes drugs, nutrition supplements, surgery or a combination of all these options (Duchmann and Zeitz 2005). By tendency, surgical treatment (removals) has been reserved for refractory disease and other complications. According to Van Assche et al. (2010), about 80 % of patients have to undergo surgery at some point. Although data regarding the health care costs of inflammatory bowel disease is limited, studies estimate the annual disease-attributable costs of IBD in the U.S. to be in a range from about USD 14 billion to USD 30 billion (Kappelman et al. 2007; Park and Bass 2011; CCFA 2015). In sample studies of U.S. children and adults with inflammatory bowel disease, researchers find that the mean treatment costs for Crohn's disease range from about USD 5000 (Kappelman et al. 2007; CCFA 2015) to USD 19,000 (Gibson et al. 2008; Yu et al. 2008; Venu and Cohen 2011) per year, depending on the applied therapy spectrum. Observing the drug product range, Isaacs et al. (2005) estimated that the number of products under study for the treatment of IBD increased from three products and one target in 1993 to more than 30 products and more than 10 targets in 2005. According to an industry report by Datamonitor (2010) and a research summary by Dutton (2013), new drugs could potentially drive sales of IBD related drugs from USD 4.26 billion in 2011 to USD 5–7 billion in 2019.

Summarizing the circumstances that inflammatory bowel disease brings in its train, both the incentive to improve the life of patients, as well as the economic burden of IBD encourage to improve the situation. Considering the presented state of research as well as internal surveys with patient advisory councils at C3N (Baebler et al. 2011), the demand for online and computer-mediated medical intelligence in IBD is very high.

3 Analyzing the IBD Patient Community Network (2010–2011)

In preparation of the netnographic patient community analysis, the five biggest English speaking public IBD-related Facebook groups were identified. The initial screening revealed that more than 40 IBD-related Facebook groups were active that time. Similar to an individual's Facebook profile page, Facebook group pages enable users to connect to these entities by "liking" the page or becoming a group member. Once a user liked or joined a group, he received updates on new links and discussions within the group via the Facebook News Feed.

For an initial analysis of the underlying network structure within the Facebook groups, each a sample of 500 random and anonymized members was selected. The sample represented each about 3–10 % of the network and allowed a first insight into the connectedness of group members, i.e. the friendship network. The visualization of networks was conducted with Gephi, an open-source visualization platform (http://gephi.org, cf. Bastian et al. 2009). In terms of privacy, it should be highlighted that the analysis was exclusively focused on the group's network and discussion board as a whole.[1] The study did explicitly not encompass an analysis of single group members or individual profiles. There was no information collected that could be linked to a living individual, just as there was no interaction between the investigator and subject or any manipulative experimental setting. It was ensured to comply with data protection and security with regard to individual privacy and research ethics as approved by the Institutional Review Boards at C3N (Cincinnati Children's Hospital).

Figure 1 exemplarily shows the network structure in one of the five Facebook groups, depicting a network with very low connectedness among members (low-density network). The figure is a sociogram, i.e. a graph that visually represents the interrelationships within a group, where actors are visualized as nodes (points) and edges (lines) that represent a connection between actors. The bigger a node, the more connections (degrees) it has. The visualization suggests only few connections with star-like networks (one central connector) as opposed to a more desirable "galaxy" of interconnected nodes. The analysis of anonymous IDs also revealed one other insight: 97.5 % of members belonged to only one of our selected Facebook groups on IBD. This result was quite surprising as one might assume that patients "leverage" the risk of missing information by joining several groups at the same time. However, it should be added that this argument is certainly limited as we only observe a subsample.

With regard to connectedness, Metcalfe's law (Metcalfe 1995) suggests that the value of a communications network is proportional to the square of the size of the network. However, networks tend to become less dense when they grow in size. This means that there is an inverse correlation between the overall connectedness (density) and the number of group members (network size). As a network grows in size, it becomes more difficult to establish stable social relationships (cf. Dunbar 1992; Wellman 2012). Correspondingly, as network density decreases, "structural

[1] Information on an online patient community is worthy of protection, even if—like in this case—the available data is publicly exposed. With respect to privacy and the ongoing ethics discussion in the computational social sciences, the analysis of interconnectedness is limited to randomized subsamples of information. It should be underlined, that our returning information certainly has a model character, but still seems to confirm what could be learned through close collaboration with patient councils.

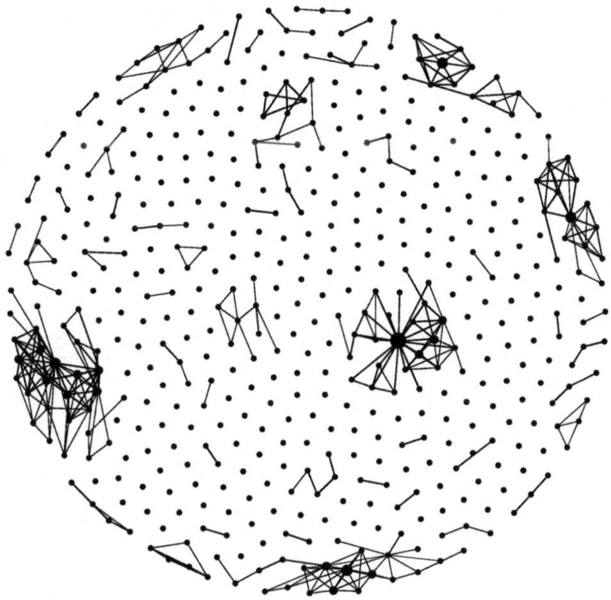

Fig. 1 Friendship network structure of a public IBD-related group with more than 24,000 members (subsample of 500 members)

holes" are likely to open and can be a source of information loss (Burt 2001). This effect is particularly important when information has to travel from highly connected members to less connected members, mostly in a network's periphery (or vice versa).

Aside from the low-density network structure of the groups, further insights on the communication pattern and content seemed interesting. The communication and sentiment analysis was conducted with Condor, an application developed at the MIT Center for Collective Intelligence (Gloor and Zhao 2004). Condor enabled to parse public discussions in one of the selected Facebook groups, i.e. posts, likes, comments and their respective date and time, covering the timeframe from November 2006 until June 2010. The dataset was generated by requesting publicly available Facebook posts and comments in the selected group through the Facebook Graph API. We collected an aggregated total of 12,000 records of posts and comments across all five groups. All information that Condor accessed was congruent with one-to-many communication that any member of the selected public Facebook groups could potentially browse through.

Table 1 presents a categorization of the most frequent discussion terms in a major public group with more than 24,000 members.

As Table 1 suggests, negative communication sentiments and a variety of uncertainties (cf. *Emotions*) dominated the discussion. In particular, the sentiment analysis revealed that experiences with doctors and nutrition ("eat") are of high importance.

In a second step of the analysis, the co-appearance of terms by betweenness centrality was visualized (Fig. 2). Betweenness centrality is a social network

Table 1 Public discussion topics of an IBD-related Facebook group with more than 24,000 members. By category and count of words

Disease	Emotions	Symptoms	Circumstances	Therapy	Social contacts	Activities
2908 crohn	2346 *feel*	1228 *flare*	1112 diagnosed	1830 *doctor*	1608 people	3137 *eat*
2622 cause	1652 pain	804 effects	906 body	1236 remicade	515 doctors	985 started
1344 disease	1391 *hope*	717 blood	788 meds	933 surgery	454 school	982 experience
598 ibd	1353 bad	682 colon	608 drink	848 drug	419 mom	647 helps
468 colitis	1255 luck	638 stomach	602 remission	847 prednisone	380 family	586 tried
	1025 thanks	524 weight	513 bathroom	813 hospital	369 friends	448 heard
	981 sick	307 tired	349 food	609 humira	345 guys	384 remember
	824 hard	222 inflammation	154 alcohol	431 imuran	250 college	384 change
	761 feeling			423 treatment	235 insurance	354 advice
	609 worse			371 infusion	140 parents	198 inform
	439 sorry			311 colonoscopy		
	250 horrible			273 asacol		
	219 happy			266 pentasa		
	178 worried			138 azathioprine		

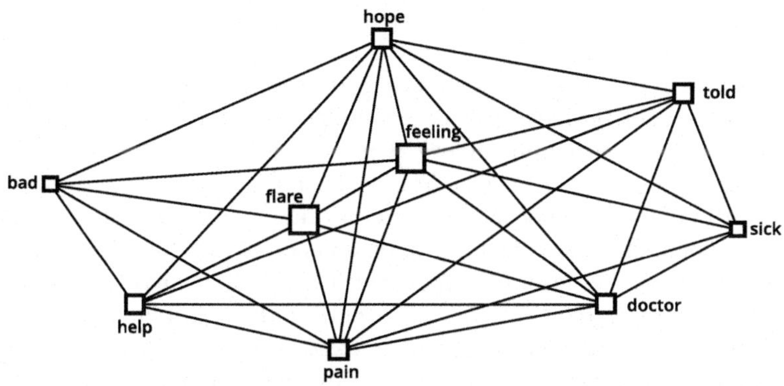

Fig. 2 The top 9 co-appearing words by communication frequency. Facebook group with 24,000 members, 12,007 posts, by betweenness centrality

measure and helps to center those terms in the center of a network visualization that are important connectors to other terms in the group discussion. Such an analysis was helpful in establishing a relationship between the use of certain words and to see how certain terms were connected.

The term network indicates that "feeling" and "flare" ("flares" or "flare-ups" are one perceived disease activity) co-appeared most often within the post and comments of the analyzed Facebook group. In a broader perspective, the visualization points out that most of the discussions were mostly about the symptoms and feelings that patients experienced.

Taken together, the sentiment analysis summarized in Table 1 and Fig. 2 suggest that members of IBD-related Facebook groups

1. share their emotional state,
2. are in pain,
3. frequently use the bathroom and
4. are very worried about their surroundings, for example in school. Last but not least, they are
5. very open in sharing their individual best practice with food and experimentations.

The semantic analysis provided a very precise impression of an IBD patient's challenges in daily life. Taken together, the discussion sentiments are rather of a negative nature, which potentially discourages a continuous interaction of patients. Such a communication culture may also entail contagious effects. Investigations of a large real-world social network, collected over a 20-year period, suggest that people's happiness depends on the happiness of others with whom they are connected (Fowler and Christakis 2008). Such insights can be used to precisely address and solve problems with regard to a newly developed application. For example, success stories and more positive sentiments (through a currency of "thankfulness" for sharing information) could be good incentives to visit the online community more frequently.

In a third step, the analysis focused on communication patterns and structures within the Facebook groups. The contribution to a group's discussion can be measured with the "contribution index", measuring the ratio of sending and receiving information (Gloor et al. 2003). The contribution index analysis yielded that there was a maximum of six members across the aggregated dataset of all five groups who dominated the content creation and communication. Such dominance can cause problems, because topics covered in discussions may be biased by the interest of a few. Only about 1 % of users significantly contribute to the discussion through new content creation, comments or likes. Roughly only about 40–50 % of these posts would receive a comment or like by other group members. More than 95 % of users in our sample did not make any contribution, as for example by posting new content, liking posts or commenting on them.

Checking for the public statistics on newly joining users among the five selected groups, it could be observed that fewer and fewer members were joining the network—in fact, two out of five groups had a decreasing number of group members toward the end of 2010. One reason for the negative linear trend might be a natural saturation, as other public and closed IBD-related Facebook groups are created. The more speculative assumption is that potential new entrants were demotivated by their first impression of the discussion boards. As negative emotions in the groups appear to take up much space, they do not provide a good incentive for patients to join and engage. Maybe, "bad news" is not the kind of news patients search for, in particular if they hold up on "hope" (see Fig. 2). Taken together, the analysis in this section uncovered a loosely coupled network with following key characteristics: There were

1. very few connected and active patients, there was
2. a rather "problem-" than "solution-"oriented discussion sentiment, and
3. a decreasing number of new group entrants could be observed.

The key question of the analysis was now, which impact such network structures and patterns might have on the diffusion of information, for example of a new therapeutic innovation. In the next section, the diffusion of innovation for the case of whipworm therapy will be analyzed. This therapy emerged around the year of 2005 in science and news as a new promising therapy for IBD patients.

4 Tracing the Whipworm: A Dynamic Communication Analysis

> "The etiology and pathogenesis of inflammatory bowel disease has puzzled investigators for decades" and epidemiologic theories of a "hygiene hypothesis" had not been subjected to direct clinical trials with intentional inoculation with infectious agents until now." (Cohen 2005)

Since about 2005, experimental and clinical studies sustain the idea that helminths might provide protection against IBD (Elliott et al. 2003; Weinstock et al. 2005; Summers et al. 2005; Ruyssers et al. 2008, 2010; Flowers and Hopkins 2013). The clinical studies showed that the treatment of IBD patients with "trichuris suis" (pig whipworm) ova lead to a decrease in the Crohn's disease and ulcerative colitis disease activity index (Summers et al. 2005).

Cohen (2005) concludes that intentionally infecting patients with (porcine whip-) worms makes headlines. The idea of being infected with living parasites could be psychologically tough to accept for patients (Ruyssers et al. 2008), especially with regard to side-effects.

Unlike the human whipworm (trichuris trichiura), trichuris suis does not spread within the human body as it is not able to deal with the human pathogene structure (Cohen 2005). As such, it does not cause an ingestion of the ovary, noninvasive larvae and a colonization of the colon. Still, therapeutic human helminth colonization needs to be examined for possible adverse side effects (Summers et al. (2003) Reddy and Fried 2009).

According to Ruyssers et al. (2008), the therapy with whipworms might bear a residual risk, which is that helminths might invade other tissues in the human host and cause pathology (Ruyssers et al. 2008). To minimize the risks of a therapy with living parasites, current research focuses on the documentation and classification of immunosuppressive molecules that contribute to the protective effect of helminths (Ruyssers et al. 2008; Heylen et al. 2014). In other words, this yet novel stream of research aims to mimic the whipworm's effect with the use of convenient and non-stigmatized pills, which were recently studied in multi-center clinical trials (Weinstock and Elliott 2013).

Being informed about the promising research studies on whipworm therapy and their exposure in magazines like *The New York Times* (Velasquez-Manoff 2008), a further netnographic analysis was conducted, aiming to of track the diffusion of the idea of whipworms as an IBD therapy. In particular, a quantification of scientific publications related to the alternative IBD whipworm therapy as well as a "coolhunting" analysis in the World Wide Web (Gloor and Cooper 2007) was conducted. Such an analysis enabled deeper insights into the external presence of the term "whipworm" that could potentially diffuse into the discussion of the Facebook groups. The diffusion analysis assumes two simplified models of information flow: (1) Information on innovation diffuses from research and news to doctors and from doctors to patients, (2) or directly from research and news to patients, provided information is available online.

Figure 3 indicates the number of general IBD publications and IBD publications with a focus on whipworm/helminthic therapy from 1990 until 2010.

Using the Publish or Perish software and the Google Scholar database in February 2011, scientific papers with the terms "*whipworm*", "*hookworm*", "*trichuris suis*" or "*helminth*" in their title or keywords were queried. While the analysis provides certainly only a rough estimate of the worldwide research volume, the publication data at least resonates with previously mentioned research studies and the first major publication wave on whipworms, reaching its peak in

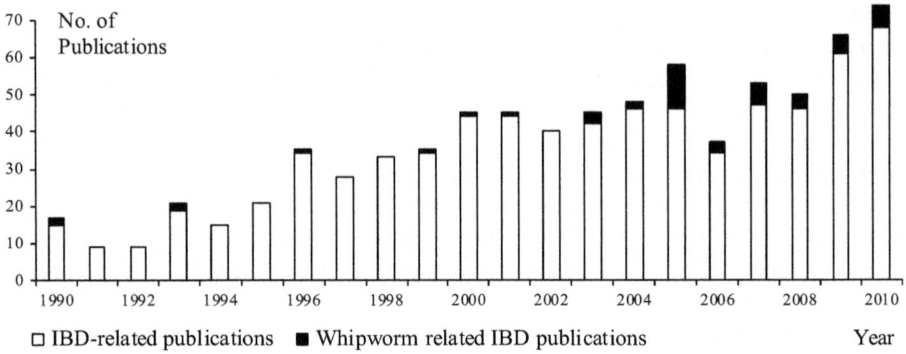

Fig. 3 Number of publications on IBD therapy and whipworm-related IBD therapy

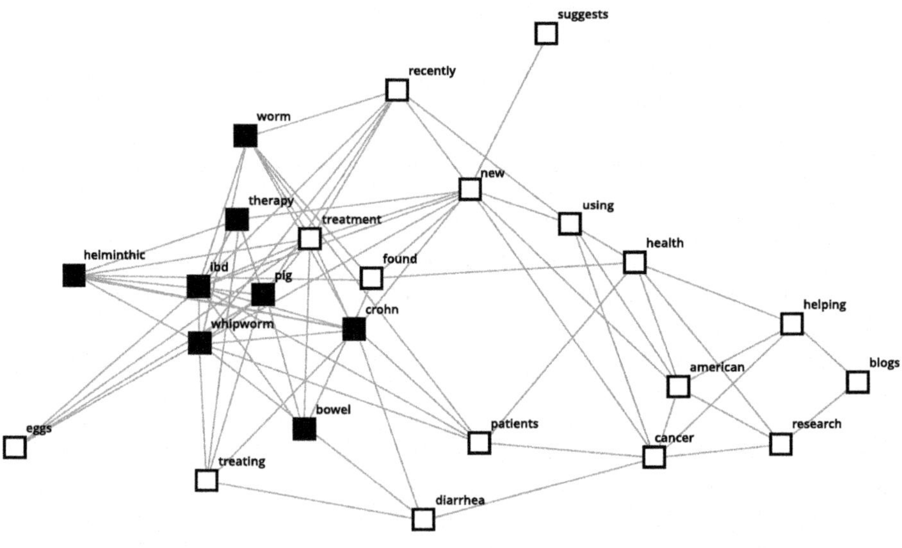

Fig. 4 Co-appearance of the term "whipworm" in top Google search results (by betweenness centrality, 2 degrees depth, top 50 Google Search results, February 2011)

2005. As it appears, the research on whipworm therapy has been trendy since then and might suggest that such coverage should theoretically induce communications about the innovation within online patient networks.

In order to check the World Wide Web's knowledge about whipworm, an additional Condor web crawl analysis was conducted. A web crawl analysis fetches thousands of results that a Google search query on "whipworm" returns and structures the available information according to the source, repeating terms and their connectedness.

The graph visualization in Fig. 4 is a structured snapshot of the World Wide Web's knowledge about whipworms in February 2011. The graphic shows that

Google search results on "whipworm" provided information about IBD and whipworm therapy in articles, blogs and other content. The term graph indicates that whipworm theory seemed to be a known "IBD" and "crohn" therapy alternative ("helped", "using", "treatment") in the Internet. However, as the neighborhood to the terms "recently" and "new" accentuates, it was relatively a relatively new therapy at that time.

Given the evident presence of helminthic therapy in research and web news, the diffusion of the topic of whipworm therapy within the selected IBD related Facebook group was now subject to investigation. For instance, following posts or comment excerpts from the selected group reflected the discussion about the whipworm therapy (paraphrased for privacy reasons):

> "I found a new study on whipworms, which may help put Crohn's in remission. It's really interesting. Although some people are wondering how someone could swallow a worm, I would do anything to get rid of my symptoms. Tell me what are your thoughts?" (2008)

> "I'm glad you gave the alternative therapies a try. The trichuris suis whipworm is something that not a lot of people know about. I'm glad that it got you back where you want to be. Rock on!" (2009)

> "'Dr. Elliott said that in Argentina, researchers found that patients with multiple sclerosis who were infected with the human whipworm had milder cases and fewer flare-ups of their disease over a period of four and a half years' [Quote of the New York Times Article by Velasquez-Manoff (2008)—Any thoughts on that?" (2010)]

These are examples of messages, potentially created by innovator- or early-adopter-type users (Rogers 2003[1962]).

Figure 5 visualizes Facebook group members and their betweenness centrality in group discussions from June 2006 until June 2009. Betweenness centrality is a measure that explains a users' influence on the transfer of information through the network. According to Kidane and Gloor (2007), betweenness centrality is predictive for creative activity, as the betweenness of a node qualifies to measure the extent, to which a user plays the part of an information gatekeeper, controlling the

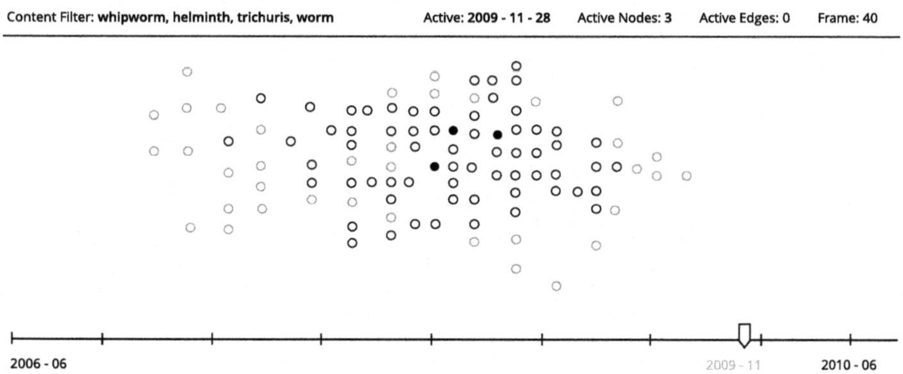

Fig. 5 "Whipworm" as a discussion topic in communication of one IBD-related Facebook groups with 24,000 members, by actor betweenness centrality (11/2009)

access and the flow of information (Gloor 2006). Creativity of individuals often appears with the oscillation between different groups and systems. Very often, users with high betweenness centrality are known innovator type users (Ryan and Gross 1943; Rogers 2003[1962]), opinion leaders (Katz 1957; Katz and Lazarsfeld 1957). Betweenness centrality has one important implication for a patient community in practice: By social contagion theory (Aral and Walker 2011), the most between members in the friendship network are in a position to influence their friends (or friends of friends), e.g. with the communication of new innovations such as whipworm therapy. The higher the betweenness centrality of an actor, the more central he appears in the visualization (Fig. 5). If a member posted content relating to whipworm, the respective node is highlighted in black.

The analysis suggests that from June 2006 until June 2010, the term "whipworm" (helminths, trichuris or worm) appears only twice (November 2006, November 2009). In both cases, the discussion on the new innovation dissolved very quickly. There was neither a considerable spread of information nor any echo through comments on the topic in the group network. While the posts about whipworms in the observed network were done by rather centrally positioned members, their information did also not diffuse into the group network's periphery, i.e. through comments by less active or connected members. Assuming that the top influential users by betweenness centrality were identified, one should have observed a more prolonged and broader information spread of the whipworm therapy within the network and course of time.

With a deeper look into the dataset, it seems remarkable that the discussion about whipworm appears together with the terms "heard" and "doctor". A check of the anonymized posts confirmed that patients "heard" about the "whipworm" therapy from their "doctor". So far, the research-doctor-patient diffusion model was partially confirmed.

Complementing the previous analysis, Fig. 6 shows the betweenness centrality of different terms, including content in posts and comments in the selected

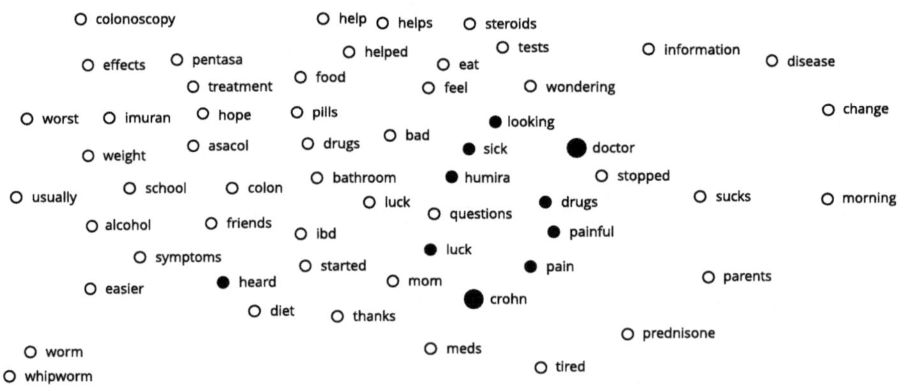

Fig. 6 Discussion terms in the group communication of a groups with 24,000 members, by betweenness centrality (06/2006–06/2010)

Facebook group with 24,000 members from 2006 to 2010. Data shows that the whipworm therapy does not significantly appear in the discussion sentiment. Rather, classical drugs ("pentasa", "humira", "steroids") take center stage, just as discussions about "pain", "doctor" and "feelings" (cf. Table 1). The discussion about "whipworms" is located in the far periphery of the overall communication (lower left), so that the average user would very unlikely stumble upon related information in posts or comments when visiting a Facebook group.

It is arguable that the social environment of diffusion plays an important role also for online patient networks (Emerson 1962; Lyytinen and Damsgaard 2001). One reason for the low level of communication might be that adopting living helminths as a therapy is not compatible with the social and individual norm. It should further be taken into account that there is a relation between high hygiene standards and the occurrence of IBD. Having that knowledge might indirectly lead to the conclusion that such a patient population has a lower likelihood to cheer for an apparently unappetizing worm. Another reason might be the lack of experience in the own social network and peer structure, and the reliance on others as source of information (Midgley and Dowling 1993). One could argue that trust is particularly low in those cases, were patients are not connected with each other, as shown in Fig. 1. A certain number of trusted members within the personal network must have adopted and posted positive outcomes about helminthic therapy before new patients would jump on the bandwagon. Social proof (Cialdini 2001) is a precondition for cooperation and innovation adoption. All that being said, what seems to be at the core of all observations is that the network's low density hinders a better diffusion of innovation. A higher density in the friendship network and less centralized discussions might certainly contribute toward a better spread of information within the network and incentivize more feedback loops.

5 Creating a Collaborative Online Patient Network (2012: Ongoing)

On the basis of the results of the patient community anamnesis, a mobile application named "YouMeIBD" is proposed. Alongside the prototype application development, undertaken by an interdisciplinary student class at MIT, the application development concentrates on three questions:

1. Which socio-psychological and socio-technical factors constitute connectedness? (*enablers*)
2. Which emotional factors drive patients to collaborate and form strong ties? (*incentives*) and
3. How can mechanisms be created that foster the spread of new innovations? (*creativity and diffusion*)

It can be concluded that following main network characteristics should be addressed with a solution designed toward helping IBD patients to better connect online:

1. A network's density must be increased to better connect patients and to support the diffusion of innovations.
2. Information within the network must be better structured as for example in Facebook group discussions. Also, information should be differentiated with regard to their quality, for instance through a collective sorting mechanism. Emotional signals and feelings need a different communication channel than relevant information.
3. A network should harness both the social and the knowledge graph. Patients need to share more relevant information with each other in a trusted environment. While the cause of IBD is still puzzling researchers, more collectively structured information can be contributory to a patient's individual solution/therapy/everyday life. In terms of co-development, a platform should channel in-formation on alternative or young medical approaches, simultaneously addressing researchers, doctors and patients. In this context, crowdfunding, for instance, has the potential to support innovative processes outside the laboratory (cf. https://patient-innovation.com/).
4. Patients need a place with success stories and positive emotions. IBD patients are likely to conceal their disease toward friends and might be in need of social support. It is important to think about the "currency" users deal with: As patients seek for a more positive and constructive dialog, the values of love, (intrinsic motivation) and glory (peer recognition) should be addressed as important motivators (cf. Malone et al. 2009). A virtual community, enabling to establish connections to distant others with similar interests, can potentially sustain social needs that are not locally met (Wellman 1992; Haythornthwaite 2005).
5. An online community should provide an opportunity to collect—self-reported—patient data on a large scale, permitting researchers to analyze aggregated patient information.
6. Recent studies show that patients with IBD often do not receive an optimal medical therapy (Trivedi and Keefer 2015), which is also reflected in the communication sentiments. In preparation of the platform development, the MIT Center for Collective Intelligence and the Cincinnati Children's Hospital conducted a quick patient survey in 2011, comprising 57 responses (Baebler et al. 2011). While most patients confirmed they try to use Facebook to connect online, they expressed their need for a more efficient and trustful online platform. Symptoms, treatment options and their social situation are the key contents that patients want to discuss about in a trustworthy environment. Thus, a network must address an individual user's need with regard to his interests, symptoms and medications.

All these points together, resulting from an extensive community analysis, are factors to be considered in the creation of an online social network for IBD patients. The following figures demonstrate the main functions of the mobile application "YouMeIBD".

The starting page of "YouMeIBD" (Fig. 7) invites users to login with their current Facebook account (*Login*). Using a user's Facebook credentials comes with

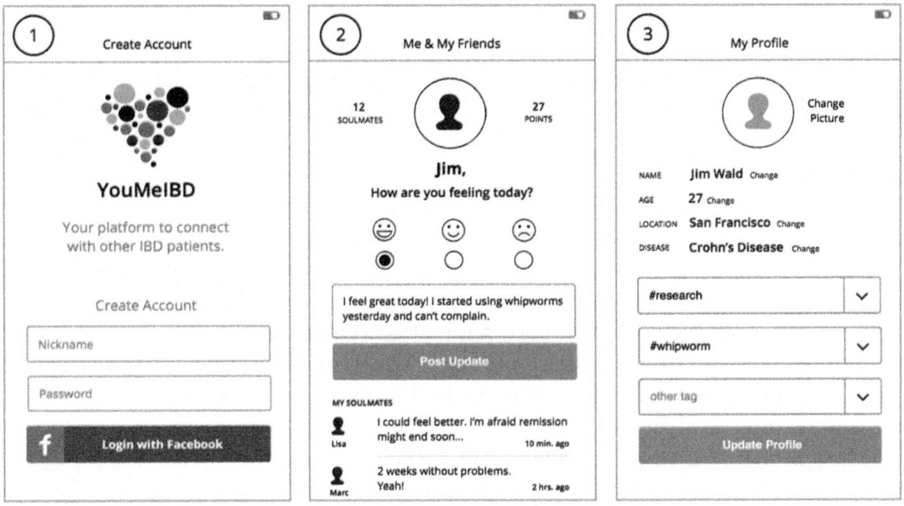

Fig. 7 YouMeIBD functions: Login, Me and My Friends, My Profile

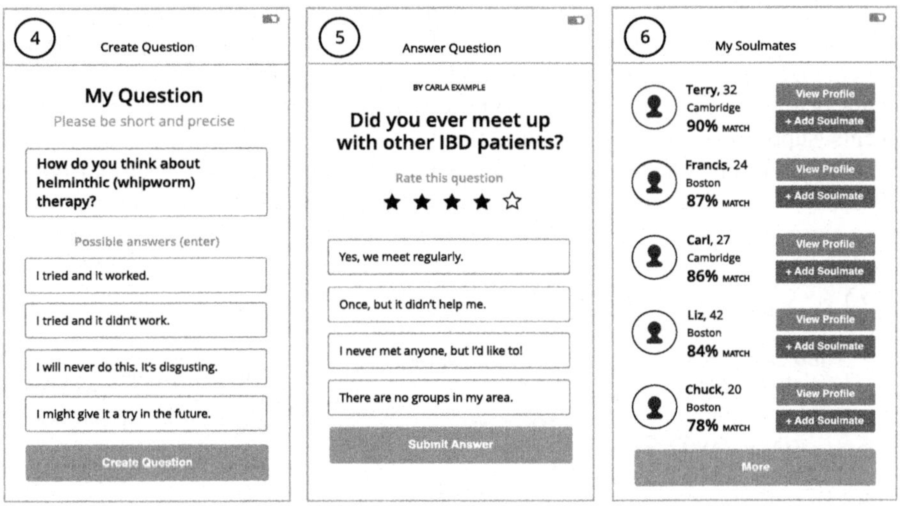

Fig. 8 YouMeIBD functions: Create Question, Answer Question, Matches

the advantage that it is an easy way to catch information a user was already willing to expose. For instance, his profile picture, age, gender, location information, friends and likes. The latter are especially important as they can provide the matching algorithm with relevant data (Fig. 8). Like on online dating websites, common music, movie or website interests, group belongings and mutual friends are good factors to facilitate connections, even though they rather seem to be "soft factors" in a patient community. Since decades, research claims that common interests are a good predictor of homophily (Lazarsfeld and Merton 1954; Byrne 1971; McPherson et al. 2001) and thus promising in creating a denser network with many strong connections among patients. Probably, there is a strong correlation between the willingness to share health data and the level of trust and empathy for peers.

Me and My Friends serves to update a user's profile, emotional mood and further allows sending messages to friends in their network. Such friendships are named "Soulmates". Users can see the most recent status updates by their peers and get an impression on their thoughts and emotions. Another sub-element is a profile page *My Profile* where users can add tags that matter to them, as e.g. their symptoms or current medication. In addition to profile and question data, these self-tags can be used to improve the matching of patients, i.e. matching a beginner in a certain therapy method with an experienced expert.

The *Questions* function as shown in Fig. 8 provides users with the opportunity to create questions. Correspondingly, the *Answers* function asks a user to rate and answer questions by other users.

Based on algorithmic matching of Facebook data, common tags and answered questions, users will finally be able to *Find Soulmates* who share mutual attributes and interests. For each user, a score of matching is calculated and displayed with supplementary information on the match. As electronic relationships deepen (Rheingold 1993; Kendall 2002), online connectivity often induces face-to-face contacts in the real world. The *Meetings* function (see Fig. 9) allows users to create events, supporting real-world connectedness.

Another future functionality could be the opportunity to create virtual online "flash teams" of expert patients, doctors and researchers to collaboratively

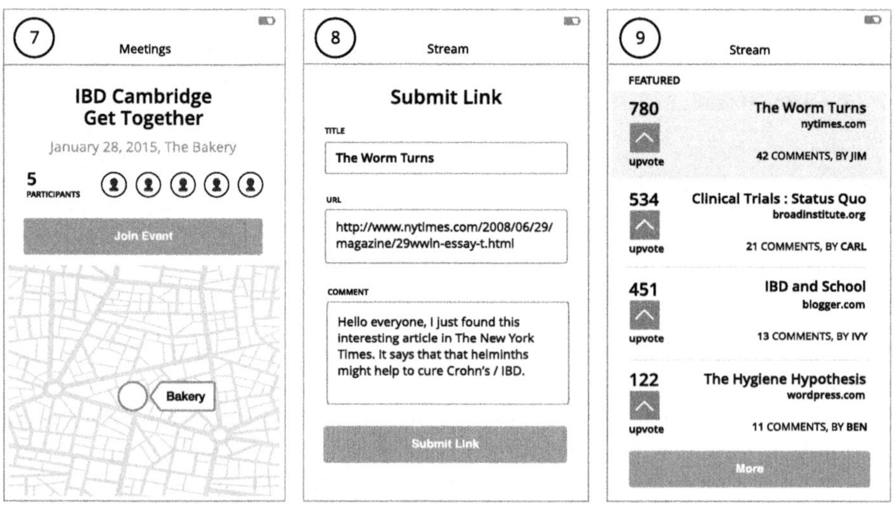

Fig. 9 YouMeIBD functions: Meetings, Stream—Submit Link, Stream—Index

investigate certain information that might be interesting to specific patient groups (Retelny et al. 2014). Within a set timeframe, patients could start a flash team of crowdworking patients that aims to summarize scientific studies on whipworm therapy or the status of current clinical trials. Current online collaboration software such as Slack, Google Docs or Dropbox could support the coordination and collective information gathering. Intrinsically motivated and equipped with expert knowledge, patient flash teams could potentially perform better than teams in laboratory settings.

The intention of the *Stream* function is to channel relevant news (therapies, research, stories, blog entries). The stream serves as an information system, relaying, amplifying, and structuring information. Functionally, users can submit and upvote links that seem helpful or interesting for other patients. Contents are then ordered by their overall (upvote) score. The more relevant an information seems to other users, the more points the author of the content will receive. By doing so, YouMeIBD aims at implementing a "*Hacker News for Patients*". Hacker News (http://news.ycombinator.com) is a programming, technology and hacks focused social news feed, that applies a time- and point-oriented algorithm. The feed, that was started by the startup accelerator Y Combinator in 2007, enables expert users to submit links to the website, that can subsequently be up-voted by users of the platform. The more up-votes a website link receives within a certain amount of time, the higher the link will be ranked on the website. Each link can be clicked and commented by users of the system. Hacker News or a more product-related system called "Product Hunt" (http://producthunt.com) became popular as efficiently working hubs for information on new technologies and software. Potentially, a patient community focused on a specific disease could harness such an infrastructure to collaboratively create and filter relevant links. Such a mechanism comes with two benefits:

1. In case a link (information) is ranked high, it could get faster response from the community. As Malone et al. (2009) state, *Create* and *Decide* are two of the four main underlying processes in a collective intelligent system. While *Create* describes the collective innovation and co-creation process, *Decide* represents the process of selection and evaluation of given options, e.g. through collective voting mechanisms. As such, the patient crowd would be able to prioritize relevant information.
2. Information that otherwise would not have found its way into a patient community, could now be elevated. For instance, there could be a link to an IBD patient's findings on self-tracking content that may never have been discovered by a doctor or scientific journal. As the nature of the medical innovation system leads to years of development time, especially young patients run out of patience. Medicine is a highly regulated arena in which new drugs and therapies must undergo extensive testing and approval processes before they can be offered to the market. A recent estimate suggests that it takes 8–12 years and costs ranging from USD 0.5 billion to USD 2 billion in order to bring a new drug to the market (DiMasi et al. 2003; Adams and Van Brantner 2006; Flowers 2014;

Flowers and Hopkins 2013). On the other hand, studies by Von Hippel (1986) have shown that 'lead users' often experience emerging needs and may prototype products and services that can satisfy these needs that are not met by the market. User innovators also draw their innovations from 'local knowledge'; knowledge that is distinct from the types of knowledge that is generated within firms. This 'sticky local information' (Von Hippel 1994) that users acquire is often costly to transfer to producers or hard to find within a clinical setting.

In the context of IBD, where therapies may require a decade or more of research and clinical trials before they overcome regulatory approval, some users may 'side-step' the innovation process (Flowers and Hopkins 2013, Flowers 2014) and actively diffuse their own innovation (Harhoff et al. 2003). Here, a collaborative sorting mechanism can contribute to rank information on (user) innovation from network peripheries that would otherwise not have been visible.

6 Summary and Outlook

This contribution started with an exemplary analysis on the pattern and profile of an online IBD patient community. It could be learned that coolhunting and "community snapshots" can provide very valuable information on a community's characteristics, its problems and needs.

Besides analyzing the low-density structure of the network, a sentiment analysis provided insights into the emotionality and content of communication. This article further explained how a high network centrality and low network density hindered the diffusion of an innovation, that counts at least for the case of whipworms.

Insights from computational social science helped to design a prototype concept, addressing the identified problems. The efficiency of the proposed application prototype will be subject to future empirical investigation.

Initially targeted for the IBD community, YouMeIBD is a non-profit prototype and to be extended to other chronic disease groups. The model could equally be applied in other patient communities of chronic diseases or any disease where belonging and cohesion do not only support individual well-being but also the diffusion of information and innovation. The access to such a mobile web platform can be limited by the ability and practice to communicate online, particularly for elderly or handicapped patients. However, as Internet affinity and technological aids will accompany the next generation of patients, one can be optimistic that this group of patients will be able to access online patient platforms.

Started in 2010, five student classes contributed to the YouMeIBD project. Class by class, the project went one step further toward a real world application for IBD patients. On the open source project websites of COINs classes (cf. COINs Class 2010, 2011, 2012, 2013, 2014, 2015) and at http://c3nproject.org/innovations/patient-engagement-community/youmeibd you may follow the recent development of the application until July 2015. Everyone who is interested in continuing on our model the produced mockups and functions is invited to get in touch.

Acknowledgments This contribution represents the work of a team consisting of more than 15 students, patients, clinicians, designers, researchers and developers. Prof. Dr. Peter A. Gloor at the MIT Center for Collective Intelligence and the Collaborative Chronic Care Network (C3N) team at Cincinnati Children's Hospital initiated this research project. Hauke Führes, Linda Bäbler, Jonas Lauener and Leslie Marticke contributed to the first YouMeIBD prototype application described in this article. Since then, five interdisciplinary and international student classes contributed to the project (cf. COINs Class 2010, 2011, 2012, 2013, 2014, 2015). I like to thank the Dr. Werner Jackstädt Foundation for their generous support.

References

Adams CP, Brantner VV (2006) Estimating the cost of new drug development: is it really $802 million? Health Aff 25(2):420–428

Alic MSM (2000) Inflammatory bowel diseases are diseases of higher socioeconomic status: dogma or reality? Am J Gastroenterol 95:3332–3333. doi:10.1016/S0002-9270(00)02123-7

Aral S, Walker D (2011) Creating social contagion through viral product design: a randomized trial of peer influence in networks. Manag Sci 57:1623–1639. doi:10.1287/mnsc.1110.1421

Baebler L, Gloor P, Kaminski J, Marticke L, Dellal G (2011) YouApp—it's all about YOU: finding patients like myself on Facebook. In: Proceedings of the 3rd international conference on Collaborative Innovation Networks COINs 2011, Basel, Switzerland, 8–10 September 2011. http://www.ickn.org/documents/COINs11_YouApp.pdf. Accessed 1 Apr 2015

Bastian M, Heymann S, Jacomy M (2009) Gephi: an open source software for exploring and manipulating networks. Third international AAAI conference on Weblogs and Social Media. https://www.aaai.org/ocs/index.php/ICWSM/09/paper/view/154/1009. Accessed 1 May 2015

Bernstein CN, Kraut A, Blanchard JF, Rawsthorne P, Yu N, Walld R (2001) The relationship between inflammatory bowel disease and socioeconomic variables. Am J Gastroenterol 96:2117–2125. doi:10.1016/S0002-9270(01)02509-6

Burisch J, Munkholm P (2013) Inflammatory bowel disease epidemiology. Curr Opin Gastroenterol 29:357–362. doi:10.1097/MOG.0b013e32836229fb

Burisch J, Jess T, Martinato M, Lakatos PL (2013) The burden of inflammatory bowel disease in Europe. J Crohns Colitis 7:322–337. doi:10.1016/j.crohns.2013.01.010

Burt RS (2001) Structural holes versus network closure as social capital. In: Lin N, Cook KS, Burt RS (eds) Social capital theory and research. Aldine de Gruyter, New York, pp 31–56

Byrne D (1971) The attraction paradigm. Academic, New York

CCFA (2015) Crohn's and Colitis Foundation of America. Fact book. http://www.ccfa.org/assets/pdfs/updatedibdfactbook.pdf. Accessed 1 May 2015

CDC (2014) Center for Disease Control and Prevention. http://www.cdc.gov/ibd/ibd-epidemiology.htm. Accessed 20 Nov 2014

Christakis NA, Fowler JH (2011) Connected: the surprising power of our social networks and how they shape our lives. Little, Brown, Boston, p 256

Cialdini RB (2001) The science of persuasion. Sci Am 284:76–81. doi:10.1038/scientificamerican0201-76

Cohen RD (2002) The quality of life in patients with Crohn's disease. Aliment Pharmacol Ther 16:1603–1609. doi:10.1046/j.1365-2036.2002.01323.x

Cohen RD (2005) Worms, germs and IBD: is it your mother's fault? Gastroenterology 129:1127–1128. doi:10.1053/j.gastro.2005.06.076, discussion 1128–9

COINs Class (2010). https://sites.google.com/site/coincourse2010/home. Accessed 1 Apr 2015

COINs Class (2011). https://sites.google.com/site/coincourse2011/home. Accessed 1 Apr 2015

COINs Class (2012). https://sites.google.com/site/coincourse2012/home. Accessed 1 Apr 2015

COINs Class (2013). https://sites.google.com/site/coincourse2013/home. Accessed 1 Apr 2015

COINs Class (2014). https://sites.google.com/site/coincourse2014/home. Accessed 1 Apr 2015

COINs Class (2015). https://sites.google.com/site/coincourse2015/home. Accessed 1 Apr 2015

Cooke WT (1981) Factors in the management of Crohn's disease: a discussion paper. J R Soc Med 74:757
Crohn BB, Ginzburg L, Oppenheimer GD (1984) Regional ileitis. A pathological and clinical entity. JAMA 251:73–79. doi:10.1001/jama.251.1.73
Datamonitor (2010) Commercial insight: inflammatory Bowel disease—future market prospects rely on addressing cost and safety. Research and Markets. Abstract: http://goo.gl/x6JSZw. Accessed 20 Nov 2014
DiMasi JA, Hansen RW, Grabowski HG (2003) The price of innovation: new estimates of drug development costs. J Health Econ 22:151–185. doi:10.1016/S0167-6296(02)00126-1
Duchmann R, Zeitz M (2005) Crohn's disease: current pathogenetic paradigms. Mucosal Immunol 3:1265–1286
Dunbar RIM (1992) Neocortex size as a constraint on group size in primates. J Hum Evol 22:469–493. doi:10.1016/0047-2484(92)90081-J
Dutton G (2013) Big need in IBD: drugs to slow progression. Genetic Eng Biotechnol News 33 (14):14–14. doi:10.1089/gen.33.14.05
Economou M, Pappas G (2008) New global map of Crohn's disease: genetic, environmental, and socioeconomic correlations. Inflamm Bowel Dis 14:709–720. doi:10.1002/ibd.20352
Elliott DE, Weinstock JV (2012) Helminth-host immunological interactions: prevention and control of immune-mediated diseases. Ann N Y Acad Sci 1247:83–96. doi:10.1111/j.1749-6632.2011.06292.x
Elliott DE, Li J, Blum A, Metwali A, Qadir K, Urban JF, Weinstock JV (2003) Exposure to schistosome eggs protects mice from TNBS-induced colitis. Am J Physiol Gastrointest Liver Physiol 284:G385–G391. doi:10.1152/ajpgi.00049.2002
Elliott DE, Summers RW, Weinstock JV (2007) Helminths as governors of immune-mediated inflammation. Int J Parasitol 37:457–464. doi:10.1016/j.ijpara.2006.12.009
Emerson RM (1962) Power-dependence relations. Am Sociol Rev 27:31. doi:10.2307/2089716
Eysenbach G, Powell J, Englesakis M, Rizo C, Stern A (2004) Health related virtual communities and electronic support groups: systematic review of the effects of online peer to peer interactions. BMJ 328:1166. doi:10.1136/bmj.328.7449.1166
Fiocchi C (1998) Inflammatory cowel disease: etiology and pathogenesis. Gastroenterology 115:182–205. doi:10.1016/S0016-5085(98)70381-6
Fowler JH, Christakis NA (2008) Dynamic spread of happiness in a large social network: longitudinal analysis over 20 years in the Framingham Heart Study. BMJ 337:a2338
Flowers S (2014) Medical user innovation in the context of chronic disease: the creation of Helminthic therapy. Workshop on medical user innovation and medical commons, NYU School of Law, 15–17 May 2014. Working paper. http://goo.gl/VVdyWQ. Accessed 20 Nov 2014
Flowers S, Hopkins M (2013) Autoimmune disease: patients self-treat with parasitic worms. Nature 493:163. doi:10.1038/493163c
Fuehres H, Kaminski J, Gloor P, Zhang X (2011) Finding a cure for Crohn's disease—analyzing medical conditions in online communities. In: Proceedings of the Sunbelt 2011, St. Pete's Beach, Florida, 10–13 February 2011
Gallant MP (2003) The influence of social support on chronic illness self-management: a review and directions for research. Health Educ Behav 30:170–195. doi:10.1177/1090198102251030
Garn H, Renz H (2007) Epidemiological and immunological evidence for the hygiene hypothesis. Immunobiology 212:441–452. doi:10.1016/j.imbio.2007.03.006
Gazzard BG, Price HL, Libby GW, Dawson AM (1978) The social toll of Crohn's disease. Br Med J 2:1117–1119. doi:10.1136/bmj.2.6145.1117
Geboes K, Collins S (1998) Structural abnormalities of the nervous system in Crohn's disease and ulcerative colitis. Neurogastroenterol Motil 10:189–202. doi:10.1046/j.1365-2982.1998.00102.x

Gibson TB, Ng E, Ozminkowski RJ, Wang S, Burton WN, Goetzel RZ, Maclean R (2008) The direct and indirect cost burden of Crohn's disease and ulcerative colitis. J Occup Environ Med 50:1261–1272. doi:10.1097/JOM.0b013e318181b8ca

Gloor PA (2006) Swarm creativity: competitive advantage through collaborative innovation networks. Oxford University Press, New York

Gloor PA, Cooper S (2007) Coolhunting: chasing down the next big thing. AMACOM, New York

Gloor PA, Zhao Y (2004) TeCFlow—a temporal communication flow visualizer for social network analysis. ACM CSCW Workshop on Social Networks, pp 1–4

Gloor PA, Laubacher R, Dynes SBC, Zhao Y (2003) Visualization of communication patterns in collaborative innovation networks—analysis of some W3C working groups. In: Proceedings of the twelfth international Conference on Information and Knowledge Management—CIKM'03 56. doi:10.1145/956873.956875

Gloor PA, Grippa F, Borgert A, Colletti R, Dellal G, Margolis P, Seid M (2011) Towards growing a COIN in a medical research community. Procedia Soc Behav Sci 26. In: Proceedings COINs 2010, collaborative innovations networks conference, Savannah, GA, 7–9 October 2010. doi:10.1016/j.sbspro.2011.10.557

Harhoff D, Henkel J, Von Hippel E (2003) Profiting from voluntary information spillovers: how users benefit by freely revealing their innovations. Res Policy 32(10):1753–1769

Haythornthwaite C (2005) Social networks and internet connectivity effects. Inf Commun Soc 8:125–147. doi:10.1080/13691180500146185

Heylen M, Ruyssers NE, Gielis EM, Vanhomwegen E, Pelckmans PA, Moreels TG, De Man JG, De Winter BY (2014) Of worms, mice and man: an overview of experimental and clinical helminth-based therapy for inflammatory bowel disease. Pharmacol Ther 143:153–167. doi:10.1016/j.pharmthera.2014.02.011

Isaacs KL, Lewis JD, Sandborn WJ, Sands BE, Targan SR (2005) State of the art: IBD therapy and clinical trials in IBD. Inflamm Bowel Dis 11(Suppl 1):S3–S12. doi:10.1097/01.MIB.0000184852.84558.b2

Kaminski J, Gloor P, Marticke L (2012) YouMeIBD—an interactive online matchmaker for patients of IBD/Crohn's disease, Stanford Medicine X, Stanford University, Palo Alto, 28—30 September 2012. http://medicinex.stanford.edu/gloor-kaminski-abstract/. Accessed 20 Nov 2014

Kappelman MD, Rifas-Shiman SL, Kleinman K, Ollendorf D, Bousvaros A, Grand RJ, Finkelstein JA (2007) The prevalence and geographic distribution of Crohn's disease and ulcerative colitis in the United States. Clin Gastroenterol Hepatol 5:1424–1429. doi:10.1016/j.cgh.2007.07.012

Katz E (1957) The two-step flow of communication: an up-to-date report on an hypothesis. Public Opin Q 21:61. doi:10.1086/266687

Katz E, Lazarsfeld PF (1957) Personal influence. Free Press, New York

Kendall L (2002) Hanging out in the virtual pub: masculinities and relationships online. University of California Press, Berkeley

Kidane YH, Gloor PA (2007) Correlating temporal communication patterns of the Eclipse open source community with performance and creativity. Comput Math Organ Theory 13:17–27. doi:10.1007/s10588-006-9006-3

Lakatos PL (2006) Recent trends in the epidemiology of inflammatory bowel diseases: up or down? World J Gastroenterol 12:6102–6108

Lashner BA, Loftus EV (2006) True or false? The hygiene hypothesis for Crohn's disease. Am J Gastroenterol 101:1003–1004. doi:10.1111/j.1572-0241.2006.00563.x

Lazarsfeld PF, Merton RK (1954) Friendship as a social process: a substantive and methodological analysis. Free Control Mod Soc 18:18–66

Lazer D, Pentland A, Adamic L, Aral S, Barabási A-L, Brewer D, Christakis N, Contractor N, Fowler J, Gutmann M, Jebara T, King G, Macy M, Roy D, van Alstyne M (2009) Computational social science. Science 323:721–723. doi:10.1126/science.1167742

Loftus EV (2004) Clinical epidemiology of inflammatory bowel disease: incidence, prevalence, and environmental influences. Gastroenterology 126:1504–1517. doi:10.1053/j.gastro.2004.01.063

Loftus EV (2007) The burden of inflammatory bowel disease in the United States: a moving target? Clin Gastroenterol Hepatol 5:1383–1384. doi:10.1016/j.cgh.2007.10.016

Longobardi T, Jacobs P, Bernstein CN (2003) Work losses related to inflammatory bowel disease in the United States: results from the National Health Interview Survey. Am J Gastroenterol 98:1064–1072. doi:10.1111/j.1572-0241.2003.07285.x

Lyytinen K, Damsgaard J (2001) What's wrong with the diffusion of innovation theory? The case of a complex and networked technology. Reports Aalborg University Department of Computer Science R985010 187:1–20

Malone TW, Laubacher R, Dellarocas C (2009) Harnessing crowds : mapping the genome of collective intelligence. Elements 1:1–20. doi:10.2139/ssrn.1381502

McLeod RS, Churchill DN, Lock AM, Vanderburgh S, Cohen Z (1991) Quality of life of patients with ulcerative colitis preoperatively and postoperatively. Gastroenterology 101:1307–1313

McPherson M, Smith-Lovin L, Cook JM (2001) Birds of a feather: homophily in social networks. Annu Rev Sociol 27:415–444. doi:10.1146/annurev.soc.27.1.415

Metcalfe B (1995) Metcalfe's law: a network becomes more valuable as it reaches more users. InfoWorld 17:53–54

Midgley DF, Dowling GR (1993) A longitudinal study of product form innovation: the interaction between predispositions and social messages. J Consum Res 19:611. doi:10.1086/209326

Park KT, Bass D (2011) Inflammatory bowel disease-attributable costs and cost-effective strategies in the United States: a review. Inflamm Bowel Dis 17:1603–1609. doi:10.1002/ibd.21488

Pentland A (2014) Social physics: how good ideas spread. Penguin Press, New York

Portier K, Greer GE, Rokach L, Ofek N, Wang Y, Biyani P, Yu M, Banerjee S, Zhao K, Mitra P, Yen J (2013) Understanding topics and sentiment in an online cancer survivor community. J Natl Cancer Inst Monogr 2013:195–198. doi:10.1093/jncimonographs/lgt025

Probert CS, Brown M (2008) Are there any ethnic groups that are more likely to develop IBD? Inflamm Bowel Dis 14(Suppl 2):S24–S25. doi:10.1002/ibd.20601

Reddy A, Fried B (2009) An update on the use of helminths to treat Crohn's and other autoimmunune diseases. Parasitol Res 104:217–221. doi:10.1007/s00436-008-1297-5

Retelny D, Robaszkiewicz S, To A, Lasecki W, Patel J, Rahmati N, Doshi T, Valentine M, Bernstein MS (2014) Expert crowdsourcing with flash teams. In: Proceedings of the 27th annual ACM symposium on User interface software and technology, ACM, 2014. doi:10.1145/2642918.2647409

Rheingold H (1993) The virtual community: homesteading on the electronic frontier. Addison-Wesley, Reading

Rogers EM (2003[1962]) Diffusion of innovations, 5th edn. Free Press, New York

Ruyssers NE, De Winter BY, De Man JG, Loukas A, Herman AG, Pelckmans PA, Moreels TG (2008) Worms and the treatment of inflammatory bowel disease: are molecules the answer? Clin Dev Immunol 2008:1–7. doi:10.1155/2008/567314

Ruyssers NE, De Winter BY, De Man JG, Ruyssers ND, Van Gils AJ, Loukas A, Pearson MS, Weinstock JV, Pelckmans PA, Moreels TG (2010) Schistosoma mansoni proteins attenuate gastrointestinal motility disturbances during experimental colitis in mice. World J Gastroenterol 16:703–712. doi:10.3748/wjg.v16.i6.703

Ryan B, Gross NC (1943) The diffusion of hybrid seed corn in two Iowa communities. Rural Sociol 8:15–24

Sajadinejad MS, Asgari K, Molavi H, Kalantari M, Adibi P (2012) Psychological issues in inflammatory bowel disease: an overview. Gastroenterol Res Pract 2012. doi:10.1155/2012/106502

Sonnenberg A (2009) Demographic characteristics of hospitalized IBD patients. Dig Dis Sci 54:2449–2455. doi:10.1007/s10620-009-0973-3

Strachan DP (2000) Family size, infection and atopy: the first decade of the "hygiene hypothesis". Thorax 55(Suppl 1):S2–S10. doi:10.1136/thorax.55.suppl_1.S2

Summers RW, Elliott DE, Qadir K, Urban JF, Thompson R, Weinstock JV (2003) Trichuris suis seems to be safe and possibly effective in the treatment of inflammatory bowel disease. Am J Gastroenterol 98:2034–2041. doi:10.1111/j.1572-0241.2003.07660.x

Summers RW, Elliott DE, Urban JF, Thompson R, Weinstock JV (2005) Trichuris suis therapy in Crohn's disease. Gut 54:87–90. doi:10.1136/gut.2004.041749

Thukkani N, Williams JL, Sonnenberg A (2011) Epidemiologic characteristics of patients with inflammatory bowel disease undergoing colonoscopy. Inflamm Bowel Dis 17:1333–1337. doi:10.1002/ibd.21513

Trivedi I, Keefer L (2015) The emerging adult with inflammatory bowel disease: challenges and recommendations for the adult gastroenterologist. Gastroenterol Res Pract. doi:10.1155/2015/260807

Valente T (2010) Social networks and health: models, methods, and applications. Oxford University Press, New York

Van Assche G, Dignass A, Panes J, Beaugerie L, Karagiannis J, Allez M, Ochsenkühn T, Orchard T, Rogler G, Louis E, Kupcinskas L, Mantzaris G, Travis S, Stange E (2010) The second European evidence-based consensus on the diagnosis and management of Crohn's disease: definitions and diagnosis. J Crohns Colitis 4:7–27. doi:10.1016/j.crohns.2009.12.003

Velasquez-Manoff M (2008) The worm turns. New York Times, June 29 2008. http://www.nytimes.com/2008/06/29/magazine/29wwln-essay-t.html. Accessed 20 Nov 2014

Venu N, Cohen RD (2011) The new economic reality in the world of IBD. In: Cohen RD (ed) Inflammatory bowel disease: diagnosis and therapeutics. Springer, New York. doi:10.1007/978-1-60327-433-3_19

Von Hippel E (1986) Lead users: a source of novel product concepts. Manag Sci 32(7):791–805

Von Hippel E (1994) "Sticky information" and the locus of problem solving: implications for innovation. Manag Sci 40:429–439. doi:10.1287/mnsc.40.4.429

Wagner EH (2001) Meeting the needs of chronically ill people. Br Med J 323:945–946. doi:10.1136/bmj.323.7319.945

Wasserman S, Faust K (1994) Social network analysis: methods and applications. Cambridge University Press, Cambridge

Weinstock JV, Elliott DE (2013) Translatability of helminth therapy in inflammatory bowel diseases. Int J Parasitol 43:245–251. doi:10.1016/j.ijpara.2012.10.016

Weinstock JV, Summers RW, Elliott DE, Qadir K, Urban JF, Thompson R (2002) The possible link between de-worming and the emergence of immunological disease. J Lab Clin Med 139:334–338. doi:10.1067/mlc.2002.124343

Weinstock JV, Summers RW, Elliott DE (2005) Role of helminths in regulating mucosal inflammation. Springer Semin Immunopathol 27:249–271. doi:10.1007/s00281-005-0209-3

Wellman B (1988) Structural analysis: from method and metaphor to theory and substance. In: Wellman B, Berkowitz SD (eds) Social structures: a network approach. Cambridge University Press, Cambridge

Wellman B (1992) Which ties provide what kinds of support? Adv Group Process 9:207–235

Wellman B (2012) Is Dunbar's number up? Br J Psychol 103:174–176. doi:10.1111/j.2044-8295.2011.02075.x

Wicks P, Massagli M, Frost J, Brownstein C, Okun S, Vaughan T, Bradley R, Heywood J (2010) Sharing health data for better outcomes on PatientsLikeMe. J Med Internet Res. doi:10.2196/jmir.1549

Wicks P, Vaughan TE, Massagli MP, Heywood J (2011) Accelerated clinical discovery using self-reported patient data collected online and a patient-matching algorithm. Nat Biotechnol 29:411–414. doi:10.1038/nbt.1837

Xavier RJ, Podolsky DK (2007) Unravelling the pathogenesis of inflammatory bowel disease. Nature 448:427–434. doi:10.1038/nature06005

Yu AP, Cabanilla LA, Wu EQ, Mulani PM, Chao J (2008) The costs of Crohn's disease in the United States and other Western countries: a systematic review. Curr Med Res Opin 24:319–328. doi:10.1185/030079908X260790

Jermain Kaminski is a technology developer and data scientist. He believes that network visualizations are a window to the soul of an organization. His work is focused on computational social science and graph technology with applications in areas such as Bitcoin, crowdfunding, movies, patient communities, soccer and startup teams. In 2011, Jermain was part of the founding team at the MIT Center for Collective Intelligence that started the YouMeIBD project.

Jermain Kaminski is a recent visiting Ph.D. researcher at MIT Media Lab's Macro Connections Group and member of RWTH Aachen's Technology Entrepreneurship Group. He studied economics at Witten-Herdecke University and the Massachusetts Institute of Technology, followed by startup experiences in Cambridge and San Francisco. Jermain is a co-founder of Moviegalaxies, a website visualizing character interaction networks in movies. He was an invited speaker at conferences such as Stanford Medicine X, TEDMed, Collective Intelligence, Falling Walls and re: publica. Jermaine Kaminski is a Fellow of the Royal Society of Arts.

Patients' Complaints and Managers' Responses as a Process of Institutional Interaction

Susanna Palomäki and Anni Vanhala

Abstract

This article is based on a study conducted in a Finnish hospital and the patients' objections handled and managed inside the hospital. The aim of our study is to describe the nature of the objection process as an institutional interaction and give an outlook for the handling of dissatisfaction in the future. The data used consists of 229 objection documents and 93 replies to a survey directed at customers making objections. The method used is thematic content analysis. A written objection passing to the managerial level distances the actual event and the party involved from each other and prevents the immediate handling of issues. The administrative process does not distract the hospital staff from their actual work and ensures that customer data is transmitted directly to management level. In our study patients and relatives were willing to engage in more debate than the hospital staff could accommodate. Communication is not a guarantee that the information will be utilized in services, unless the value of the source of information is recognized. A change in the interaction framework from a "patient challenges and hospital defends" process to joint analysis by the parties involved requires a change in attitudes. Making the role of the customer more active and appreciating his or her contribution in a boundaryless hospital produces a more equitable relationship and partnership.

Keywords

Complaint • Response • Objection process • Institutional interaction • Customer relationship • Complaint management • Stakeholder management • Finland

S. Palomäki (✉)
University of Tampere, Tampere 33014, Finland
e-mail: palomaki.m.susanna@student.uta.fi

A. Vanhala
Tampere University Hospital, Tampere, PO Box 2000 33521, Finland
e-mail: anni.vanhala@pshp.fi

H. Albach et al. (eds.), *Boundaryless Hospital*, DOI 10.1007/978-3-662-49012-9_18

1 Introduction

The requirements of customer-oriented objectives and evidence-based practices are part of the control and management of health care functions. Providing information to the customer and increasing the customer's possibilities for choice and inclusion provide opportunities for a more balanced interaction between the professional and the customer. The goal is a well-informed customer who makes choices together with the health care provider. Thus, the responsibility for making choices can be shared between the customer and the professional (Härter et al. 2011; Scholl et al. 2011; Beresford and Carr 2012; Juhila et al. 2014). The flow of information, and communication, may reveal problems in customer-oriented health care services (Wofford et al. 2004; European Commission 2012; Paterson 2013). Communication is not a guarantee that the information will be utilized in services, unless the value of the source of information is recognized. Kaseva (2011), in a literature review on social and health development, found that customer influence was inadequate.

Our article is based on research conducted at a Finnish university hospital. The data used consists of objection documents and replies to a survey directed at customers making objections. A customer who is dissatisfied with his or her care or handling can raise an objection based on the Act on the Status and Rights of Patients (1992/785). Generally, an objection concerns unfortunate comments made during contacts, a lack of consideration or knowledge, or treatment-related misunderstandings. The health care official responsible for objections is not an independent party in the issue brought up by the customer. At best, an objection may provide a fast and flexible opportunity to get things fixed (Pajukoski 2010).

In our study, we are interested in the causes of objections, the responses to objections, and in the customer feedback on the effectiveness of the objection process. We ask what significance the making of an objection has to the customer and the health care system, and what effects it has on the customer relationship. Finally, we consider how active customer involvement, and the abandonment of interaction based on authority relationships, will affect the handling of dissatisfaction in the future, in the boundaryless hospital.

2 The Active Citizen in Health Care

An objection is one of the procedures prescribed for the implementation of citizen's legal rights. The most important rights of the patient can be divided under four heads: the right to good health and medical care, and good patient handling; access to care; the right to access personal information; and the right to self-determination (Valvira 2012). Patients who are dissatisfied with their care and handling can complain to the director responsible for health care in the health care unit (Act on the Status and Rights of Patients 1992/785). The director must respond to the objection within a reasonable time. No appeal can be lodged against the response. However, making an objection does not limit the customer's right of appeal or ability to take his/her complaint to the regional state administrative agencies, the administrative court, or to Finland's National Supervisory Authority for Welfare and Health (Valvira), the Parliamentary Ombudsman or the Data Protection Supervisor. An objection differs from these in that it is handled internally by the organization.

The patient has the right to ask questions, get clarification, and express his or her views, and must be consulted (Etene 2011). Demonstration of dissatisfaction with services relates to discussion on the implementation of the rights of citizens (Valokivi 2008; Hirschman 1970). The Act on the Status and Rights of Patients came into force in 1993. The law was scheduled to enter into force during the reforms following the recession of the 1990s, when the viewpoint was increasingly economic and the aim was cost control. Instead of protecting social and health care services, the emphasis was typically placed upon service-related procedural rights (Julkunen 2006). The Act on the Status and Rights of Patients does not provide direct entitlement to treatment, but rather the availability of services is affected, e.g., by personnel and finance, as well as views on the effectiveness of treatment. The Act on the Status and Rights of Patients is considered goal-oriented and pro-active in nature; it seeks to strengthen the patient's right to self-determination and offers citizens the legal grounds on which to demand the health care services they need (Mattila 2011; Kotkas 2009).

In addition to health care legislation, expansion of health markets is intended to promote the position of the health care customer. Increased freedom of choice in care facilities is expected to strengthen customer-oriented services. Freedom of choice may be illusory in relation to the accessibility of services and the financial resources of customers (Mattila 2011). Emphasis on the perspective of the service consumer may raise the threshold for customers to express criticism and discontent. However, from a competitive viewpoint expressions of discontent and provision of feedback should be viewed positively in health care markets. When correctly handled, demonstrations of discontent support the mission of the organization. Customer feedback can be used to correct and improve services, support staff morale and commitment, and strengthen the trust of customers in the service provider (Cook 2012).

Confidence in health care can be considered significant, because citizens' trust in public institutions promotes generalized trust between strangers. Such confidence affects the ability of society to function, since generalized trust has been shown to increase psychological well-being, and strengthen the functionality of democracy and even economic activity. The views of citizens on the reliability of institutions are largely based on their views on the activities of their representatives. The individual's experience of the fairness and reliability of people in positions of responsibility affects their trust in other citizens. The practices of public institutions act as a benchmark when assessing the acceptability and fairness of various functions in society (Kouvo 2014; Rothstein and Stolle 2007; Uslaner 2002). A well-ordered objection process can strengthen the trust of customers not only in health care but in other services provided by their society.

3 Research Subject

Little research on health care objections has been published in Finland (Vanhala and Palomäki 2015). Instead, research on appeals and claims has been done, particularly in the fields of medical and health sciences (Kuosmanen et al. 2008) and law (Ellilä 2007). Internationally, complaints related to health care seem to be a phenomenon of multidisciplinary interest. They have been studied especially in health administration, and in the medical, health, nursing, and legal sciences; some research has also been conducted in the social sciences. A closely related phenomenon in the field of patient safety is complaints and their connection to malpractice risks and adverse events (Järvelin et al. 2012; Pichert et al. 2008; Hickson et al. 2007; Bismark et al. 2006). The relations of complaints to gender and age have been studied (Allen et al. 2006; Pukk et al. 2003), as well as the causes of complaints (Wofford et al. 2004), and their processing nature (Hsieh 2012) and significance (Paterson 2013). Complaints are also one of the instruments used to measure the quality of health care (Debono and Travaglia 2009).

Familiarization with the knowledge and experience of people who have suffered during medical care or been disappointed by a customer visit is required in order to improve both medical and social processes (Ocloo 2010). Our research deals with the objection process as a social phenomenon. We examine objection procedures in terms of interaction between the citizen and the authority. The interaction between the official and the customer is goal-oriented and asymmetrical, and participation in the interaction is regulated by structures for action (Mäkitalo 2005; Thornborrow 2002; Drew and Heritage 1992). Legislation and the institution of health care management make objection a process of administrative bureaucracy. Bureaucracy is associated with the processing of individuals and with a routine way of conceptualizing customers' life situations and of making decisions (Mäkitalo 2002; Lipsky 1980; Prottas 1979). Criticism of bureaucracy often focuses on its "assembly-line" processing, in which people are never regarded as individuals and the language of authority does not reach the citizen (Palomäki 2012).

4 Data and Methods

In most cases, the objection process begins with the patient filling out a hospital form designed for this purpose. Also some e-mail messages, letters from patients and relatives, and messages from the customer feedback system end up in objection processing. The persons responsible for the process and for preparing responses are area managers. The written response often includes "sub responses", from which the full response to the maker of the objection is created. In addition to managers, those directly affected by the objection, e.g., the attending doctor or nurse usually participates in providing a response. Objections are usually not filed into the patient record. This aims at keeping the patient's treatment and related dissatisfaction separate from each other.

The hospital we studied responded to 307 objections in 2012. A total of 900 responses were made to complaints, claims, notices and requests for clarification. In relation to days of treatment and number of outpatient visits, the number of objections was small, at one objection for rather less than 3000 treatment days and outpatient visits. It is worthwhile to become familiar with objections, since matters repeated in these may be more broadly applicable to the situations that people encounter in health care. As a research topic, objection is a sensitive matter from the viewpoint of the customer, employee and organization alike, since it deals with events relating to failure in customer relationships. We hope that our research will stimulate discussion of the status and rights of the health care customer, from individual cases to a more general level, in order to develop the service system.

Before research began, the research project received the assent of the hospital's Ethics Committee and a research permit from the respective organization. We concentrated the choice of data on objections and the responses returned. In addition to documents, the data included replies to a survey directed at customers making objections. The data selection process is described in Fig. 1.

The documents are stored separately from patient records by the administration of the hospitals' different departments. Replies to questionnaires are stored in the hospital and are available only to the researchers of this project. We studied the materials, collected data, and made observations for analysis on those premises. The anonymity of persons appearing in the research data was secured. The empirical data is reliable from the viewpoint of the studied phenomenon; the questionnaire answers are from people making objections and the documents are produced by

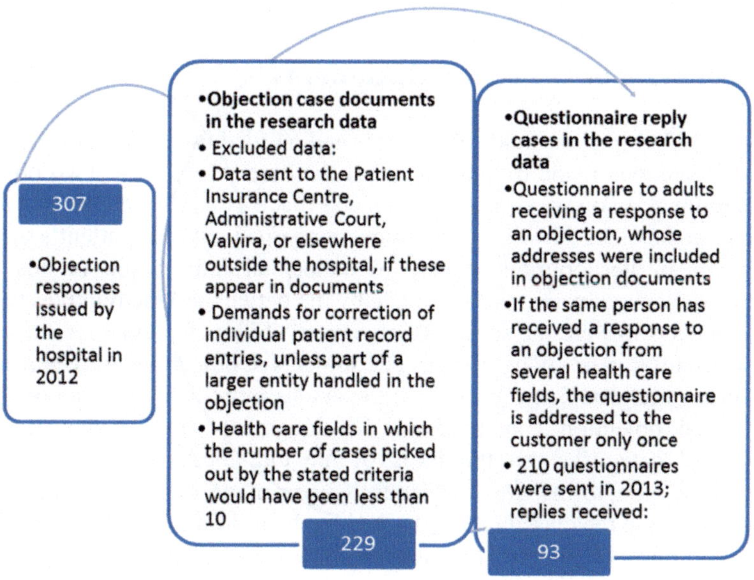

Fig. 1 Formation of the research data

patients, relatives, and loved ones, as well as by hospital staff and administrative management. If the documents revealed a claim, complaint or other issue outside the hospital, in addition to the objection, we did not include it, nor did we send a questionnaire, since we intended to focus the research on the hospitals' internal processes. The exclusion criterion was not exhaustive, since we could not know for certain about the flow of external processes. Nine such issues, not recorded in the hospital objection documents, were pending.

Sampling produced more than 2/3 of the objection data for the entire year. The response rate for the survey was 44.3 %. We discovered that we had gathered a wide range of issues for objection, from serious irreversible events to transient or correctable matters. Having examined the material, we found that it included common, recurring themes and features, in relation to the studied phenomenon, but also some exceptions. We analyzed the data by categorization using qualitative content analysis. Content analysis is a broad theoretical framework for producing answers to specific research questions. Marked items are collected together while classes, themes and types are identified from the material (Tuomi and Sarajärvi 2011; Cavanagh 1997; Weber 1990). Data collection involved creating concise summaries and interpretations, since the material included more than a 1000 pages of documents and 93 answers to five-page questionnaires. We describe the content of the material both numerically and verbally. We are looking for answers to questions concerning the makers and content of objections, as well as the providers and content of responses to objections. We also surveyed the views of people making objections on the objection process and on the effect that the subject and process of the objection had on the customer relationship. On this basis, we interpreted the significance of objections to the customer and to health care players.

5 Analysis of Objection Documents

There were 167 objections made by patients and 64 filed by relatives or loved ones, including objections made by parents about the care of children. Two objections were exceptional: In one case the objection was made by a representative of another institution; in the other the objection was not concerned with the patient's own care, but with his or her opinion of care in a hospital unit, based on his or her observations. A few objections were made by the patient and the relatives together. Of the patients who were the subject of objections, 132 were women, 69 were men, and 28 were children or young people. The subjects of objections were spread quite evenly across age groups, from toddlers to persons more than 90 years of age.

We sorted objection content from the documents into organization-based pre-structured categories on the basis of the classification used on hospital-produced objection forms. Most objections were made on these forms, and we selected from these the classification marked by the person making the objection. A small proportion of objections were statements sent by e-mail, texts collected from the hospital's customer feedback system, or statements made without the use of forms or the questions guiding their use. In these cases, we made an interpretive decision as researchers on the category to which the objection should belong on the basis of its content.

Two hundred and twenty six cases were included in the analysis of responses given to objections. In three cases, the response had been handled through negotiation or by telephone, and these were not included in the study. The average case processing time, i.e., the time after which a response was sent to the person making the objection, was 30 days (Patient ombudsman's report 2012, unpublished). Preparation of a written response involved three people on average per objection. The responses included "sub responses", from which the full response to the maker of the objection was created. The number of people involved in producing a response varied by field, with the greatest number involved in children's and women's diseases (3.7 persons per response) and fewest in psychiatry (2 persons per response).

With few exceptions, responses followed a single formula: The response was provided by the principal director in the hierarchy of the health care field and the manager immediately following in the division of responsibilities. Both provided responses based on their official position, seldom as parties involved in the content of the objection, such as attending physicians. In addition to managers, those directly concerned in the objection, i.e., persons involved in encounters between relatives and nurses, took part in preparing responses. Most responses were provided by doctors. Other occupational categories of responders (63 cases) were nurse, nursing sister, senior nurse, speech therapist, orderly, ward clerk, social worker or physiotherapist. Table 1 describes the content of objections and Table 2 the content of responses.

5.1 Subject of Objections

Objections concerned with treatment and procedure dealt with inadequate and incorrect diagnosis or treatment, harm caused by treatment, delays and refusal of treatment, lack of self-determination or comprehensiveness, being "bounced around" from place to place, and uncertainty in treatment, planning, or continuity. Content concerning conduct and patient handling covered unfriendliness of staff, depreciation and "bypassing" of patients and relatives, failure to listen,

Table 1 Subject of objections (n = 229)

Content of objections	Number of objections
Treatment and procedures	190
Patient handling and conduct	116
Access to information	62
Prescription of medications	29
Certificates and statements	18
Confidentiality	9
Other (informal description of the subject of the objection)	19

indifference, rudeness or aggression towards the patient or a relative, and questioning the patient's experience, need, or pain. Content under the heading of lack of information included provision of inadequate or incorrect information to the patient or a relative, conflicting information, such as differing expert opinions on lines of treatment, or confusion, such as the wrong patient record being used at reception or sent to a patient's home. Other subject matter included prescriptions, certificates and statements as well as confidentiality. Medication was questioned and errors in the administration of drugs reported. There were delays in delivery of certificates and statements, and errors in their content. Violations of staff confidentiality were also reported and the hospital's practice of discussing patient information in the hearing of other patients was also considered a problem.

Table 2 Subject of responses (n = 226)

Content of responses	Number of responses
Medical information and report	198
Regret	176
Questioning	133
Promise	92
Admission	74
Apology	63
Medical information and patient record + Questioning + regret	91
Medical information and patient record + Acknowledgement + regret and apology	58

The heading "Other" contained customers' informal descriptions of the subject of objections. Their content covered delayed or denied admission to treatment, difficulties in obtaining a referral, patient fees, appointment booking ambiguities, ambiguity in obtaining commitment to pay or proposal that it will be awarded, disappearance of the patient's property during treatment, deficiencies in the storage of patient records, difficulty in obtaining the text of medical records, and the questioning attitude of hospital staff towards personnel at other care facilities.

Most objections were related to treatment and procedure, patient handling or conduct, and access to information. Treatment and procedure was often used as a kind of umbrella term, formed from a variety of content. Treatment and procedure occurred in conjunction with conduct and patient handling in 103 objections, and access to information in 48 objections. The above-mentioned three items, treatment and procedure, conduct and patient handling, and access to information, appeared together in 30 objections.

5.2 Subject of Responses

The majority of responses contained treatment-related medical information, such as excerpts from patient records, laboratory values, or information on medication. The responses highlighted entries in the patient's medical record on the basis of which they attempted to clarify the course of events, e.g., during treatment on a ward. Typically, they contain regrets, especially about the experience of the patient or relative.

Objections relating to conduct and patient handling seemed also to receive responses that questioned or denied the bad conduct or patient handling, or gave a neutral account. For example, in situations where the patient complained about the bad conduct of a doctor or nurse, the employee, responding to the patient via the director, usually denied having behaved inappropriately or treated the patient badly. In the response sent to the patient, the director took a neutral position on the matter, but regretted the experience of the patient or relative. The responses did not include descriptions of the patients' or relatives' bad conduct and inappropriate treatment of hospital staff. An apology occurred in less than one third of responses. Apologies were frequently given for error, wrongful actions, injury, or things said or done. An apology was often veiled by denial or doubt of the event portrayed in the objection, for instance by using such formulae as: "if I behaved offensively, I apologize." In some situations, a supervisor apologized for the actions of subordinates.

Most responses questioned the doubts and accusations presented in the objection and showed the doubt to be unfounded, and the actions of the hospital and its staff to be correct or in line with accepted practice and orthodox treatment. Affirmatively, paraphrasing the content of the objection, 74 responses found that it was appropriate, at least to some extent, to draw attention to the charge, complaint, or fault. Less than 20 responses can be described as neutral. These included reports that were difficult to interpret as either affirmative or negative in relation to the content of the objection. The usual way to respond to an objection was to question the content of the objection by presenting medical criteria and documented events while, at the same time, regretting the unpleasant experience caused by an action to the patient or relative.

5.3 The Tension Caused by the Objection Process

The written objection process involves interaction between customer and professional in which the maker of the objection, arguing on the basis of lay knowledge and experience, could question expert knowledge and behaviour but only rarely overturn or challenge it. The interaction operated in two directions but was in both directions non-recurring and by nature an exchange of different kinds of information; objections highlighted knowledge from experience, while responses highlighted medical and documented information. Handling of objection content related to the conduct of staff could be skipped over in responses, when the objection involved a number of different causes of discontent. The asymmetry of interaction between the parties appears from the fact that while the objector might submit allegations concerning staff, the staff did not make corresponding allegations concerning patients or relatives. In responses, the veracity of reports by the patient or relative was questioned, but reports of staff, and the patient record, were not subject to doubt.

The relationship between customer and professional can rarely represent an equal partnership. The parties are subject to a different logic of responsibilities, obligations, rights and penalties (Duyvendak et al. 2009). The objection process implies tension between the disappointed person making the objection and the explaining and defending responder. Authorized explanation relates to the roles of experts in various fields. For example, the physician must try to clarify the cause of a disease or decrease in capacity before undertaking its treatment. Correspondingly, the ability of the expert to diagnose and treat problems is included in the rights of the patient. An expert responding to an objection might use his or her own position of authority to bypass the patient's or relative's experience of the situation (Juhila 2012; Palomäki 2012).

6 Analysis of Questionnaires

The questionnaire was partly structured, with space left for informal answers in addition to given choices. The questions on the questionnaire concentrated on information about the objector, its subject and content, the process of raising an objection and producing a response, views on the benefit and impact of the process, and proposals for development. The response rate for the survey was 44.3 % ($n = 93/210$). The majority of questionnaire respondents were female ($n = 68$), and nearly half ($n = 42$) were born in the 1950s and 1960s. In terms of socio-economic background, 51 of the respondents were employed, 36 were outside the labour market (retired, unemployed, etc.), and two were students. Objections were mostly concerned with the patients' own care ($n = 70$), but also ($n = 23$) with the care of a relative, such as a child, spouse or parent. We compiled the survey results in Table 3. Multiple choice answers were accepted. The text in italics consists of direct data extracts from the questionnaires.

6.1 Objection

In answer to the structured reply options, survey respondents most often chose as the reason for their dissatisfaction a failure to listen and to demonstrate compassion, caring and respect. Deficiencies were also identified in professional skills and special know-how, in giving reasons for examinations and treatment procedures, and in sharing a common language and understanding. Dissatisfaction applied broadly to different issues; less than half of the responses covered one or two issues while more than half contained three to seven.

All of the survey respondents had written an informal description of the reason for their objection or the events leading to it. We divided free-form replies on the basis of their content into admission to treatment, access to information, disagreement on treatment or line of treatment, conduct and patient handling, and malpractice. If a single free-form reply referred to more than one subject of objection, we interpreted the answers in such a way that an answer was included in only one of the

Table 3 Answers to the questionnaires (n = 93 answered forms)

Objection subject	Number of responses
Did not listen/believe	59
Compassion, caring	47
Respect	44
Professional skill, competence	38
Justifying examinations/treatments	27
Common language (did not understand what the caregiver said)	9
Free-form replies	
Conduct and patient handling	28
Malpractice	26
Disagreement on treatment/line of treatment	18
Access to information	12
Access to treatment	12
Objection functionality	
Objection led to the expected result	20
Objection did not lead to the expected result	54
Objection led partly to the expected result	8
The response met expectations	23
The response did not meet expectations	54
The response partly met expectations	12
The objection is a very successful practice	36
The objection is not a very successful practice	57
Objection effects	
Positively affected received care/handling	11
Negatively affected received care/handling	12
Did not affect received care/handling	57
Negatively affected own attitude towards hospital/staff	61
Positively affected own attitude towards hospital/staff	1
Did not affect own attitude towards hospital/staff	25

content categories, according to the type of content with which the answer was most concerned. We mostly found content concerned with conduct and patient handling:

> When the patient tries to answer, the doctor interrupts after the second word. The doctor belittles the patient's pain. The patient is not allowed to express a personal opinion (26).

On malpractice and disputes over treatment/line of treatment the following appeared:

> I believe this unfortunate chain of events could have been avoided if a routine [name of procedure] had been done with sufficient care (16).

Survey respondents described difficulties concerning access to information:

> I phoned a month later, and they gave me no information. The information was there for a long time; the patient was left to fret and wait for a response (8).

Difficulties concerning access to treatment were often mentioned:

> No longer accepted there for treatment, even though the symptoms have increased (30).

The severity of the subjects of objection ranged from mental discomfort caused by unkind comments from nursing staff up to fatal malpractice or suspicion of such.

6.2 Objection Functionality

Answers are based on both structured and open questions. The majority of respondents felt that the objection did not lead to the desired result, the written response from the hospital did not meet expectations, and the objection process in its current form is not a very successful practice. One in ten of the free-form replies mentioned that the processing of objections should be given to a neutral party, preferably externally. One in five of the respondents thought that the objection led to the expected result, while one in four stated that the written response from the hospital met their expectations. There was satisfaction insofar as that the response from the hospital provided information and clarification about events, and the patient's illness and examinations:

> I got a more detailed explanation of my examination, showing [. . .], which I had not known, and which had not been explained to me (11).

Fulfilling expectations was often related to the objectivity and politeness of the answers. It was welcomed if a meeting was offered at the hospital to discuss the subject of the objection. It was considered appropriate that the matter should be discussed in the hospital work community and an attempt made to change and improve practices. People were also pleased when an error, ill-treatment, or undesirable course of events was admitted:

> They admitted that an incorrect assessment of the situation was made in the ward and said that in future they would consult with the on-call [specialist] (24).

An apology was considered relevant, but not exhaustive; regret is not enough, if the errors are not admitted and no attempt is made to remedy the situation. People who expressed dissatisfaction expected an admission of error or ill-treatment, a more personal conversation, and a meeting and apology or regret:

> A proper apology, regrets, a conversation with someone who would not only make excuses but really understand and do something to correct the issues (36).

Comments were made on the professional language in responses and familiarity with the objection caused disappointment:

> The response to feedback should be clear, so that people can understand it without studying medicine for 10 years (58).

> The response suggests that my objection was not even properly read (65).

The question of defending the actions of hospital staff and blaming the patient was also raised:

> I was mainly left with the feeling that the patient was at fault, but reading between the lines, though they defended their own actions and did not answer my questions, I believe that this experience was nonetheless considered, and hopefully it taught them something (43).

Many survey answers emphasized the promotion of general good care and patient handling through their own case:

> It was hoped that the situation would change for other patients in a similar position (74).

Several survey answers highlighted the bias and questionable collegiality of the hospital response; it was suspected that "old boy" relations with colleagues weighed more than the grievance raised by the customer or its correction.

6.3 Objection Effects

More than half of the survey respondents were of the opinion that the objection had no effect on future care and patient handling. However, the objection process, and the events that led up to it, had some impact on how the patient or relative was afterwards treated in the hospital. One positive effect noted was the more friendly and courteous conduct of staff. Also considered important were availability of care and changes in the care facility:

> I moved to another care unit where the doctor listened to me and designed my medication accordingly. The medication has greatly improved my general condition (33).

A negative feature reported was that the intended treatment or examination was not received after the objection, or that the treatment did not continue. The attitude of staff was thought to have changed, for example becoming disparaging; there was also a situation in which a patient had to agree to refrain from any further complaints about the staff's behaviour before their medical treatment could continue. There were also stories of teasing and deliberate delay: medical staff failing to arrive for agreed meetings, pain medication delayed, or a necessary statement not written.

The objection subject, and the objection process, had more effect on the person's own attitude than on the attitude of the hospital staff. Only one respondent found that the experience had a positive effect on his or her own attitude. Some respondents considered that there was no effect, and most thought that their personal attitude towards the hospital and its staff had become more negative. Many described a fear of the hospital and believed that the situation could lead to them avoiding treatment:

> I fear and hate landing in hospital, for myself or others (56).
>
> I won't go to that doctor at the outpatient clinic; if there is no other option, I'll do without treatment (62).

People making objections described their attitude as having become more observant. They will be more able in the future to demand help and to discover and question the treatment guidelines and actions of the hospital. Generally, trust has been damaged:

> I have serious reservations; it's a place where you can't be sure how people will treat you (18).
>
> It undermines your belief that this hospital provides the most skilled and highest level of care (7).

On the other hand, the standards demanded of care and patient handling have increased:

> In hospital reception, the expectation of clear patient information has increased, as well as the expectation of appropriate handling of patients (50).

The objection process has raised expectations about the staff's ability to communicate.

6.4 Developing the Objection Process

We looked at the open questions for ideas with which to develop the objection process. One fifth of respondents thought the hospital's internal processing unreliable. In their view, handling of the objection process should be given to a neutral party, preferably outside the hospital. Most respondents thought that a better substitute for the written objection procedure would be a discussion handled by a third party:

> I said in my objection that I hoped for a personal discussion about my situation, but that didn't happen (53).
>
> Discussion would give more to the patient and to the hospital (70).

Provision of direct feedback for all hospital visits was also highlighted as a replacement for the objection. It was proposed that a discussion should be held after a period on the ward, prior to leaving the hospital, in which opinions would be sought on the care provided. However, busy staff and inadequate human resources were seen as a reason for not handling issues immediately.

6.5 Information, Care and Compensation

The tangible importance of the objection process to the customer lies in obtaining information and clarification about care and examinations. Grievances drawn to the attention of management, and the arguments and demands produced by the objector, fostered access to care and examinations. Coordinating the prioritization of resources and care, and the fair and equal handling of patients, are key health care issues (Lammintakanen 2005). Increased freedom of choice in care facilities can reduce emerging care needs and delays in responding to them, but not divergent views on the care required. The importance of interaction is enhanced in situations where no connection can be found between the medical findings and the customer's experience of pain or functional limitations (Palomäki 2012). With the help of the objection, the patient's situation was again and possibly more comprehensively, assessed.

Concretisation is more difficult with matters relating to compensation and the conciliation of issues at the emotional level than with information and care. The objection process involves the upkeeping of moral order (Jayyusi 1991; Raitakari and Juhila 2011) and the drawing of a distinction as to what is acceptable in health care services and what is not. The order can be broken, e.g., by a nurse or doctor being rude to a relative or indifferent to a patient's pain. Objections function as a correction or reinforcement of the moral order, e.g., when the hospital board rules on acceptable actions and conduct. The response may compensate and atone for what happened also when an error has occurred or damage was caused during treatment. Although the regrets and apologies in the hospital's responses were not always considered convincing by questionnaire respondents, they were often mentioned, which confirms their importance in the objection process.

7 Conclusions

A written objection passing through the executive and managerial level distances the actual event and the parties involved from each other. The written process also prevents the natural and immediate handling of issues in care units. On the other hand, the administrative process provides security to the hospital staff by giving them peace to work and ensuring that customer data is transmitted directly to management level. In our study, patients and relatives were willing to engage in more and broader debate than the time and capacity of hospital staff and those responding to objections could accommodate.

What seems to be problematic in objection practices is finding evidence of a given conduct or good patient handling. They are not based on what is called medical knowledge, in fact, proving it by entries in the patient record is only possible in exceptional cases. No doubt, the situation, time, place and the patient's illness all affect the expectations regarding staff conduct in terms of how holistic and empathetic, considerate and respectful it should be. Legislation is of little help when considering the boundaries of good patient handling, rather, this is a matter of professional ethics and is dealt with in the codes of conduct and guidelines for various professional groups. Judging by the objection, however, patients and family members seem to expect respect, empathy, and often also a comprehensive grasp of the patient's situation. If these are found to be deficient, the result may be a loss of trust and respect towards health care staff. In some cases, mistrust may be so universal that any attempt to provide good treatment by the health care practitioners will be interpreted as a failure. This could be seen in some of the objections, in which a sweeping dissatisfaction was expressed with treatment, access to information and conduct of staff. The challenge here is how to recognize the experiences of inappropriate and disrespectful conduct mentioned in the objections and how to take them into account in responses based on medical and documented information. Parallel to developing procedural and administrative processes, we should pay more attention to the content of objections and the ensuing responses, and make sure that the response deals with the issue presented by the customer.

In many of the survey answers, rather than self-interest, the objectors emphasized the possibility that someone else might avoid a similar situation and that the responsible care management entity would learn from what happened. Even difficult experiences did not unequivocally destroy confidence in the professionalism of the staff or the organization's goal of good services. Even in the midst of change, the Finnish health care system enjoys very broad public confidence (Klavus 2010). Questioning that confidence can be useful if rising demands from citizens lead to improvements in the quality of care and in maintaining a good level of health care.

Health care is a balancing act between a non-individual process and the coordination of the patient's individual physical, psychological and social needs (Koivuniemi et al. 2014). Technologically and procedurally, the performance might seem to head straight for the goal, but the customer may feel badly treated, unless his or her needs are taken into account comprehensively. The value of customer-oriented services is in danger of being forgotten while techniques and procedures are emphasized (Beresford 2014; Sennet 2003). Transition from production-oriented models that focus upon shortcomings to a human-centred approach involves a change in thinking for both customers and professionals.

A change in the interaction framework of objections from a "patient challenges and hospital defends" process to collective analysis by the parties involved requires a change in attitudes. Making the role of the customer more active creates a more equitable relation and partnership between the parties and may improve patient satisfaction and experience (Kennedy et al. 2014). Courage is needed also to question the customer's role in the events leading to objections. How might each of the parties have avoided the undesirable outcome? This kind of conversation requires trust between the parties. In addition, it requires both tact and discretion from health care staff with respect to what has occurred and to the customer's life situation. The customer's active participation in the treatment process requires a genuine appreciation for his or her contribution. Participation involves the assumption that the customer's actions have some effect on the service process (Julkunen and Heikkilä 2007; Thompson 2007), even when it does not always fully succeed.

The customers of the *boundaryless hospital* are not passive patients but players who have access to knowledge, experience and expertise. They participate via the Internet in managing health and care information relating to them and in monitoring the fulfilment of their customer-hospital relationship. They compare health care services with other services and their relationship with traditional authorities, such as medical experts, has changed from subordination to partnership. Information is available and options offered, and feedback on the customer relationship flows in both directions, from the customer to the caregiver and vice versa. Both customers and professionals are encouraged to bring up problems and engage in open discussion. Customers and professionals rely increasingly on each other in solving problems. A problem forum jointly selected by professionals and customers deals with expressions of dissatisfaction concerning solutions with which neither the hospital representative nor the customer is satisfied. The most recently handled customer feedbacks and solutions to customer relations problems, and their impact on hospital actions, can be read on the *boundaryless hospital* website. The value of customer-oriented services is especially stressed when techniques and procedures are the subject of development in the *boundaryless hospital*.

References

Act on the Status and Rights of Patients (1992/785) http://www.finlex.fi/fi/laki/ajantasa/1992/19920785. Accessed 20 July 2015, sect 10

Allen PD, Nelson WH, Gruman C et al (2006) Nursing home complaints: who's complaining and what's gender got to do with it? J Gerontol Soc Work 47:89–106. doi:10.1300/J083v4n01_07

Beresford P (2014) Personalisation: from solution to problem? In: Beresford P (ed) Personalisation. Policy Press, University of Bristol, Bristol, pp 1–26

Beresford P, Carr S (eds) (2012) Social care service users and user involvement. Jessica Kingsley Publisher, London

Bismark MM, Brennan TA, Paterson RJ et al (2006) Relationship between complaints and quality of care in New Zealand: a descriptive analysis of complainants and noncomplainants following adverse events. BMJ Qual Saf 15:17–22. doi:10.1136/qshc.2005.015743

Cavanagh S (1997) Content analysis: concepts, methods and applications. Nurse Res 4:5–16

Cook S (2012) Complaint management excellence. Creating customer loyalty through service recovery. Kogan Page, London, PA

Debono D, Travaglia J (2009) Complaints and patient satisfaction: a comprehensive review of the literature. Centre for Clinical Governance Research in Health, University of New South Wales, Sydney, NSW

Drew P, Heritage J (1992) Analyzing talk at work: an introduction. In: Drew P, Heritage J (eds) Talk at work. Interaction in institutional settings. Cambridge University Press, Cambridge, pp 3–65

Duyvendak JW, Hoijtink M, Tonkens E (2009) Post-patients perspectives: user-based logics and a never ending inequality between users and professionals. In: Otto H-U, Polutta A, Ziegler H (eds) Evidence-based practice: modernising the knowledge base of social work? Barbara Budrich Publishers, Leverkusen Opladen, pp 31–45

Ellilä K (2007) Terveyskantelun oikeusperusteet; kuntaterveyspalveluiden potilasoikeuksien toteutuminen (Public health-care claims during the years 1994–2007 in Finland). Pilot-kustannus, Helsinki

Etene (2011) Sosiaali- ja terveysalan eettinen perusta. ETENE-julkaisuja 32. Valtakunnallinen sosiaali- ja terveysalan eettinen neuvottelukunta ETENE. (Ethical grounds for the social and health care field. ETENE-publications 32. The National Advisory Board on Social Welfare and Health Care Ethics ETENE.) Sosiaali- ja terveysministeriö, Helsinki

European Commission (2012) Patient involvement Eurobarometer Qualitative Study. Aggregate Report. http://ec.europa.eu/health/healthcare/docs/eurobaro_patient_involvement_2012_en.pdf- Accessed 14 July 2015, p 13

Hickson GB, Federspiel CF, Blackford J et al (2007) Patient complaints and malpractice risk in a regional healthcare center. South Med J 100(8):791–796. doi:10.1097/SMJ.0b013e318063bd75

Hirschman AO (1970) Exit, voice, and loyalty. Responses to decline in firms, organizations, and states. Harvard University Press, Cambridge, London

Hsieh YS (2012) An explanatory study of complaints handling and nature. Int J Nurs Pract 18:471–480. doi:10.1111/j.1440-172X.2012.02057.x

Härter M, Elwyn G, van der Weijden T (2011) Policy and practice developments in the implementation of shared decision-making: an international perspective. Z Evid Fortbild Qual Gesundh wesen 105:229–233. doi:10.1016/j.zefq.2011.04.018

Järvelin J, Häkkinen U, Rosenqvist G et al (2012) Factors predisposing to claims and compensations for patient injuries following total hip and knee arthroplasty. Acta Orthop 83 (2):190–196. doi:10.3109/17453674.2012.672089

Jayyusi L (1991) Values and moral judgment: communicative praxis as a moral order. In: Button G (ed) Ethnomethodology and the human sciences. Cambridge University Press, Cambridge, pp 227–251

Juhila K (2012) Ongelmat, niiden selittäminen ja kategoriat (Problem explanations and categories). In: Jokinen A, Juhila K, Suoninen E (eds) Kategoriat, kulttuuri ja moraali (Categories, culture and morale). Vastapaino, Tampere, pp 131–173

Juhila K, Hall C, Günther K et al (2014) Accepting and negotiating service users' choices in mental health transition meetings. Social Policy & Administration 49(5):612–630. doi:10.1111/spol.12082

Julkunen R (2006) Kuka vastaa? Hyvinvointivaltion rajat ja julkinen vastuu (Who's responsible? The limits of the welfare state and public responsibility). Stakes, Helsinki

Julkunen I, Heikkilä M (2007) User involvement in personal social services. In: Valkenburg B, Van Berkel R (eds) Making it personal. Individualising activation services in the EU. The Policy Press University of Bristol, Bristol, pp 87–103

Kaseva K (2011) Asiakkaan asema, itsemääräämınen ja vaikutusmahdollisuudet sosiaali- ja terveydenhuollon kehittämisessä—integroitu kirjallisuuskatsaus (Customer status, self-determination and influence in the development of health and social care: an integrated review of the literature). Sosiaali- ja terveysministeriön raportteja ja muistioita (Reports and memorandums of the Ministry of Social Affairs and Health) 16, Helsinki

Klavus J (2010) Suomalaisten terveys, terveyspalvelujen käyttö ja kokemukset palveluista (Finnish health, use of health services, and experiences of services). In: Vaarama M, Moisio P, Karvonen S (eds) Suomalaisten hyvinvointi 2010 (Finnish welfare, 2010). Terveyden ja

hyvinvoinnin laitos (National Institute for Health and Welfare), Yliopistopaino, Helsinki, pp 28–43
Kennedy D, Fasolino J, Gullen D (2014) Improving the patient experience through provider communication skills building. Patient Experience J 1(1):56–60, http://pxjournal.org/journal/vol1/iss1/10
Koivuniemi K, Holmberg-Marttila D, Hirsso P et al (2014) Terveydenhuollon kompassi. Avain asiakkuuteen (Health care compass: a key to customership). Kustannus Oy Duodecim, Riga
Kotkas T (2009) Terveyden ja sosiaalisen turvallisuuden hallinnointi 2000-luvun Suomessa. Menettelylliset oikeudet ja aktiivinen kansalaisuus (Administration of health and social security in Finland in the 2000s: procedural rights and active citizenship), vol 107. Lakimies, Helsinki, pp. 207–225
Kouvo A (2014) Luottamuksen lähteet. Vertaileva tutkimus yleistynyttä luottamusta synnyttävistä mekanismeista (The sources of generalized trust—A comparative study). Annales Universitatis Turkuensis C 381, Turku
Kuosmanen L, Kaltiala-Heino R, Suominen S et al (2008) Patient complaints in Finland 2000–2004: a retrospective register study. J Med Ethics 34(11):788–792. doi:10.1136/jme.2008.024463
Lammintakanen J (2005) Health care priorisation—Evolution of the concept, research and policy process, vol 116, E. Social Sciences. Kuopio University Publications, Kuopio
Lipsky M (1980) Street-Level Bureaucracy. Dilemmas of the individual in public services. Russell Sage, New York
Mattila Y (2011) Suuria käännekohtia vai tasaista kehitystä. Tutkimus Suomen terveydenhuollon suuntaviivoista. (Major turning points or measured progress? A study of development trends in Finnish health care. Helsinki: The Social Insurance Institution of Finland, Studies in social security and health 116:2011) Juvenes Print- Tampereen yliopistopaino oy, Tampere, pp. 219–230
Mäkitalo Å (2002) Categorizing work: knowing, arguing and social dilemmas in vocational guidance. Acta Universitatis Gothenburgensis, Göteborg
Mäkitalo Å (2005) The record as a formative tool. A study of immanent pedagogy in a practice of vocational guidance. Qual Soc Work 4(4):431–449. doi:10.1177/1473325005058645
Ocloo J (2010) Harmed patients gaining voice: challenging dominant perspectives in the construction of medical harm and patient safety reforms. Soc Sci Med 71(3):510–516. doi:10.1016/j.socscimed.2010.03.050
Pajukoski M (2010) Mitä oikeusturva on (What is legal protection)? In: Pajukoski M (ed) Pääseekö asiakas oikeuksiinsa (Will customers have their rights)? Sosiaali- ja terveydenhuollon ulkopuoliset tekijät-työryhmä. Raportti III (Workgroup on external influences on social and health care: Report III). Yliopistopaino, Helsinki, pp 11–41
Palomäki S (2012) Asiakkaiden osallisuus kuntoutustutkimusprosessissa. Asiakkaiden kokemuksia osallisuudesta ja kuntoutustutkimuksen oikea-aikaisuudesta Tampereen yliopistollisessa sairaalassa. (Clients' participation in the rehabilitation assessment process. Clients' experiencies of participation and the timeliness of the process in Rehabilitation Assessment Outpatient Clinic.) Professional licentiate's Thesis. School of Social Sciences and Humanities, University of Tampere
Paterson R (2013) Not so random: patient complaints and 'frequent flier' doctors. BMJ Qual Saf 22:525–527. doi:10.1136/bmjqs-2013-001902
Pichert JW, Hickson G, Moore I (2008) Using patient complaints to promote patient safety. In: Advances in patient safety: new directions and alternative approaches 2: culture and redesign. Agency for Healthcare Research and Quality, Rockville, MD
Pukk K, Lundberg J, Penaloza-Pesantes RV et al (2003) Do women simply complain more? National patient injury claims data show gender and age differences. Qual Manag Health Care 12(4):225–31
Prottas JM (1979) People-processing. The street-level Bureaucraut in Public Service Bureaucracies. Lexington Books, Toronto

Raitakari S, Juhila K (2011) Moraalinen järjestys ja aikuisuuden odotukset ammatillisessa vuorovaikutuksessa: esimerkkinä mielenterveyskuntoutus. (Moral order of adulthood in mental health rehabilitation). In: Pehkonen A, Väänänen-Fomin A (eds) Sosiaalityön arvot ja etiikka. Ps-kustannus, Juva, pp 189–214

Rothstein B, Stolle D (2007) The quality of government and social capital. A theory of political institutions and generalised trust. Göteborg University, Göteborg, pp 1–44, QOG Working Paper Series 2

Scholl I, Koelewijn-van Loon M, Sepucha K et al (2011) Measurement of shared decision making—a review of instruments. Z Evid Fortbild Qual Gesundh wesen 105:313–324. doi:10.1016/j.zefq.2011.04.012

Sennet R (2003) Respect in a world of inequality. W.W. Norton & Company, New York

Thornborrow J (2002) Power talk. Language and interaction in institutional discourse. Pearson Education, Harlow, London

Thompson AGH (2007) The meaning of patient involvement and participation in health care consultations: a taxonomy. Soc Sci Med 64:1297–1310. doi:10.1016/j.socscimed.2006.11.002

Tuomi J, Sarajärvi A (2011) Laadullinen tutkimus ja sisällönanalyysi (Qualitative research and content analysis). Tammi, Helsinki

Uslaner EM (2002) The moral foundation of trust. Cambridge University Press, Cambridge

Valokivi H (2008) Kansalainen asiakkaana: tutkimus vanhusten ja lainrikkojien osallisuudesta, oikeuksista ja velvollisuuksista. (Citizen as a client. A research on participation, rights and responsibilities of elderly people and offenders.) Acta Universitatis Tamperensis 1286. University Press, Tampere

Valvira (2012) National Supervisory Authority for Welfare and Health, Finland. Patient's charter. Brochures 1:2012, Valvira, Helsinki

Vanhala A, Palomäki S (2015) Muistutus institutionaalisena vuorovaikutuksena terveydenhuollossa. Sosiaalilääketieteellinen aikakauslehti. (Objection as Institutional Interaction in Healthcare. Journal of Social Medicine) (forthcoming)

Weber RP (1990) Basic content analysis, 2nd edn. SAGE Publications, Newbury Park

Wofford MM, Wofford JL, Bothra J et al (2004) Patients' complaints about physician behaviors: a qualitative study. Acad Med 79(2):134–138

Susanna Palomäki is a Licentiate of Social Sciences and is doing doctoral studies at the University of Tampere, Finland. She works as a social worker at an outpatient clinic for adolescent psychiatry in Tampere University Hospital. She has specialised in rehabilitating social work and her licentiate's thesis concerned clients' participation in the rehabilitation assessment process. The interest in researching client status in service systems has encouraged her to take up the topic of complaints with her colleague and coauthor.

Anni Vanhala is a Doctor of Social Sciences. Her research activities have been focused on institutional practices and interaction, social and health care work carried out in institutions. Her current position is a Leading Social Worker and acting as a Patient Ombudsman in Tampere University Hospital. She has also had teaching duties of social work and social sciences.

Innovations by and for Patients, and Their Place in the Future Health Care System

Leid Zejnilović, Pedro Oliveira, and Helena Canhão

Abstract

The innovation management literature recently brought forward an important, but largely ignored role that patients have in health care—as a source of important new solutions for medical care. Several studies have documented health-related innovations made by lay people, specifically the phenomenon of patient innovation and its potential to improve patient well-being and the health care system. In this paper we synthesize the extant findings of patient innovation research, and explore the current limits of patient innovation, including its value and impact. In particular, we discuss the implications that the phenomenon may have on health care systems and the value that society may harness from innovative patients. We use insights from a multiple case study to address barriers to patient innovation—solution development and diffusion—and elaborate on ways to improve it. We further explore patient innovation and its role in future health care by looking into three unique initiatives that aim to facilitate interactions among patients and improve social welfare.

Keywords

Patient innovation • Innovation activity • Collaboration • Solution sharing • Patient involvement • Innovation in health care • Portugal

1 Introduction

Recent findings of innovation management scholars suggest that debates on the future of patient-centric health care should explicitly address the ways to integrate patients' innovative capacity and develop it further. National-level measurements

L. Zejnilović (✉) • P. Oliveira • H. Canhão
Catolica-Lisbon School of Business and Economics, Palma de Cima, 1649-023 Lisbon, Portugal
e-mail: lz@clsbe.lisboa.ucp.pt

H. Albach et al. (eds.), *Boundaryless Hospital*, DOI 10.1007/978-3-662-49012-9_19

of innovation by consumers in the USA, UK, Finland, and Japan, have demonstrated the phenomenon of health-related innovations made by citizens (De Jong et al. 2014; Ogawa and Pongtanalert 2011; von Hippel et al. 2012). Qualitative and quantitative research of innovation activity among patients afflicted with rare and rheumatic diseases documented the phenomenon, and provided evidence of its potential to improve both the health care system and the patients' well-being (Habicht et al. 2012; Oliveira et al. 2015). Also, a number of commercial and non-profit initiatives have recently emerged with the aim to advance the potential of patients to develop novel health care-related solutions. To exemplify, consider the following initiatives: (a) the website *PatientsLikeMe* which facilitates the collection and analysis of patients' vital health indicators in relation to their medical interventions and sharing these data with other patients; (b) *Patient-innovation* which is a website that offers a venue for patients, caregivers, and collaborators to share and evaluate patient-developed solutions; and (c) *Enabling-thefuture.org*, a collaborative community that develops customizable, modular, 3D-printable prosthetic hands.

Each of these examples focuses on different market niches, and offers unique experimental settings for finding ways to better integrate patients in the health care system. Together, the examples also represent the beginning of the wave of approaches that combine technology and social components to bring health care closer to the patients and their real needs.

In this paper we briefly review the foundation behind the shift towards patient-driven innovation in health care and the extant views on patient-centric health care. Then we review the findings related to patient innovation, and provide a short presentation of multiple case study analysis of patient innovation and solution sharing. We conclude with a discussion on how health care could embrace patient innovation, informed by the results from the case studies and the three initiatives mentioned above.

2 Health Care for and by Patients, a Literature Review

2.1 Patient-Centered Health

Patient-centered health care has been promoted and discussed since the work of Balint et al. (1969). In 2001, the Institute of Medicine issued a report in which patient-centered health care is defined as "...care that is respectful of and responsive to individual patient preferences, needs and values, and assuring that patient's values guide all clinical decisions" (IOM 2001, p. 40). They further elaborated on patient-centered care by identifying four distinct levels:

- the level of the individual patient's experience;
- the clinical microsystem level where patients participate in the overall design of the service and programs;

- the organizational level where patients participate in key committees to improve all aspects at the organizational level; and
- the environmental level where interactions with regulators and policies stimulate stronger engagement of patients and their families (IOM 2001).

This holistic approach to improving the quality of health care via stronger involvement of patients in all aspects of the health care system reflects the fundamental shift in thinking about the future of the system. Until now, the efforts to lift the boundaries between health care institutions and the patients were not sufficient to systematically integrate the innovation activities of patients in delivery of health care services. The emerging initiatives, some of which we also discuss here, suggest that the situation is improving.

There are two main reasons for the surge of interest in the role of patients in health care. One reason is technological advancement. Technology enables almost effortless access to information and easy networking among patients (Ferguson 2007; Sands and DeBronkart 2013). A number of studies have shown that people invest significant efforts to search for and share health-related information (e.g., see the review by Anker et al. 2011). The type of information they search for depends on their health status; the search may be about a specific health condition and its management, or about disease prevention (Brashers et al. 2002). This independent information acquisition has shifted the power balance, as the medical professionals' authority that was built largely upon information asymmetry is now challenged by informed patients (Sands et al. 2013). The second reason for the surge of interest in a stronger patient role in health care is financial. In the twentieth century, life expectancy at birth increased by about 30 years (WHO 2011), resulting from advancements in medical science and the socio-economic development. In addition, many infectious diseases have been put under control. As the world's population is getting older, non-communicable diseases and chronic conditions have taken over as the main cause of death (Suzman et al. 2014; Lozano et al. 2012; WHO 2011). The downside of this development is that an already costly health care system with unsustainable spending levels is expected to grow even more so as the percentage of the elderlies increases significantly and medical science finds even more innovative but expensive treatments. Therefore, any new opportunity that may both improve individual well-being and address the cost issue is warmly welcomed by all the stakeholders in the health care value chain. A logical step is to empower those with the strongest need and incentives to contribute—patients.

There is growing evidence that the future health care can rely more upon strong involvement of patients. Empowering patients to self-manage their chronic diseases both enhances health and diminishes costs (Ahn et al. 2013). Patients also lead medical research (Frydman 2009), organize clinical trials and seek alternatives to cure themselves, sometimes with considerable risks (Akst 2013; Sands et al. 2013). Although there is a recognition that patients may respond to both usual and new situations in novel ways (Hibbard et al. 2004; Sands and DeBronkart 2013), the innovative capacity of patients has only recently captured the attention of researchers (Flowers 2014; Habicht et al. 2012).

2.2 Patients as Consumers and Developers of Health Care Products and Services

Patients are the "end users" of health care services. Innovation management scholars have long recognized that users engage in innovative behavior as they experience unmet and pressing needs (von Hippel 1976, 1988, 2010). When they innovate in expectation of benefits from personal use of the innovations, they are referred to as "user innovators" (von Hippel 1988). The phenomenon of user innovation is well established in the academic literature. There is substantial evidence of high prevalence of user innovation in various fields ranging from industrial and consumer products, like scientific instruments, printed circuit CAD software; to equipment for radical sports such as mountain biking, kite surfing or kayaking; and this phenomenon even extends to services like commercial and retail banking services, and mobile banking (von Hippel 2010; Oliveira and von Hippel 2011; van der Boor et al. 2014). Recent studies indicate that the user innovation in health care follows the general patterns of other product and services industries (Habicht et al. 2012; Oliveira et al. 2015). To overcome difficulties imposed by their health disorder, or the disease of people close to them, patients and caregivers often innovate. To emphasize the health care context, we refer to user innovation by patients and caregivers as to patient innovation.

Considering the extent of the phenomenon, survey evidence from studies of user innovation at national level helps establish its general boundaries. Current estimates are that 4–6 % of citizens in the US, Japan, Finland, and the UK modify or create new products and services for personal use; up to 7 % of these innovations are classified as health care products (De Jong et al. 2014; von Hippel et al. 2012). A recent study that focused on rare disease patients and their non-professional caregivers shows that the frequency of user innovation may be higher for underserved communities: 52 % of the respondents reported having developed a solution that were new to them, of which 16 % were validated as new to the medical community (Oliveira et al. 2015).

The solutions that are picked-up in surveys or otherwise observed are only a fraction of the overall innovation activity among patients and caregivers. Several authors who studied sports communities, noticed the fall-offs in user innovation activity during the progress from an idea to a diffused solution (Lüthje et al. 2005). They asked members of sports communities if they have ever had an idea for a new or improved product (e.g., for an outdoor-related product or mountain biking equipment) and how far they had developed it. In the study of sports-related product consumers, Lüthje (2004) observed that 37 % of the sample reported having ideas for new or improved products, but only 9 % of the users reported building product prototypes or marketable products. In another study on mountain biking by Lüthje et al. (2005), users with ideas comprised about 38.7 % of the sample, whereas 16 % of these developed a usable prototype. Although a considerable percentage of users are a source of innovative ideas, a large percentage drops out and does not reach the prototype stage. This suggests that there is potential to further improve user innovation.

With regard to the value of the solutions developed by patients, there is evidence of patients reporting improvements in the quality of life when applying the solutions (Oliveira et al. 2015). Furthermore, Shcherbatiuk (2012) identified a number of successful cases of patient innovations that made a significant impact on medical practice. The value of a particular innovation can only be achieved when it diffuses—when it is adopted and used by other people. User innovations diffuse either within peer-to-peer networks, or through a producer that offers the innovation in a market (Baldwin et al. 2006; De Jong et al. 2014; Harhoff et al. 2003). Survey evidence shows that diffusion of user innovations is low: in general population surveys, the fraction of diffused innovations varied from 5 to 17 %, with the most common diffusion pathway being peer-to-peer exchanges (De Jong et al. 2014; Ogawa and Pongtanalert 2011; von Hippel et al. 2012). Low diffusion levels are recognized as a new type of market failure (von Hippel et al. 2014).

The user innovators develop solutions for their use, without considering the value of their solutions for others. Therefore, their decision not to diffuse is individually rational but puts society in the loss (von Hippel et al. 2014). De Jong et al. (2014) explored this topic further, and found that less than one-third of users with innovative solutions, in a representative sample of Finnish citizens, actually made the effort to share it with others. The only argument that was found to be explanatory for the lack of diffusion is that the innovators do not find the effort (or cost) to diffuse worthwhile (De Jong et al. 2014; von Hippel et al. 2014). The most important implications of this conclusion are: those who search for solutions and cannot find one may wastefully duplicate design and development efforts for something that already exists; and the search for a solution may result in an inferior need-solution match than what could have been attained if an existing better solution had been made available to the searching party.

Patients have potentials to contribute to the advancement of medical care. For those interested to improve the outcomes of the patient innovation activity, and to integrate them in the future health care system, it may be useful to learn more about innovation development and barriers in this process.

3 The Critical Factors for Progression of Patient Innovation Activity: Multiple Case Study

In this section, we discuss results of a multiple case analysis conducted in Portugal in 2014, among caregivers and patients afflicted with diseases such as Angelman syndrome, epidermolysis bullosa, hemiparesis and spinal cord injuries (Oliveira 2014).

The multiple case study methodology (Eisenhardt and Eisenhardt 1989; Yin 2009) was applied to explore the fall-offs of patient innovation activity as it progressed from an idea to a diffused solution. One of the particular aims of the study, of relevance for this paper, was to explore the barriers to the development of patient innovations and their diffusion.

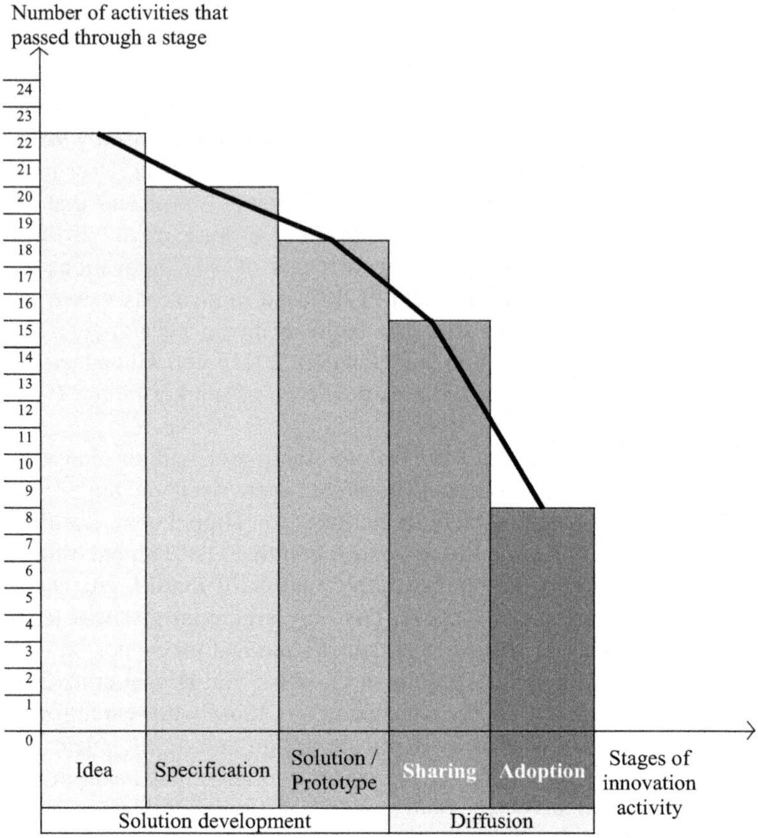

Fig. 1 Fall-offs in innovation activity - the number of cases that passed through each of the stages

The unit of analysis in the study is an innovation activity by a single patient. The activity may occur in any of the development stages—an idea, a specified solution, a functional prototype, or an adopted solution.

The data source is a set of 15 in-depth semi-structured interviews with patients at a medical and rehabilitation center in Portugal and other patient innovators that were known to us through the Patient-Innovation project (Oliveira 2014). The study was approved by the Ethics Committee of the medical and rehabilitation center. As suggested by Yin (2009), two types of cases were considered: "holistic" cases, when an interviewee has only one example, and "embedded" cases, when an interviewee has two or more examples of innovation activities. The interviews yielded 4 "holistic" and 26 "embedded" cases distributed along the innovation process continuum from an idea to an adopted solution as shown in Fig. 1.[1]

[1] All the cases are archived in the library of the Catholic University of Portugal (Oliveira 2014).

The interviewees were selected based on the recommendation of the health professionals, with an aim to provide as many cases as possible to fill the stages of the fall-offs diagram. To contrast the cases of active patients, those who develop solutions, two patients who were fully compliant with their treatment and doctors' requests were also interviewed. These two cases are not presented in Fig. 1, as there was no innovation activity reported—the interviewees felt that their needs were fully met by the regular health care (services). Also, six cases of adoption from the interviewed patients were omitted from the diagram in Fig. 1.

The cases revealed a number of factors that may inhibit the development and diffusion of innovations. We continue in next sub-section with a brief discussion about these factors by grouping them into two categories: collaboration and incentives.

3.1 Collaboration

In the observed cases, collaboration repeatedly appeared to be important for innovation and diffusion. The collaborating parties were patients and caregivers, people with complementary skills, and medical professionals. We next discuss how each of these groups helps patients in developing solutions and their diffusion.

3.1.1 Access to the Community of Patients

Peer communities are important in all phases of solution development (Hienerth and Lettl 2011). The patient innovators would often approach other patients to request help to develop their innovations. Communication with other patients helped them mature ideas, assess their viability, and also refine methodologies for developing solutions. For example, a patient with tetraplegia got interested in developing a type of a surfboard for personal use. The advice he obtained from other patients afflicted with tetraplegia, who shared his interest in surfing, was instrumental to help the patient decide what features he wanted and eventually to build the board.

The community can also help further develop prototypes with their usage-related feedback, and help diffuse solutions by publishing individual experiences. The personal accounts and the spread of the information through networks of personal contacts increases solutions' observability and trialability, which are important factors for the adoption of the solutions (Rogers 2003). Indeed, in several of the cases the adoption only happened when the patients were able to see a solution and give it a try by building it with the developer's help.

The critical challenge, with respect to patient innovations in general and their diffusion in particular, is to organize the patients' communities in order to effectively channel their innovation activity and have the information available and accessible to the others. We will discuss this challenge and potential ways to address it in this section and Sect. 4.

3.1.2 Complementary Skills

People with complementary skills can be instrumental in the early phase of idea development. These people can provide assessment of the idea's viability and propose important modifications. Also, where it is needed, they are the ones that provide the services to help with the implementation. In our sample, a person who works with metal helped a patient with the spinal cord injury and her parents make a metal piece to attach a specialized transportation chair to the car floor. A carpenter helped another person with a spinal cord injury to design her bathroom and improve the function of taking a bath independently. In several other examples, however, it took a long time for the patients to find a willing individual with the skills to complete development of their solutions. In some cases, unfortunately, the patient innovator never connected with a skilled peer.

To find individuals with complementary skills, patients first used their closest ties, their family, friends, and then peers. In cases when this search gave no results, the patients also sometimes attempted to make contacts with people they found online who appeared to have the skills and showed a willingness to engage in such an interaction.

Complementary skills are an important resource and an obstacle to the development of patient innovations. Therefore, creating a venue where patients and caregivers could match with people with complementary skills is an important aim to be considered by both policy makers and entrepreneurs in health.

3.1.3 Expertise from Medical Professionals

Given the health care context, we emphasize that medical professionals' expertise is both critical to the diffusion of and an impediment to patient innovation. Although the majority of the reported innovations were about coping with a disease, and not about something that would directly interest doctors, interviewees reported medical expertise as one of the major impediment in ideation and implementation.

An ample example of the positive role that medical professionals have in fostering development of safe solutions is the case of mediating the exchange of experiences in drug therapy among patients. One caregiver reported engaging in an activity inside a community of caregivers who discussed mixtures of drug therapies and experimenting them. But before she would start giving a new therapy—drugs cocktail—to her son, she would consult her son's doctor. In this case, the doctor-patient relationship was such that the patient felt free to share important information with the doctor that they jointly assessed. They assessed the drug cocktail for safety and efficacy. That the quality of doctor-patient relationship is not always conducive for such sharing was shown by research in Australia: A survey revealed that the majority of the respondents indicated that they were not sharing information about complementary and alternative treatments with their doctors (Williamson et al. 2008). The main reason for this, as reported in the survey, was that no one ever asked the patients about what else they were doing besides the regular health care.

Research conducted among medical professionals (Hibbard et al. 2010; Stewart et al. 2000) and experts' narrative evidence (Berwick 2009) suggest that there still exists discomfort with giving patients the power to interpret independently and evaluate the medical professional's information, and hence to make their own health-related decisions. The most likely effect of ignoring these needs and wants is the degradation of an important communication channel between patients and medical professionals. Maintaining a trustful doctor-patient relationship enables learning on both ends and helps improving the well-being of patients, which is after all an ultimate objective of health care systems.

The cooperation between patients and health professionals along with the mechanisms that facilitate this cooperation are something policy makers and regulators should consider addressing in accordance with health care institutions.

3.2 The Perception of the Solution's Value, and the Incentives for Sharing

An important property that may affect a solution's development, sharing and adoption is the perception of the solution's value. Habicht et al. (2012) showed that patients sometimes go to a great length to develop the solutions. This is what happened to Tal Golesworthy and his development of external aortic root support. This is an example of what the authors refer to as a pressing need situation. In our study, most of the innovations were simple solutions or technical aids. The interviewees reported that as the commercial alternatives to their solutions, if they existed, were inappropriate for their needs, they had to come (up) with their own alternatives. For majority of the cases, the innovators reached the diffusion stage (see Fig. 1). If the solution was not shared, we explored the reasons for not sharing it. One of the reasons was that no one asked the developers for their solution, and they did not see the value in investing efforts and inform others about it—they had solved their problem and this was sufficient. This is a typical situation that was discussed earlier in the text—the lack of incentives to diffuse (von Hippel et al. 2014). Another reason for not sharing a solution was that the patient innovators moved on to other problems and forgot about their solution, as it was only needed for a short period (see Table 1 for the causes of fall-offs). We identified three developed solutions that were not shared (Fig. 1), although the developers were content with the outcome—the solutions had served their purpose as intended. The developers expressed willingness to share the solutions with others, if there was a convenient way to do that.

When solutions are shared, insufficiency of information may impact the likelihood of others adopting these patient/caregivers' solution. This is especially salient to free sharing of information about user innovations (Harhoff et al. 2003). For example, one of the patients reported a fairly complex technical solution for controlling doors, blinds, lights, and other elements in his house—a type of "smart home" solution. However, the information that he shares for free with the others is insufficient to replicate the solution. User-friendliness was not a priority for the developer who did this for himself. This is reflected in the lack of comprehensive organization of the source code of his software, and the lack of documentation related to hardware units

Table 1 The causes of the innovation activity fall-offs, as reported by patients and caregivers

Cause of a fall-off	Final stage of innovation activity progression			
	Idea	Specification	Solution/ prototype	Sharing
Lack of time to pursue further the development	√	√		
Lack of technical knowledge	√	√		
Lack of resources (financial and material)		√		
Lack of support (or discouragement)		√		
Existence of alternatives (inferior but functional solutions)		√		
Lack of a community of peers			√	
Low perceived value of the solution for others			√	√
Lack of an observable demand for a solution			√	
Expectancy of a short exposure to a problem	√			
Short duration of use/need for a solution			√	
Lack of a feasible value appropriation mechanism			√	
High perceived costs for further engagement			√	√
Uncertainty about outcome/a solution's fit (no possibility to try a solution and/or observe its efficiency)	√	√		√
Safety and legal concerns			√	√
High acquisition cost (no/poor information, complex or costly solution)				√

and how to make hardware and software work. The adoption of the solution required high investment from an adopting party. The alternative to costly adoption on one's own would be that the developer installs the product. On the developer's side, as the solution serves the intended function, there was no incentive to invest further efforts to make the solution more accessible to others. This leads to the situation that a solution potentially useful for others remains unobservable or unattainable to others. Even though other solutions for "smart homes" may exist, it is very likely that a patient with mobility issues develops features that producers of general purpose solutions do not take into consideration.

In case of the "smart home" solution and in few other cases, when the developers thought that there might be a commercial interest for their solution, they reported as an obstacle the uncertainty about feasible way to protect their intellectual property and appropriate value from what they saw as an innovation. In addition, safety and legal concerns were adding to already high perceived costs of further pursuing solution development on a commercial basis.

From the cases discussed here, we may conclude that an active solicitation of solutions by patients is a potentially useful strategy to surface these solutions. Yet, without the infrastructure that allows easy solution sharing, but also adequate support to explain solutions and make them easy to replicate, any attempt to incentivize the diffusion of patient innovations may fall short.

In Table 1 we summarize the main reasons the interviewees reported for terminating innovation activities in their respective stages—the causes of the innovation activity fall-offs.

4 Should Health Care Embrace Patient Innovation, and How?

There are many reasons why health care should embrace patient innovation. In this section, we discuss potential ways of embracing it, based on the discussion in the previous section and the three initiatives mentioned in the introduction of this paper.

4.1 The Collaborative Force of Patients

The communities of patients and individuals with complementary skills have great potentials to improve provision of medical care. An excellent example of their collaborative force is the development of customizable prosthetic hands, made using 3D printers. The idea came from Richard Van As, a carpenter who initiated the development of a mechanical, and later a 3D printed prosthetic hand, with a puppeteer, Ivan Owen. After their initial success, Richard developed a company to further pursue the project–RoboHand (2015). Ivan opted for an open-source development of customizable prosthetic hands, and helped creating a community of volunteers-Enabling the Future-who "...use 3D printing to give the world a 'Helping Hand'" (Enabling the Future 2015). Figure 2 shows an image of a modular device developed by these volunteers using an open-source collaborative development paradigm. This is among the first development of the kind in health care, where the efforts of many individual volunteer developers have been integrated into a single release–eNable Raptor Hand 1.0.

There are sophisticated, technology powered, but expensive hands on the market that outperform the 3D printed hands as the one shown in Fig. 2. However, the 3D printed prosthetic hands are a viable alternative for those that cannot afford or do not need the advanced features. Both closed-mode development (by "RoboHand" company) and the open and collaborative innovation approach have resulted in comparable solutions, developed over a period of about 1 year. Based on the information provided on the respective websites, the open-source community delivered over 1500 free hands (Enabling the Future 2015), while its firm-driven counterpart delivered over 200 hands (RoboHand 2015). The ability to easily change the design as needed, and get it at almost no cost, makes the open-source 3D hand an attractive option for many people worldwide.

There are two important takeaways from studying the EnablingtheFuture.org community that could be applied to designing the hospitals of the future and addressing some health policy issues. The community of patients and individuals with complementary skills made a remarkable product because they had the venue

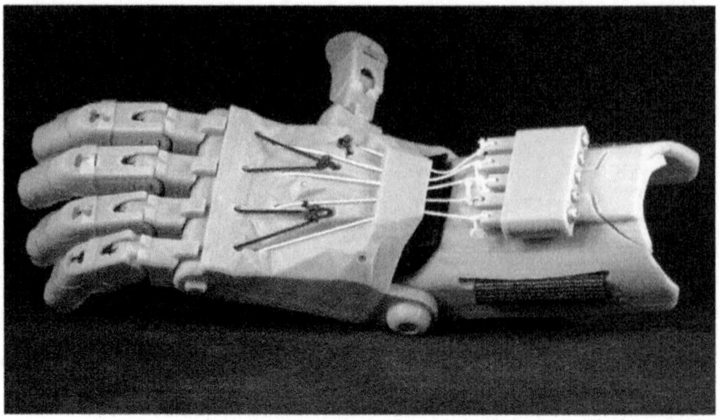

Fig. 2 User-developed prosthetic hand—open-source collaborative development mode (e-Nable Raptor 2015)

to meet, sticky information about what they need, and tools to build incrementally upon the work of the others. It is not hard to imagine the convenience for patients to have places in the hospitals where medical professionals could collaborate with them to customize modular technical aids and print them on the spot.

Therefore, policy makers could consider ways to support the development of other health related products by engaging open source communities of patients and volunteers, and explore ways to integrate these into the health care practice.

4.2 The Integrative Role of Health Care Professionals

Patient innovation activity and the activity of health care professionals are complementary rather than competing activities (Oliveira et al. 2015). Surveys show that health care professionals have an important impact on their patients' health-related behavior. Xiao et al. (2014) found that health care providers were the most trusted source of health information. Given the health-related context, questions of safety are often associated with the untested solutions that patients come up with. Even in the case of seemingly benign solutions, like wearing tights all day long for patients with epidermolysis bullosa, or a chair for transportation in a car, discussing potential safety issues with medical professionals may be useful. Recall the case of the mother who experiments with drug cocktails: This case suggests that the communication between patients and medical professionals also has to take the innovation activity and experimentation by patients into consideration.

To create a more supportive environment for patient innovation, it is necessary to raise the awareness about patient innovation from the early days at medical, nursing, and other health care professional schools. Successful identification of potential patient innovators is important, as they can contribute to improve other people's quality of life in two ways: first by participating in new product/service development with other patients, and commercial or research entities—as lead users (von Hippel 2010), and secondly, by sharing their innovations. In the latter case, and as mentioned earlier, the problem is that users rarely come out to share innovations. Another intervention at a policy level would be to teach health professionals and give them tools to identify these innovative patients and caregivers. An investment in such an educational program for health care professionals and monitoring its implementation is a low-cost but potentially very worthy investment. Fortunately, there are many tools that are also valuable for educational purpose about the topic of patient innovation, and we will next discuss some of them.

4.3 Infrastructures for Sharing Solutions and Health-Related Data

As mentioned earlier, patients need a venue to easily share their solutions, collaboratively improve them and evaluate the solutions' efficiency with as little effort as possible. One example of such a venue is the website Patient-innovation.com. The most significant benefits of the site are its focus on patients and caregivers and cross-pollination of knowledge between different health disorders. The focus on patients is important for building a trusted community of peers, within which they can share their solutions. This trust is reinforced by the fact that the site is made in recognition of the value of patient innovation activity. This may also contribute to the development of the identity and a stronger association of the community members with the ideals of patient innovation. The second benefit is the knowledge sharing that is possible due to the coding mechanism applied when solutions are posted. After writing the solution description, the submitting party may select additional labels for the solution, including a disease name, symptoms addressed, and a set of tags associated with the solution—such as activities, devices, therapy and the part of the body it concerns. If the solutions are correctly coded, communities that previously not considered each other's solutions may be connected. For example, an individual who searches for a solution related to gastrointestinal problems that bothers him, may connect with a community of those undergoing a chemotherapy who are also experiencing similar problems. The website allows individuals to leave their feedback about the solution's efficiency and engage in communication about the solution.

The knowledge that is stored on the sites like Patient-innovation.com is also useful for those trying to learn about diseases by observing the types of problems and solutions that patients and caregivers are posting. The solutions developed by patients represent externalized tacit knowledge about their health disorder. This is valuable to researchers, health professionals, and to other patients who would like to learn what can they expect from living with a disease.

Technology has not only enabled patients to connect with one another, but also capture, organize, share and compare large amounts of their health-related data. An example of a website that helps patients in this activity is PatientsLikeMe.com. On this website patients can store their vital health indicators and associate them with a treatment they have been using. These longitudinal data sets about health and therapies, shared by numerous patients from around the world, are the most significant benefit of this website. The data represent a valuable asset for researchers interested in the efficiency of specific treatments and can help advance medical science. The website also offers data for sale.

The websites mentioned above are only a few examples of different initiatives that aim to connect patients and health care professionals. They have been selected for this paper for being both patient-centered and novel initiatives that may help expand our views on the future of health care. Also, they are a voice that advocates for the availability of patient-developed solutions and personal health data.

5 Conclusion

Patient innovation is a natural part of any patient-centered initiative that looks towards the future of health care. Patients, with experiential knowledge about living with health disorders and their innovative solutions, can help advance medical care. Their activity is complementary to the pursuits of health care professionals. Moreover, developing synergies among health care professionals, patients and others interested in health care, is an important goal. The challenge is to create an institutional environment where these synergies can freely develop.

Patients and caregivers are already making their own space within the system, by developing open source prosthesis models, novel treatments for rare diseases, and even discovering new health disorders. Without an infrastructure that allows credible information exchange and provides support for ensuring safety, the efforts of many (innovative) people may fall short.

The popularity of ongoing initiatives that we have briefly described in the paper, suggests that there is a critical mass of those who want to implement fully patient-centered health care. Experimentation with different approaches to mobilize untapped innovation potential and establish evidence-based benchmarks about health care interventions, provide opportunities to learn about how to organize future health care. But the ball is now in the policy makers' and the health care professionals' court. They need to decide if and how to support innovative patients and health care innovation initiatives that empower them, and ultimately help improving individual well-being.

References

Ahn S, Basu R, Smith M et al (2013) The impact of chronic disease self-management programs: healthcare savings through a community-based intervention. BMC Public Health 13:1141

Akst J (2013) Do-it-yourself medicine. http://www.the-scientist.com/?articles.view/articleNo/34433/title/Do-It-Yourself-Medicine/. Accessed 23 Jul 2015

Anker AE, Reinhart AM, Feeley TH (2011) Health information seeking: a review of measures and methods. Patient Educ Couns 82(3):346–54

Baldwin CY, Hienerth C, von Hippel E (2006) How user innovations become commercial products: a theoretical investigation and case study. Res Policy 35(9):1291–1313

Balint M, Ball D, Hare M (1969) Training medical students in patient-centered medicine. Compr Psychiatry 10(4):249–258

Berwick DM (2009) What "patient-centered" should mean: confessions of an extremist. Health Aff (Project Hope) 28(4):555–65

Brashers DE, Goldsmith DJ, Hsieh E (2002) Information seeking and avoiding in health contexts. Hum Commun Res 28(2):258–271

De Jong JPJ, von Hippel E, Gault F et al (2014) The diffusion of consumer-developed innovations: patterns in Finland. Res Policy 44(10):1856–1865. doi:10.2139/ssrn.2426498, Accessed 23 Jul 2015

Eisenhardt KM, Eisenhardt M (1989) Building theories from case study research. Acad Manage Rev 14(4):532–550

Enabling the Future (2015) http://enablingthefuture.org/. Accessed 23 Jul 2015

e-Nable Raptor (2015) http://enablingthefuture.org/upper-limb-prosthetics/the-raptor-hand/. Accessed 20 Jul 2015

Ferguson T (2007) E-patient: how they can help us heal healthcare. http://e-patients.net/e-Patients_White_Paper.pdf. Accessed 23 Jul 2015

Flowers S (2014) Medical user innovation in the context of chronic disease: the creation of Helminthic therapy. Paper presented at the Workshop on Medical User Innovation and Medical Commons, New York University School of Law, 15–17 May 2014

Frydman G (2009) Patient-driven research: rich opportunities and real risks. J Participatory Med 1:6–10

Habicht H, Oliveira P, Shcherbatiuk V (2012) User innovators: when patients set out to help themselves and end up helping many. Die Unternehmung 66(3):277–294

Harhoff D, Henkel J, von Hippel E (2003) Profiting from voluntary information spillovers: how users benefit by freely revealing their innovations. Res Policy 32(10):1753–1769

Hibbard J, Collins P, Mahoney E et al (2010) The development and testing of a measure assessing clinician beliefs about patient self-management. Health Expect 13(1):65–72

Hibbard J, Stockard J, Mahoney E et al (2004) Development of the patient activation measure (PAM): conceptualizing and measuring activation in patients and consumers. Health Serv Res 39(4):1005–26

Hienerth C, Lettl C (2011) Exploring how peer communities enable lead user innovations to become standard equipment in the industry: community pull effects. J Prod Innovat Manag 28 (S1):175–195

IOM (2001) Crossing the quality chasm: a new health system for the 21st century. The National Academies Press, Washington, DC, p 40

Lozano R, Naghavi M, Foreman K et al (2012) Global and regional mortality from 235 causes of death for 20 age groups in 1990 and 2010: a systematic analysis for the Global Burden of Disease Study 2010. The Lancet 380(9859):2095–2128

Lüthje C (2004) Characteristics of innovating users in a consumer goods field: an empirical study of sport-related product consumers. Technovation 24:683–695

Lüthje C, Herstatt C, von Hippel E (2005) User-innovators and "local" information: the case of mountain biking. Res Policy 34(6):951–965

Ogawa S, Pongtanalert, K (2011). Visualizing invisible innovation continent: evidence from global consumer innovation surveys. doi:10.2139/ssrn.1876186 Accessed 23 Jul 2015

Oliveira R (2014) Patients and caregivers as sources of innovative ideas and solutions: a multiple-case study approach. Master thesis (Católica-Lisbon School of Business and Economics), Catholic University of Portugal

Oliveira P, von Hippel E (2011) Users as service innovators: the case of banking services. Res Policy 40(6):806–818

Oliveira P, Zejnilovic L, Canhao H et al (2015) Innovation by patients with rare diseases and chronic needs. Orphanet J Rare Dis 10(41)

Rogers EM (2003) Diffusion of innovations, 5th edn. Free Press, New York

RoboHand (2015) http://www.robohand.net/. Accessed 23 Jul 2015

Sands D, DeBronkart D, Topol E (2013) Let patients help! A patient engagement handbook—how doctors, nurses, patiens and caregivers can partner for better care. CreateSpace.com, 2013

Shcherbatiuk (2012) Users as developers and entrepreneurs of medical treatments treatments/ devices: the case of patients and their families and friends. Master thesis (Católica-Lisbon School of Business and Economics), Catholic University of Portugal

Stewart M, Brown JB, Donner A et al (2000) The impact of patient-centered care on outcomes. J Fam Pract 49(09):796–804

Suzman R, Beard JR, Boerma T (2014) Health in an ageing world-what do we know? Lancet 6736 (14):14–16

van der Boor P, Oliveira P, Veloso F (2014) Users as innovators in developing countries: the global sources of innovation and diffusion in mobile banking services. Res Policy 43(9):1594–1607

von Hippel E (1976) The dominant role of users in the scientific instrument innovation process. Res Policy 5:212–239

von Hippel E (1988) The sources of innovation. Oxford University Press, New York

von Hippel E (2010) Open user innovation. In: Hall B, Rosenberg N (eds) Handbook of the economics of innovation, vol 1. Elsevier, Amsterdam, pp 411–427

von Hippel E, De Jong JPJ, Flowers S (2012) Comparing business and household sector innovation in consumer products: findings from a representative study in the United Kingdom. Manage Sci 58(9):1669–1681

von Hippel E, DeMonaco HJ, De Jong, JPJ (2014) Market failure in the diffusion of user innovations: the case of "Off-Label" innovations by medical clinicians? doi: 10.2139/ssrn. 2275562 Accessed 23 Jul 2015

WHO (2011) Global health and aging. World Health Organization, US National Institute of Aging. http://www.who.int/ageing/publications/global_health/en/. Accessed 04 May 2015

Williamson M, Tudball J, Toms M, Garden F et al (2008) Information use and needs of complementary medicines users. National Prescribing Service, Sydney

Xiao N, Sharman R, Rao HR et al (2014) Factors influencing online health information search: an empirical analysis of a national cancer-related survey. Decis Support Syst 57:417–427

Yin RK (2009) Case study research: design and methods. In: Bickman L, Rog DJ (eds) Applied social research methods series, 4th edn. Sage, Thousand Oaks

Leid Zejnilović is a Postdoctoral Fellow at Catolica-Lisbon School of Business and Economics, Portugal, where he also teaches in master, executive, and undergraduate programs. He is the Research and Operations Officer of Patient Innovation, a non-profit platform and social network for patients and caregivers of any disease to share their innovations. Leid Zejnilovic received his Ph.D. degree in Strategy, Entrepreneurship and Technological Change from Carnegie Mellon University, U.S.A. and Catholic University of Portugal.

Pedro Oliveira is Associate Dean for Research and Academic Director of the Lisbon MBA at the Católica-Lisbon School of Business and Economics, where he is Associate Professor. Professor Olieeira teaches in the Lisbon MBA executive masters, undergraduate and executive education programs. He is the Director of the Doctoral Program in Technological Change and Entrepreneurship jointly offered by Católica-Lisbon, University of Lisbon and Carnegie Mellon University. He is also the Director of the Health Innovation and Entrepreneurship Program (HIEP), the Program in Supply Chain Management (SCM), the Advanced Program in Entrepreneurship and Innovation Management (PAEGI), and the Program for the Acceleration of Entrepreneurial Ventures (BES Emp). He was an International Faculty Fellow at the MIT Sloan School of Management, advisor to the Portuguese Ministry of Science, Technology and Higher Education and Project Leader for Creative Commons PT (Portugal). Together with three former Lisbon MBA students, he co-founded PPL Crowdfunding Portugal. He is founder and project leader of Patient Innovation, a non-profit platform and social network for patients and caregivers of any disease to share their innovations. Pedro Oliveira received his Ph.D. in Operations, Technology and Innovation Management from The University of North Carolina at Chapel Hill, and both his M.Sc. in Operations Research and Systems Engineering and his undergraduate degree in Naval Engineering from IST. He also attended advanced training programs at Northwestern University, Kellogg School of Management, U.S.A.

Helena Canhão is Professor of Rheumatology at Lisbon Medical School, a Senior Consultant of Rheumatology at North Lisbon Medical Centre (Santa Maria Hospital, Lisbon) and Principal Investigator at Instituto de Medicina Molecular. She was the former Clinical Director of Casa dos Marcos, a medical facility of Rarissimas, the national patient association of rare diseases and currently she is the vice-president of the patient association Portuguese League Against Rheumatic Diseases.

Helen Canhao is also the Principal Investigator of several Clinical Trials at Santa Maria Hospital; National Coordinator of Reuma.pt (the Portuguese Register in Rheumatic Diseases) from Portuguese Society of Rheumatology (SPR); Co-coordinator of EpireumaPt (the Portuguese Epidemiologic Study of Rheumatic Diseases, known also as RheumaCensus) and the Principal Investigator of CoReumaPt (Portuguese Cohort Study of Rheumatic Diseases) from SPR. She is co-project leader and Chief Medical Officer of the website Patient Innovation. She is the Scientific Director of the Health Innovation Lab (HiLab), a forum that brings together leaders, professionals and entrepreneurs from the health care sector and academia to discuss, share and experiment innovative ideas and concepts. She is also Director of the Health Innovation and Entrepreneurship Program (HIEP) at Catolica-Lisbon. She received her MD and her Ph.D. in Medicine (Rheumatology) from the Lisbon Medical School (FMUL), Portugal and her M.Sc. in Medical Sciences (MMSc) from Harvard Medical School, Harvard University, U.S.A.

About the Editors

Prof. Dr. Dr. h.c. mult. Horst Albach was born in 1931 in Essen, Germany. After a year of study at Bowdoin College in Brunswick, Maine, U.S., he continued his studies of management and economics at Cologne University, Germany, where he received his doctoral degree in business economics in 1958. He taught at Darmstadt Technical University (1958–1960) and Kiel University (1960/1961), Germany, and Graz University (1960), Austria. He accepted an offer to become full Professor of Business Economics at Bonn University in 1961, co-founded the private Coblence School of Management in 1984, and taught there on leave of absence from Bonn until 1987 when he became Professor of Industrial Economics at the Freie University Berlin. After the unification of Germany, he became a Professor of Management Science at the Humboldt-Universität zu Berlin. Professor Albach holds honorary degrees from the Swedish School of Management in Stockholm, the Finnish School of Business in Helsinki, the universities of Kiel, Bielefeld, Cottbus, Graz, Alcalá de Henares, Waseda, Bowdoin College in Brunswick, ME, and the Russian Academy of Sciences. He is a member of the German order Pour le Mérite for Sciences and Arts and was its chancellor from 2004 to 2009. Since 2012 Professor Albach has been a member of the executive board of the Center for Advanced Studies in Management (CASiM) at HHL Leipzig Graduate School of Management, Leipzig, Germany.

Prof. Dr. Dr. h.c. mult. Heribert Meffert studied business administration in Munich, Germany, and wrote his habilitation about flexibility in business decisions in 1968. In 1969 he was appointed to the Chair of Business Administration at the University of Münster, where he established the first institute of marketing at a German university. In 1981 he was a founding member of the Wissenschaftliche Gesellschaft für Marketing und Unternehmensführung e. V., an academic society for marketing and management. From 1995 until 1997 he was responsible for the academic management of HHL Leipzig Graduate School of Management in Leipzig, Germany. As an emeritus professor, Heribert Meffert was Chairman of the Board of Management of the Bertelsmann Foundation from October 2002 to December 2005. He received numerous awards as well as honorary doctorates, and he was active on a number of supervisory boards and advisory committees of international companies. As a marketing researcher he has published more than 300 scientific writings and over 30 monographs. As the initiator of the AMD-Net NRW, Professor Meffert has been working since 2008 in an honorary capacity toward the improvement of the health care situation for persons with visual impairments. Professor Meffert has been serving as a member of the executive board of the Center for Advanced Studies in Management (CASiM) at HHL Leipzig Graduate School of Management since 2012.

H. Albach et al. (eds.), *Boundaryless Hospital*, DOI 10.1007/978-3-662-49012-9

Prof. Dr. Andreas Pinkwart was born in 1960 in Seelscheid, North Rhine-Westphalia, Germany. After his training as a banker he studied economics and business administration at the University of Münster and the University of Bonn where he finished his Diploma in Economics and obtained his doctoral degree (*summa cum laude*) in 1991. Subsequently, Professor Pinkwart ran the office of the Free Democratic Party's leader of the parliamentary group in the German Bundestag from 1991 to 1994. In 1994 he became a Professor of Economics and Business Administration at the School of Public Administration in Düsseldorf from where he moved to the University of Siegen in 1997. There, his qualifications equaling those of a habilitation in business economics were attested and he was appointed as a full Professor to the Chair of Business Administration, especially Small and Medium-Sized Companies. Being on sabbatical leave, Professor Pinkwart was a Member of the German Bundestag (2002–2005) and the German Bundesrat (2005–2010) as well as Minister for Innovation, Science, Research and Technology and Deputy Prime Minister of the federal state of North Rhine-Westphalia (2005–2010).

In 2011 Professor Pinkwart became the Dean of HHL Leipzig Graduate School of Management in Leipzig, Germany, and holder of the Stiftungsfonds Deutsche Bank Chair of Innovation Management and Entrepreneurship. Before he started his new positions at HHL in April 2011, he was a senior research fellow at AICGS, Johns Hopkins University, Washington. Since 2012 he has been the Academic Director of the Center for Advanced Studies in Management (CASiM) at HHL.

Prof. Dr. Dr. h.c. Ralf Reichwald studied economics and business management at the universities of Bonn, Marburg, and Munich in Germany. From 1970 to 1975 he worked at Ludwig-Maximilians-Universität München as a research associate at the Institute for Industry Research (Prof. Edmund Heinen), where he received his doctoral degree in 1973. From 1975 to 1989 he was an Associate Professor of Business Management at the University of the Federal Armed Forces, Munich. In 1990 he was appointed to the Chair of Business Administration at Technische Universität München (TUM). From 1994 to 1996 he was Dean of the Faculty of Economics and Social Sciences at TUM and from 2002 to 2005 Dean of the TUM School of Management. During this time he was also Founding Dean of the Faculty of Economics at the Technical University Freiberg, Saxony. In 1994 he received an honorary doctorate degree and in 2013 he was awarded with the title Honorary Senator of the Technical University Freiberg. Professor Reichwald is Academic Director and co-founder (2006) of the Center for Leading Innovation & Cooperation (CLIC) at HHL Leipzig Graduate School of Management. In 2010 he became a Professor of Management at HHL and Member of the Executive Board of the Center for Advances Studies in Management (CASiM). Furthermore, he has been a permanent visiting professor at the University of Tunis, El Manar, which honored him for his work in research and teaching in 2006 with the title Professor honoris causa. Since 2005 Professor Reichwald has been serving as Chair of the Advisory Board of the Peter Pribilla Foundation at the Technische Universität München (TUM).

Prof. Dr. Dr. Wilfried von Eiff is a Professor of Health Care Management at HHL Leipzig Graduate School of Management and is the Director of the Center for Hospital Management, a research institute linked to the University of Münster, Germany. Both institutions are well-known for international and national research, consulting and government advisory activities in the fields of cost–benefit analysis of medical technology and clinical procedures, strategic management and mergers and acquisitions in the health care sector, business ethics in medicine, risk management and health service research. Professor von Eiff is a founding member of the initiative Best Practice Management in Healthcare and Hospital Management, which is part of the European Hospital Management Association (EHMA). He is member of various boards of directors in health care and industry. Before, he was Director and Member of the Board of the University Clinic of Giessen, Germany, and also Managing Director of an international automotive company overseeing the fields of organization, process, logistics and IT management. He holds a doctoral degree from the Faculty of Business Administration, University of Tübingen, Germany, as well as a doctoral degree from the Faculty of Medicine, University of Giessen.

Printed by Printforce, the Netherlands